Finder

Story and Art by **Ayano Yamane**   volume **8**

CONTENTS

SUBLIME
SuBLime Manga Edition

Pray in the Abyss

Finder Series Character Introduction

Akihito Takaba

Akihito Takaba, a free-lance photographer, was chasing a scoop on a dirty politician when he first met Asami. Routinely employed by a weekly magazine, Akihito spends his time hunting for news stories. Outgoing and determined, he refuses to back down or lose hope, even in the toughest of situations. After getting caught up in an idol-stalker incident and subsequently hounded by angry fans, he winds up crashing at Asami's place and taking care of most of the household chores. He is very confident in his cooking.

Ryuichi Asami

On the surface, Ryuichi Asami is one of Japan's brightest young business-men, owning several highly successful luxury hotels and nightclubs. But under this facade lies a cunning and powerful crime lord with influence among not just the wealthy elite but also international movers and shakers. Where he came from and how he got to his current position remains unknown. While generally cold and calcu-lating, he has been known to go out of his way to protect loyal subordinates. He is known for both his intelligence and his cool good looks.

Shinji Kuroda

A detective with the Tokyo District Public Prosecutor's Office. He comes into contact with Akihito while investi-gating a case. It appears he may know Asami from an earlier time.

Shu Sudo

The manager at Club Dracaena, one of the luxurious members-only nightclubs Asami owns. Shu has feelings for his boss, Asami.

Sakazaki

The owner of several night-clubs in Tokyo's Kabukicho red-light district. Well-connected and learned, he has a wealth of information about the underworld.

Kei Kirishima

Asami's personal secretary. Constantly at his boss's side, Kei handles both Asami's business schedule and personal needs.

Pray in the Abyss

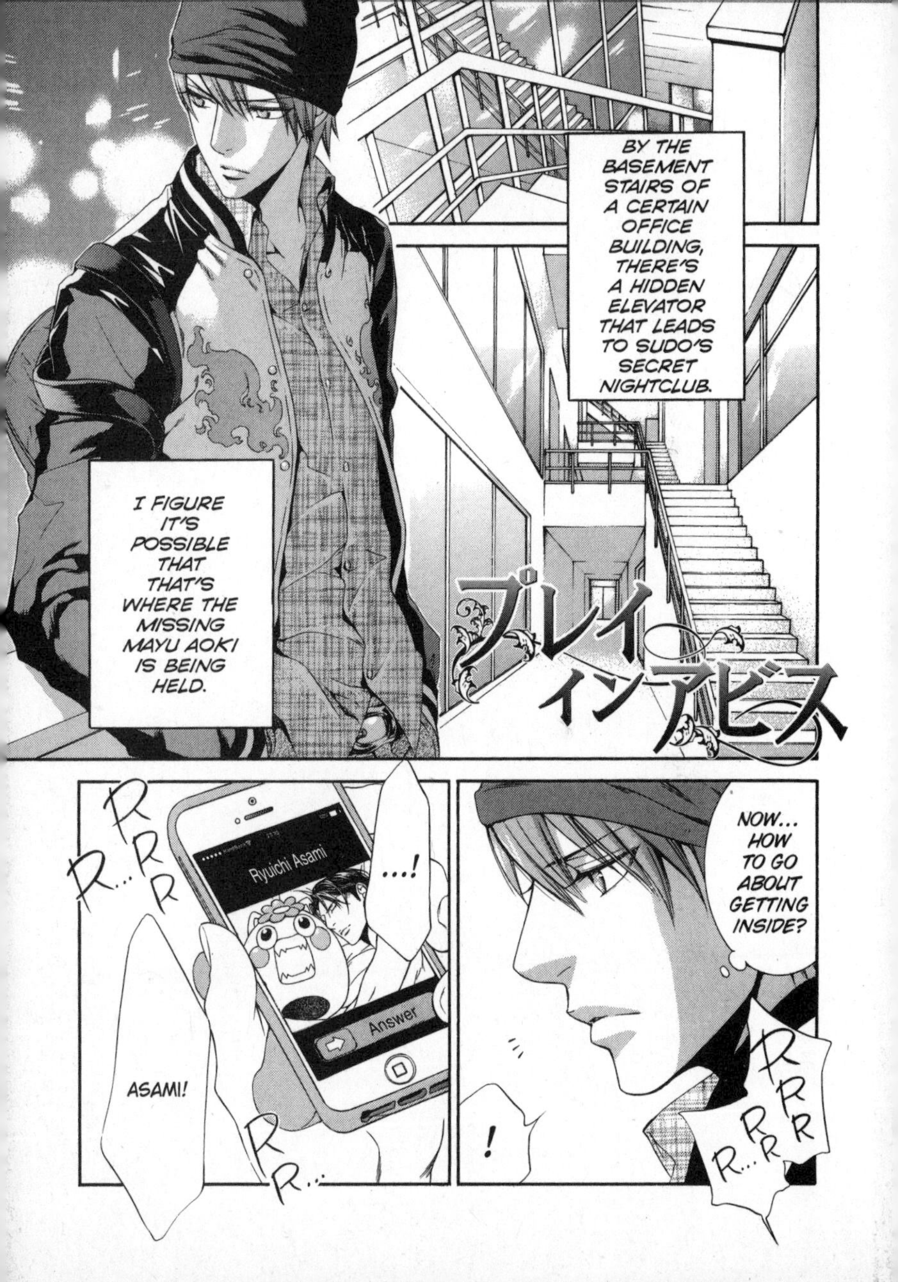
BY THE BASEMENT STAIRS OF A CERTAIN OFFICE BUILDING, THERE'S A HIDDEN ELEVATOR THAT LEADS TO SUDO'S SECRET NIGHTCLUB.
I FIGURE IT'S POSSIBLE THAT THAT'S WHERE THE MISSING MAYU AOKI IS BEING HELD.
プレイインアビス
NOW... HOW TO GO ABOUT GETTING INSIDE?
!
R... R R R R R
R... R R R
Ryuichi Asami
Answer
...!
ASAMI!
R R...

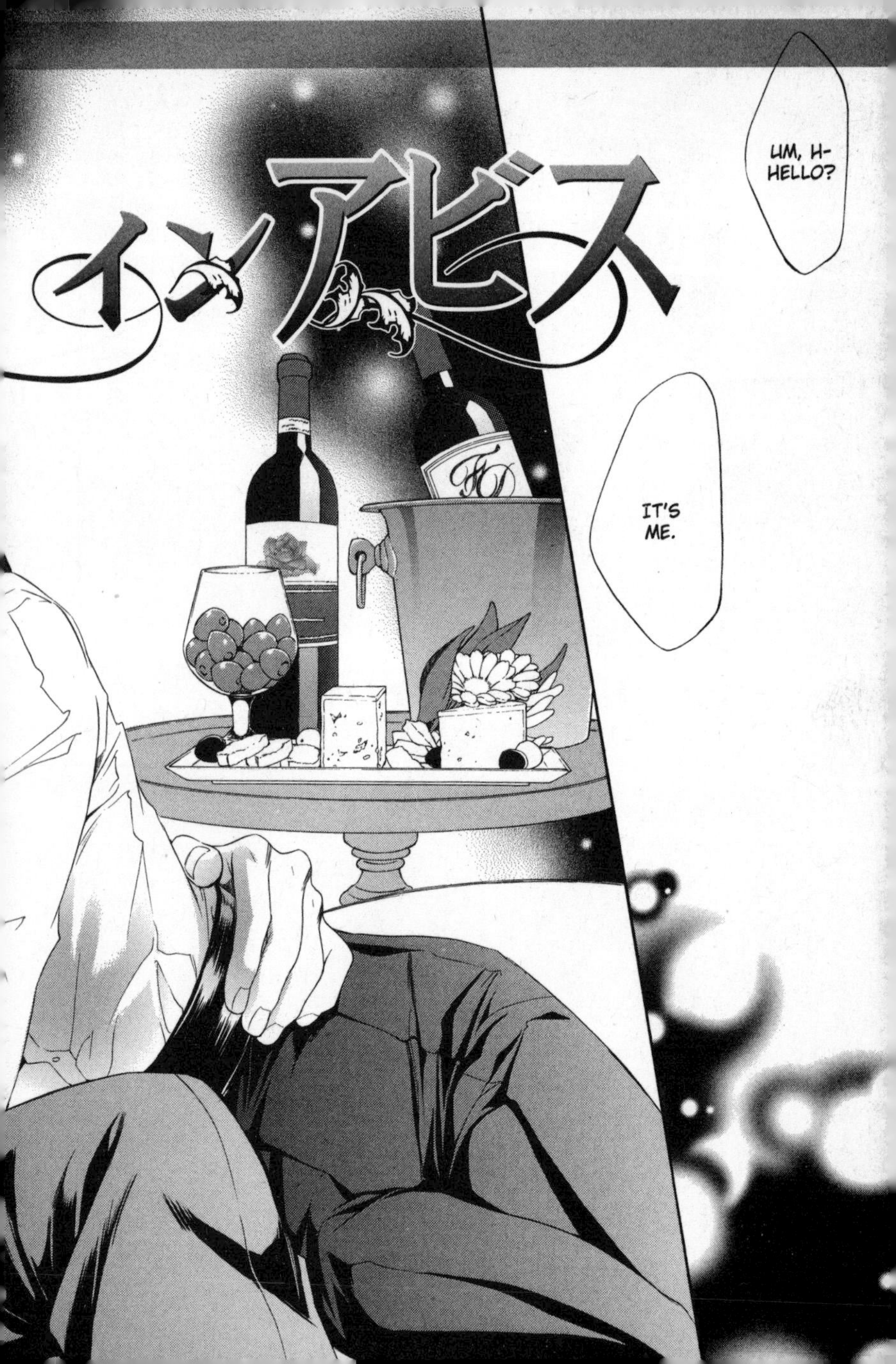
UM, H-HELLO?
インアビス
IT'S ME.

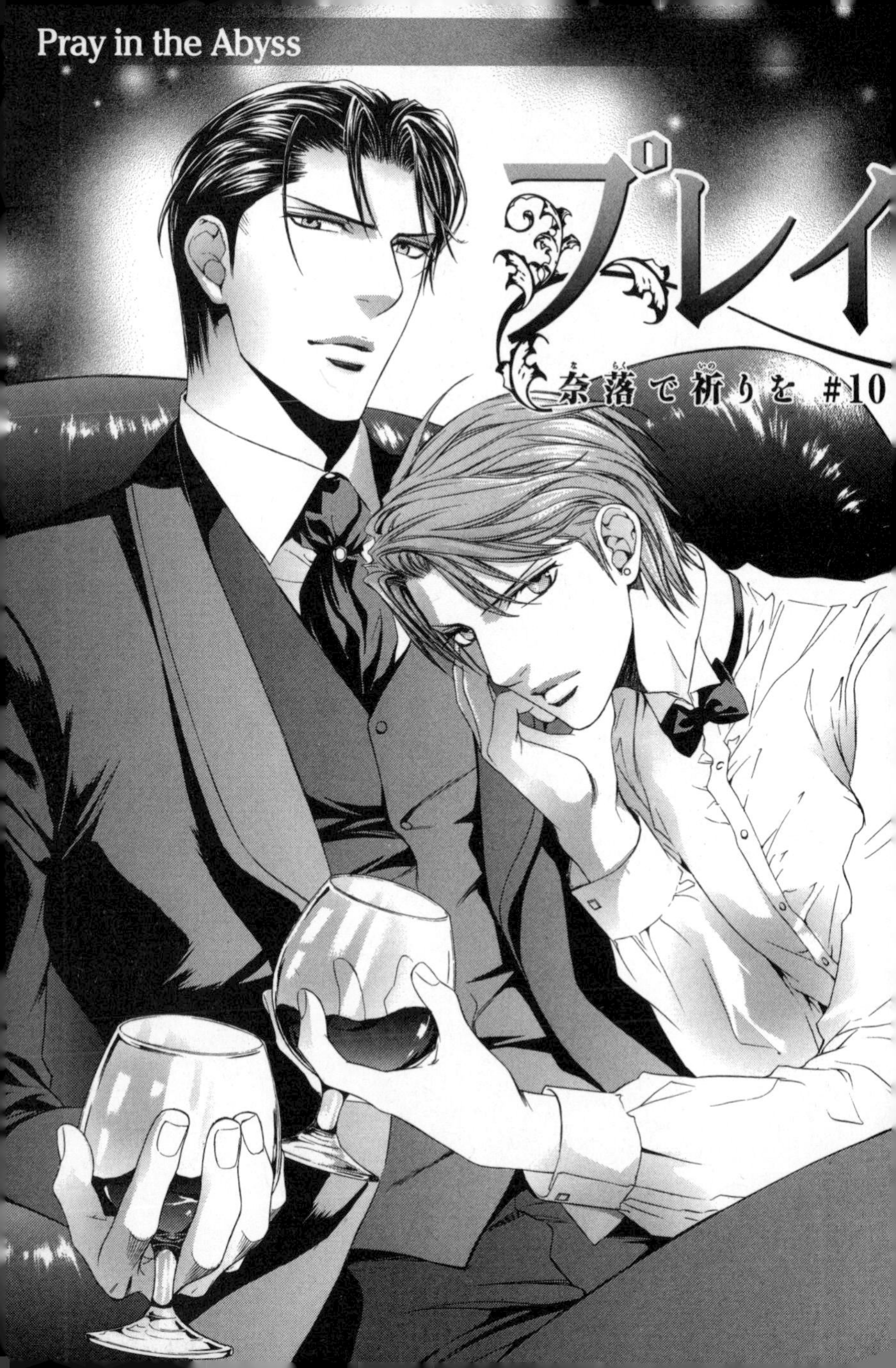
Pray in the Abyss
プレイ
奈落で祈りを #10

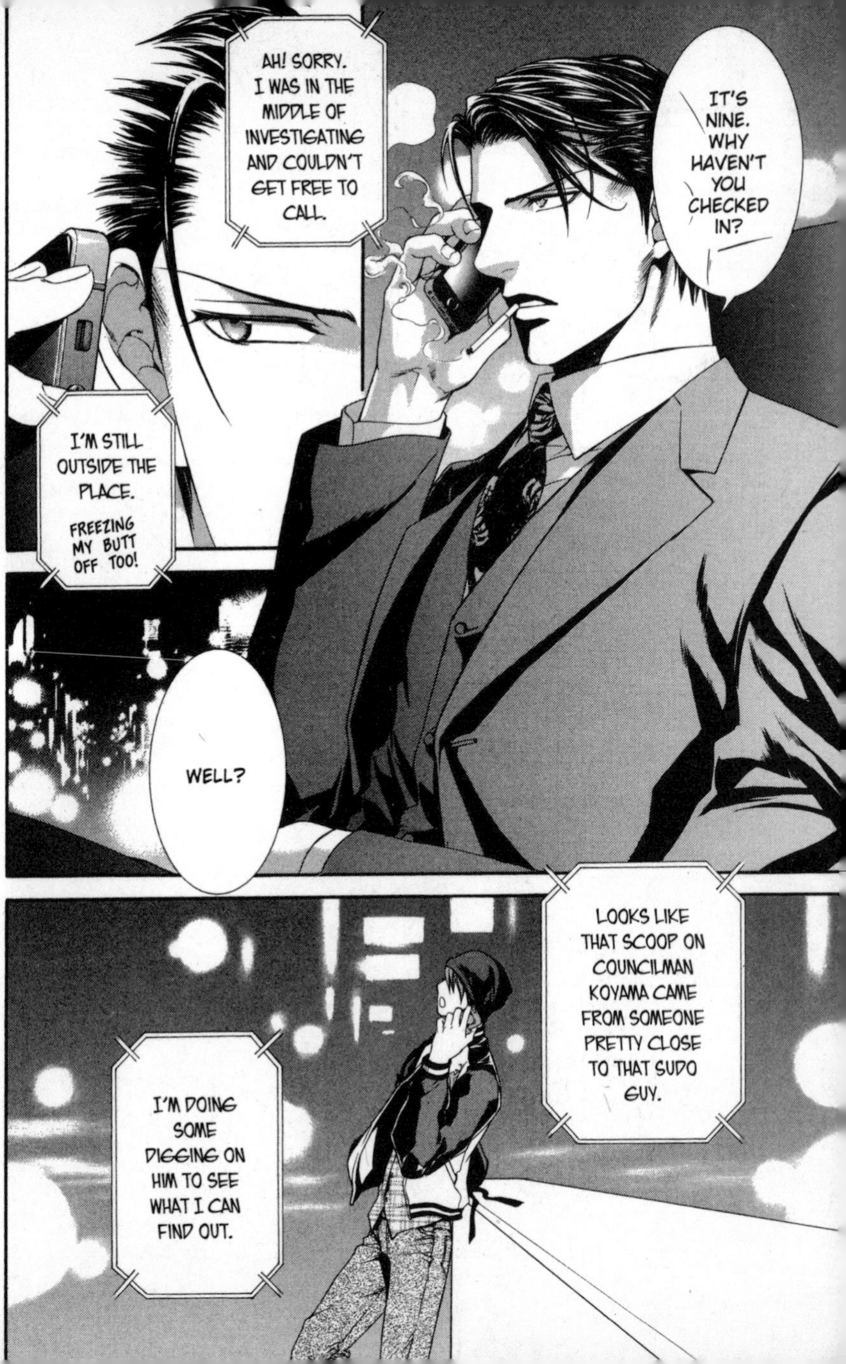
IT'S NINE. WHY HAVEN'T YOU CHECKED IN?
AH! SORRY. I WAS IN THE MIDDLE OF INVESTIGATING AND COULDN'T GET FREE TO CALL.
I'M STILL OUTSIDE THE PLACE.
FREEZING MY BUTT OFF TOO!
WELL?
LOOKS LIKE THAT SCOOP ON COUNCILMAN KOYAMA CAME FROM SOMEONE PRETTY CLOSE TO THAT SUDO GUY.
I'M DOING SOME DIGGING ON HIM TO SEE WHAT I CAN FIND OUT.

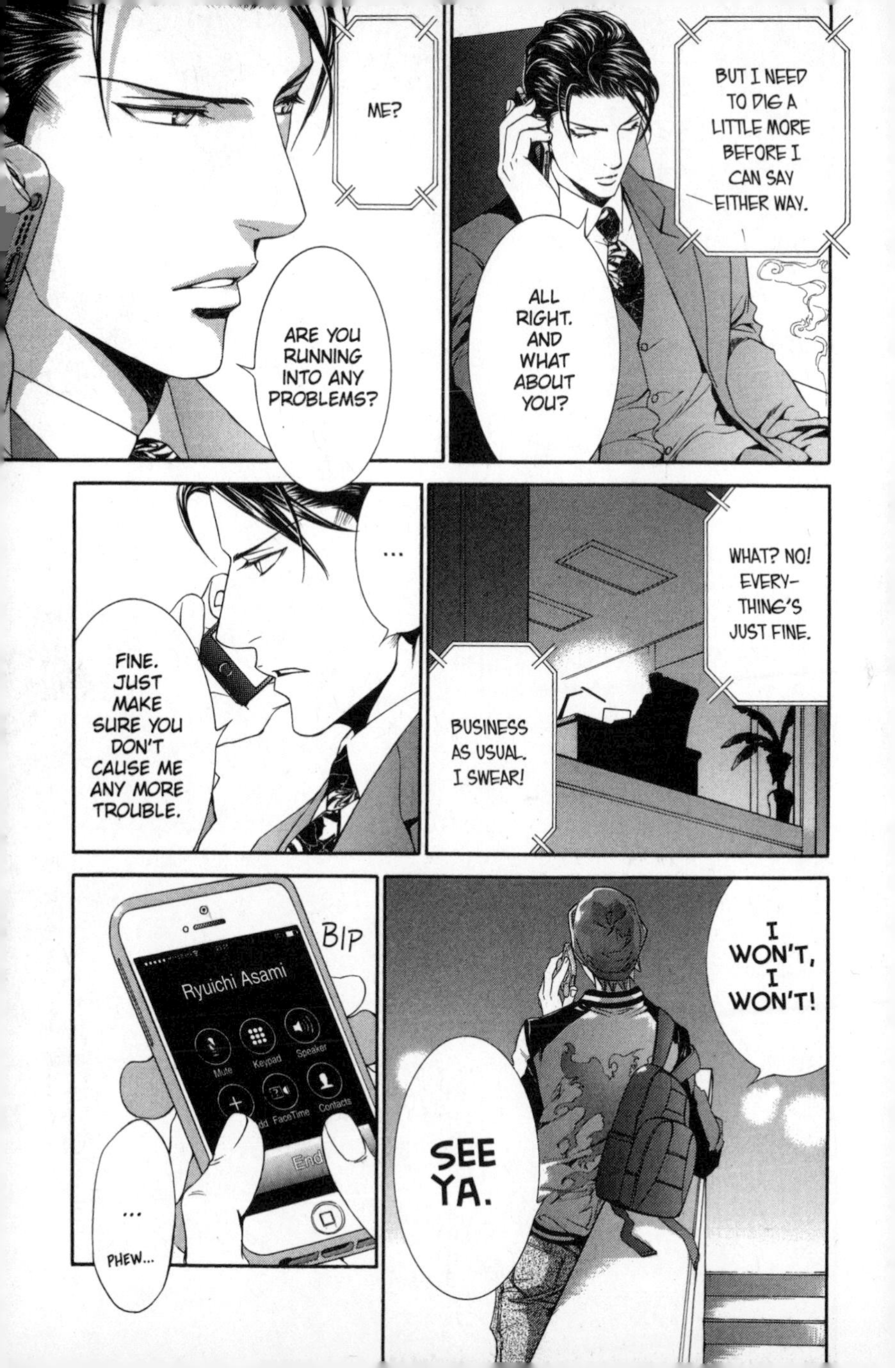
BUT I NEED TO DIG A LITTLE MORE BEFORE I CAN SAY EITHER WAY.
ALL RIGHT. AND WHAT ABOUT YOU?
ME?
ARE YOU RUNNING INTO ANY PROBLEMS?
WHAT? NO! EVERY-THING'S JUST FINE.
BUSINESS AS USUAL. I SWEAR!
...
FINE. JUST MAKE SURE YOU DON'T CAUSE ME ANY MORE TROUBLE.
I WON'T, I WON'T!
SEE YA.
BIP
Ryuichi Asami
Mute
Keypad
Speaker
FaceTime
Contacts
End
... PHEW...

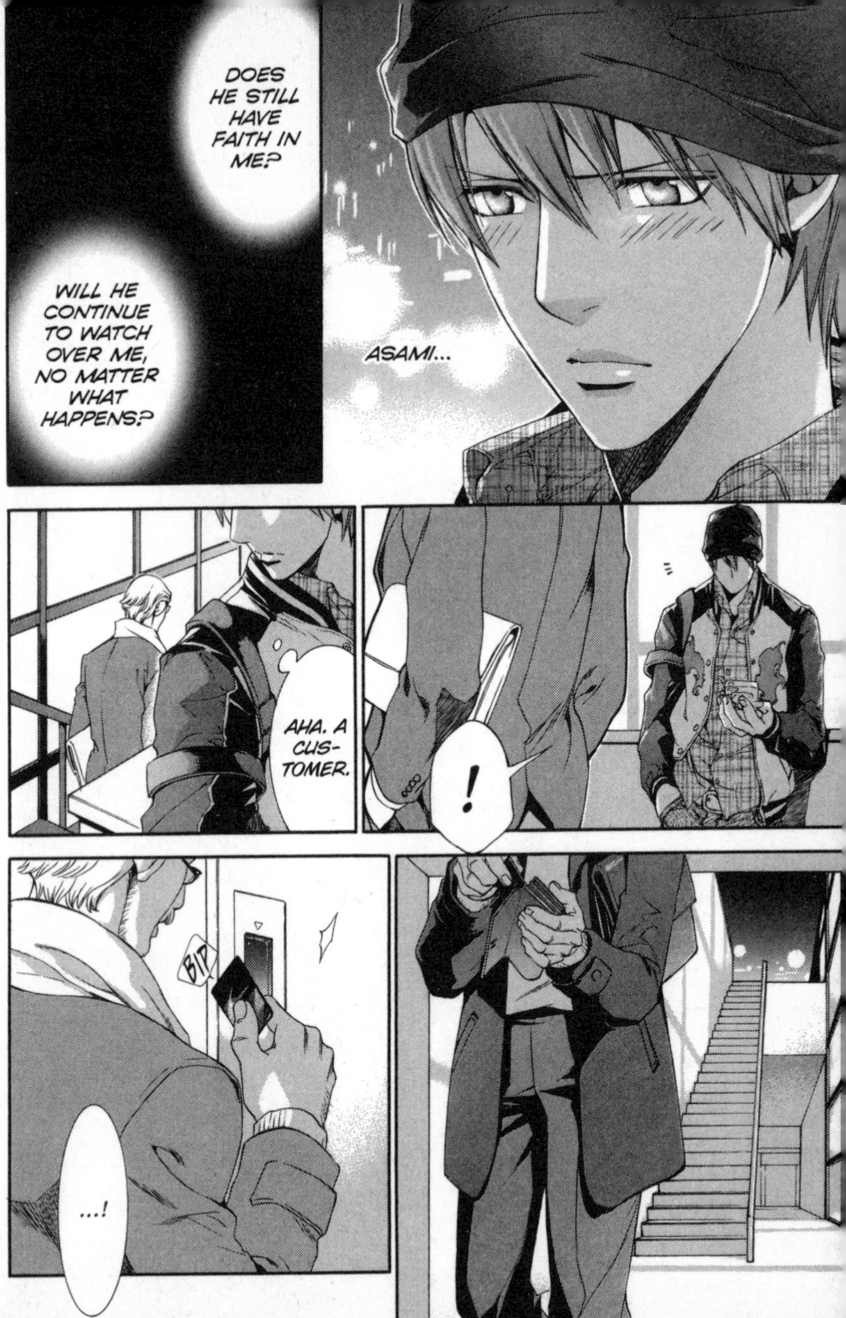
ASAMI...
DOES HE STILL HAVE FAITH IN ME?
WILL HE CONTINUE TO WATCH OVER ME, NO MATTER WHAT HAPPENS?
!
AHA. A CUS-TOMER.
BIP
...!

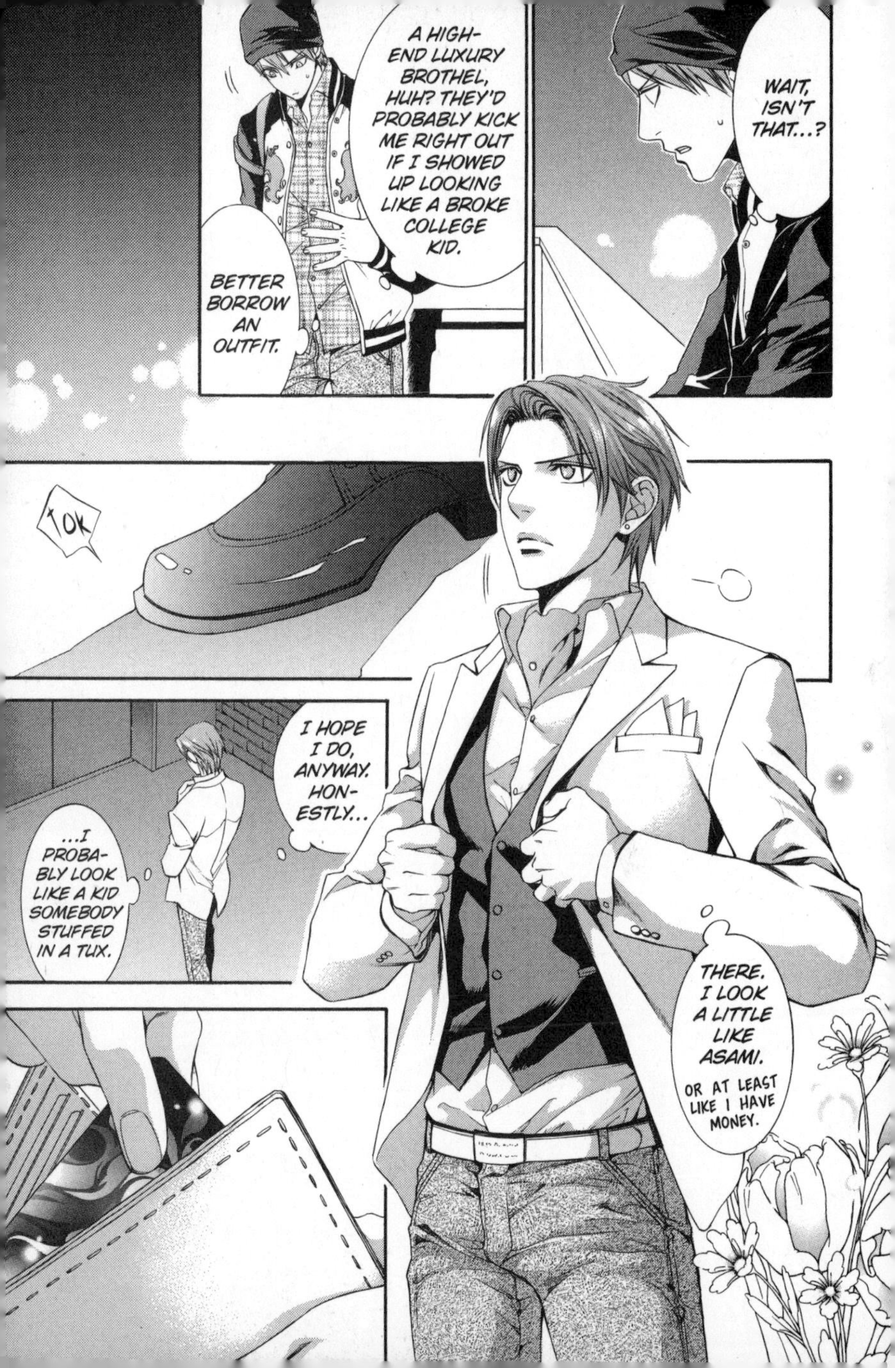
WAIT, ISN'T THAT...?
A HIGH-END LUXURY BROTHEL, HUH? THEY'D PROBABLY KICK ME RIGHT OUT IF I SHOWED UP LOOKING LIKE A BROKE COLLEGE KID.
BETTER BORROW AN OUTFIT.
THERE. I LOOK A LITTLE LIKE ASAMI.
OR AT LEAST LIKE I HAVE MONEY.
TOK
I HOPE I DO, ANYWAY. HON-ESTLY...
...I PROBA-BLY LOOK LIKE A KID SOMEBODY STUFFED IN A TUX.

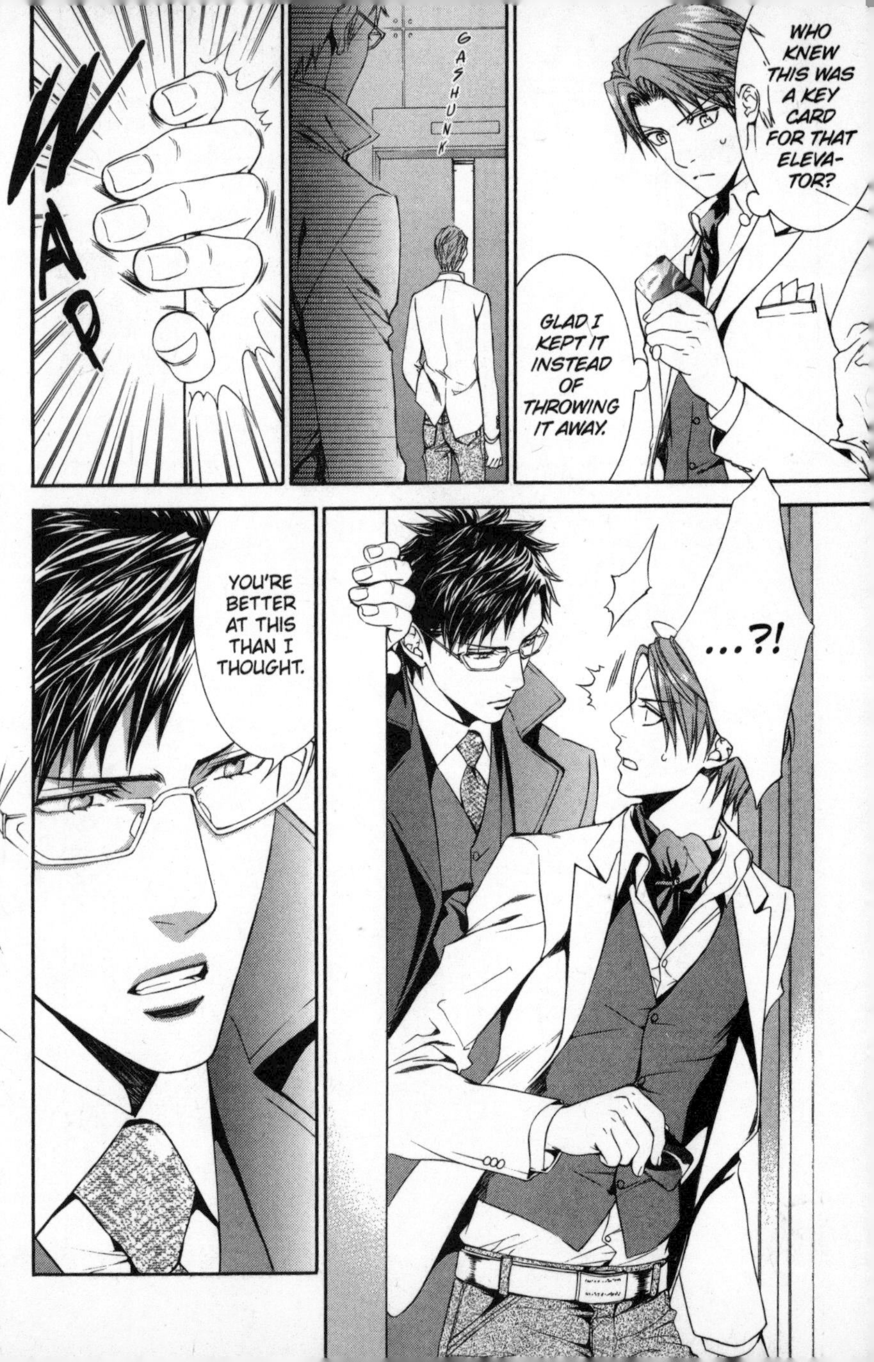
WHO KNEW THIS WAS A KEY CARD FOR THAT ELEVATOR?
GLAD I KEPT IT INSTEAD OF THROWING IT AWAY.
GASHUNK
WAP
...?!
YOU'RE BETTER AT THIS THAN I THOUGHT.

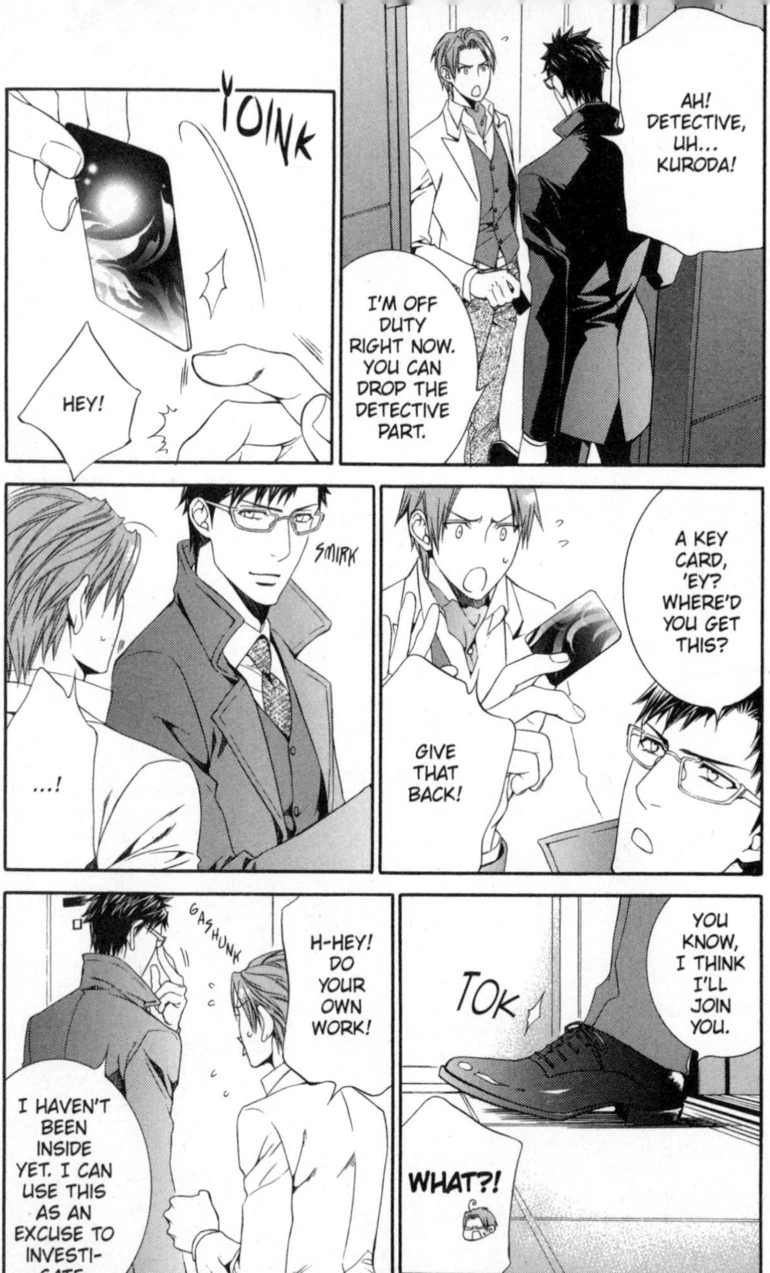
AH! DETECTIVE, UH... KURODA!
I'M OFF DUTY RIGHT NOW. YOU CAN DROP THE DETECTIVE PART.
YOINK
HEY!
A KEY CARD, 'EY? WHERE'D YOU GET THIS?
GIVE THAT BACK!
SMIRK
...!
YOU KNOW, I THINK I'LL JOIN YOU.
TOK
WHAT?!
H-HEY! DO YOUR OWN WORK!
GASHUNK
I HAVEN'T BEEN INSIDE YET. I CAN USE THIS AS AN EXCUSE TO INVESTI-GATE.

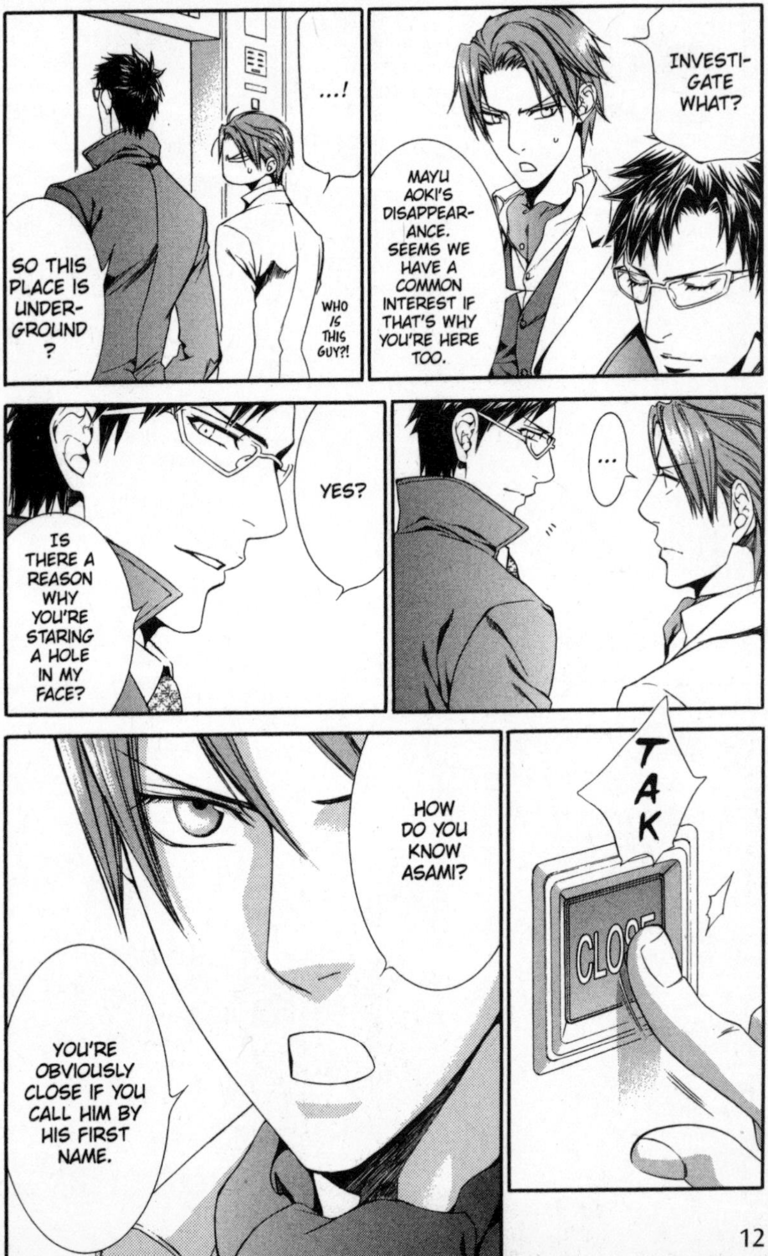
INVESTIGATE WHAT?
MAYU AOKI'S DISAPPEARANCE. SEEMS WE HAVE A COMMON INTEREST IF THAT'S WHY YOU'RE HERE TOO.
...!
WHO IS THIS GUY?!
SO THIS PLACE IS UNDERGROUND?
...
YES?
IS THERE A REASON WHY YOU'RE STARING A HOLE IN MY FACE?
TAK
CLOSE
HOW DO YOU KNOW ASAMI?
YOU'RE OBVIOUSLY CLOSE IF YOU CALL HIM BY HIS FIRST NAME.

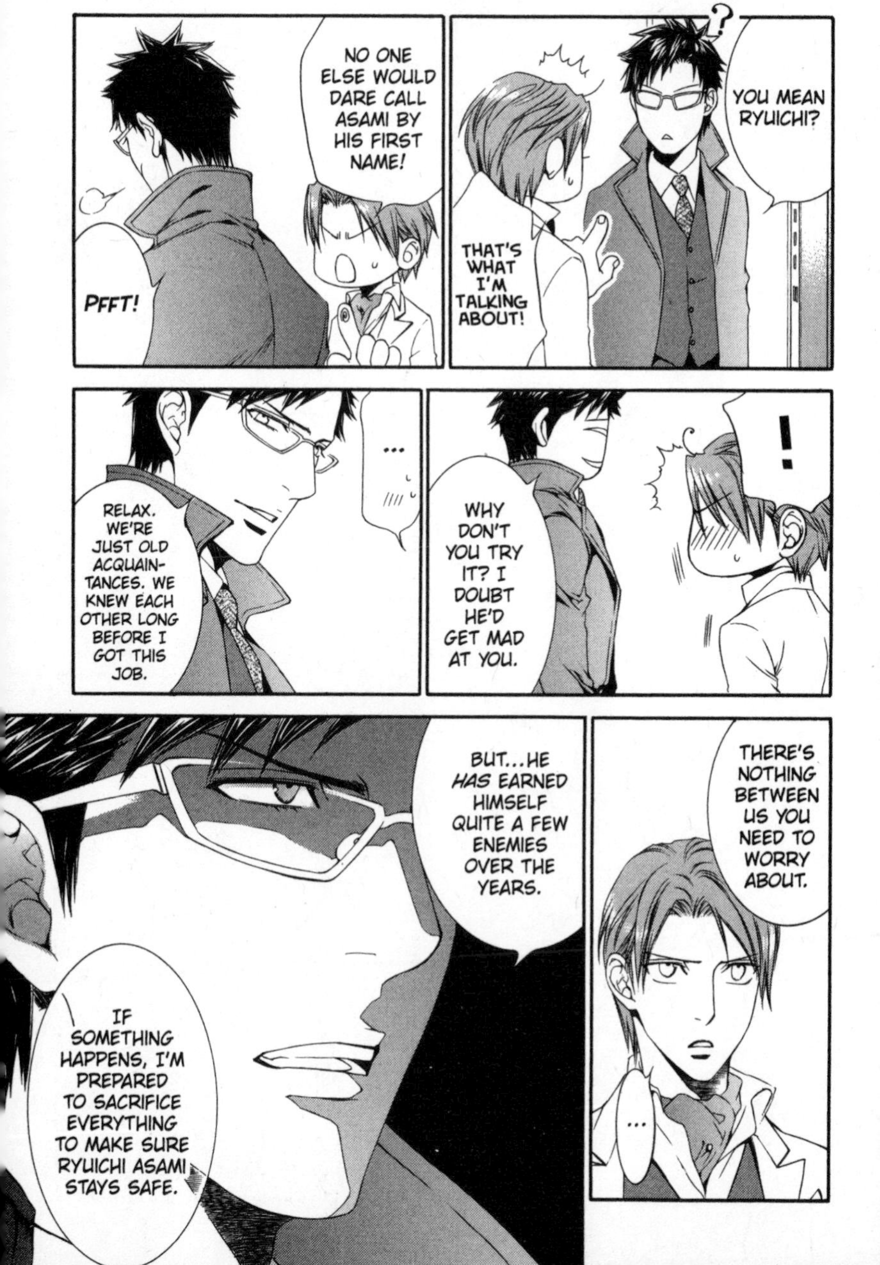
?
YOU MEAN RYUICHI?
THAT'S WHAT I'M TALKING ABOUT!
NO ONE ELSE WOULD DARE CALL ASAMI BY HIS FIRST NAME!
PFFT!
!
WHY DON'T YOU TRY IT? I DOUBT HE'D GET MAD AT YOU.
...
RELAX. WE'RE JUST OLD ACQUAIN-TANCES. WE KNEW EACH OTHER LONG BEFORE I GOT THIS JOB.
THERE'S NOTHING BETWEEN US YOU NEED TO WORRY ABOUT.
...
BUT...HE *HAS* EARNED HIMSELF QUITE A FEW ENEMIES OVER THE YEARS.
IF SOMETHING HAPPENS, I'M PREPARED TO SACRIFICE EVERYTHING TO MAKE SURE RYUICHI ASAMI STAYS SAFE.

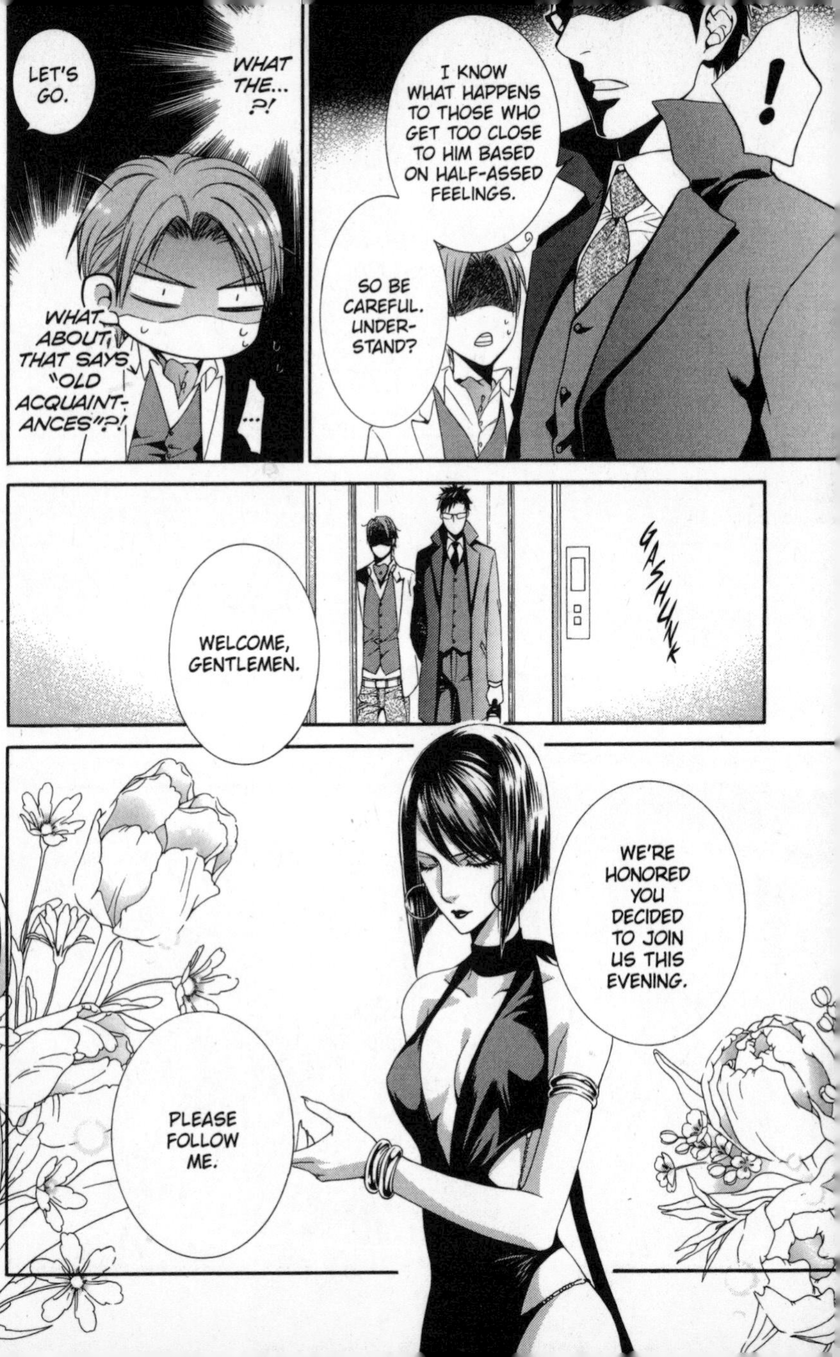
!
I KNOW WHAT HAPPENS TO THOSE WHO GET TOO CLOSE TO HIM BASED ON HALF-ASSED FEELINGS.
SO BE CAREFUL. UNDERSTAND?
...
LET'S GO.
WHAT THE... ?!
WHAT ABOUT THAT SAYS "OLD ACQUAINTANCES"?!
GASHUNK
WELCOME, GENTLEMEN.
WE'RE HONORED YOU DECIDED TO JOIN US THIS EVENING.
PLEASE FOLLOW ME.

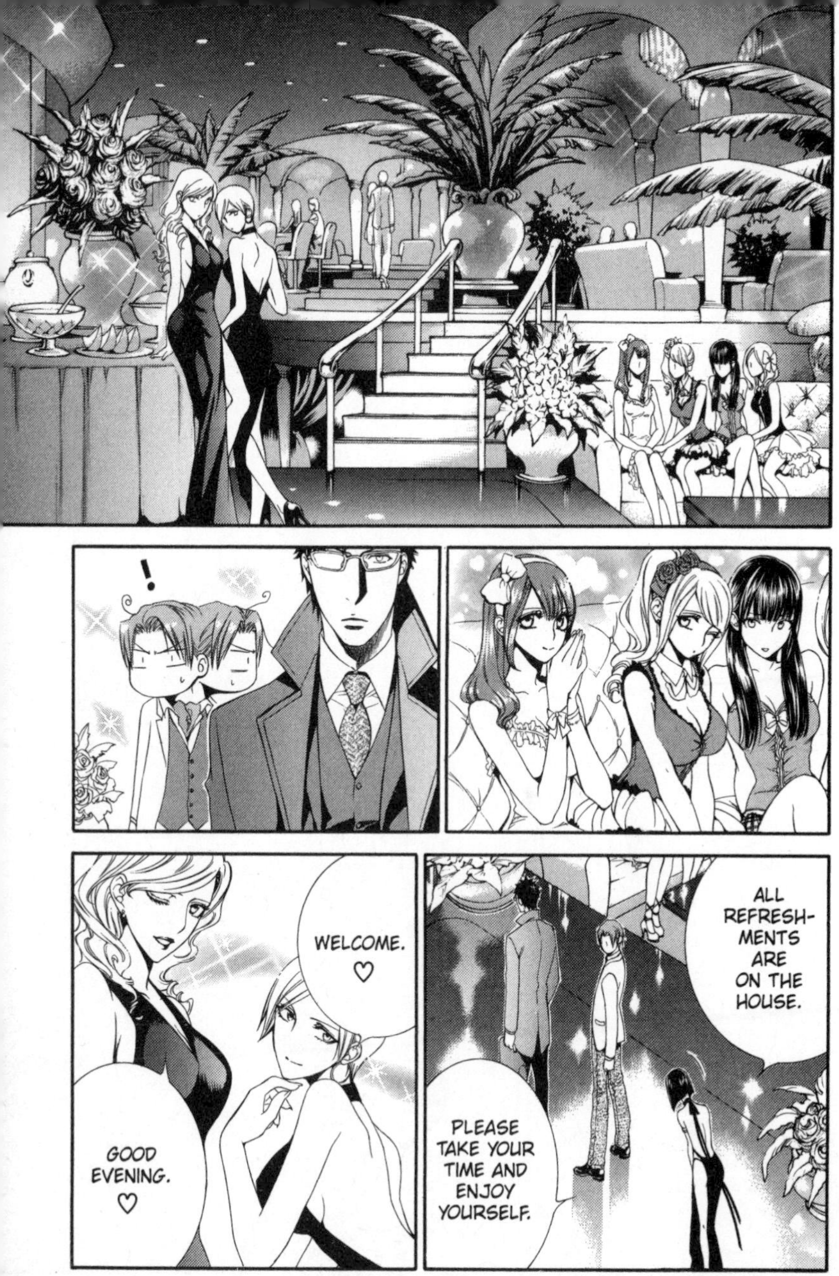
!
ALL REFRESH-MENTS ARE ON THE HOUSE.
PLEASE TAKE YOUR TIME AND ENJOY YOURSELF.
WELCOME. ♡
GOOD EVENING. ♡

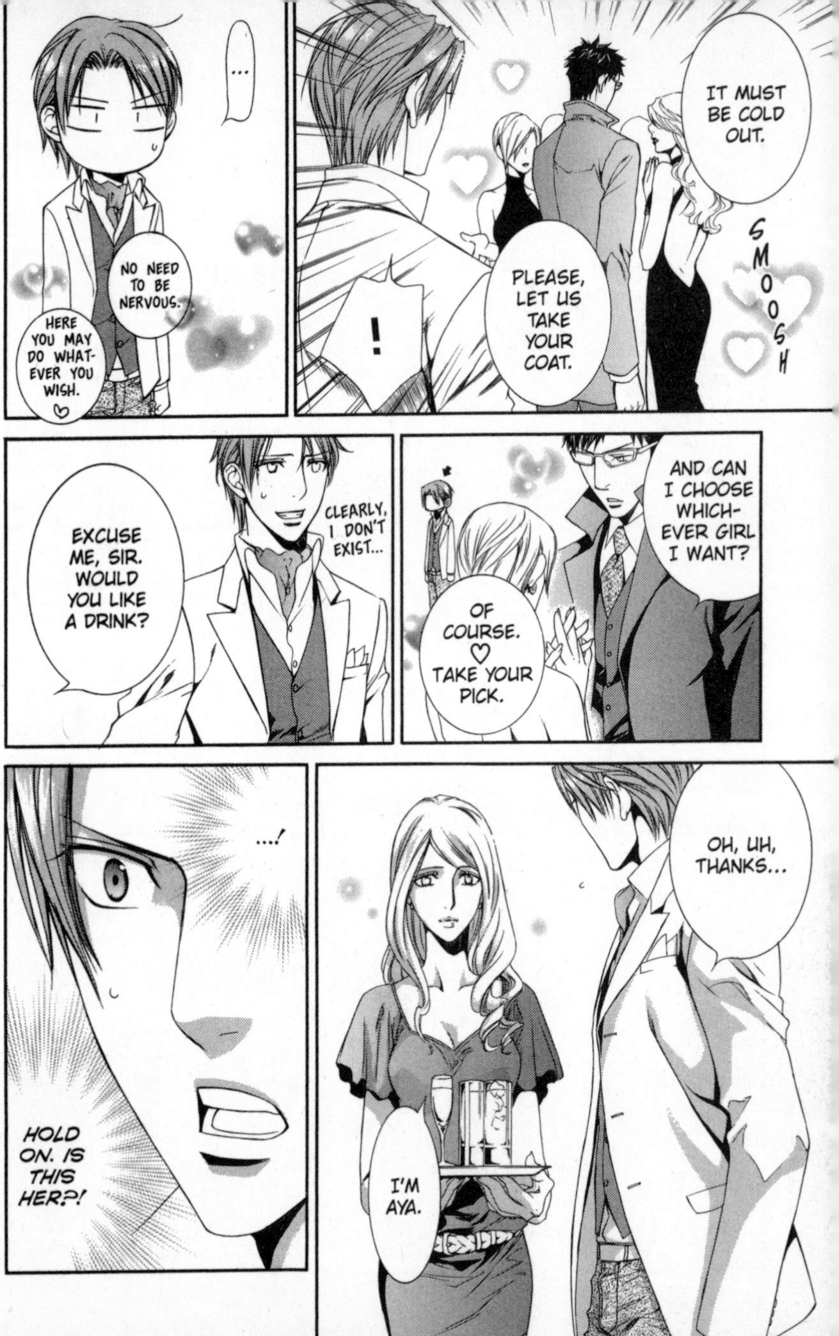
IT MUST BE COLD OUT.
SMOOSH
PLEASE, LET US TAKE YOUR COAT.
!
...
NO NEED TO BE NERVOUS.
HERE YOU MAY DO WHATEVER YOU WISH. ♡
AND CAN I CHOOSE WHICHEVER GIRL I WANT?
OF COURSE. ♡ TAKE YOUR PICK.
CLEARLY, I DON'T EXIST...
EXCUSE ME, SIR. WOULD YOU LIKE A DRINK?
OH, UH, THANKS...
I'M AYA.
...!
HOLD ON. IS THIS HER?!

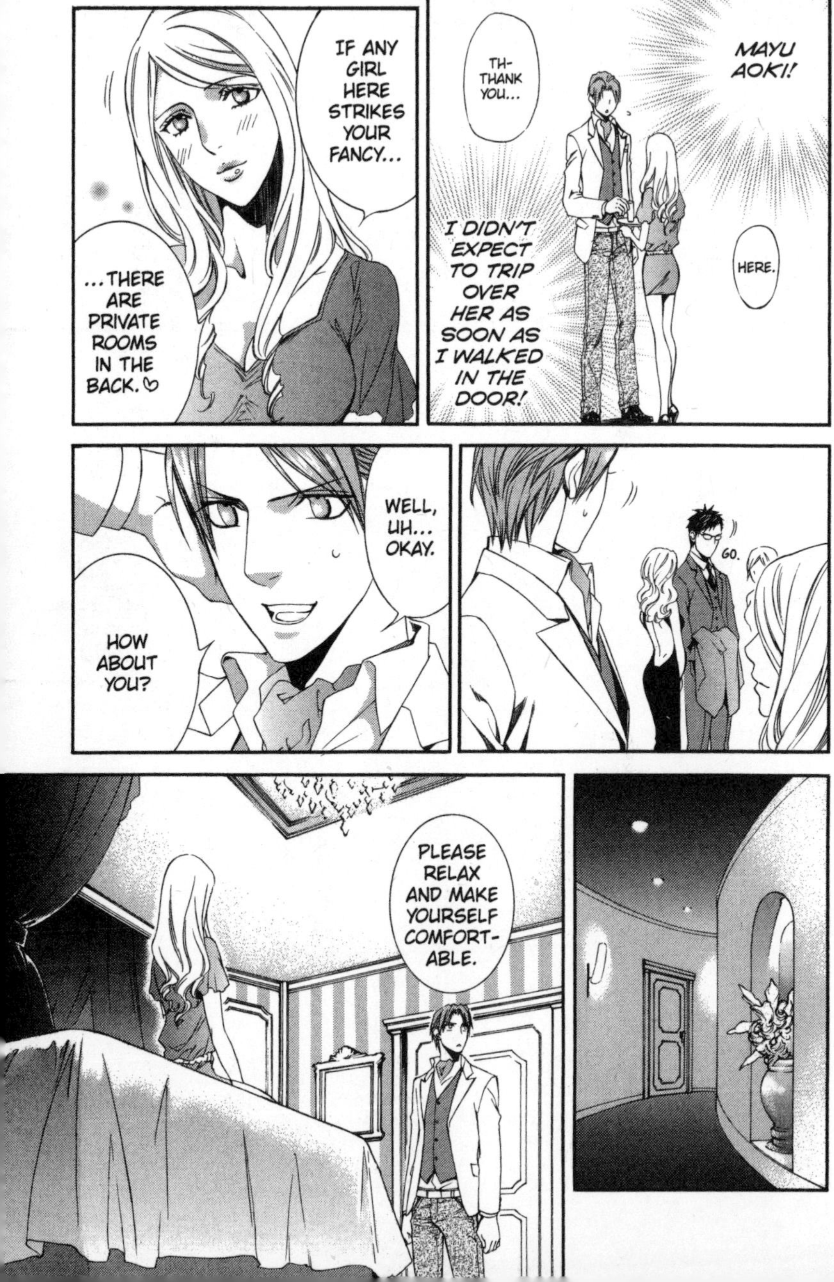
MAYU AOKI!
TH-THANK YOU...
HERE.
I DIDN'T EXPECT TO TRIP OVER HER AS SOON AS I WALKED IN THE DOOR!
IF ANY GIRL HERE STRIKES YOUR FANCY...
...THERE ARE PRIVATE ROOMS IN THE BACK. ♡
GO.
WELL, UH... OKAY.
HOW ABOUT YOU?
PLEASE RELAX AND MAKE YOURSELF COMFORT-ABLE.

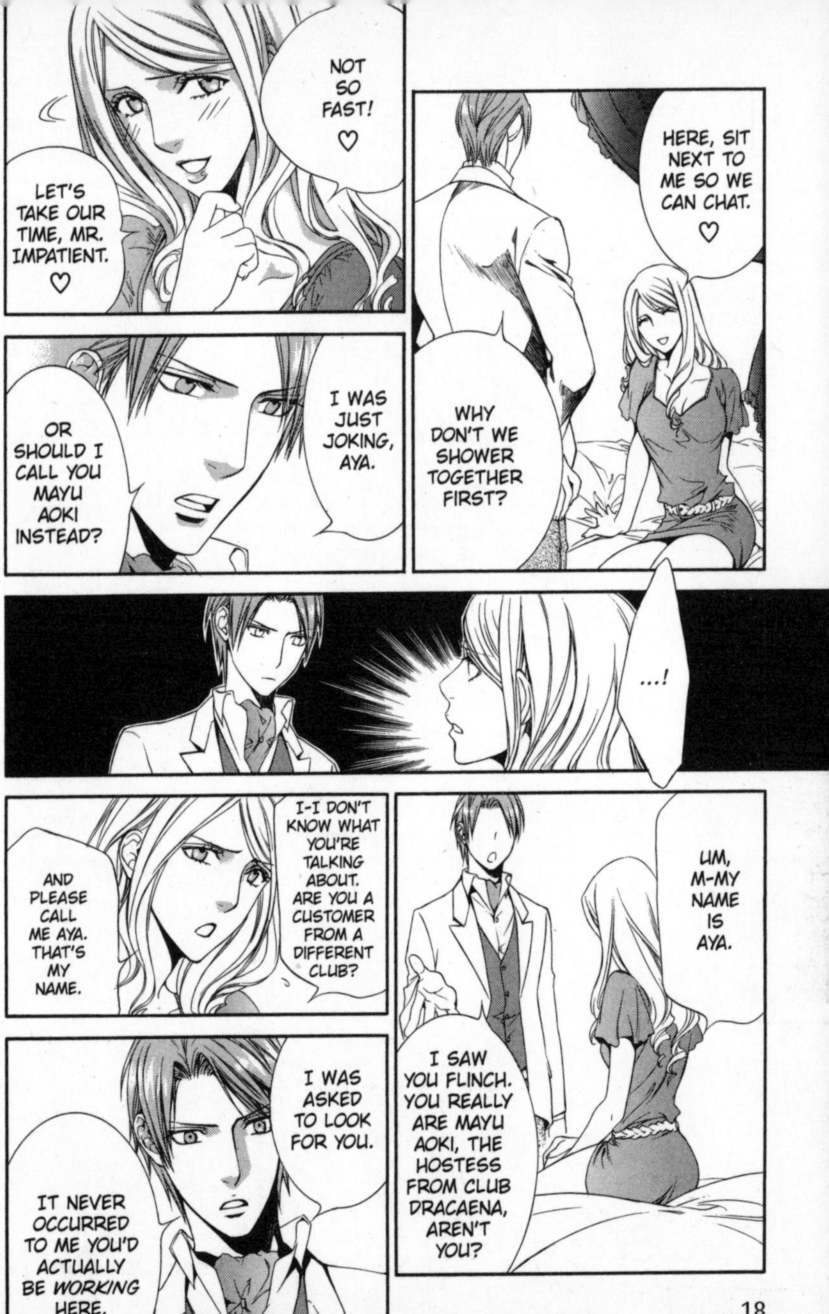
HERE, SIT NEXT TO ME SO WE CAN CHAT. ♡
WHY DON'T WE SHOWER TOGETHER FIRST?
NOT SO FAST! ♡
LET'S TAKE OUR TIME, MR. IMPATIENT. ♡
I WAS JUST JOKING, AYA.
OR SHOULD I CALL YOU MAYU AOKI INSTEAD?
...!
UM, M-MY NAME IS AYA.
I SAW YOU FLINCH. YOU REALLY ARE MAYU AOKI, THE HOSTESS FROM CLUB DRACAENA, AREN'T YOU?
I-I DON'T KNOW WHAT YOU'RE TALKING ABOUT. ARE YOU A CUSTOMER FROM A DIFFERENT CLUB?
AND PLEASE CALL ME AYA. THAT'S MY NAME.
I WAS ASKED TO LOOK FOR YOU.
IT NEVER OCCURRED TO ME YOU'D ACTUALLY BE *WORKING* HERE.

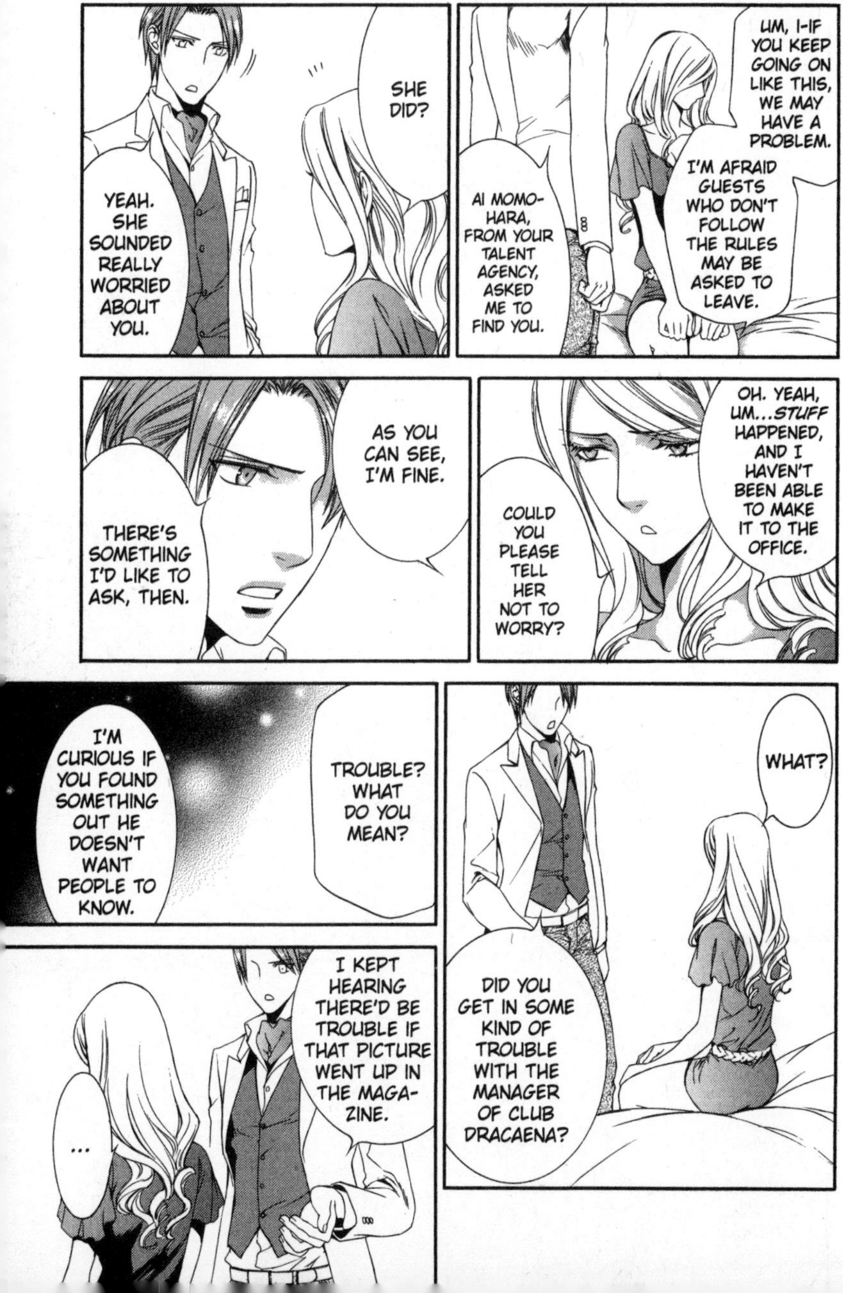

UM, I-IF YOU KEEP GOING ON LIKE THIS, WE MAY HAVE A PROBLEM.
I'M AFRAID GUESTS WHO DON'T FOLLOW THE RULES MAY BE ASKED TO LEAVE.
AI MOMOHARA, FROM YOUR TALENT AGENCY, ASKED ME TO FIND YOU.
SHE DID?
YEAH. SHE SOUNDED REALLY WORRIED ABOUT YOU.
OH. YEAH, UM...*STUFF* HAPPENED, AND I HAVEN'T BEEN ABLE TO MAKE IT TO THE OFFICE.
COULD YOU PLEASE TELL HER NOT TO WORRY?
AS YOU CAN SEE, I'M FINE.
THERE'S SOMETHING I'D LIKE TO ASK, THEN.
WHAT?
DID YOU GET IN SOME KIND OF TROUBLE WITH THE MANAGER OF CLUB DRACAENA?
TROUBLE? WHAT DO YOU MEAN?
I'M CURIOUS IF YOU FOUND SOMETHING OUT HE DOESN'T WANT PEOPLE TO KNOW.
I KEPT HEARING THERE'D BE TROUBLE IF THAT PICTURE WENT UP IN THE MAGAZINE.
...

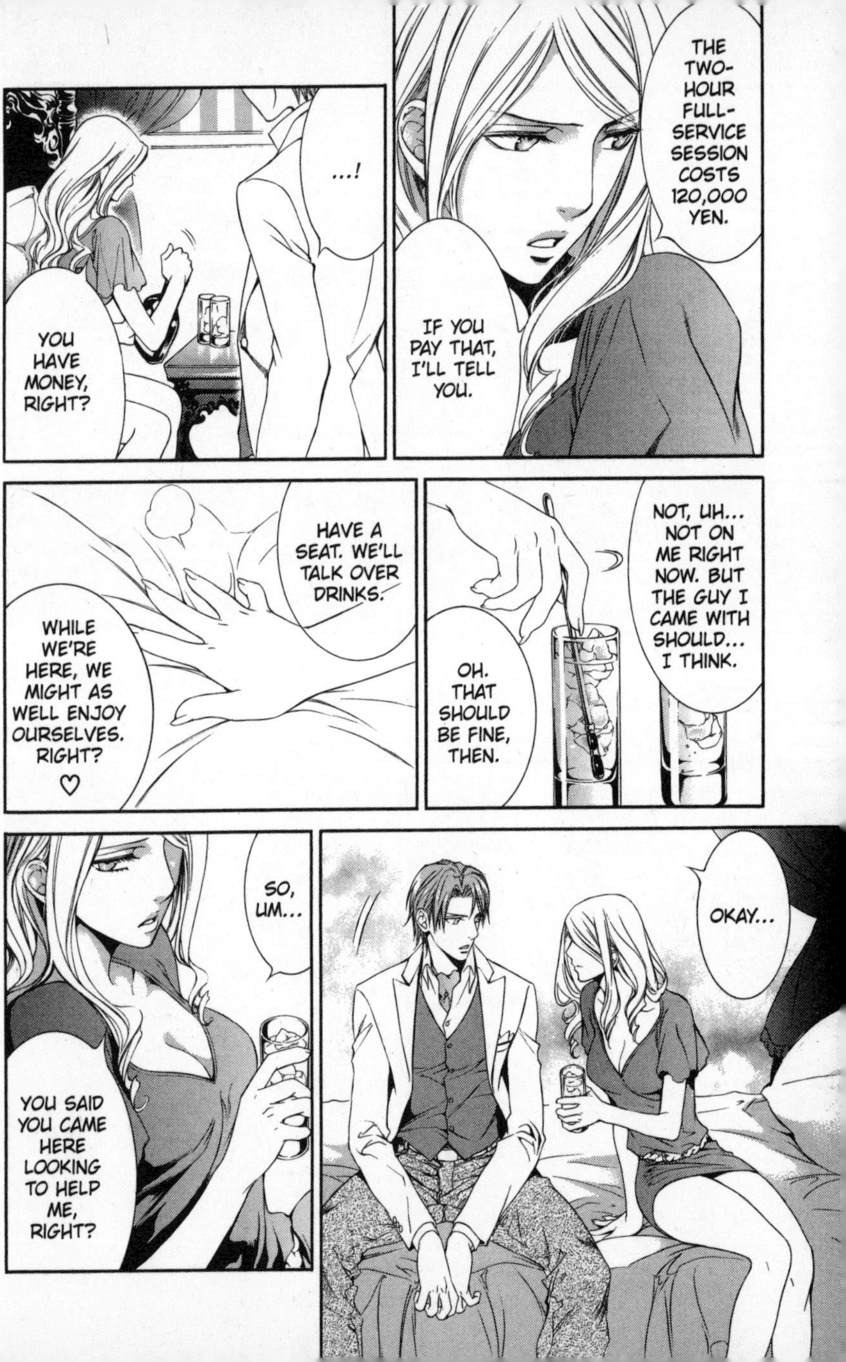
THE TWO-HOUR FULL-SERVICE SESSION COSTS 120,000 YEN.
IF YOU PAY THAT, I'LL TELL YOU.
...!
YOU HAVE MONEY, RIGHT?
NOT, UH... NOT ON ME RIGHT NOW. BUT THE GUY I CAME WITH SHOULD... I THINK.
OH. THAT SHOULD BE FINE, THEN.
HAVE A SEAT. WE'LL TALK OVER DRINKS.
WHILE WE'RE HERE, WE MIGHT AS WELL ENJOY OURSELVES. RIGHT? ♡
OKAY...
SO, UM...
YOU SAID YOU CAME HERE LOOKING TO HELP ME, RIGHT?

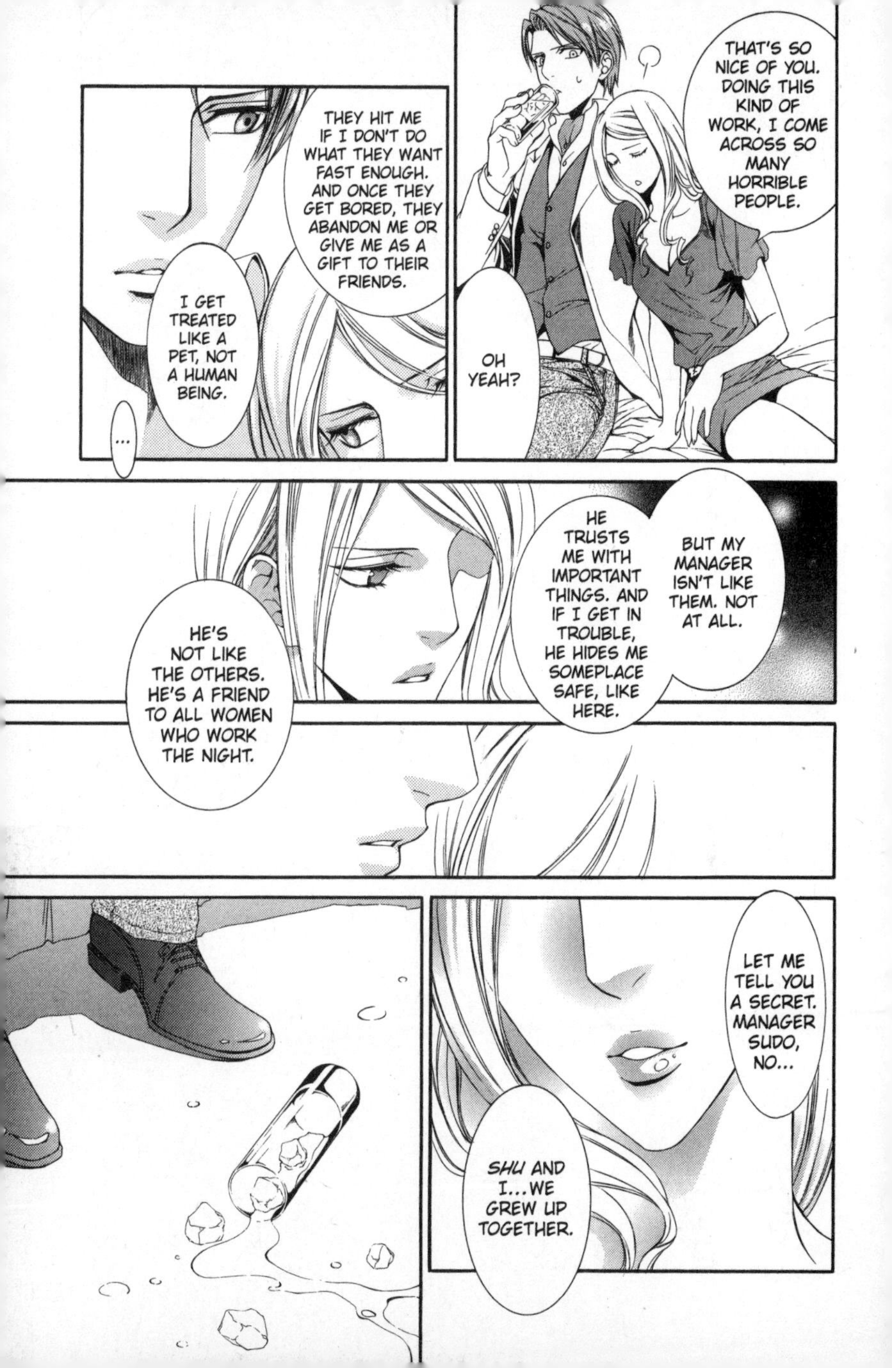

THAT'S SO NICE OF YOU. DOING THIS KIND OF WORK, I COME ACROSS SO MANY HORRIBLE PEOPLE.
OH YEAH?
THEY HIT ME IF I DON'T DO WHAT THEY WANT FAST ENOUGH. AND ONCE THEY GET BORED, THEY ABANDON ME OR GIVE ME AS A GIFT TO THEIR FRIENDS.
I GET TREATED LIKE A PET, NOT A HUMAN BEING.
...
BUT MY MANAGER ISN'T LIKE THEM. NOT AT ALL.
HE TRUSTS ME WITH IMPORTANT THINGS. AND IF I GET IN TROUBLE, HE HIDES ME SOMEPLACE SAFE, LIKE HERE.
HE'S NOT LIKE THE OTHERS. HE'S A FRIEND TO ALL WOMEN WHO WORK THE NIGHT.
LET ME TELL YOU A SECRET. MANAGER SUDO, NO...
SHU AND I...WE GREW UP TOGETHER.

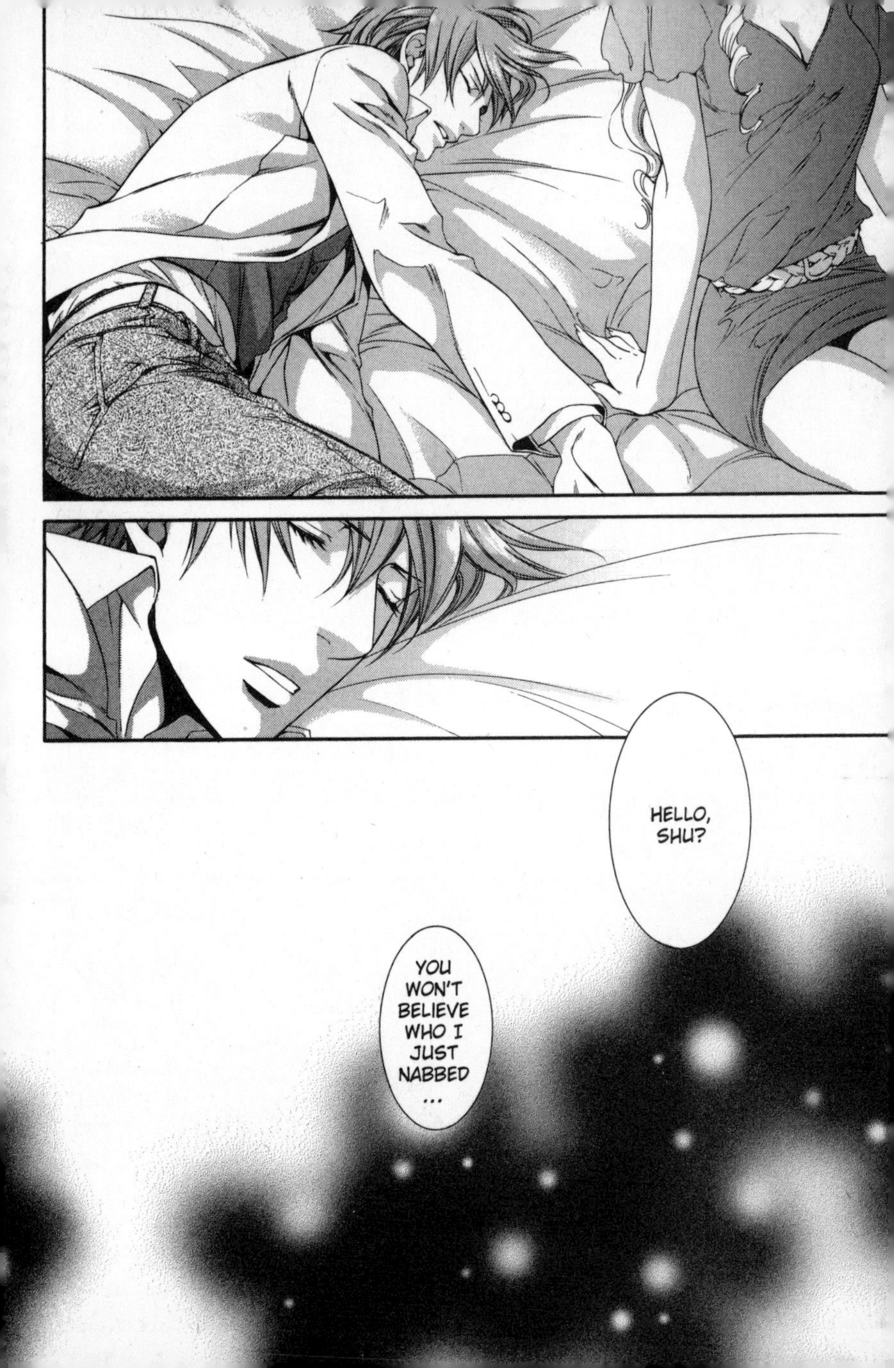
HELLO, SHU?
YOU WON'T BELIEVE WHO I JUST NABBED ...

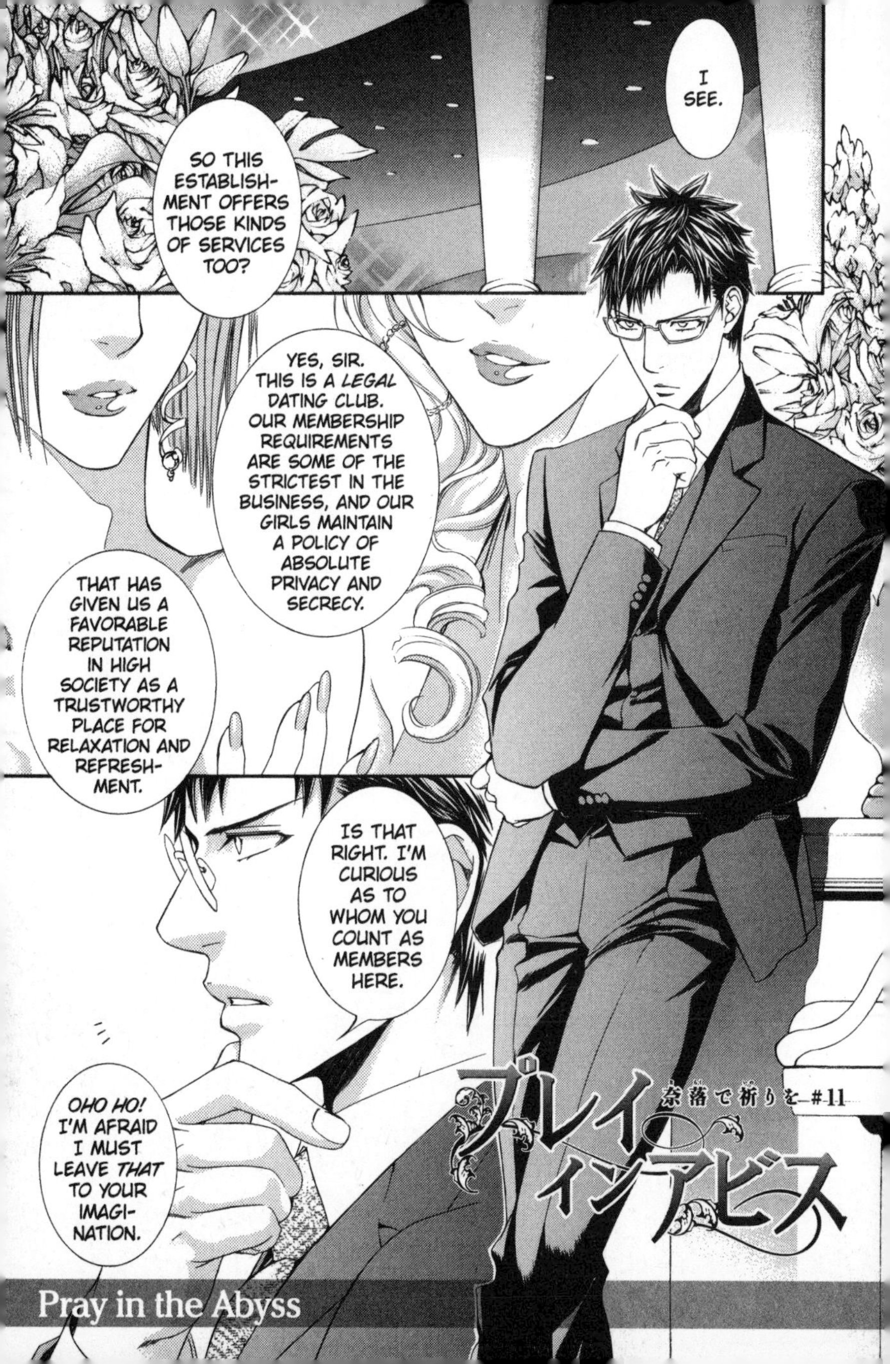
I SEE.
SO THIS ESTABLISHMENT OFFERS THOSE KINDS OF SERVICES TOO?
YES, SIR. THIS IS A *LEGAL* DATING CLUB. OUR MEMBERSHIP REQUIREMENTS ARE SOME OF THE STRICTEST IN THE BUSINESS, AND OUR GIRLS MAINTAIN A POLICY OF ABSOLUTE PRIVACY AND SECRECY.
THAT HAS GIVEN US A FAVORABLE REPUTATION IN HIGH SOCIETY AS A TRUSTWORTHY PLACE FOR RELAXATION AND REFRESHMENT.
IS THAT RIGHT. I'M CURIOUS AS TO WHOM YOU COUNT AS MEMBERS HERE.
OHO HO! I'M AFRAID I MUST LEAVE *THAT* TO YOUR IMAGINATION.
プレイ インアビス
奈落で祈りを #11
Pray in the Abyss

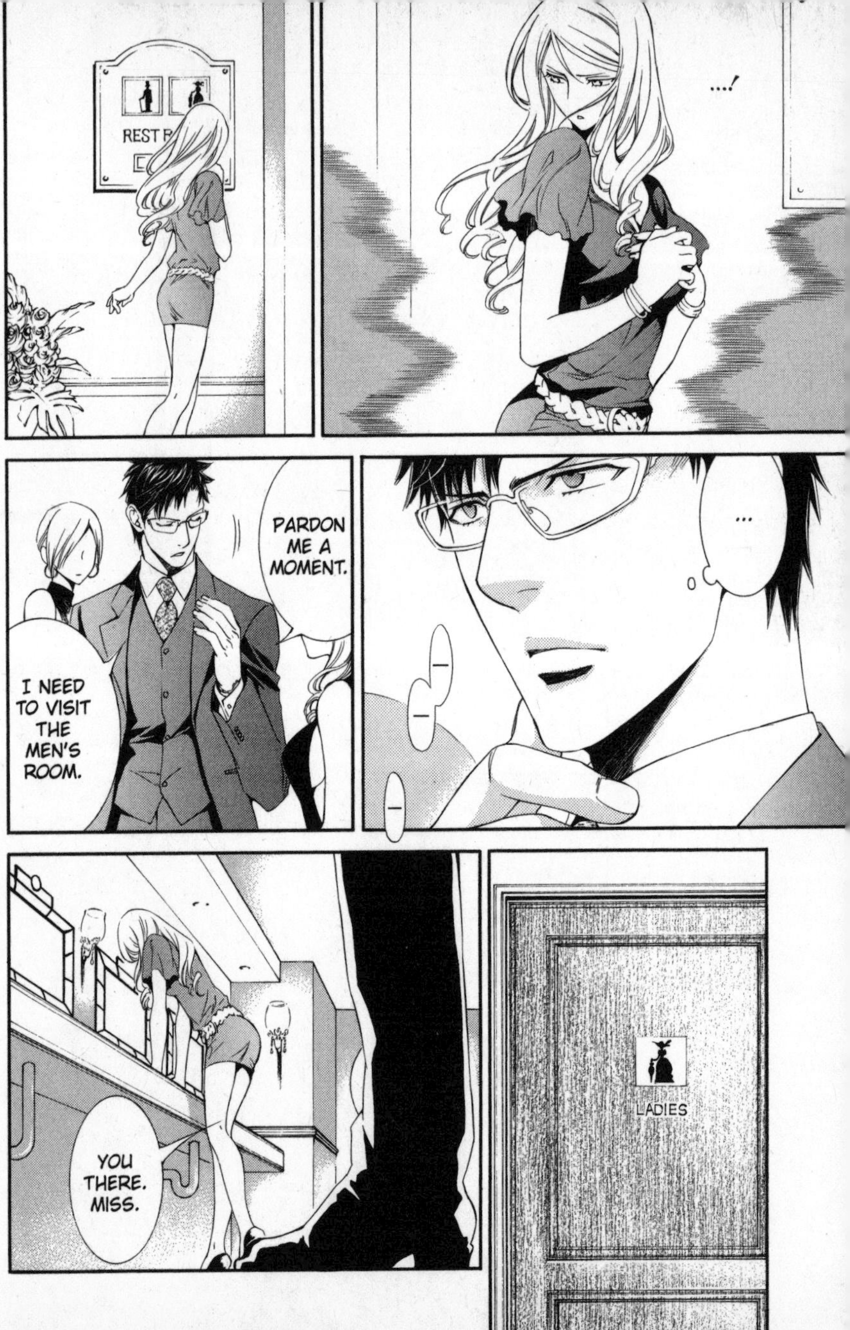
....!
...
—
—
—
PARDON ME A MOMENT.
I NEED TO VISIT THE MEN'S ROOM.
LADIES
YOU THERE. MISS.

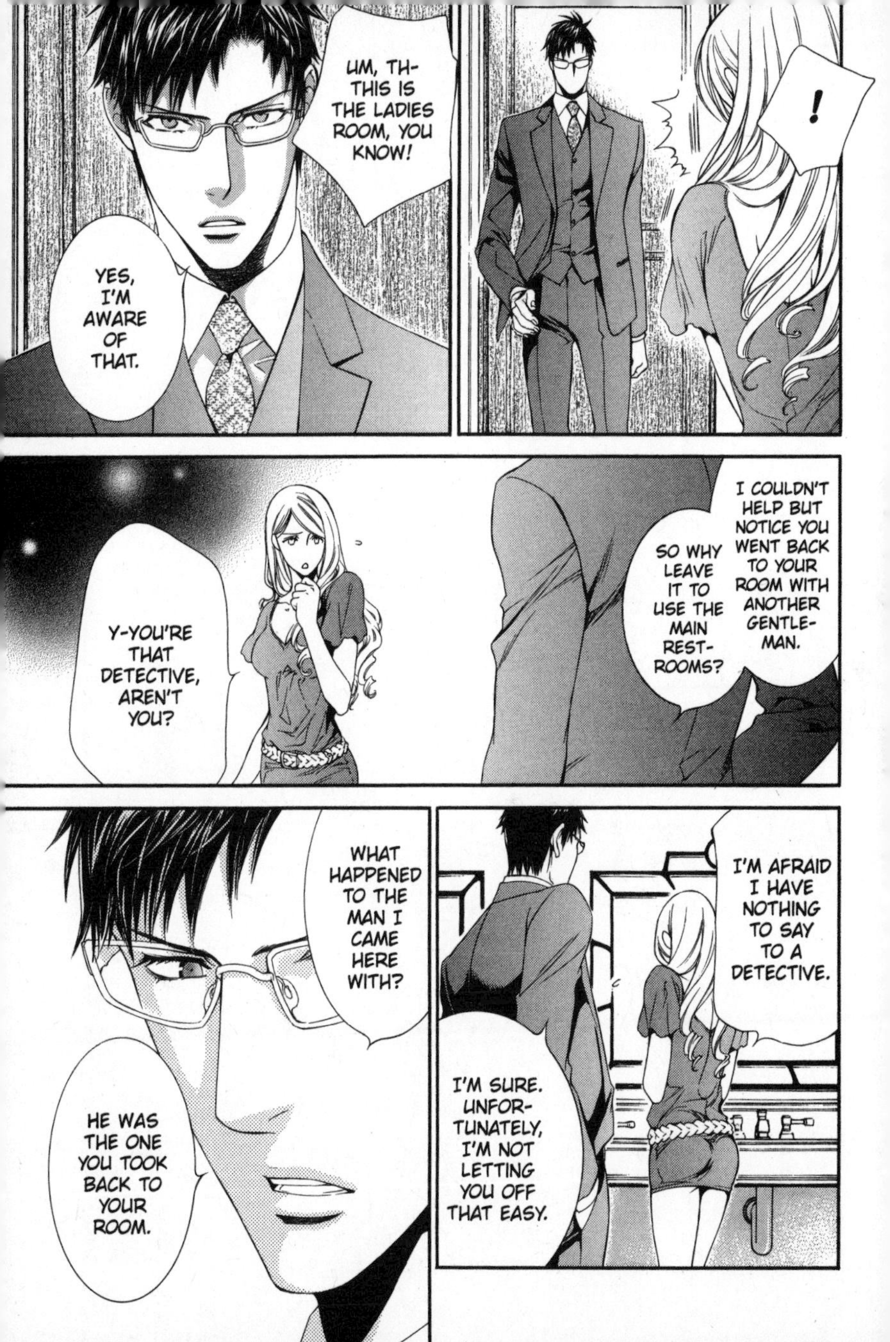
!
UM, TH-THIS IS THE LADIES ROOM, YOU KNOW!
YES, I'M AWARE OF THAT.
I COULDN'T HELP BUT NOTICE YOU WENT BACK TO YOUR ROOM WITH ANOTHER GENTLE-MAN.
SO WHY LEAVE IT TO USE THE MAIN REST-ROOMS?
Y-YOU'RE THAT DETECTIVE, AREN'T YOU?
I'M AFRAID I HAVE NOTHING TO SAY TO A DETECTIVE.
I'M SURE. UNFOR-TUNATELY, I'M NOT LETTING YOU OFF THAT EASY.
WHAT HAPPENED TO THE MAN I CAME HERE WITH?
HE WAS THE ONE YOU TOOK BACK TO YOUR ROOM.

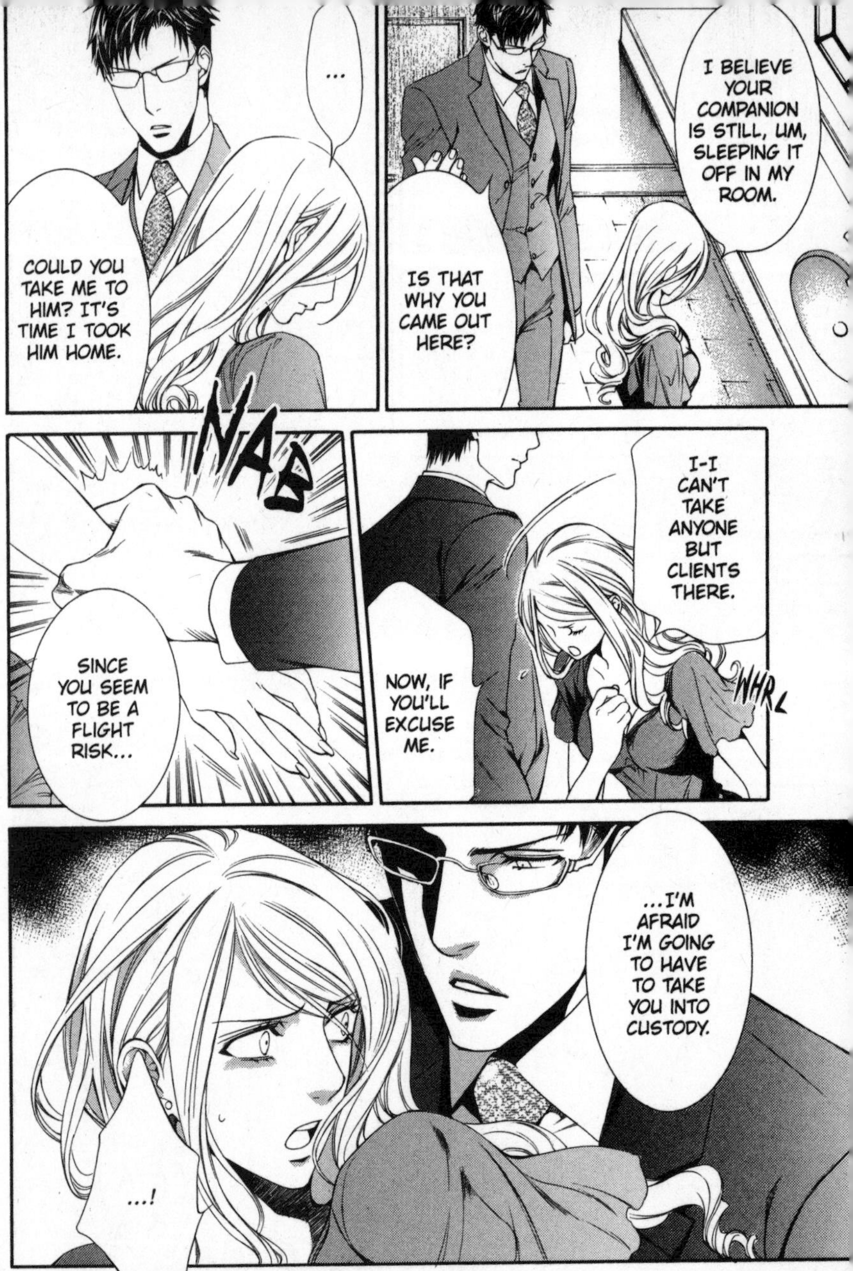
I BELIEVE YOUR COMPANION IS STILL, UM, SLEEPING IT OFF IN MY ROOM.
IS THAT WHY YOU CAME OUT HERE?
...
COULD YOU TAKE ME TO HIM? IT'S TIME I TOOK HIM HOME.
I-I CAN'T TAKE ANYONE BUT CLIENTS THERE.
NOW, IF YOU'LL EXCUSE ME.
WHRL
NAB
SINCE YOU SEEM TO BE A FLIGHT RISK...
...I'M AFRAID I'M GOING TO HAVE TO TAKE YOU INTO CUSTODY.
...!

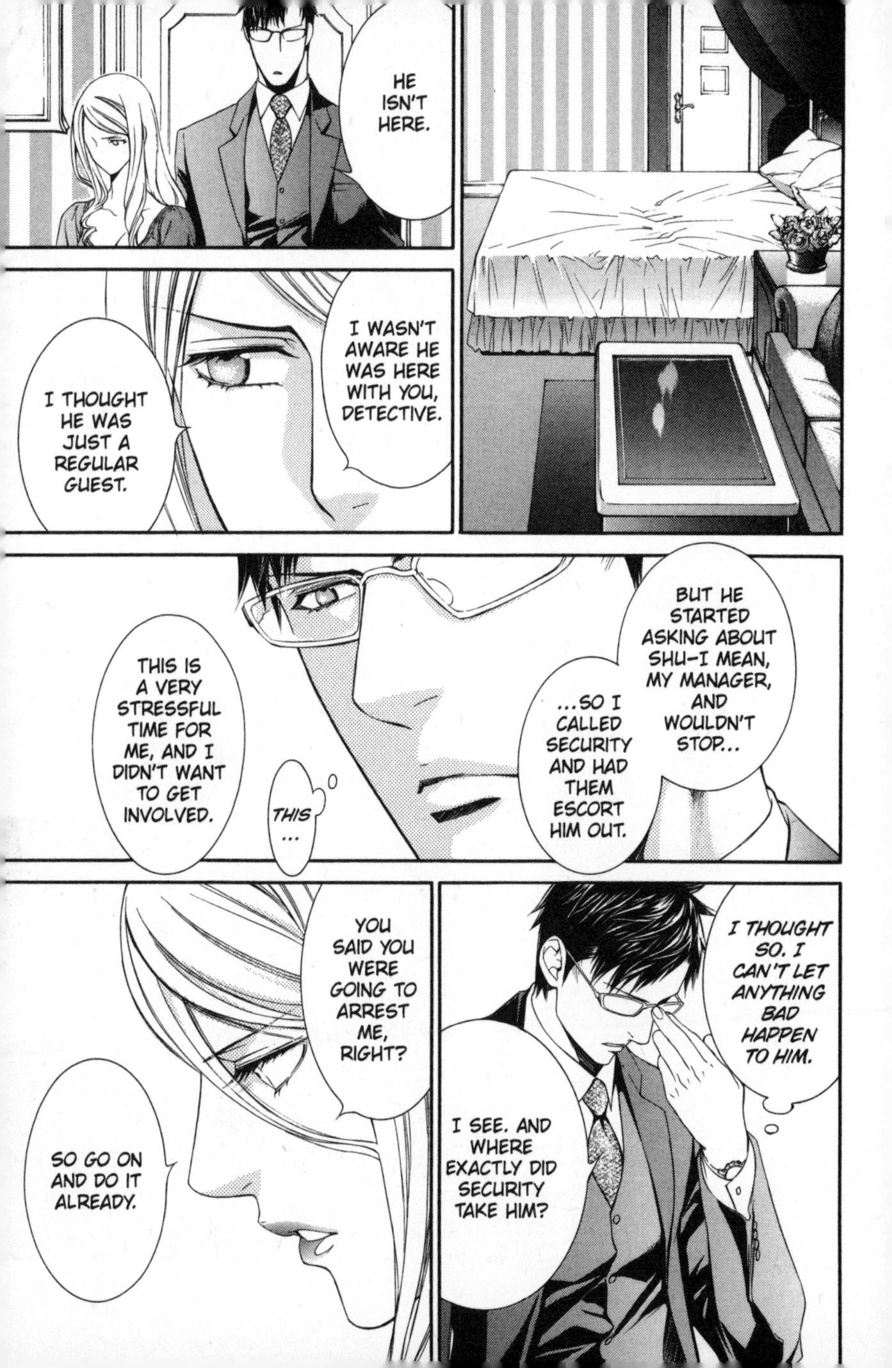
HE ISN'T HERE.
I WASN'T AWARE HE WAS HERE WITH YOU, DETECTIVE.
I THOUGHT HE WAS JUST A REGULAR GUEST.
BUT HE STARTED ASKING ABOUT SHU—I MEAN, MY MANAGER, AND WOULDN'T STOP...
...SO I CALLED SECURITY AND HAD THEM ESCORT HIM OUT.
THIS...
THIS IS A VERY STRESSFUL TIME FOR ME, AND I DIDN'T WANT TO GET INVOLVED.
I THOUGHT SO. I CAN'T LET ANYTHING BAD HAPPEN TO HIM.
I SEE. AND WHERE EXACTLY DID SECURITY TAKE HIM?
YOU SAID YOU WERE GOING TO ARREST ME, RIGHT?
SO GO ON AND DO IT ALREADY.

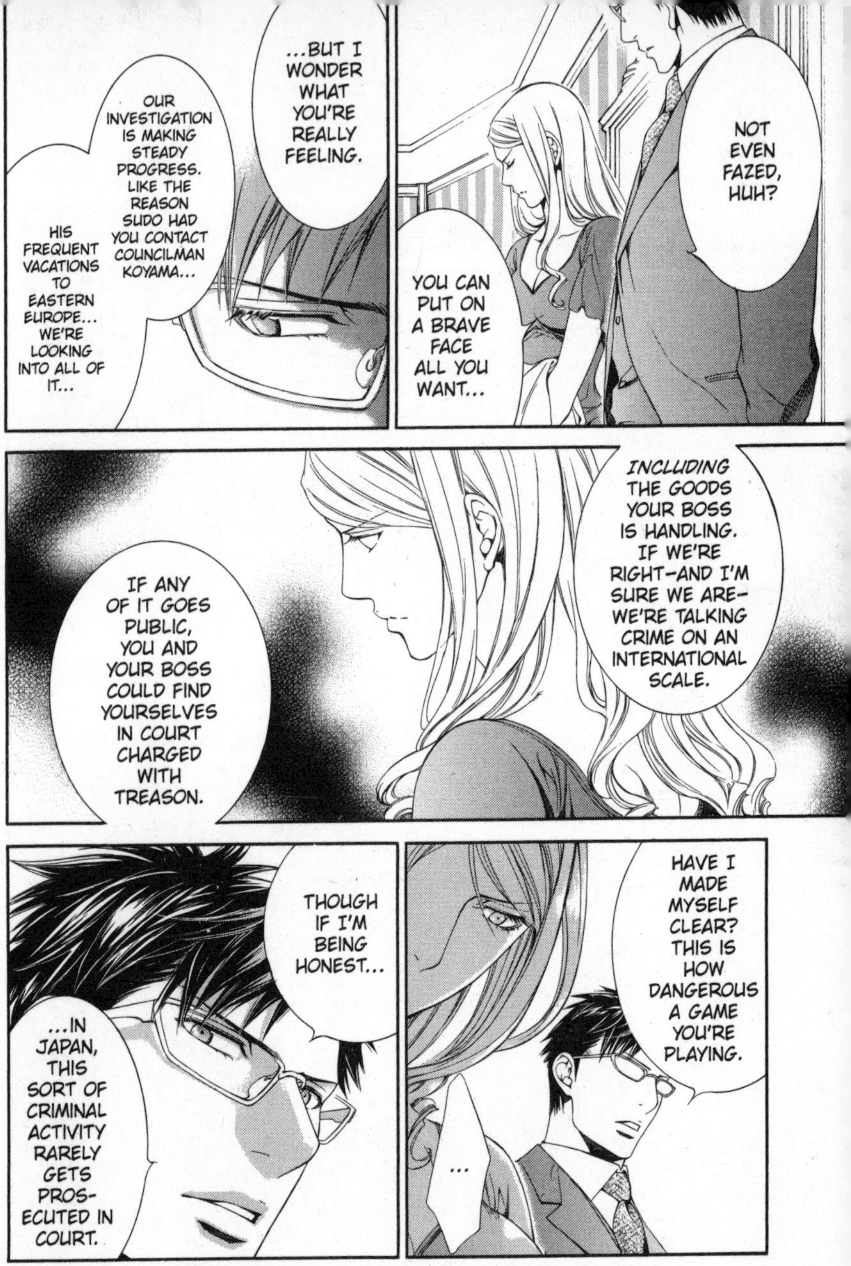
NOT EVEN FAZED, HUH?
YOU CAN PUT ON A BRAVE FACE ALL YOU WANT...
...BUT I WONDER WHAT YOU'RE REALLY FEELING.
OUR INVESTIGATION IS MAKING STEADY PROGRESS. LIKE THE REASON SUDO HAD YOU CONTACT COUNCILMAN KOYAMA...
HIS FREQUENT VACATIONS TO EASTERN EUROPE... WE'RE LOOKING INTO ALL OF IT...
INCLUDING THE GOODS YOUR BOSS IS HANDLING. IF WE'RE RIGHT—AND I'M SURE WE ARE—WE'RE TALKING CRIME ON AN INTERNATIONAL SCALE.
IF ANY OF IT GOES PUBLIC, YOU AND YOUR BOSS COULD FIND YOURSELVES IN COURT CHARGED WITH TREASON.
HAVE I MADE MYSELF CLEAR? THIS IS HOW DANGEROUS A GAME YOU'RE PLAYING.
...
THOUGH IF I'M BEING HONEST...
...IN JAPAN, THIS SORT OF CRIMINAL ACTIVITY RARELY GETS PROS-ECUTED IN COURT.

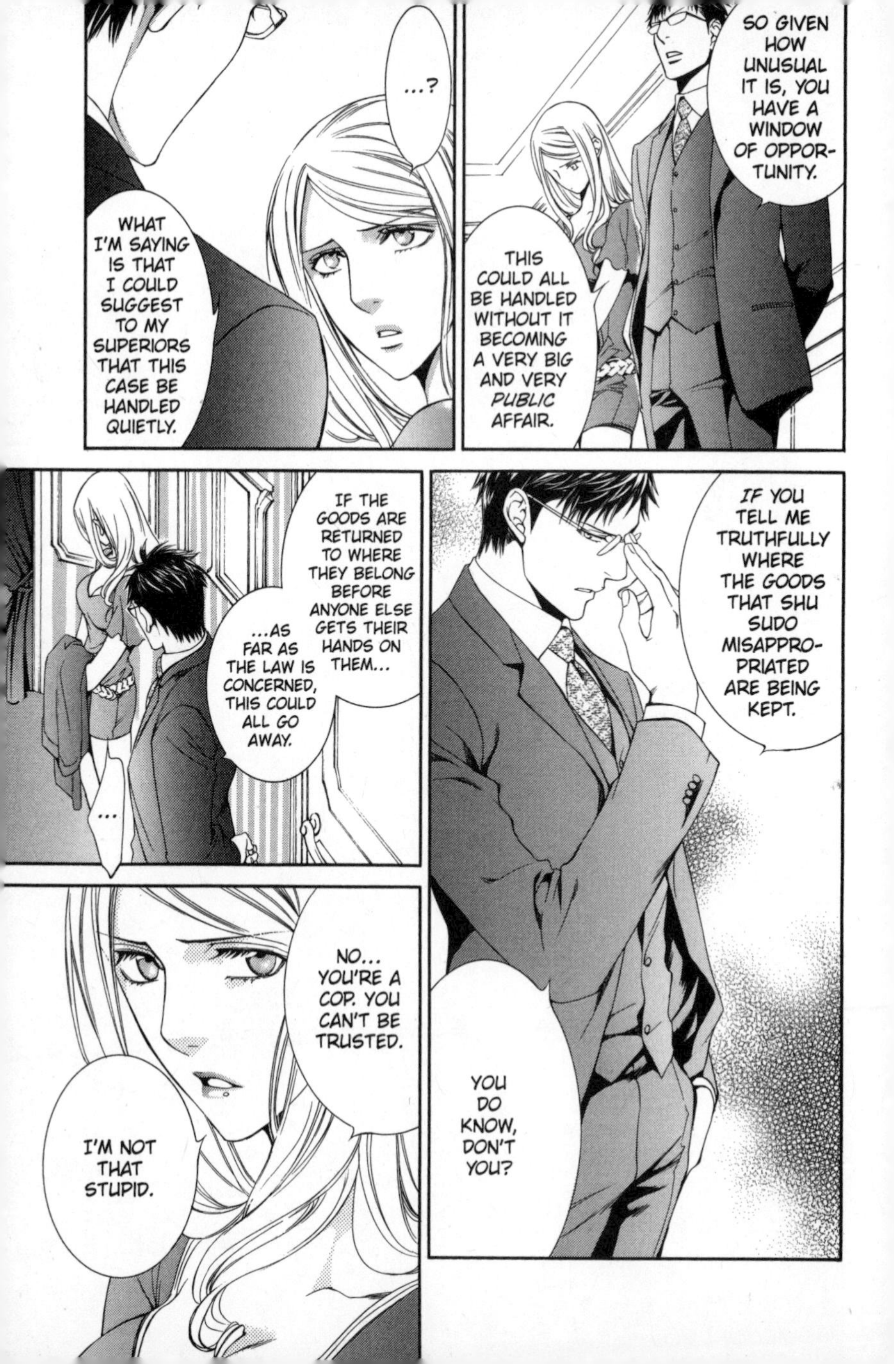
SO GIVEN HOW UNUSUAL IT IS, YOU HAVE A WINDOW OF OPPORTUNITY.
THIS COULD ALL BE HANDLED WITHOUT IT BECOMING A VERY BIG AND VERY *PUBLIC* AFFAIR.
...?
WHAT I'M SAYING IS THAT I COULD SUGGEST TO MY SUPERIORS THAT THIS CASE BE HANDLED QUIETLY.
IF YOU TELL ME TRUTHFULLY WHERE THE GOODS THAT SHU SUDO MISAPPROPRIATED ARE BEING KEPT.
YOU DO KNOW, DON'T YOU?
IF THE GOODS ARE RETURNED TO WHERE THEY BELONG BEFORE ANYONE ELSE GETS THEIR HANDS ON THEM...
...AS FAR AS THE LAW IS CONCERNED, THIS COULD ALL GO AWAY.
...
NO... YOU'RE A COP. YOU CAN'T BE TRUSTED.
I'M NOT THAT STUPID.

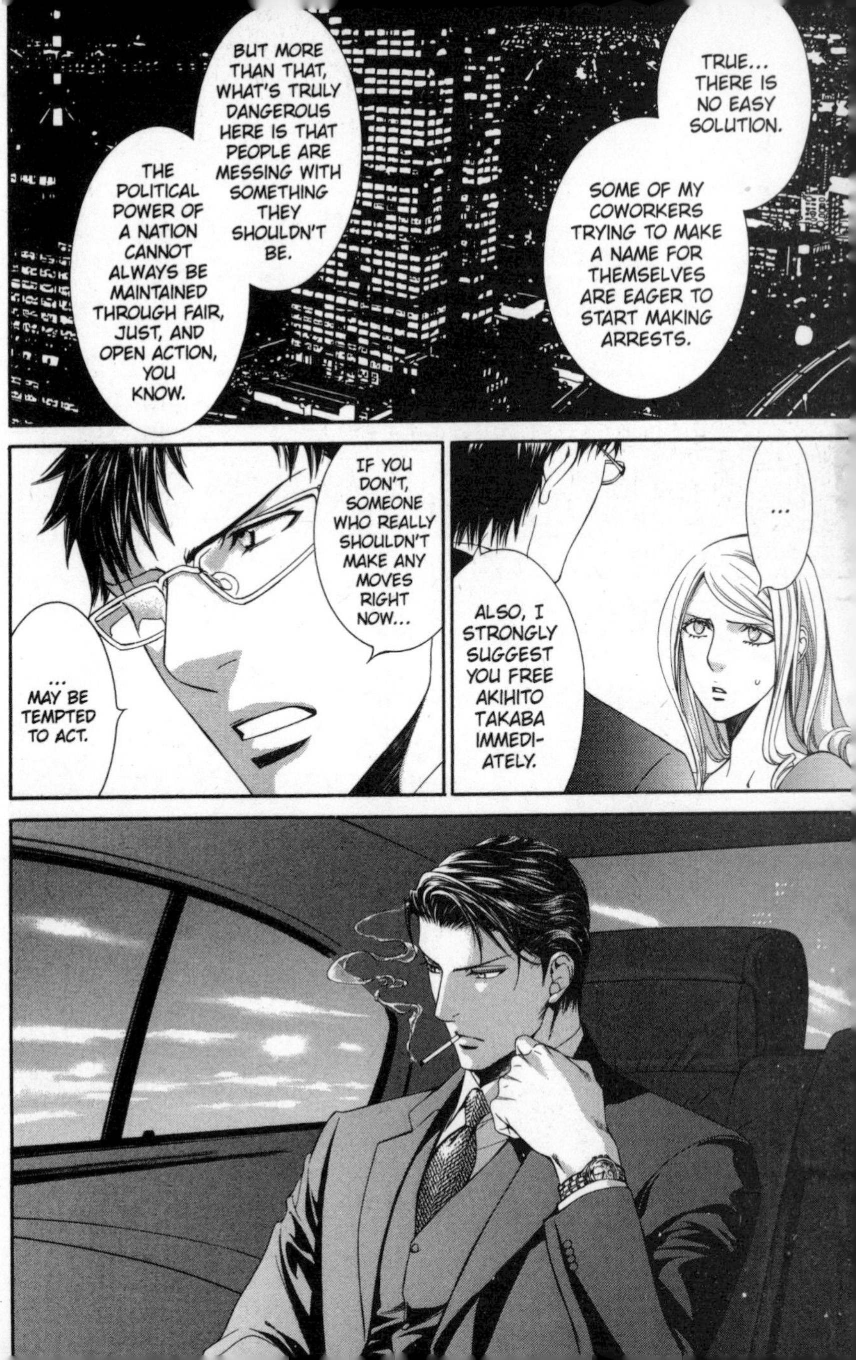
TRUE... THERE IS NO EASY SOLUTION.
SOME OF MY COWORKERS TRYING TO MAKE A NAME FOR THEMSELVES ARE EAGER TO START MAKING ARRESTS.
BUT MORE THAN THAT, WHAT'S TRULY DANGEROUS HERE IS THAT PEOPLE ARE MESSING WITH SOMETHING THEY SHOULDN'T BE.
THE POLITICAL POWER OF A NATION CANNOT ALWAYS BE MAINTAINED THROUGH FAIR, JUST, AND OPEN ACTION, YOU KNOW.
...
ALSO, I STRONGLY SUGGEST YOU FREE AKIHITO TAKABA IMMEDI-ATELY.
IF YOU DON'T, SOMEONE WHO REALLY SHOULDN'T MAKE ANY MOVES RIGHT NOW...
... MAY BE TEMPTED TO ACT.

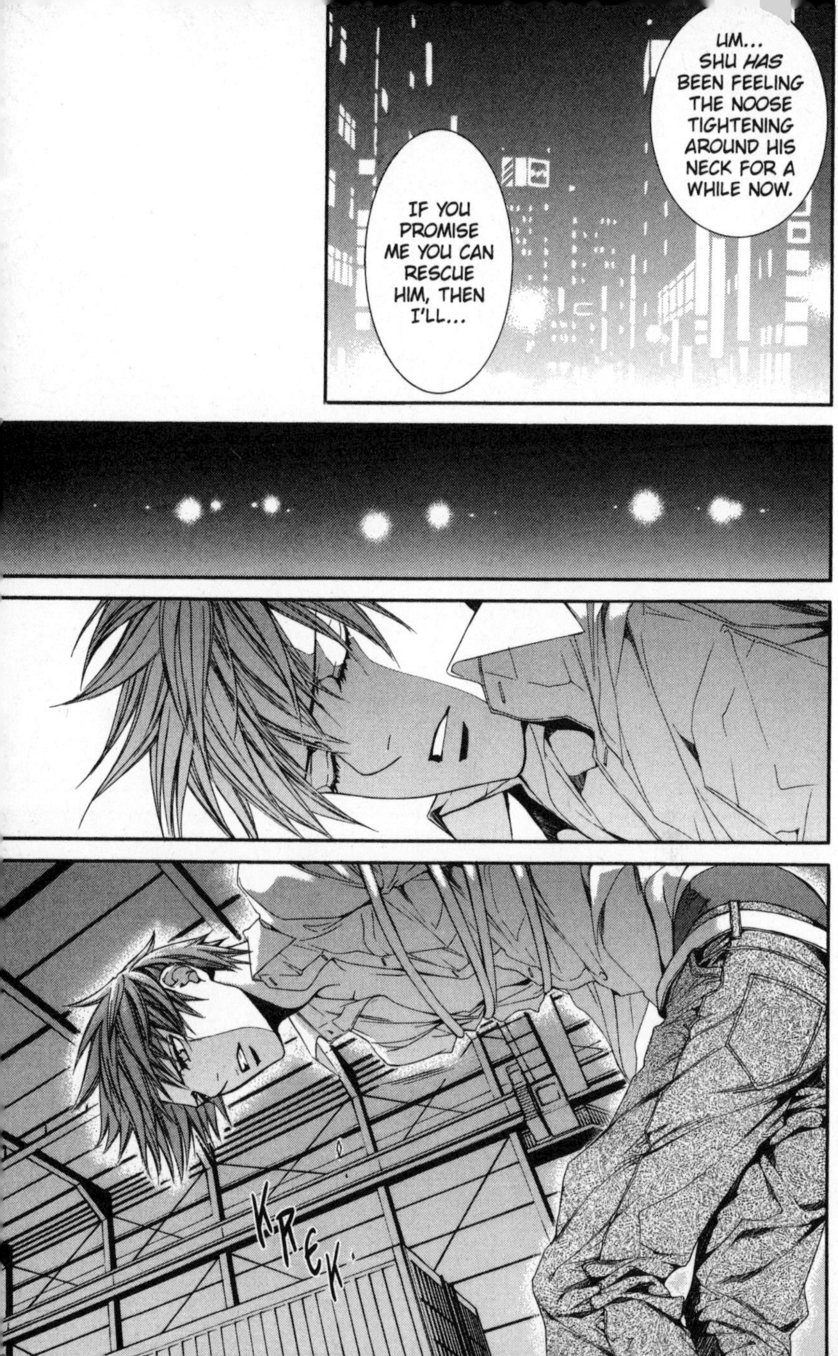
UM... SHU *HAS* BEEN FEELING THE NOOSE TIGHTENING AROUND HIS NECK FOR A WHILE NOW.
IF YOU PROMISE ME YOU CAN RESCUE HIM, THEN I'LL...
KREK

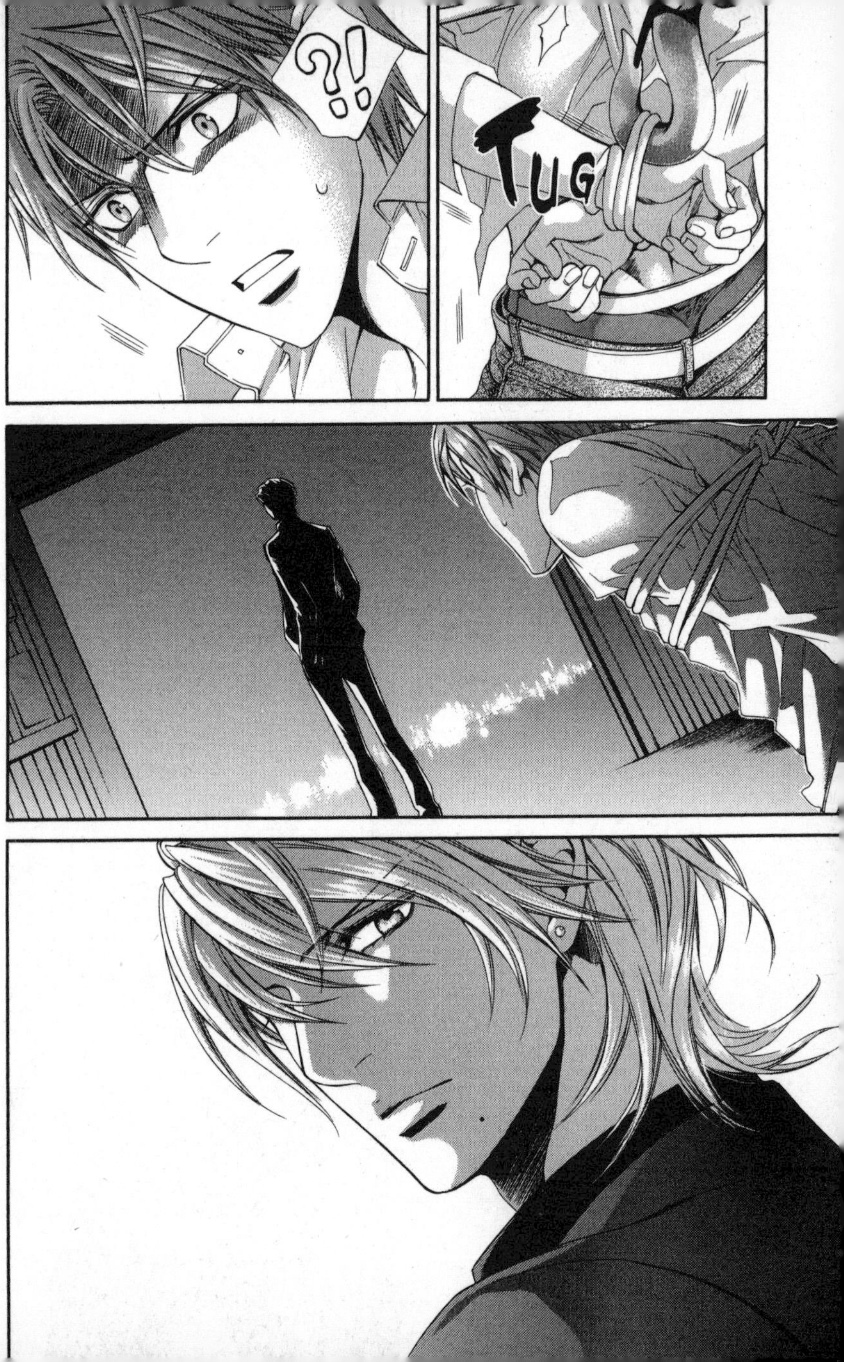
TUG
?!

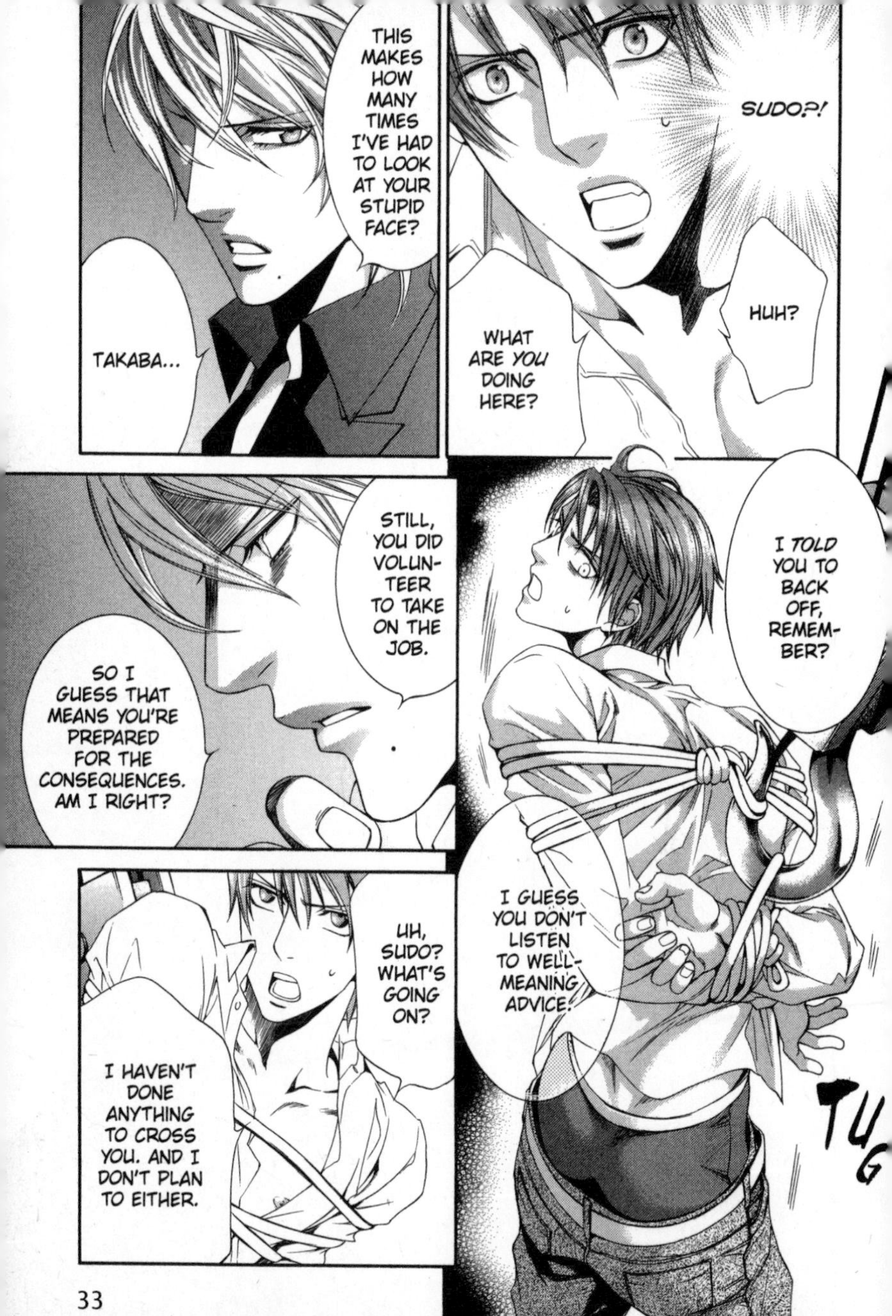
SUDO?!
HUH?
WHAT ARE *YOU* DOING HERE?
THIS MAKES HOW MANY TIMES I'VE HAD TO LOOK AT YOUR STUPID FACE?
TAKABA...
I *TOLD* YOU TO BACK OFF, REMEMBER?
I GUESS YOU DON'T LISTEN TO WELL-MEANING ADVICE.
TUG
STILL, YOU DID VOLUNTEER TO TAKE ON THE JOB.
SO I GUESS THAT MEANS YOU'RE PREPARED FOR THE CONSEQUENCES. AM I RIGHT?
UH, SUDO? WHAT'S GOING ON?
I HAVEN'T DONE ANYTHING TO CROSS YOU. AND I DON'T PLAN TO EITHER.

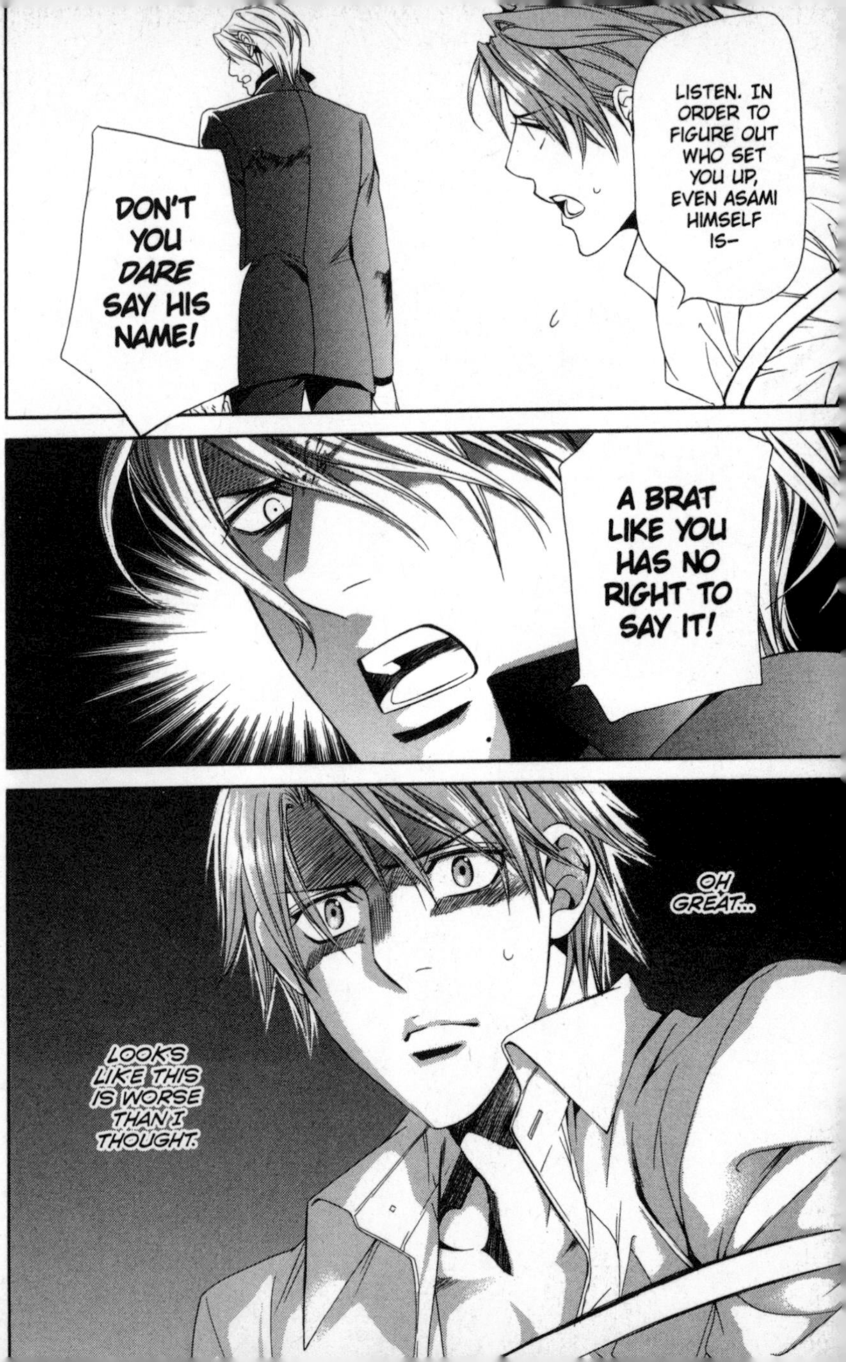
LISTEN. IN ORDER TO FIGURE OUT WHO SET YOU UP, EVEN ASAMI HIMSELF IS–
DON'T YOU DARE SAY HIS NAME!
A BRAT LIKE YOU HAS NO RIGHT TO SAY IT!
OH GREAT...
LOOKS LIKE THIS IS WORSE THAN I THOUGHT.

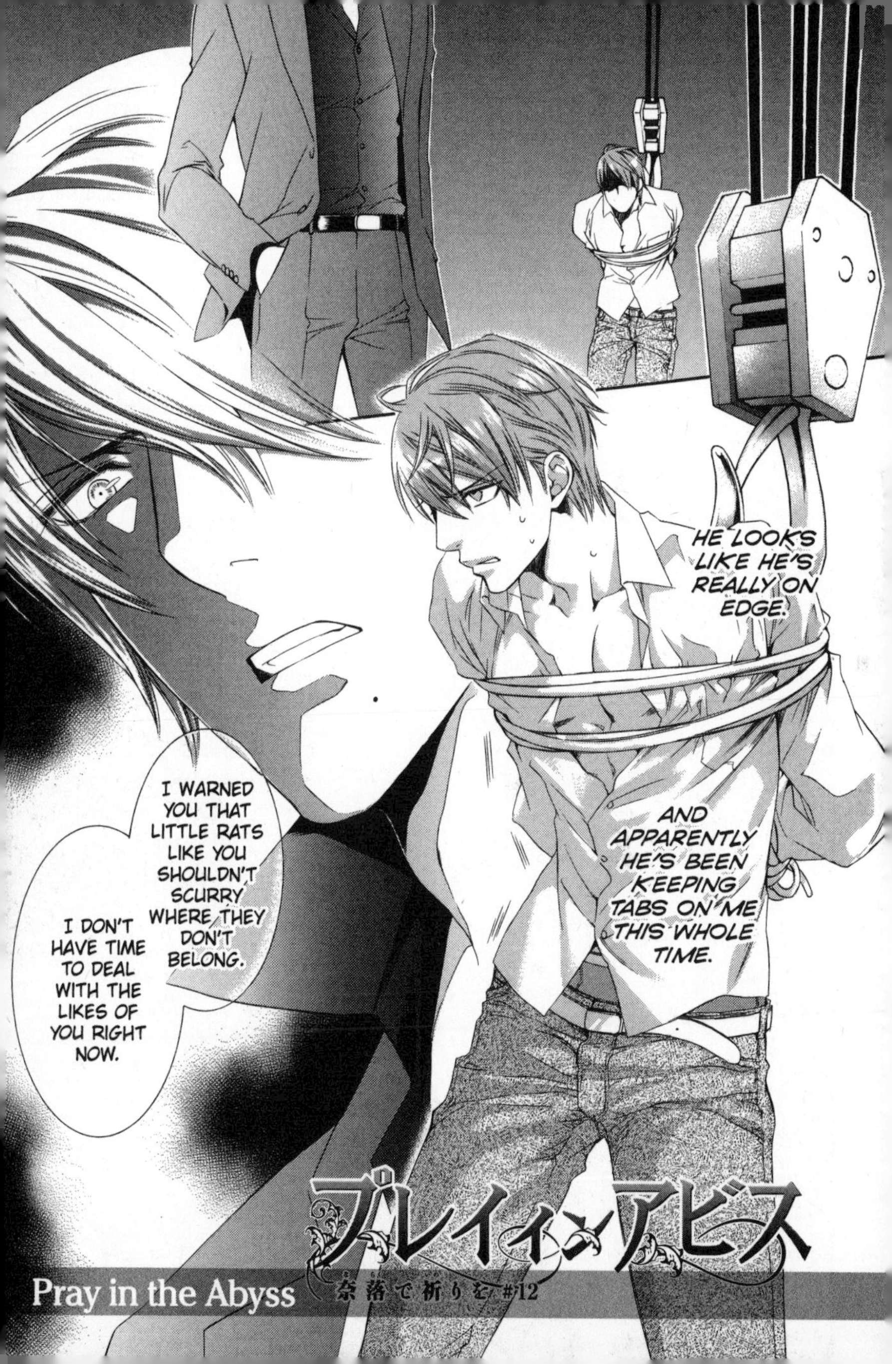
HE LOOKS LIKE HE'S REALLY ON EDGE.
AND APPARENTLY HE'S BEEN KEEPING TABS ON ME THIS WHOLE TIME.
I WARNED YOU THAT LITTLE RATS LIKE YOU SHOULDN'T SCURRY WHERE THEY DON'T BELONG.
I DON'T HAVE TIME TO DEAL WITH THE LIKES OF YOU RIGHT NOW.
プレイィンアビス
Pray in the Abyss
奈落で祈りを #12

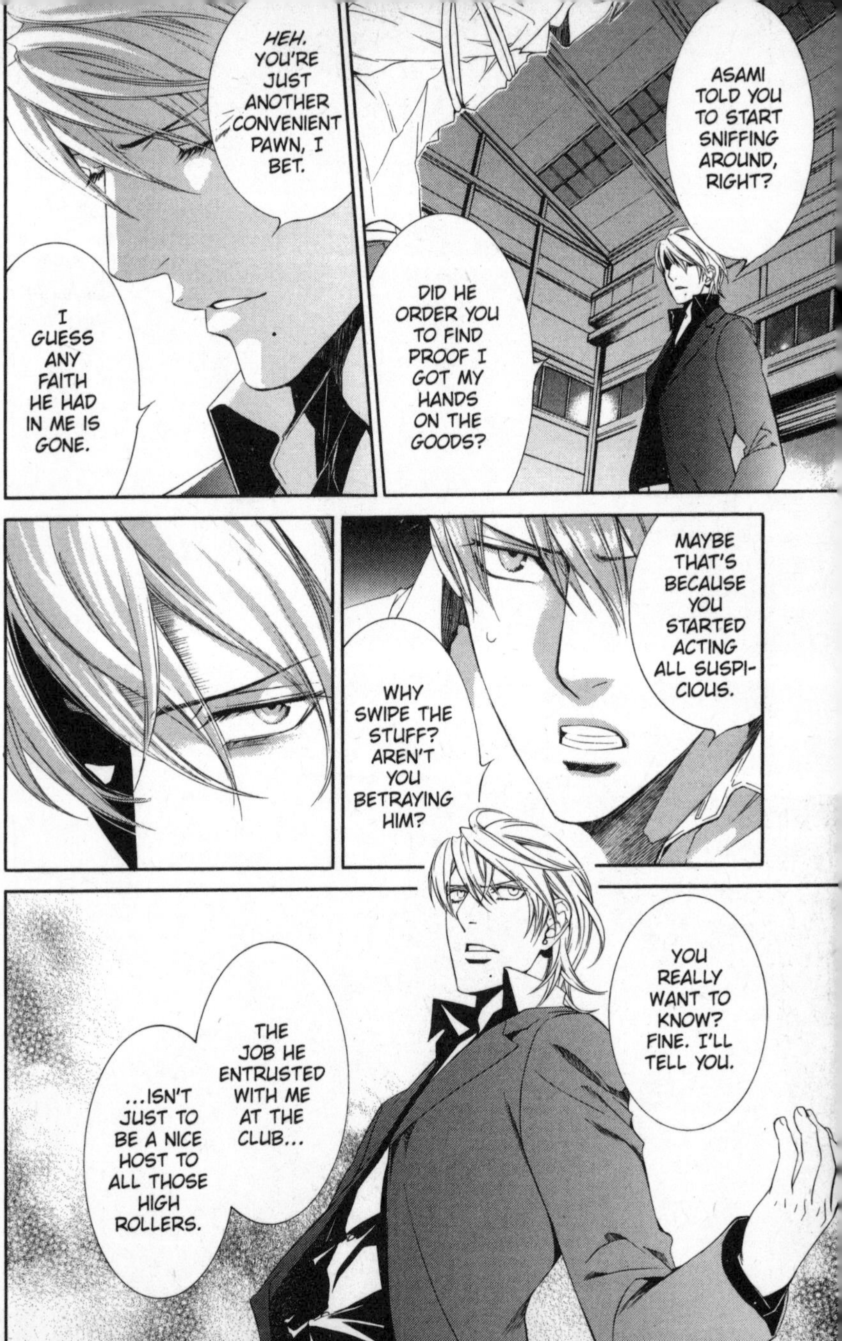
ASAMI TOLD YOU TO START SNIFFING AROUND, RIGHT?
DID HE ORDER YOU TO FIND PROOF I GOT MY HANDS ON THE GOODS?
HEH. YOU'RE JUST ANOTHER CONVENIENT PAWN, I BET.
I GUESS ANY FAITH HE HAD IN ME IS GONE.
MAYBE THAT'S BECAUSE YOU STARTED ACTING ALL SUSPICIOUS.
WHY SWIPE THE STUFF? AREN'T YOU BETRAYING HIM?
YOU REALLY WANT TO KNOW? FINE. I'LL TELL YOU.
THE JOB HE ENTRUSTED WITH ME AT THE CLUB...
...ISN'T JUST TO BE A NICE HOST TO ALL THOSE HIGH ROLLERS.

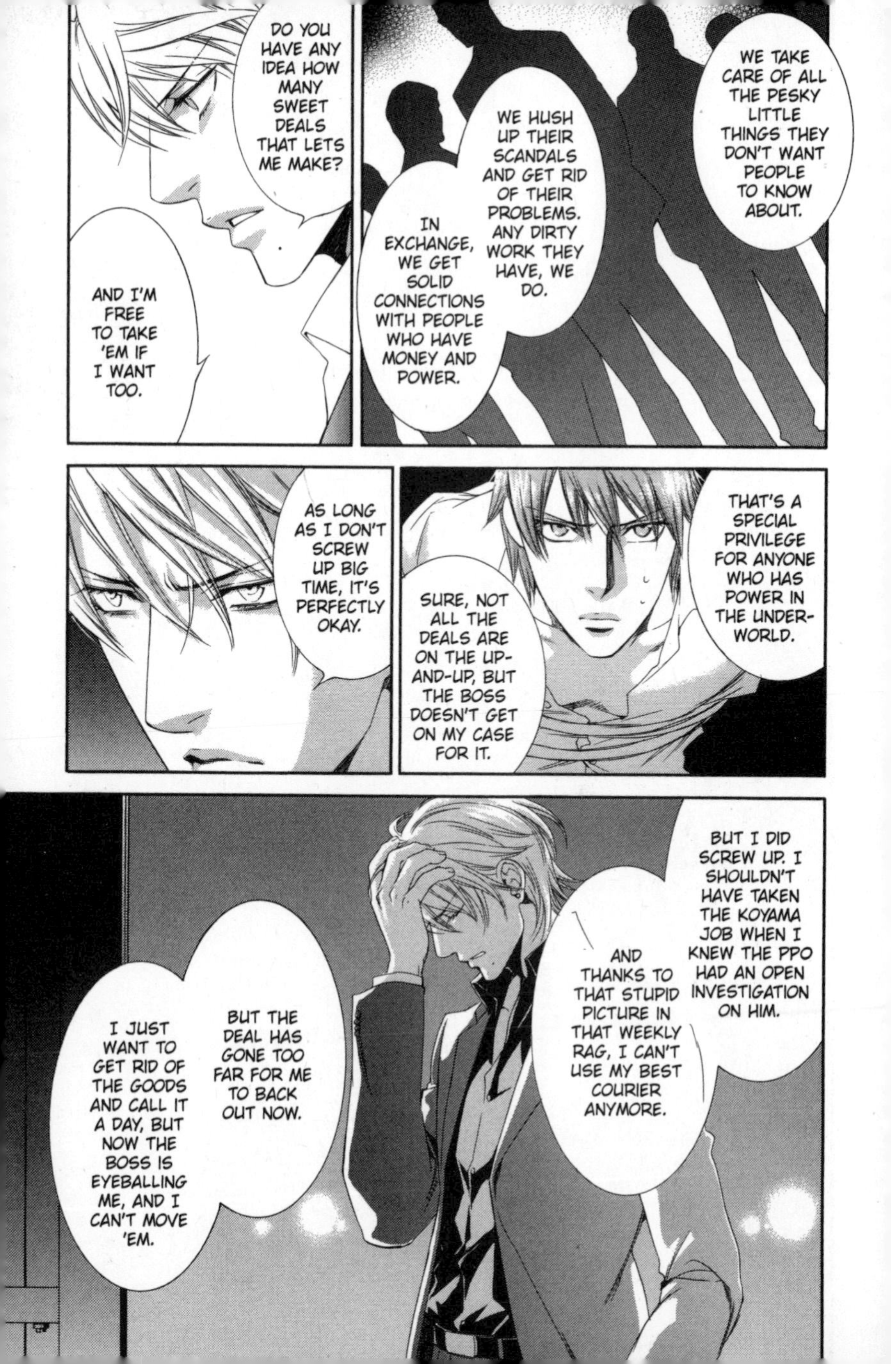
WE TAKE CARE OF ALL THE PESKY LITTLE THINGS THEY DON'T WANT PEOPLE TO KNOW ABOUT.
WE HUSH UP THEIR SCANDALS AND GET RID OF THEIR PROBLEMS. ANY DIRTY WORK THEY HAVE, WE DO.
IN EXCHANGE, WE GET SOLID CONNECTIONS WITH PEOPLE WHO HAVE MONEY AND POWER.
DO YOU HAVE ANY IDEA HOW MANY SWEET DEALS THAT LETS ME MAKE?
AND I'M FREE TO TAKE 'EM IF I WANT TOO.
THAT'S A SPECIAL PRIVILEGE FOR ANYONE WHO HAS POWER IN THE UNDER-WORLD.
SURE, NOT ALL THE DEALS ARE ON THE UP-AND-UP, BUT THE BOSS DOESN'T GET ON MY CASE FOR IT.
AS LONG AS I DON'T SCREW UP BIG TIME, IT'S PERFECTLY OKAY.
BUT I DID SCREW UP. I SHOULDN'T HAVE TAKEN THE KOYAMA JOB WHEN I KNEW THE PPO HAD AN OPEN INVESTIGATION ON HIM.
AND THANKS TO THAT STUPID PICTURE IN THAT WEEKLY RAG, I CAN'T USE MY BEST COURIER ANYMORE.
BUT THE DEAL HAS GONE TOO FAR FOR ME TO BACK OUT NOW.
I JUST WANT TO GET RID OF THE GOODS AND CALL IT A DAY, BUT NOW THE BOSS IS EYEBALLING ME, AND I CAN'T MOVE 'EM.

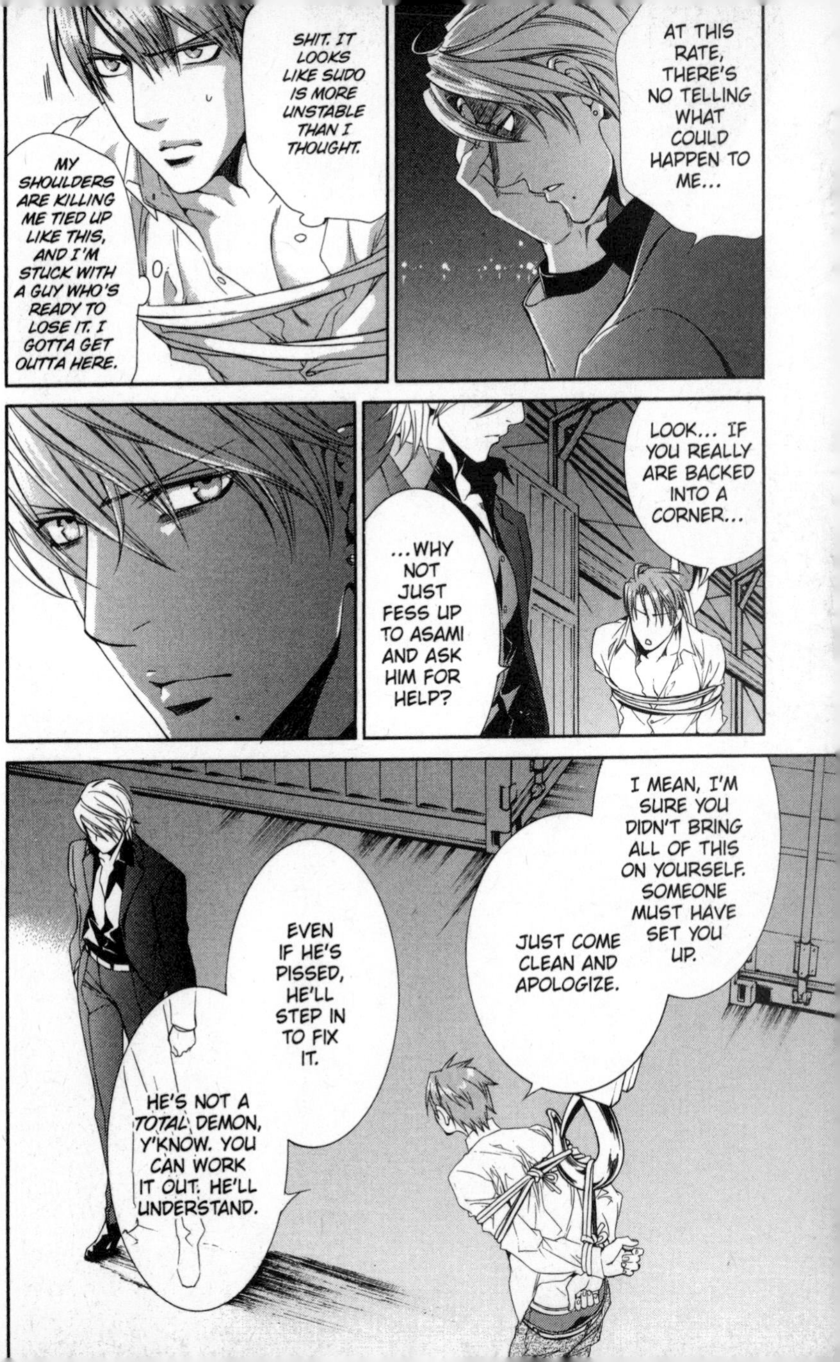
AT THIS RATE, THERE'S NO TELLING WHAT COULD HAPPEN TO ME...
SHIT. IT LOOKS LIKE SUDO IS MORE UNSTABLE THAN I THOUGHT.
MY SHOULDERS ARE KILLING ME TIED UP LIKE THIS, AND I'M STUCK WITH A GUY WHO'S READY TO LOSE IT. I GOTTA GET OUTTA HERE.
LOOK... IF YOU REALLY ARE BACKED INTO A CORNER...
...WHY NOT JUST FESS UP TO ASAMI AND ASK HIM FOR HELP?
I MEAN, I'M SURE YOU DIDN'T BRING ALL OF THIS ON YOURSELF. SOMEONE MUST HAVE SET YOU UP.
JUST COME CLEAN AND APOLOGIZE.
EVEN IF HE'S PISSED, HE'LL STEP IN TO FIX IT.
HE'S NOT A *TOTAL* DEMON, Y'KNOW. YOU CAN WORK IT OUT. HE'LL UNDERSTAND.

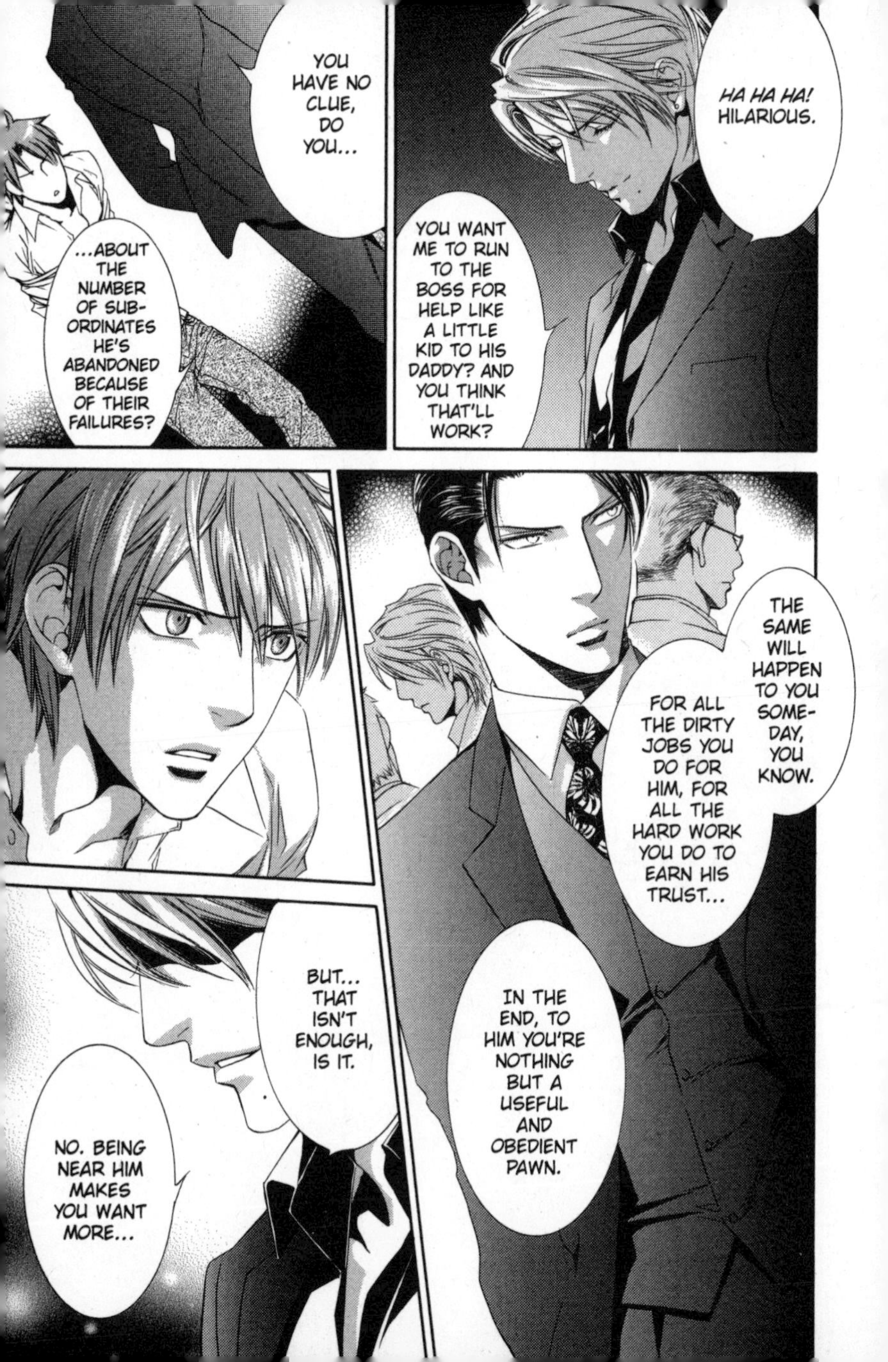
HA HA HA! HILARIOUS.
YOU WANT ME TO RUN TO THE BOSS FOR HELP LIKE A LITTLE KID TO HIS DADDY? AND YOU THINK THAT'LL WORK?
YOU HAVE NO CLUE, DO YOU...
...ABOUT THE NUMBER OF SUB-ORDINATES HE'S ABANDONED BECAUSE OF THEIR FAILURES?
THE SAME WILL HAPPEN TO YOU SOME-DAY, YOU KNOW.
FOR ALL THE DIRTY JOBS YOU DO FOR HIM, FOR ALL THE HARD WORK YOU DO TO EARN HIS TRUST...
IN THE END, TO HIM YOU'RE NOTHING BUT A USEFUL AND OBEDIENT PAWN.
BUT... THAT ISN'T ENOUGH, IS IT.
NO. BEING NEAR HIM MAKES YOU WANT MORE...

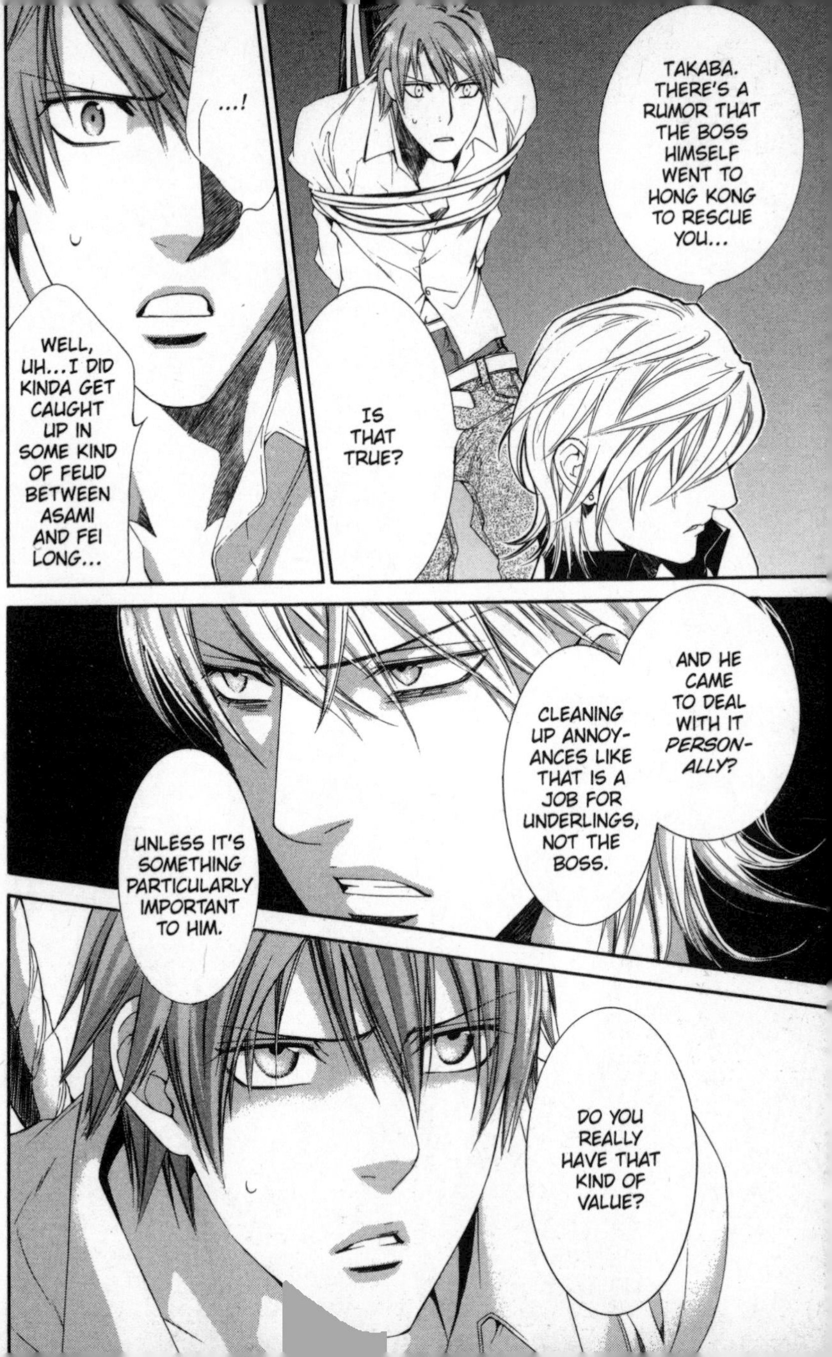
TAKABA. THERE'S A RUMOR THAT THE BOSS HIMSELF WENT TO HONG KONG TO RESCUE YOU...
IS THAT TRUE?
...!
WELL, UH...I DID KINDA GET CAUGHT UP IN SOME KIND OF FEUD BETWEEN ASAMI AND FEI LONG...
AND HE CAME TO DEAL WITH IT *PERSON-ALLY?*
CLEANING UP ANNOY-ANCES LIKE THAT IS A JOB FOR UNDERLINGS, NOT THE BOSS.
UNLESS IT'S SOMETHING PARTICULARLY IMPORTANT TO HIM.
DO YOU REALLY HAVE THAT KIND OF VALUE?

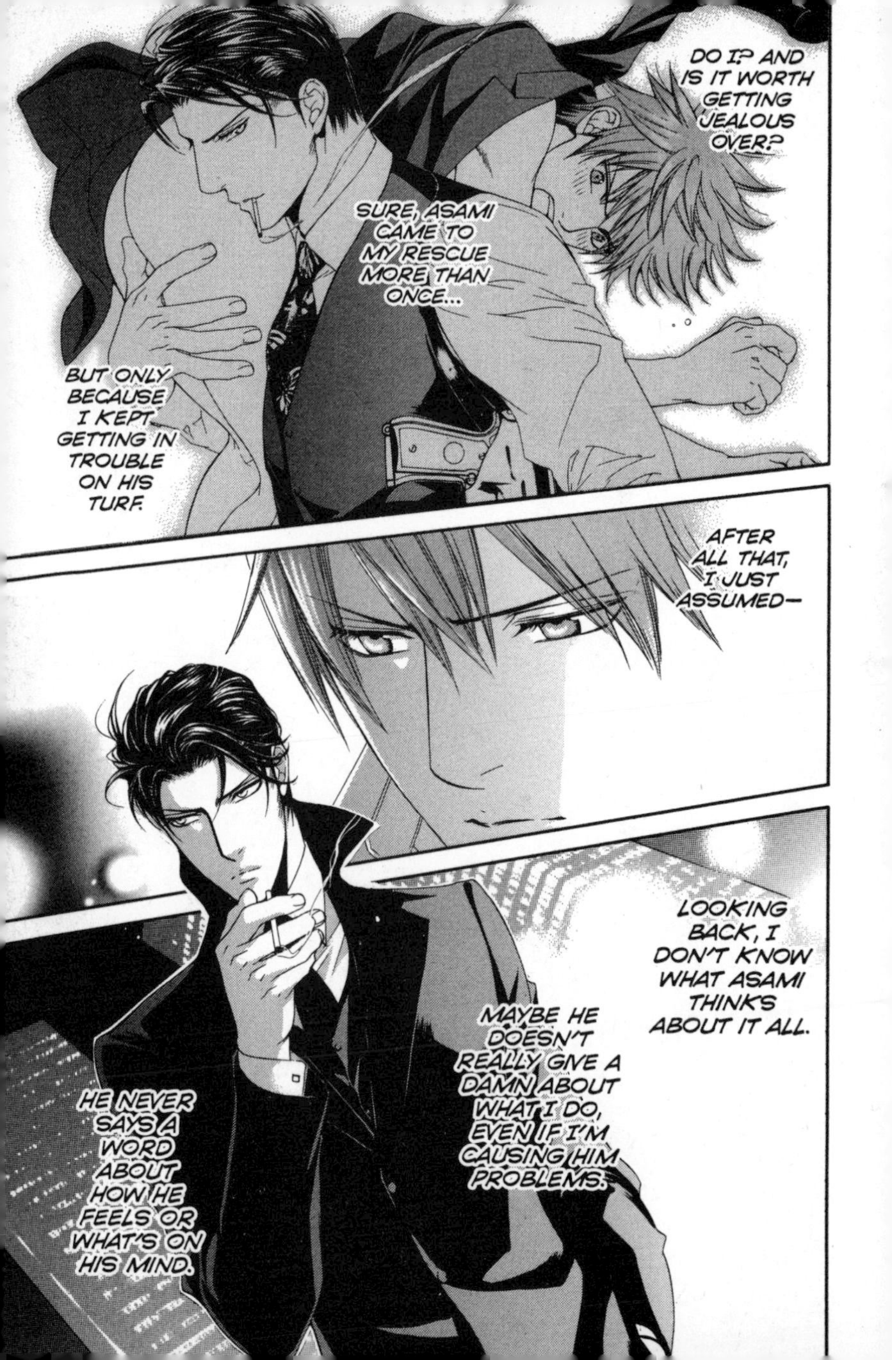
DO I? AND IS IT WORTH GETTING JEALOUS OVER?
SURE, ASAMI CAME TO MY RESCUE MORE THAN ONCE...
BUT ONLY BECAUSE I KEPT GETTING IN TROUBLE ON HIS TURF.
AFTER ALL THAT, I JUST ASSUMED—
LOOKING BACK, I DON'T KNOW WHAT ASAMI THINKS ABOUT IT ALL.
MAYBE HE DOESN'T REALLY GIVE A DAMN ABOUT WHAT I DO, EVEN IF I'M CAUSING HIM PROBLEMS.
HE NEVER SAYS A WORD ABOUT HOW HE FEELS OR WHAT'S ON HIS MIND.

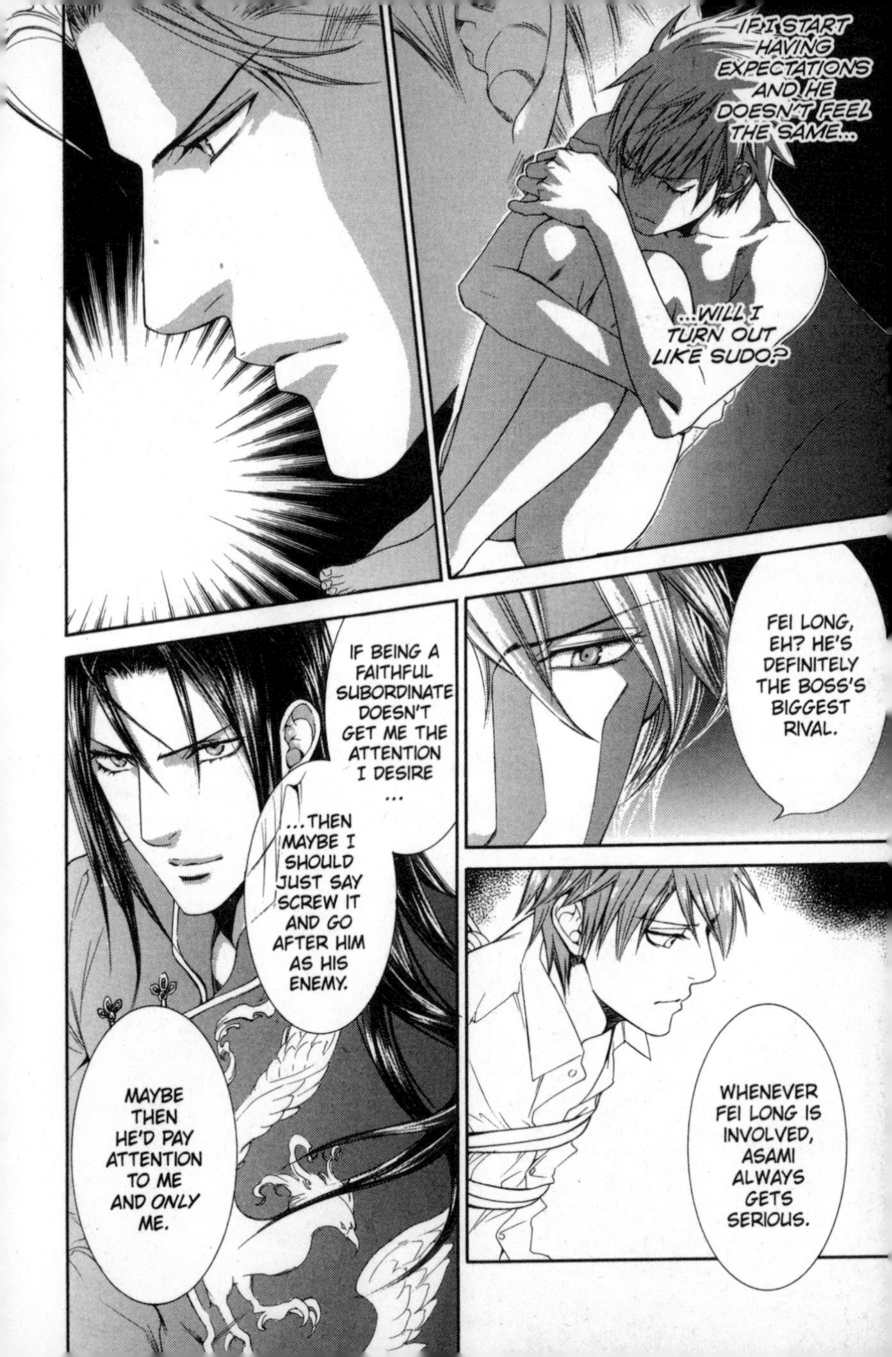
IF I START HAVING EXPECTATIONS AND HE DOESN'T FEEL THE SAME...
...WILL I TURN OUT LIKE SUDO?
FEI LONG, EH? HE'S DEFINITELY THE BOSS'S BIGGEST RIVAL.
WHENEVER FEI LONG IS INVOLVED, ASAMI ALWAYS GETS SERIOUS.
IF BEING A FAITHFUL SUBORDINATE DOESN'T GET ME THE ATTENTION I DESIRE ...
...THEN MAYBE I SHOULD JUST SAY SCREW IT AND GO AFTER HIM AS HIS ENEMY.
MAYBE THEN HE'D PAY ATTENTION TO ME AND *ONLY* ME.

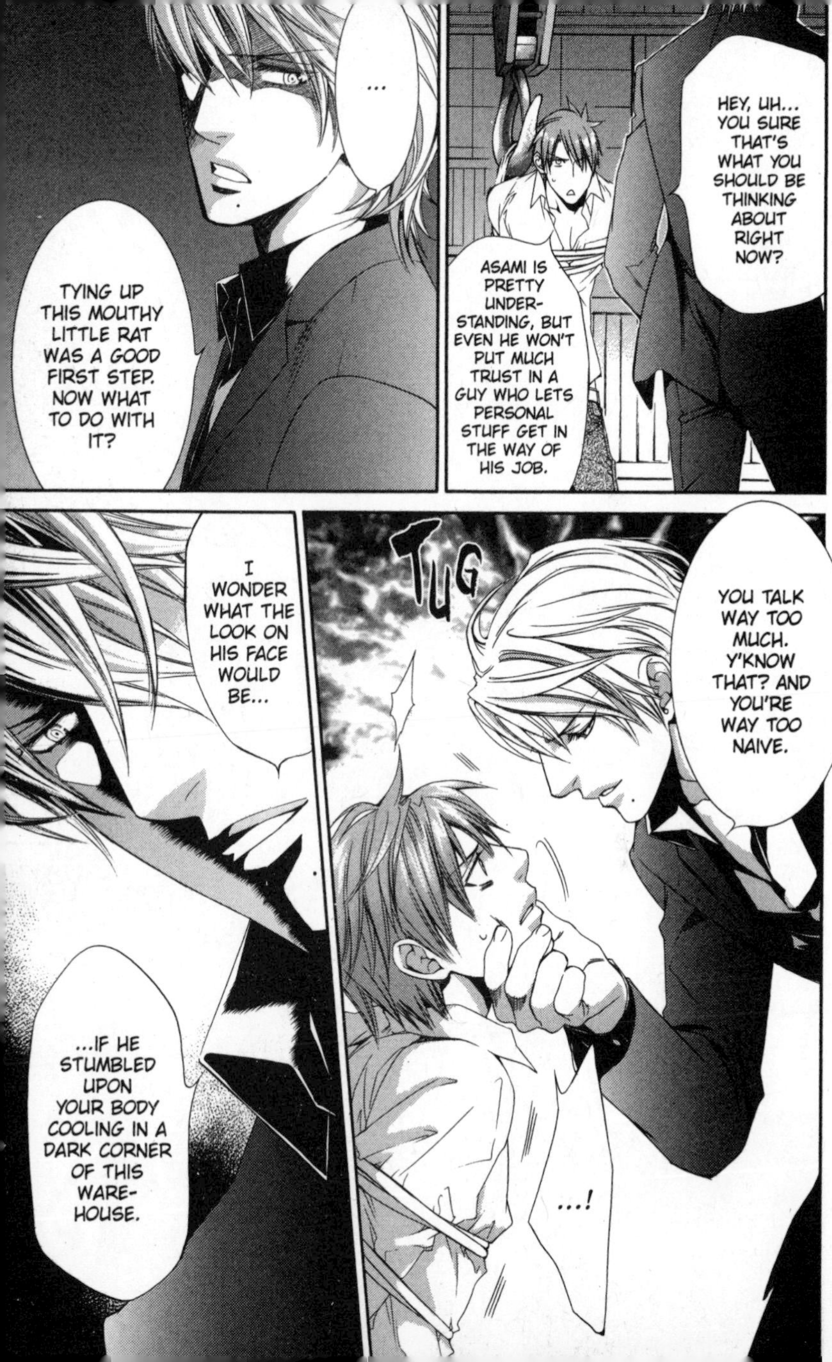
HEY, UH... YOU SURE THAT'S WHAT YOU SHOULD BE THINKING ABOUT RIGHT NOW?
ASAMI IS PRETTY UNDER-STANDING, BUT EVEN HE WON'T PUT MUCH TRUST IN A GUY WHO LETS PERSONAL STUFF GET IN THE WAY OF HIS JOB.
...
TYING UP THIS MOUTHY LITTLE RAT WAS A GOOD FIRST STEP. NOW WHAT TO DO WITH IT?
YOU TALK WAY TOO MUCH. Y'KNOW THAT? AND YOU'RE WAY TOO NAIVE.
TUG
...!
I WONDER WHAT THE LOOK ON HIS FACE WOULD BE...
...IF HE STUMBLED UPON YOUR BODY COOLING IN A DARK CORNER OF THIS WARE-HOUSE.

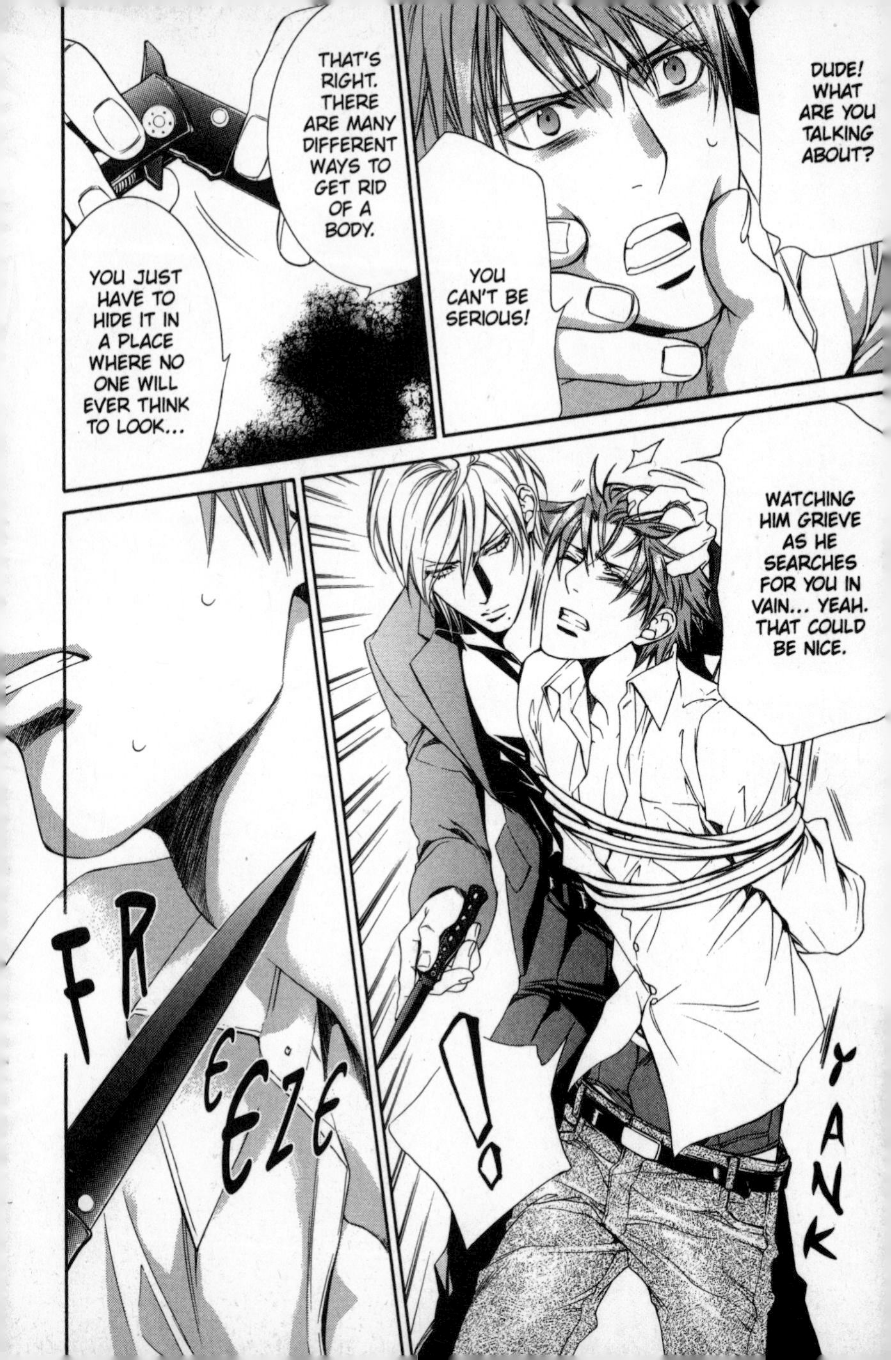
DUDE! WHAT ARE YOU TALKING ABOUT?
YOU CAN'T BE SERIOUS!
THAT'S RIGHT. THERE ARE MANY DIFFERENT WAYS TO GET RID OF A BODY.
YOU JUST HAVE TO HIDE IT IN A PLACE WHERE NO ONE WILL EVER THINK TO LOOK...
WATCHING HIM GRIEVE AS HE SEARCHES FOR YOU IN VAIN... YEAH. THAT COULD BE NICE.
YANK
!
FREEZE

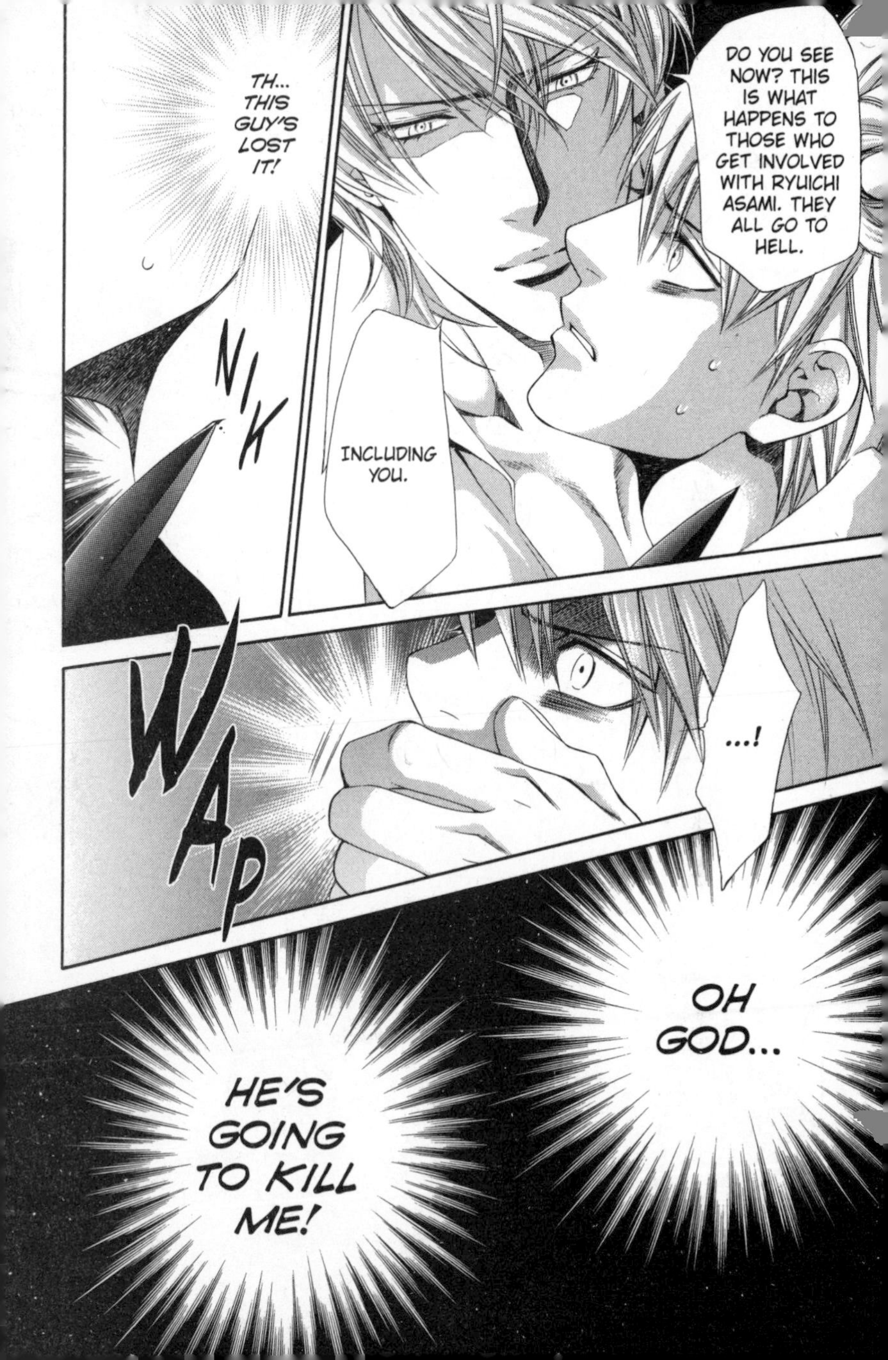

DO YOU SEE NOW? THIS IS WHAT HAPPENS TO THOSE WHO GET INVOLVED WITH RYUICHI ASAMI. THEY ALL GO TO HELL.
INCLUDING YOU.
TH... THIS GUY'S LOST IT!
NIK
...!
WAP
OH GOD...
HE'S GOING TO KILL ME!

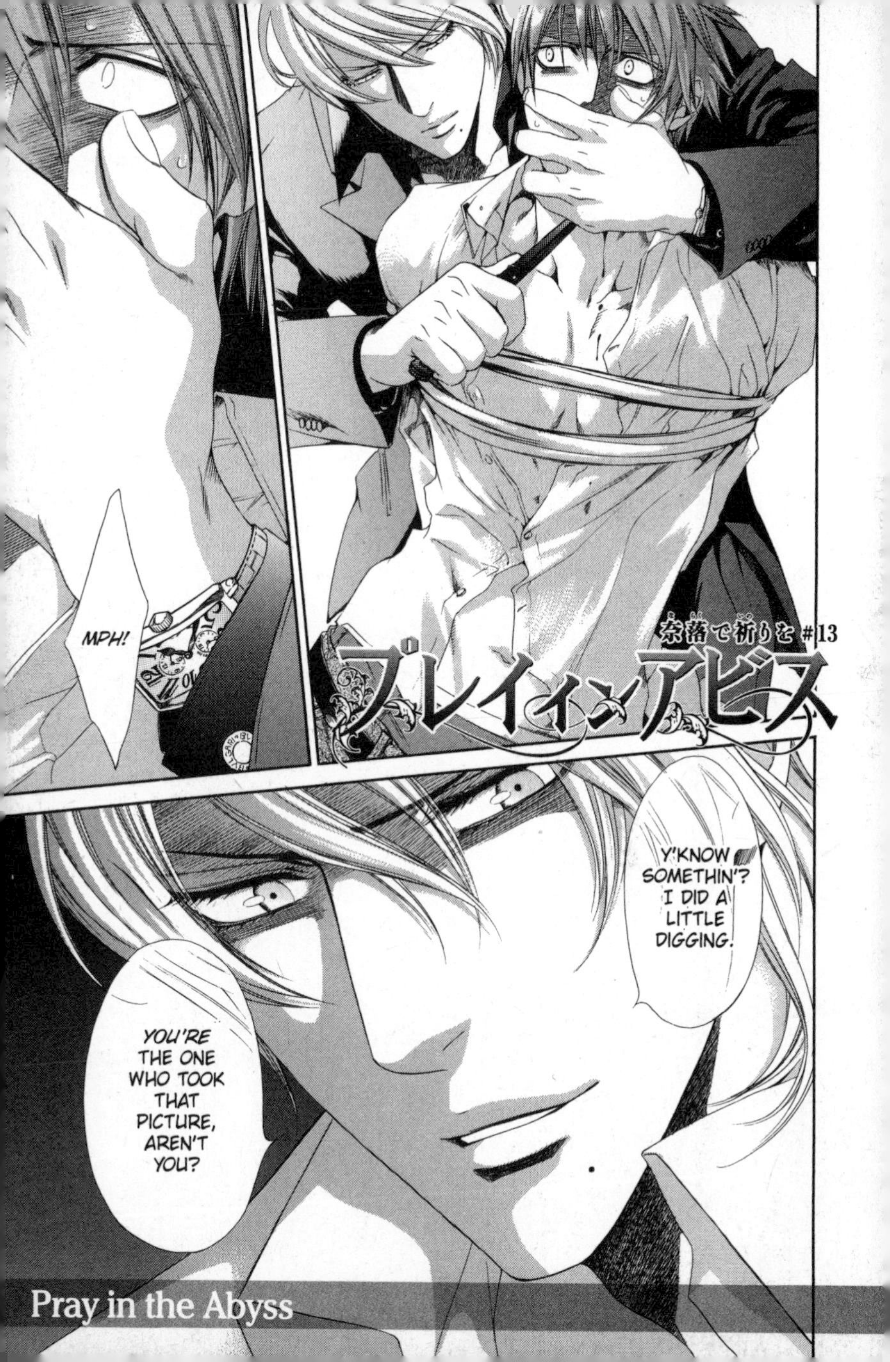
奈落で祈りを #13
プレイインアビス
MPH!
Y'KNOW SOMETHIN'? I DID A LITTLE DIGGING.
YOU'RE THE ONE WHO TOOK THAT PICTURE, AREN'T YOU?
Pray in the Abyss

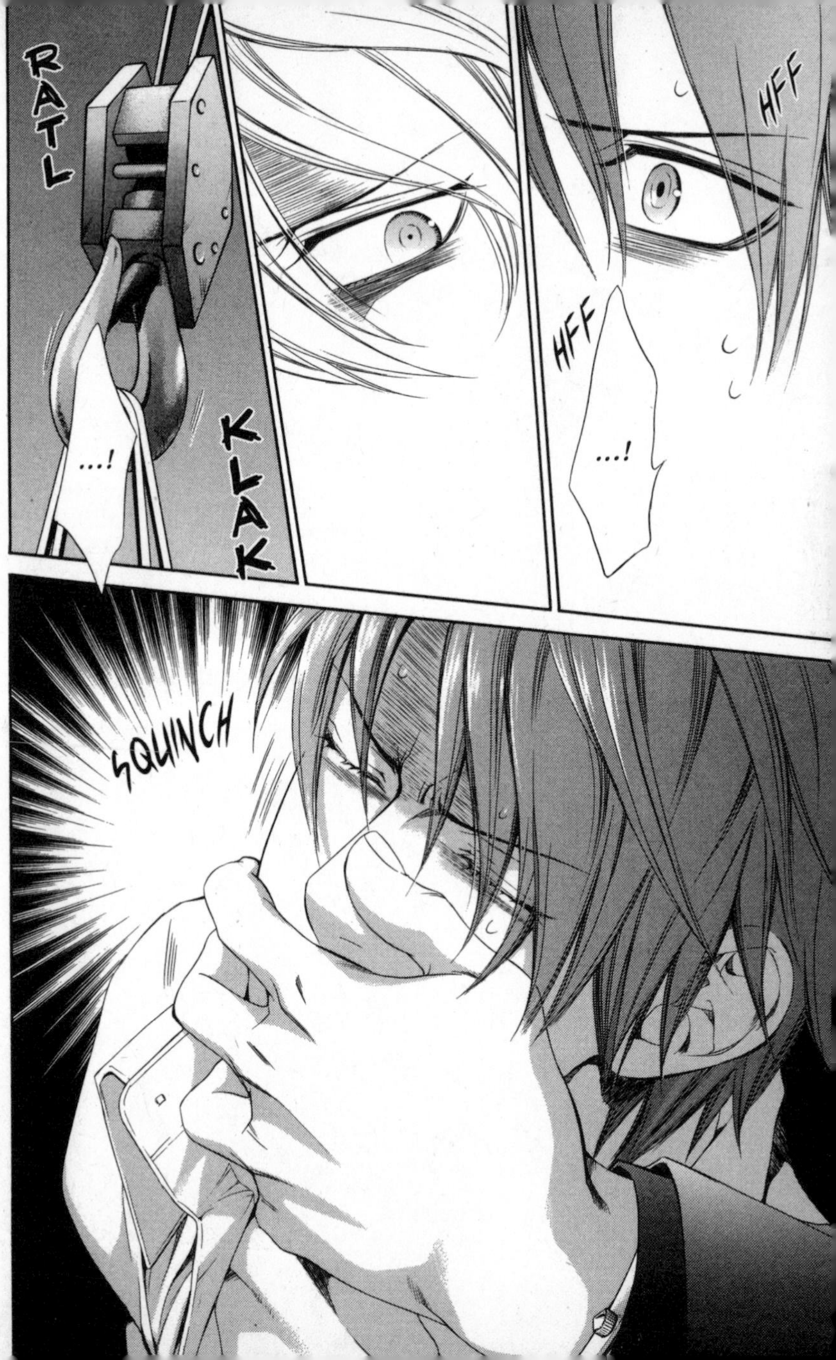
HFF
HFF
...!
KLAK
RATL
...!
SQUINCH

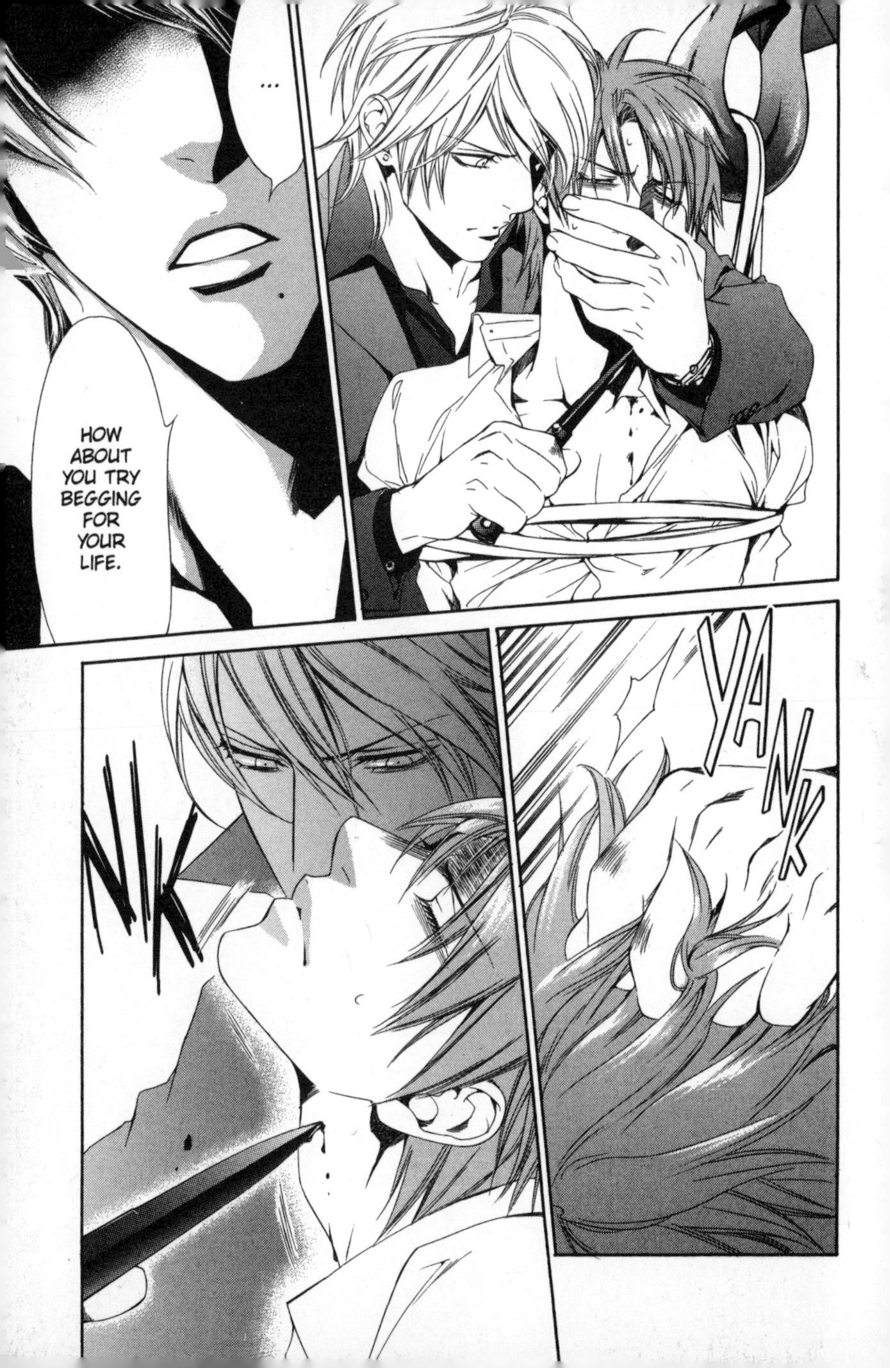
...
HOW ABOUT YOU TRY BEGGING FOR YOUR LIFE.
YANK
NK

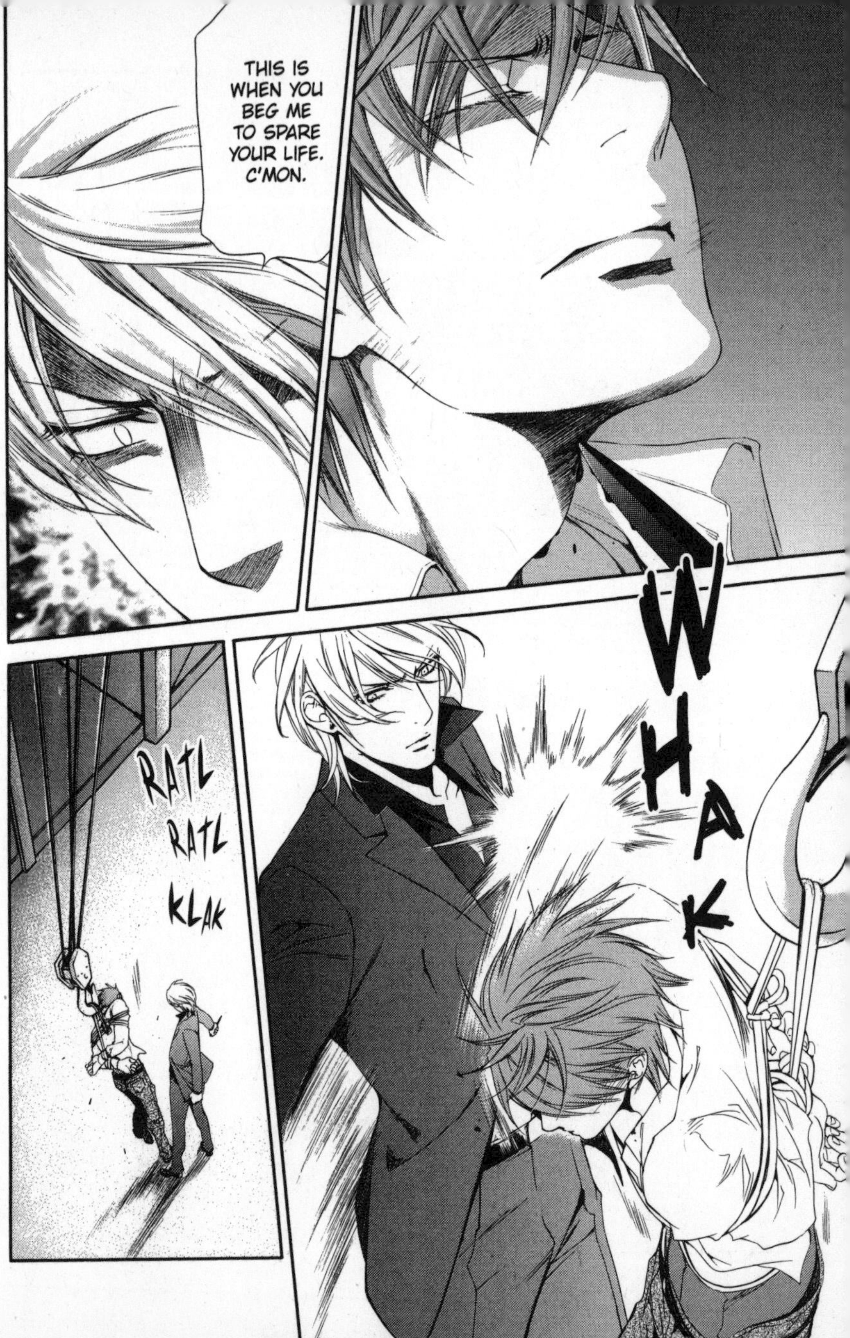
THIS IS WHEN YOU BEG ME TO SPARE YOUR LIFE. C'MON.
WHAK
RATL
RATL
KLAK

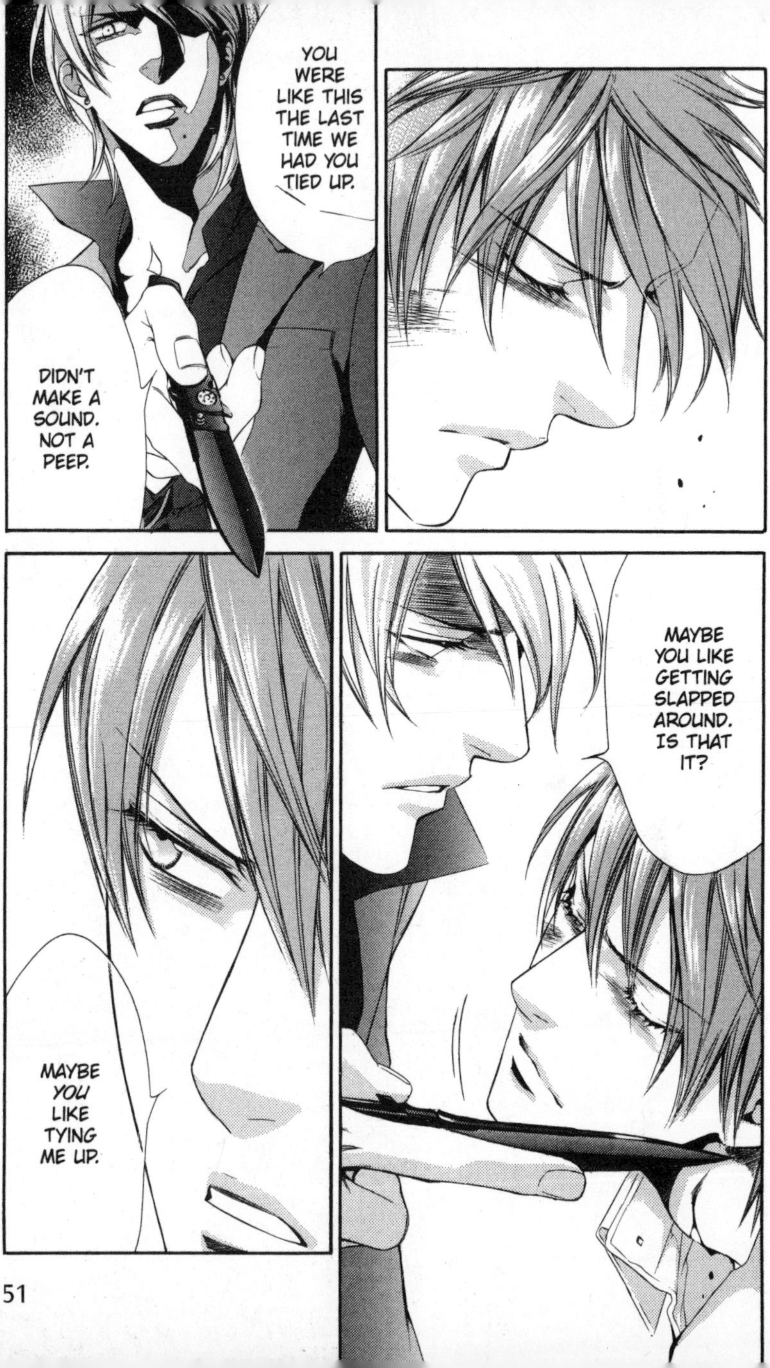
YOU WERE LIKE THIS THE LAST TIME WE HAD YOU TIED UP.
DIDN'T MAKE A SOUND. NOT A PEEP.
MAYBE YOU LIKE GETTING SLAPPED AROUND. IS THAT IT?
MAYBE *YOU* LIKE TYING ME UP.

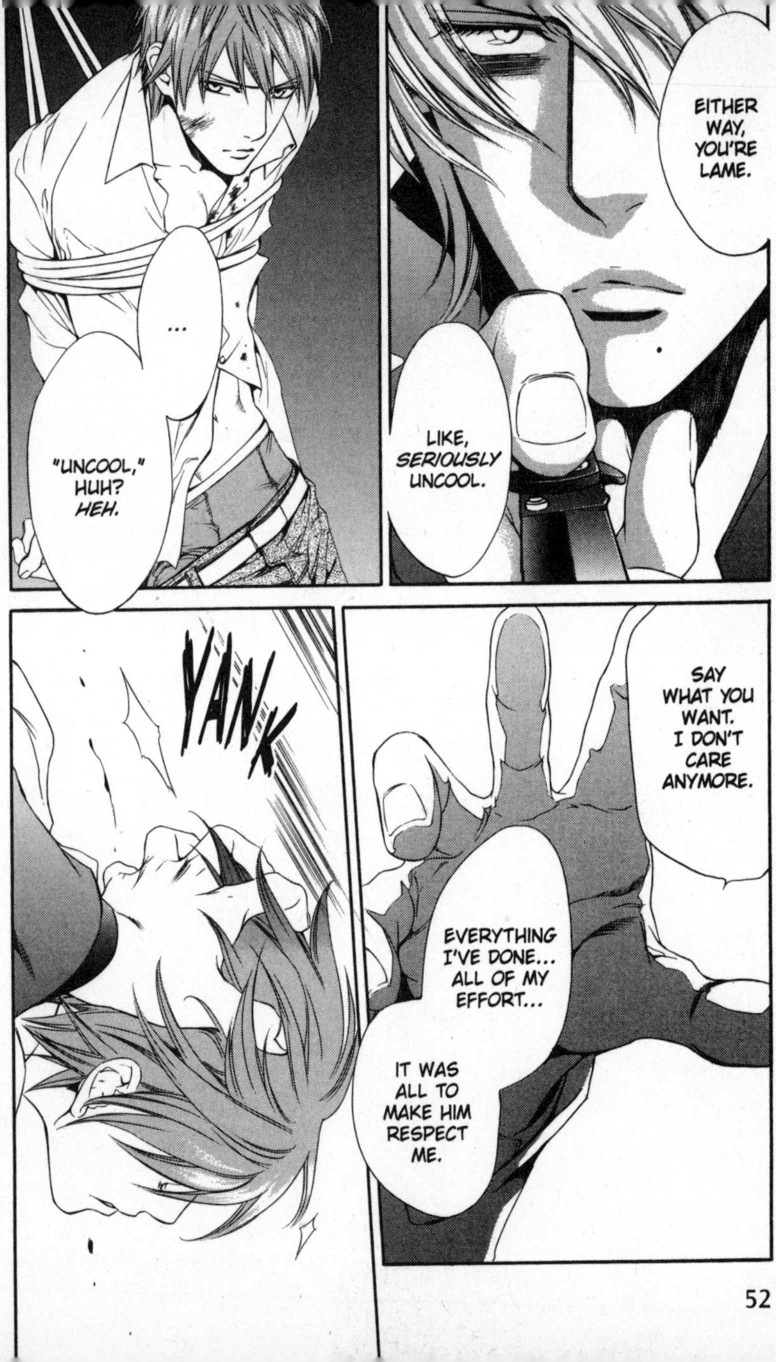
EITHER WAY, YOU'RE LAME.
LIKE, *SERIOUSLY* UNCOOL.
...
"UNCOOL," HUH? *HEH.*
SAY WHAT YOU WANT. I DON'T CARE ANYMORE.
EVERYTHING I'VE DONE... ALL OF MY EFFORT...
IT WAS ALL TO MAKE HIM RESPECT ME.
YANK

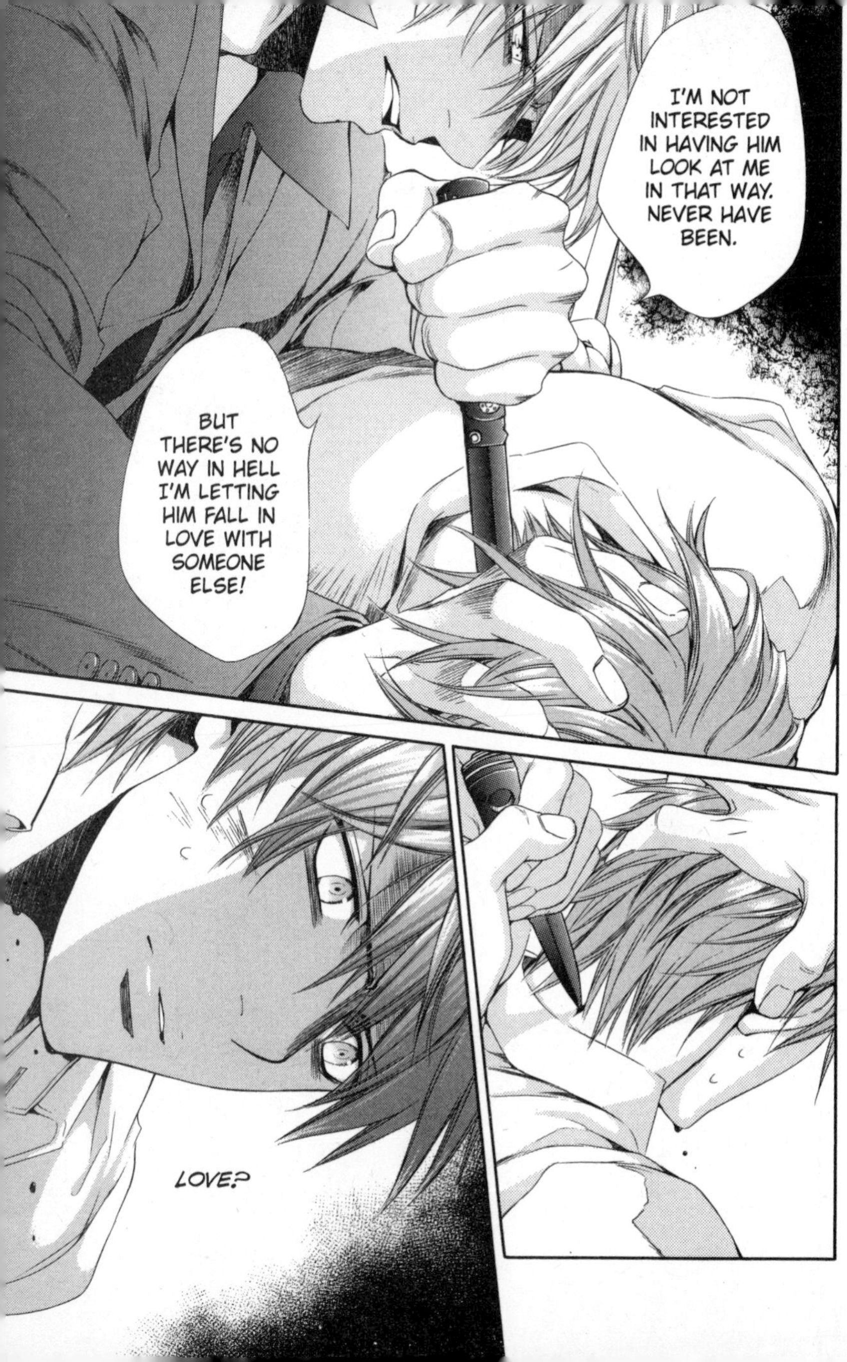
I'M NOT INTERESTED IN HAVING HIM LOOK AT ME IN THAT WAY. NEVER HAVE BEEN.
BUT THERE'S NO WAY IN HELL I'M LETTING HIM FALL IN LOVE WITH SOMEONE ELSE!
LOVE?

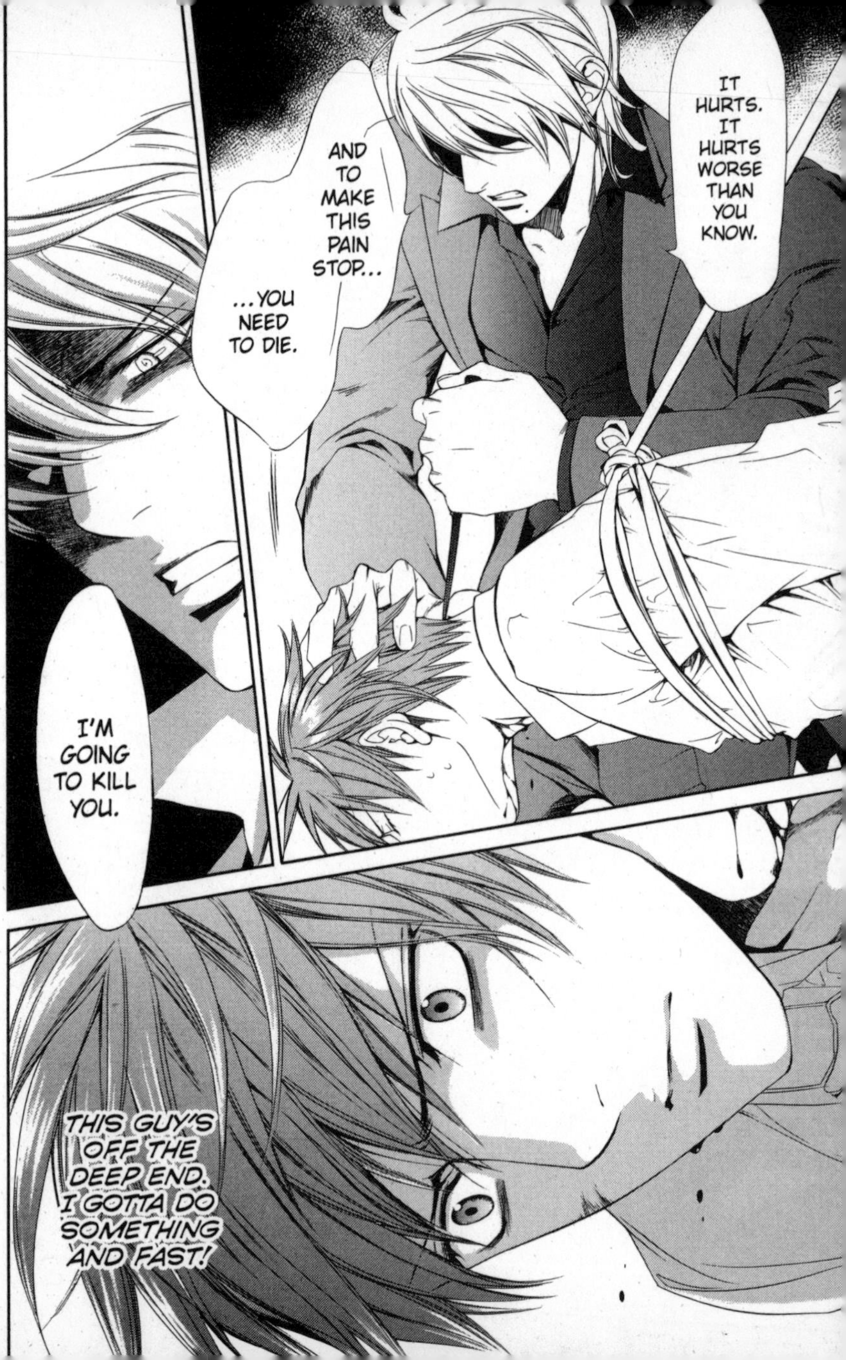
IT HURTS. IT HURTS WORSE THAN YOU KNOW.
AND TO MAKE THIS PAIN STOP...
...YOU NEED TO DIE.
I'M GOING TO KILL YOU.
THIS GUY'S OFF THE DEEP END. I GOTTA DO SOMETHING AND FAST!

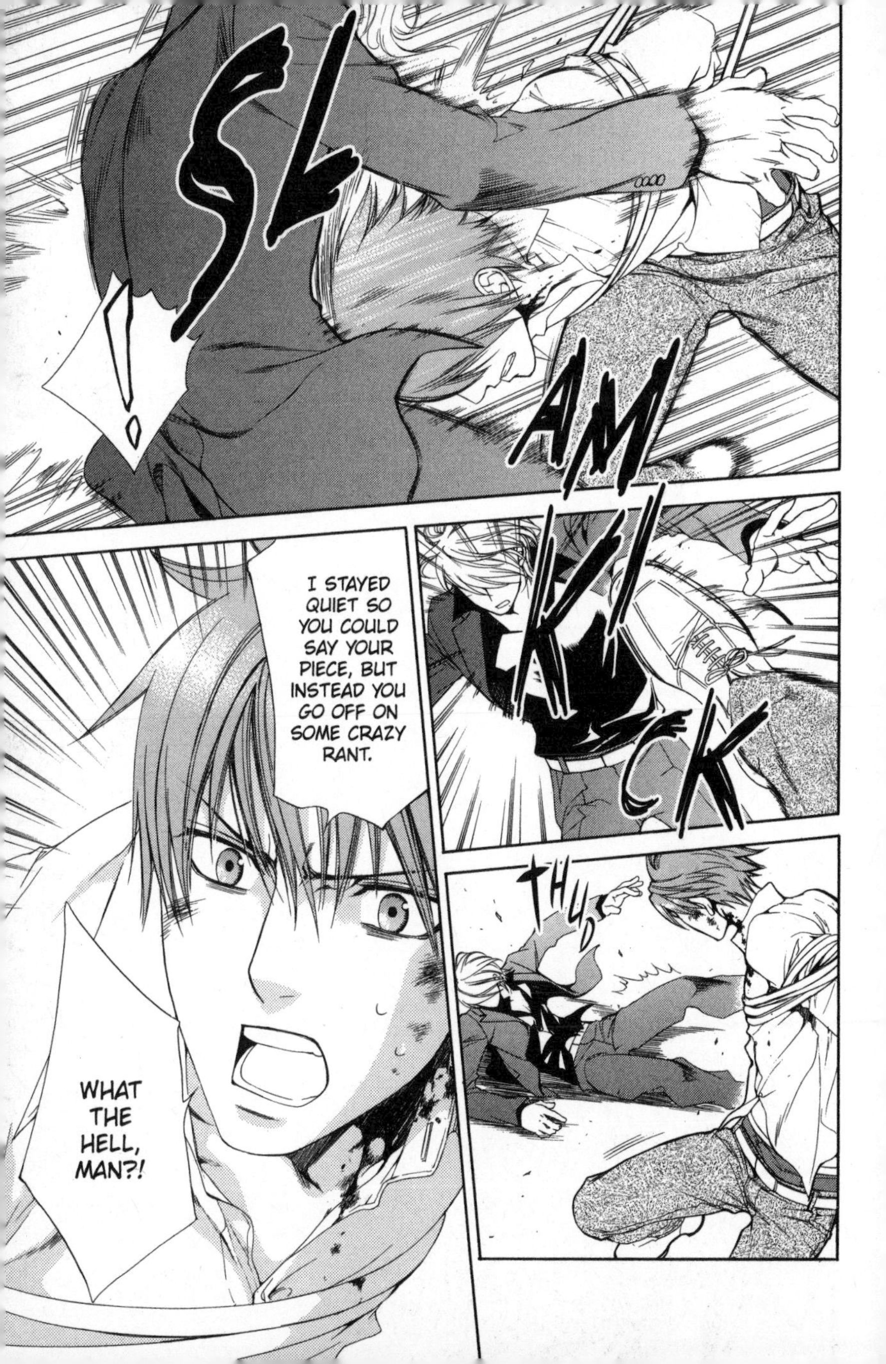
SLAM
!
KICK
THUD
I STAYED QUIET SO YOU COULD SAY YOUR PIECE, BUT INSTEAD YOU GO OFF ON SOME CRAZY RANT.
WHAT THE HELL, MAN?!

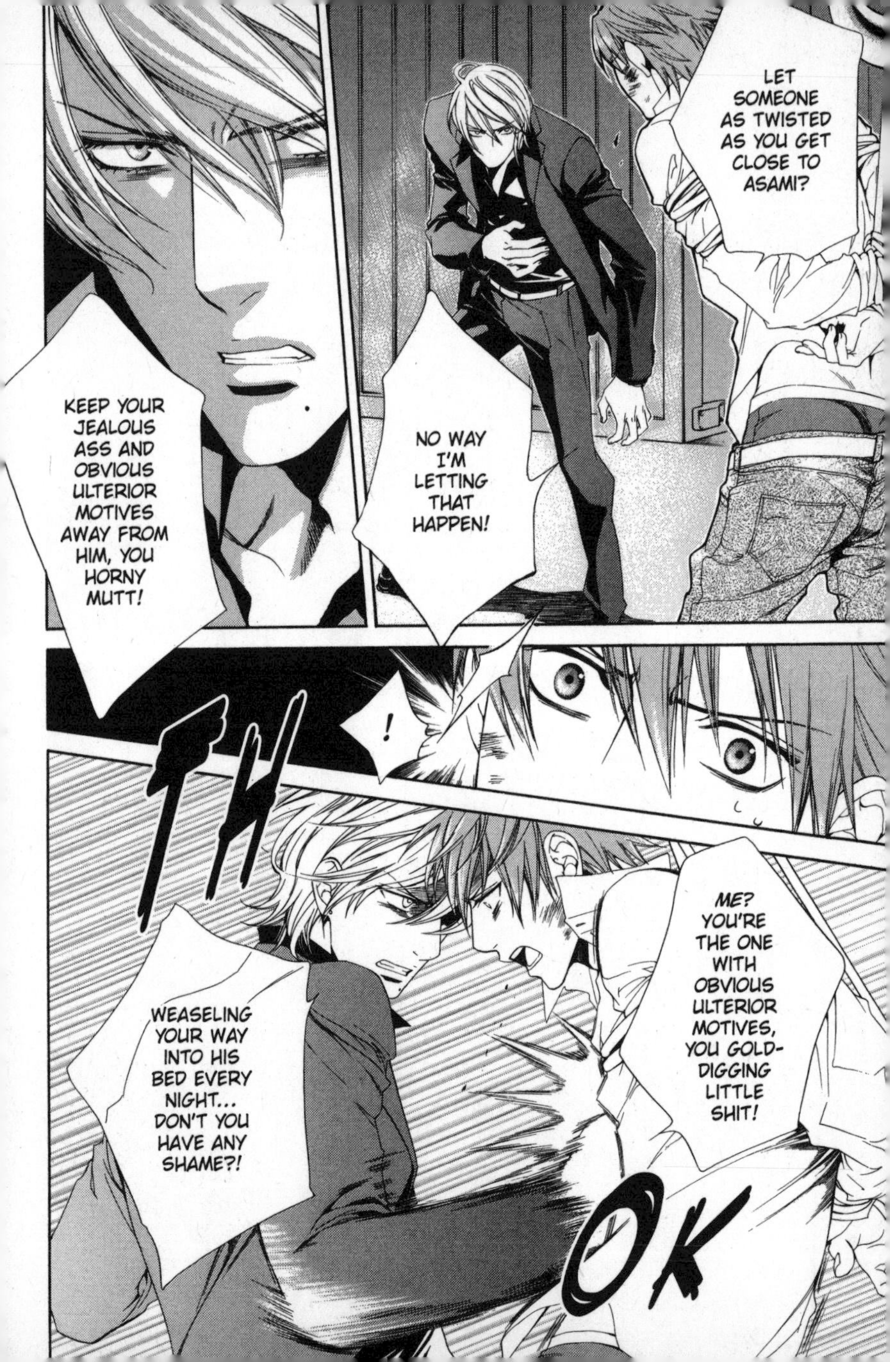
LET SOMEONE AS TWISTED AS YOU GET CLOSE TO ASAMI?
NO WAY I'M LETTING THAT HAPPEN!
KEEP YOUR JEALOUS ASS AND OBVIOUS ULTERIOR MOTIVES AWAY FROM HIM, YOU HORNY MUTT!
!
ME? YOU'RE THE ONE WITH OBVIOUS ULTERIOR MOTIVES, YOU GOLD-DIGGING LITTLE SHIT!
TH
WEASELING YOUR WAY INTO HIS BED EVERY NIGHT... DON'T YOU HAVE ANY SHAME?!
OK

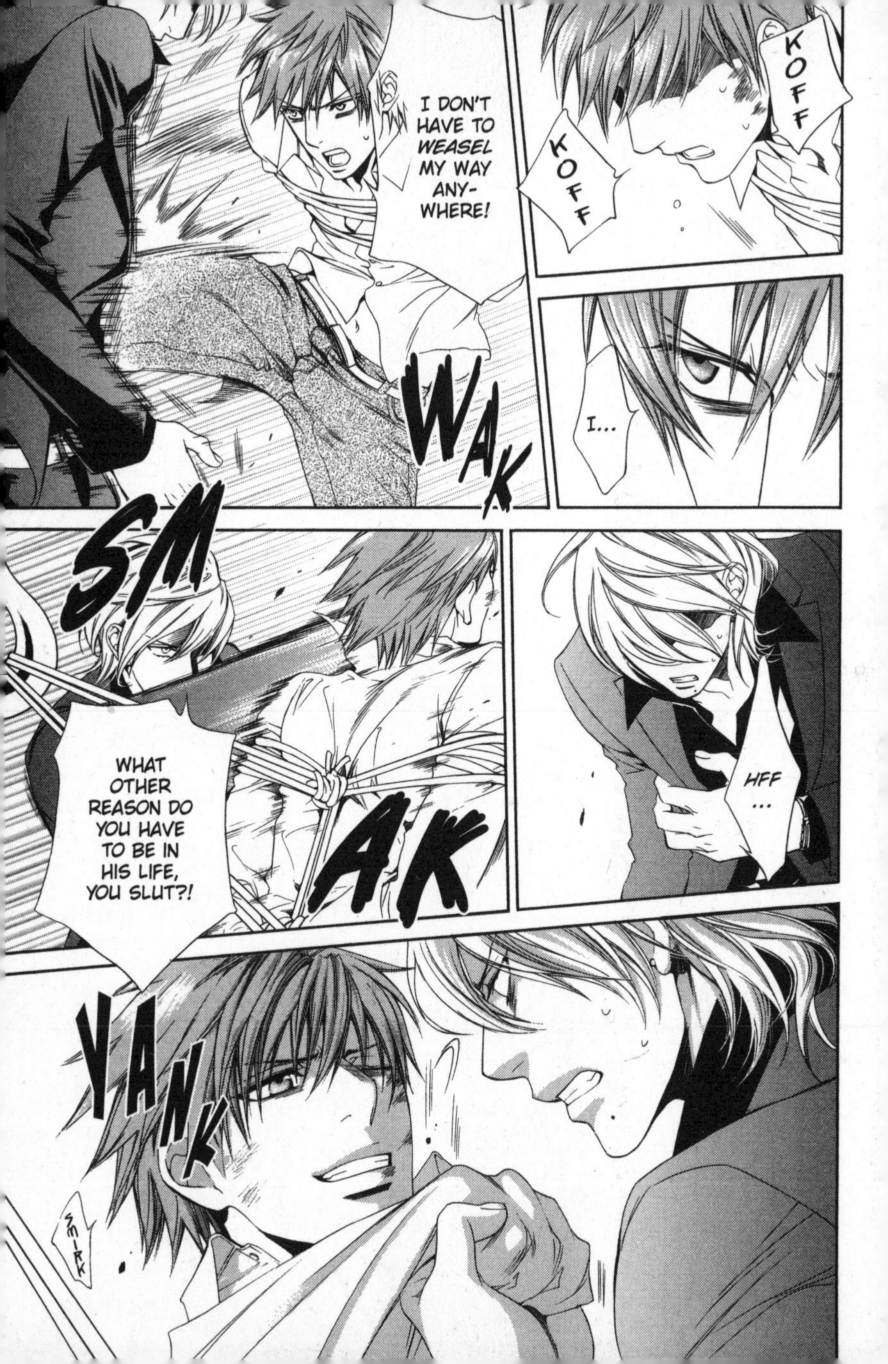
KOFF
KOFF
I...
I DON'T HAVE TO WEASEL MY WAY ANYWHERE!
WAK
HFF...
SMAK
WHAT OTHER REASON DO YOU HAVE TO BE IN HIS LIFE, YOU SLUT?!
YANK
SMIRK

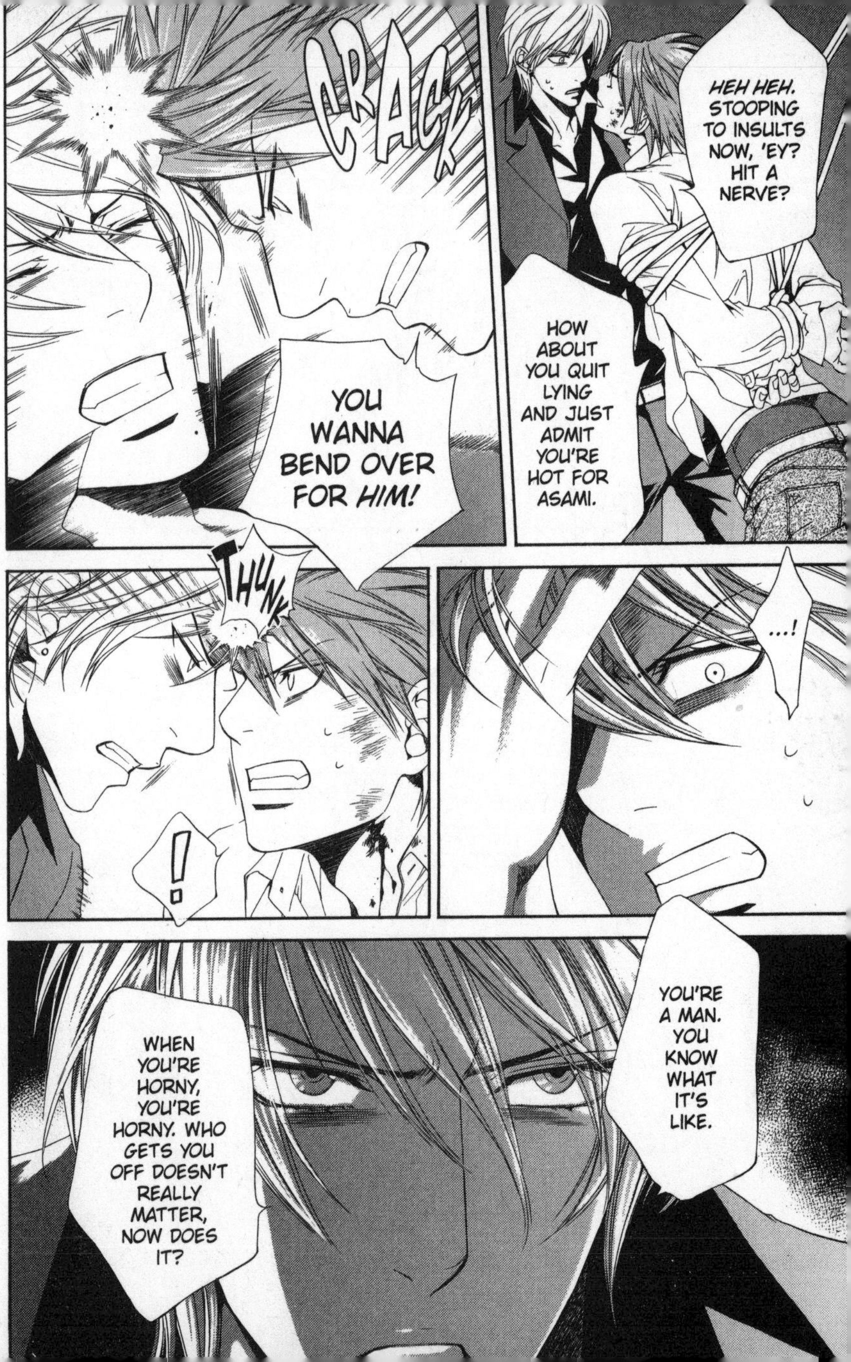
HEH HEH. STOOPING TO INSULTS NOW, 'EY? HIT A NERVE?
HOW ABOUT YOU QUIT LYING AND JUST ADMIT YOU'RE HOT FOR ASAMI.
CRACK
YOU WANNA BEND OVER FOR *HIM!*
...!
THUNK
!
YOU'RE A MAN. YOU KNOW WHAT IT'S LIKE.
WHEN YOU'RE HORNY, YOU'RE HORNY. WHO GETS YOU OFF DOESN'T REALLY MATTER, NOW DOES IT?

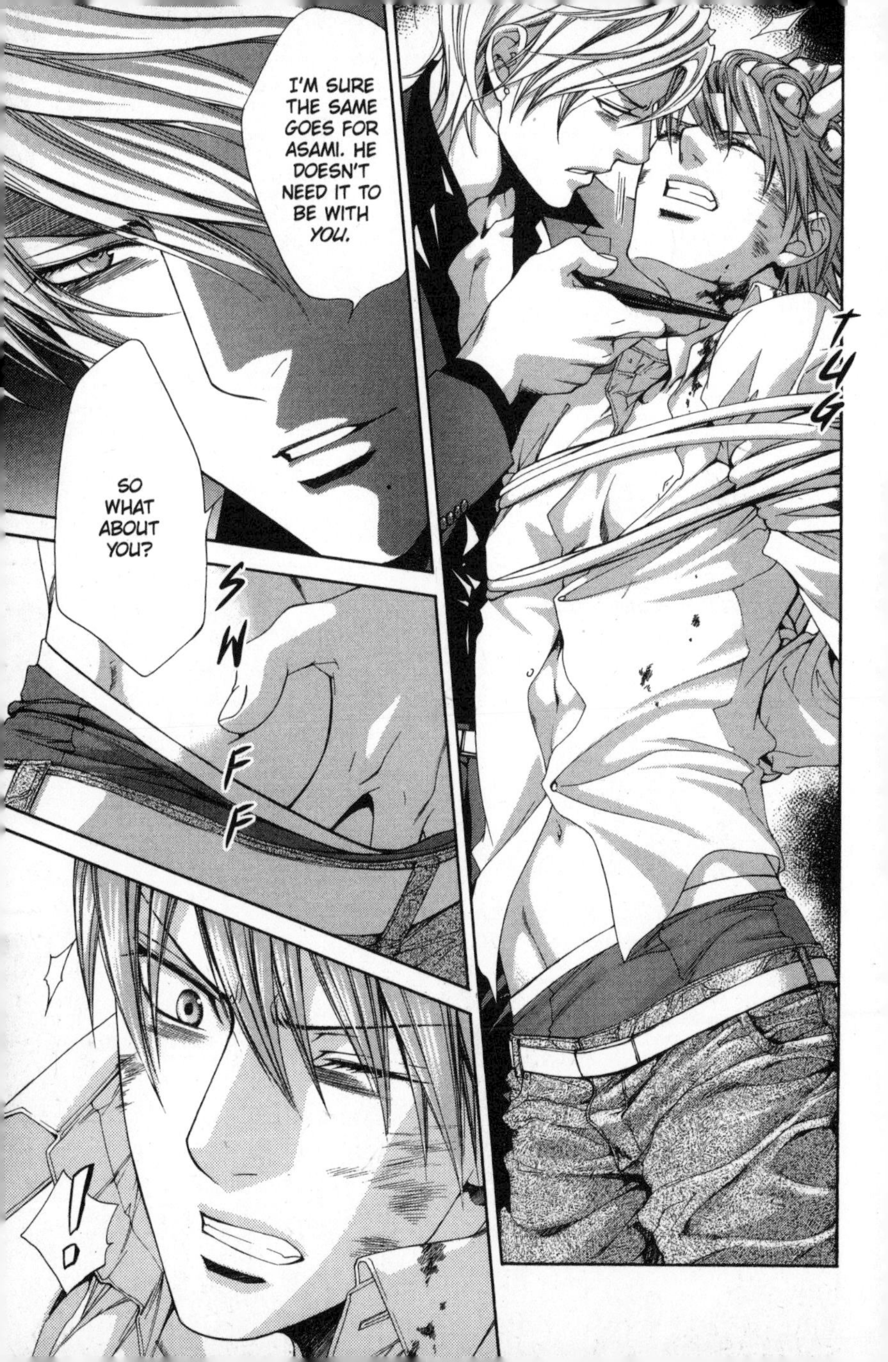
TUG
I'M SURE THE SAME GOES FOR ASAMI. HE DOESN'T NEED IT TO BE WITH *YOU.*
SO WHAT ABOUT YOU?
SWFF
!?

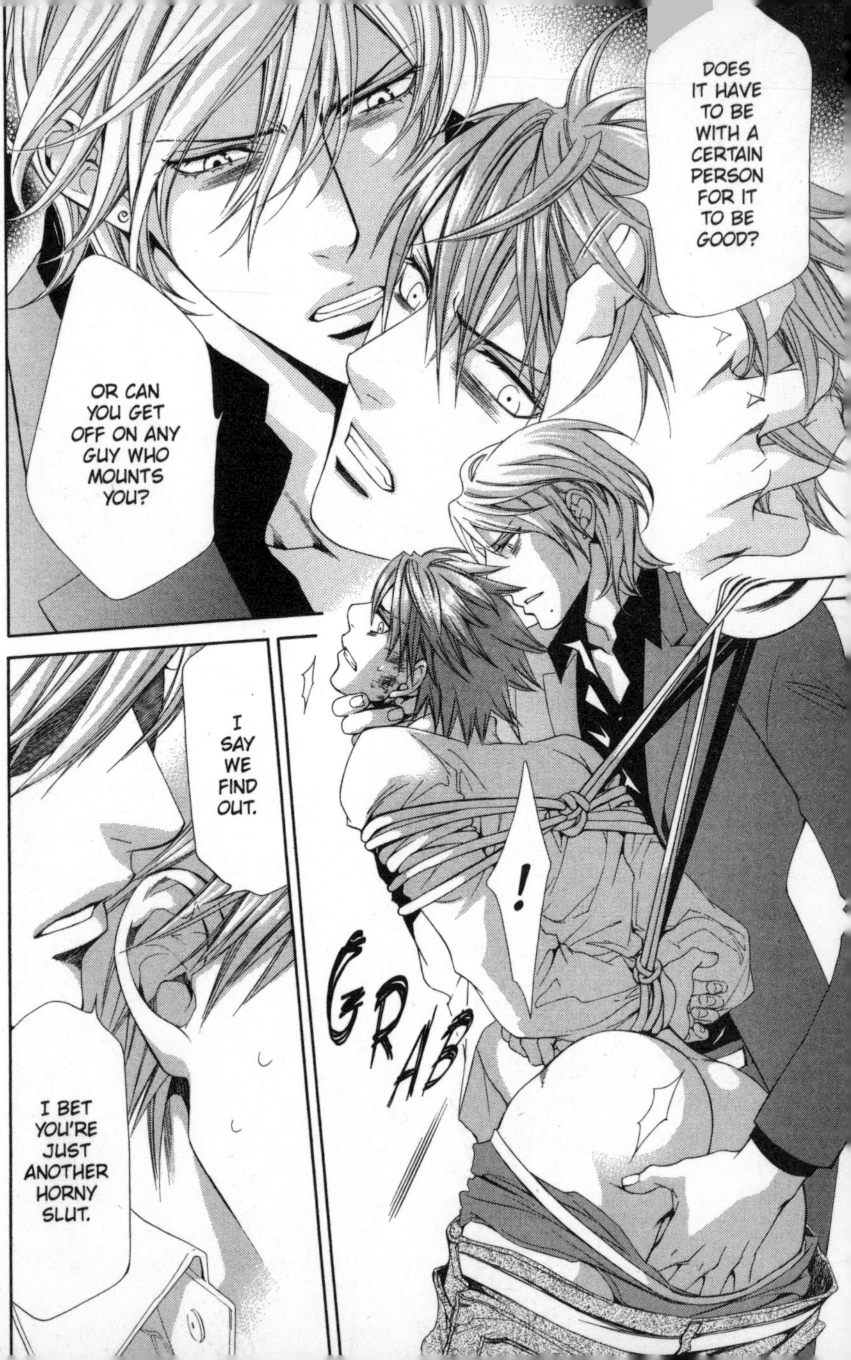
DOES IT HAVE TO BE WITH A CERTAIN PERSON FOR IT TO BE GOOD?
OR CAN YOU GET OFF ON ANY GUY WHO MOUNTS YOU?
!
GRAB
I SAY WE FIND OUT.
I BET YOU'RE JUST ANOTHER HORNY SLUT.

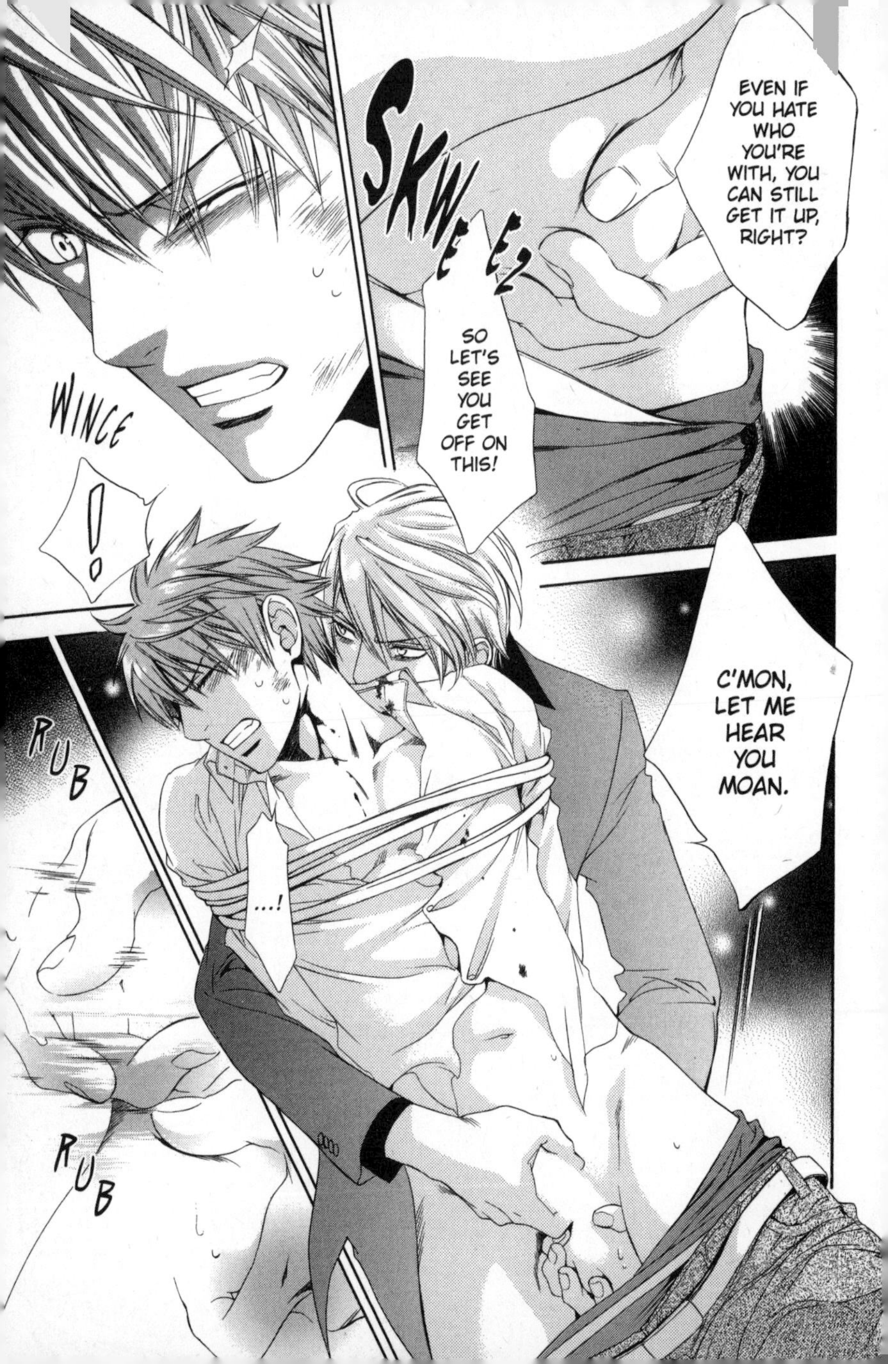
EVEN IF YOU HATE WHO YOU'RE WITH, YOU CAN STILL GET IT UP, RIGHT?
SKWEEZ
SO LET'S SEE YOU GET OFF ON THIS!
WINCE
!
C'MON, LET ME HEAR YOU MOAN.
...!
RUB
RUB

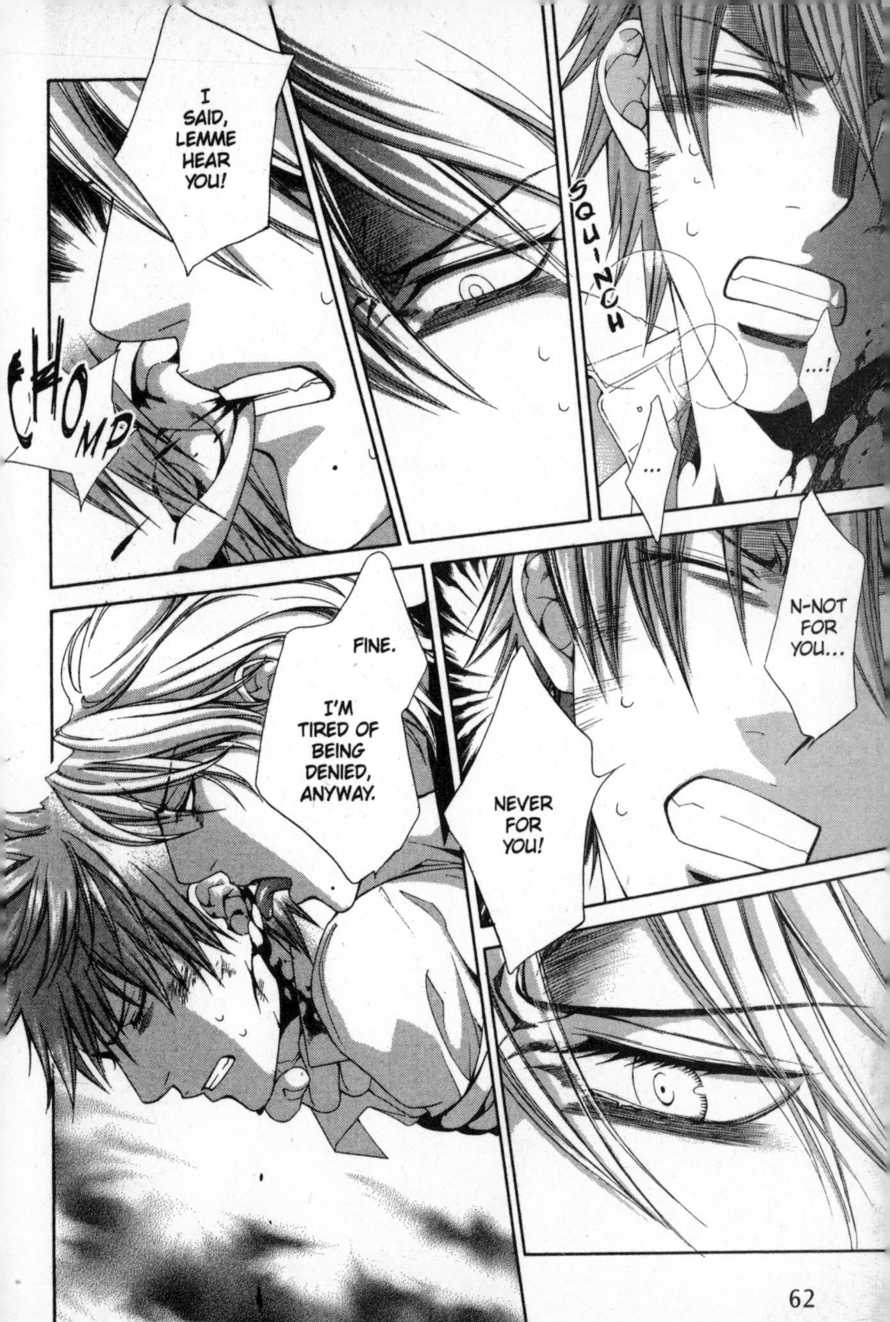
SQUI-NCH
...!
...
I SAID, LEMME HEAR YOU!
CHOMP
N-NOT FOR YOU...
NEVER FOR YOU!
FINE.
I'M TIRED OF BEING DENIED, ANYWAY.

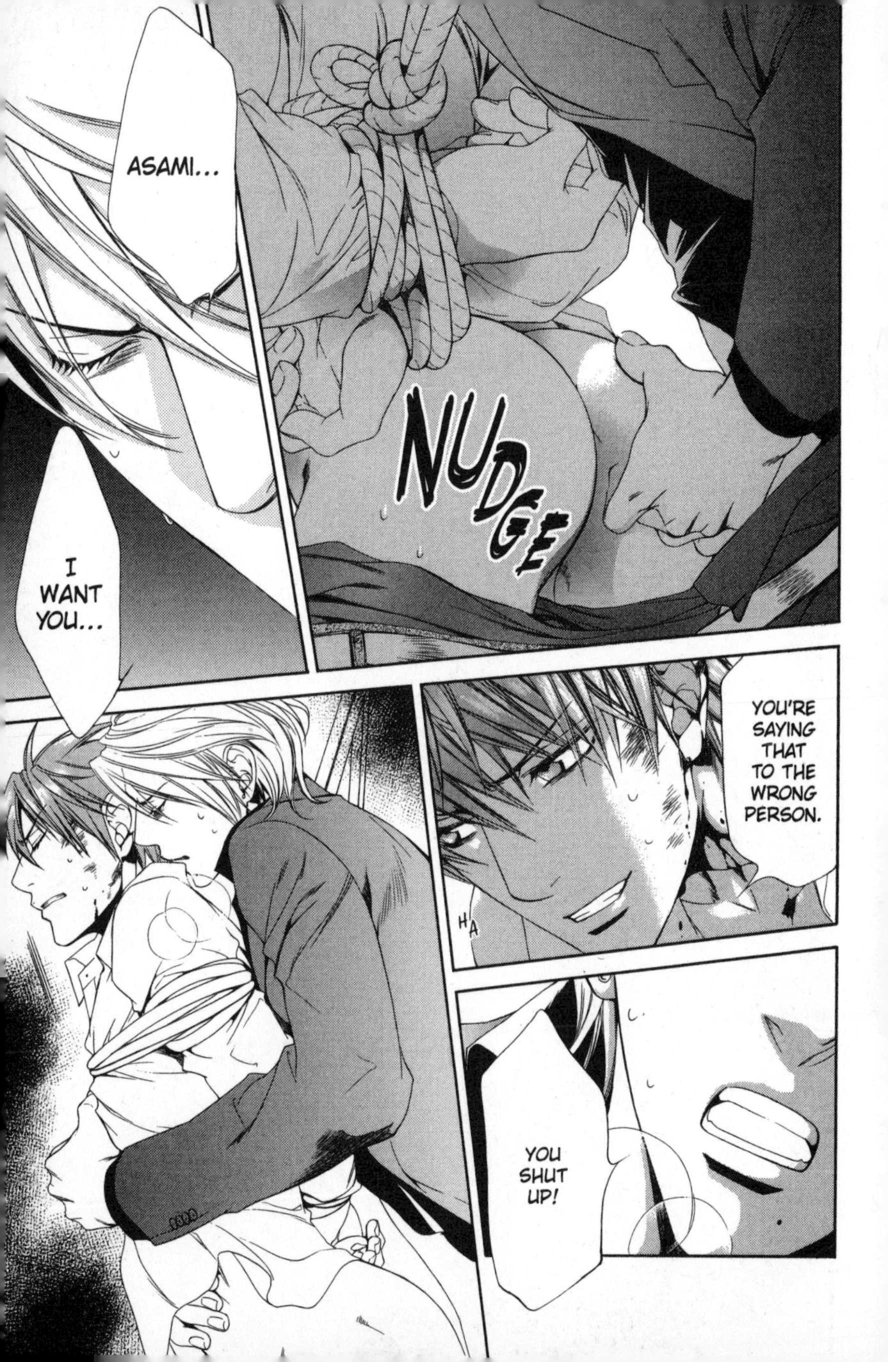
NUDGE
ASAMI...
I WANT YOU...
YOU'RE SAYING THAT TO THE WRONG PERSON.
HA
YOU SHUT UP!

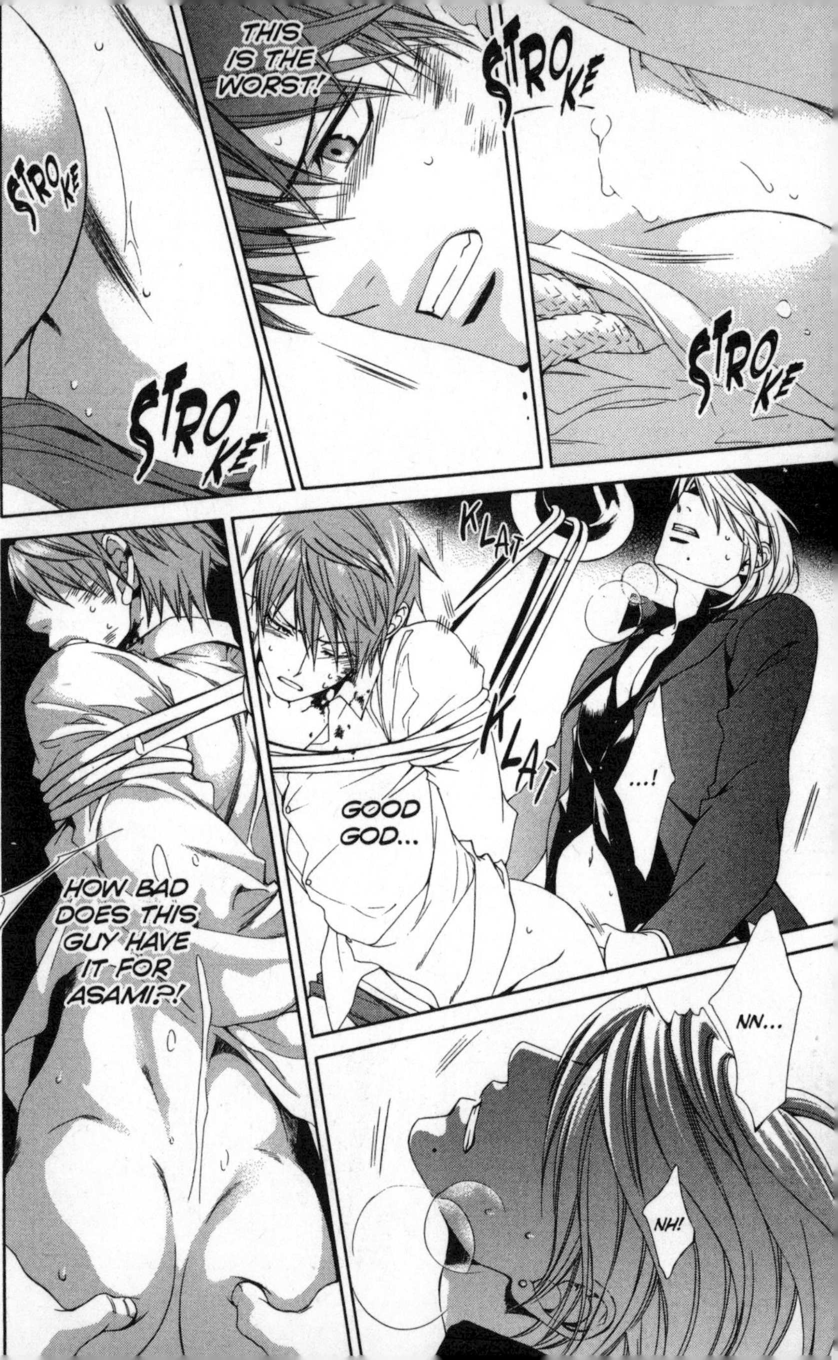
STROKE
STROKE
THIS IS THE WORST!
STROKE
STROKE
KLAT
KLAT
...!
GOOD GOD...
NN...
NH!
HOW BAD DOES THIS GUY HAVE IT FOR ASAMI?!

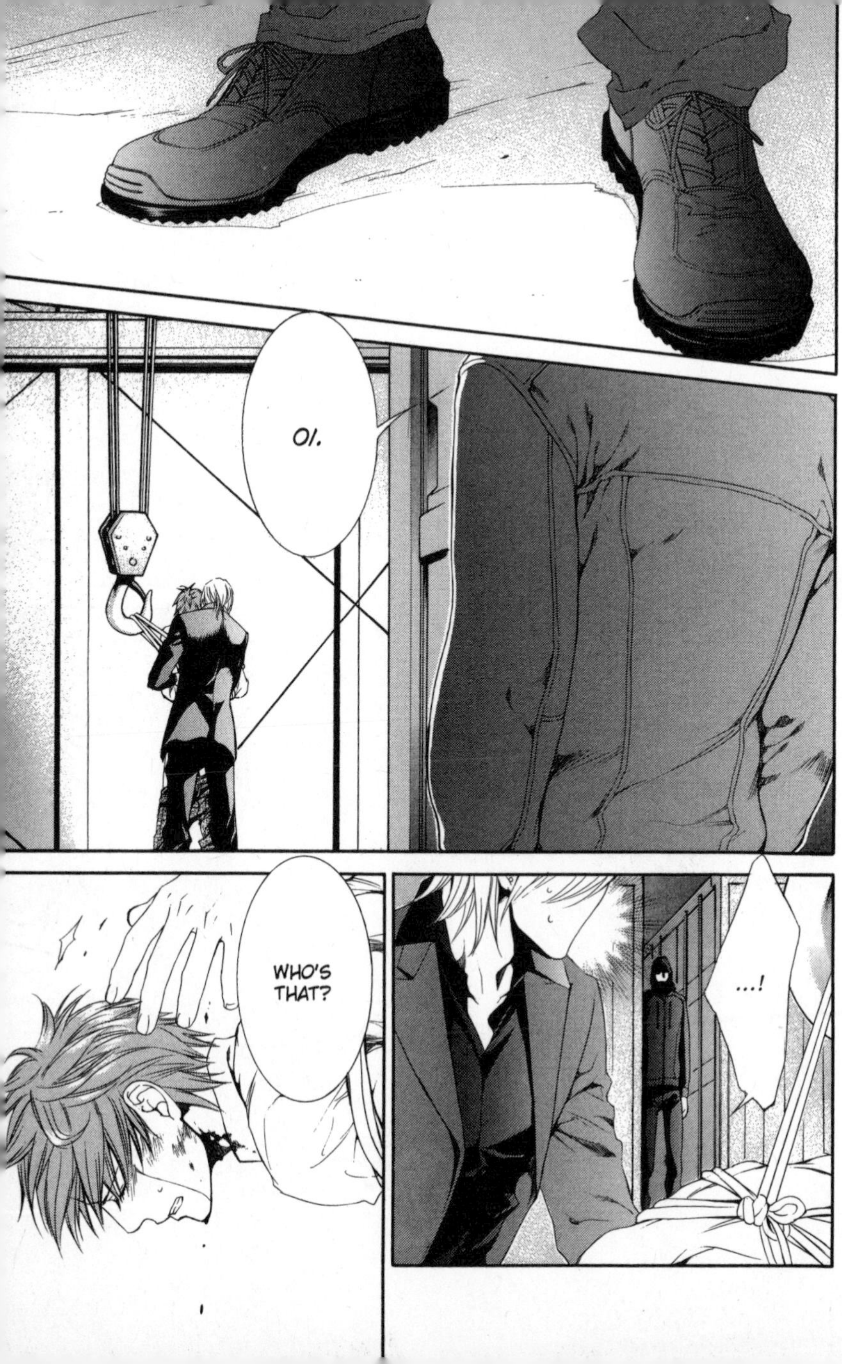
OI.
...!
WHO'S THAT?

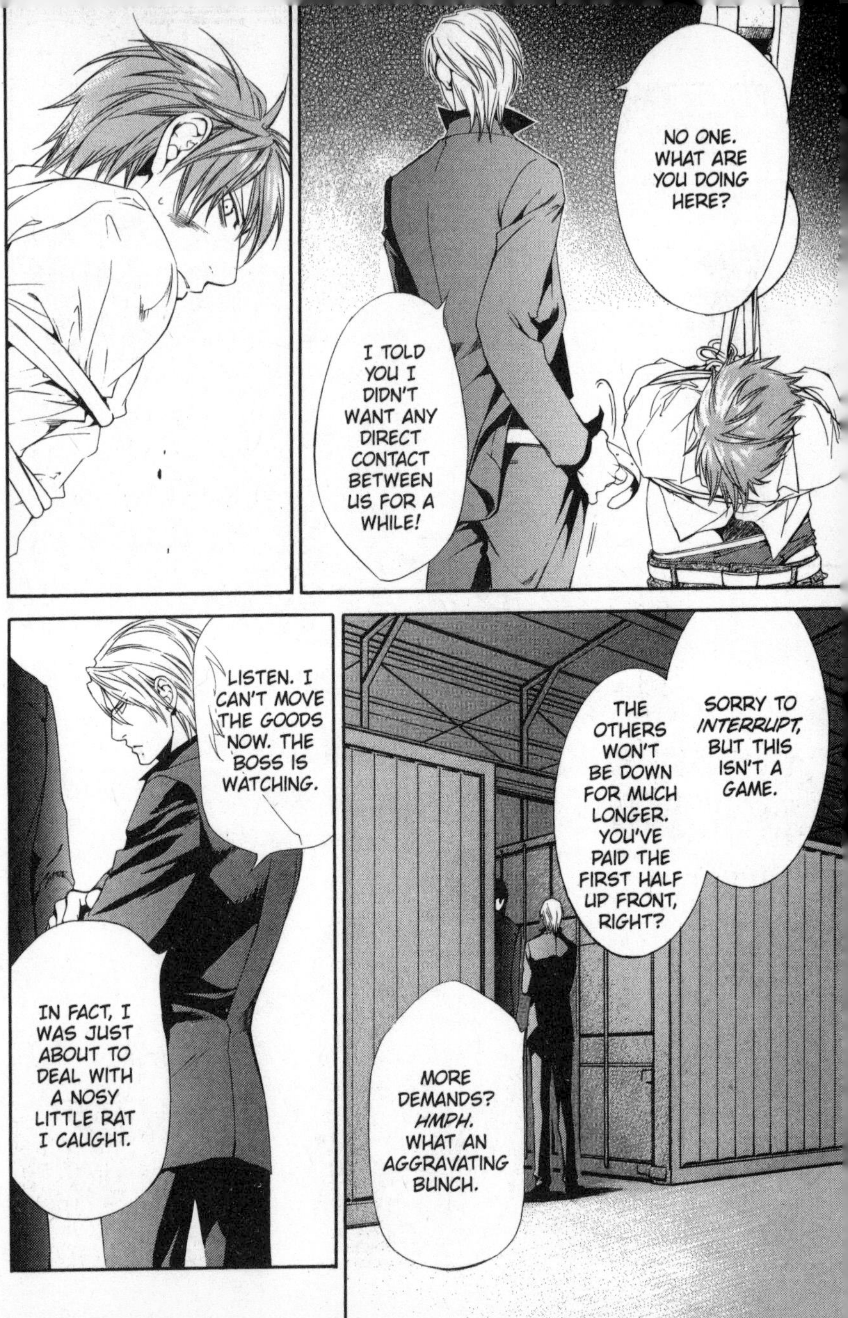
NO ONE. WHAT ARE YOU DOING HERE?
I TOLD YOU I DIDN'T WANT ANY DIRECT CONTACT BETWEEN US FOR A WHILE!
SORRY TO *INTERRUPT*, BUT THIS ISN'T A GAME.
THE OTHERS WON'T BE DOWN FOR MUCH LONGER. YOU'VE PAID THE FIRST HALF UP FRONT, RIGHT?
MORE DEMANDS? *HMPH.* WHAT AN AGGRAVATING BUNCH.
LISTEN. I CAN'T MOVE THE GOODS NOW. THE BOSS IS WATCHING.
IN FACT, I WAS JUST ABOUT TO DEAL WITH A NOSY LITTLE RAT I CAUGHT.

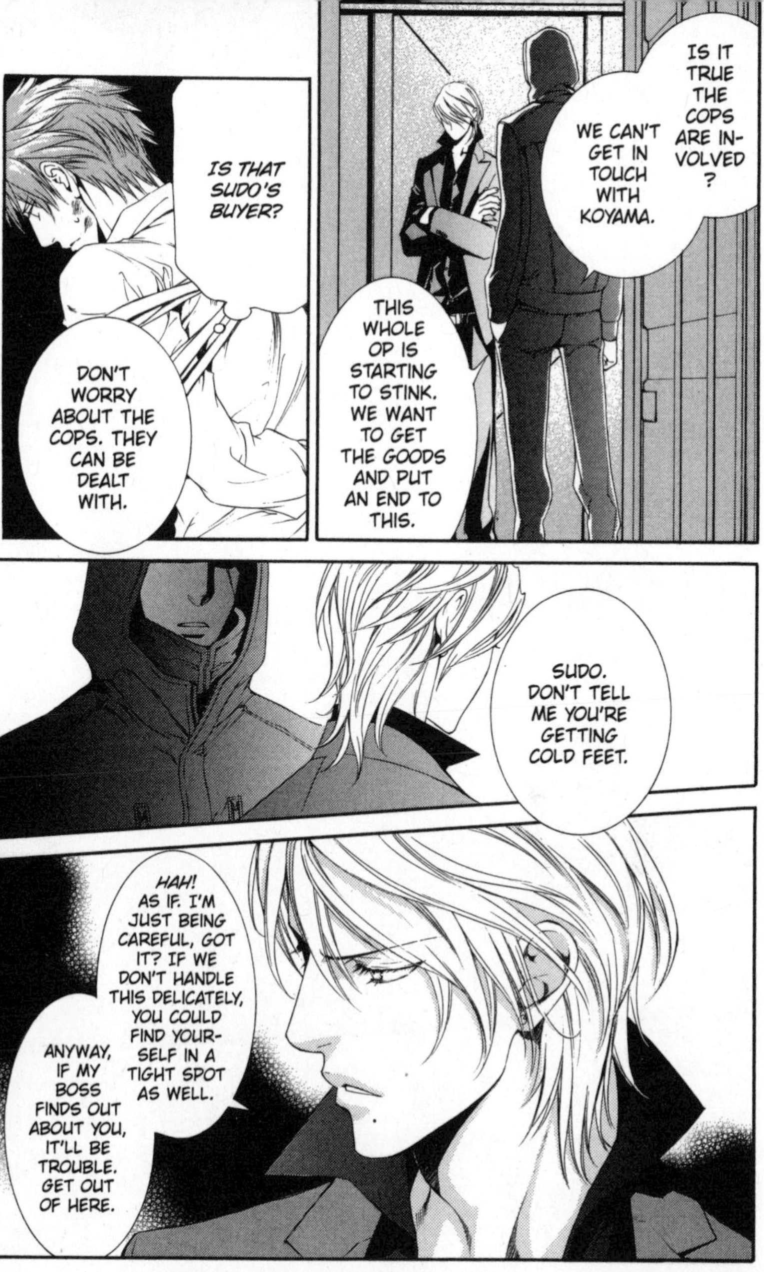
IS IT TRUE THE COPS ARE IN-VOLVED?
WE CAN'T GET IN TOUCH WITH KOYAMA.
THIS WHOLE OP IS STARTING TO STINK. WE WANT TO GET THE GOODS AND PUT AN END TO THIS.
IS THAT SUDO'S BUYER?
DON'T WORRY ABOUT THE COPS. THEY CAN BE DEALT WITH.
SUDO. DON'T TELL ME YOU'RE GETTING COLD FEET.
HAH! AS IF. I'M JUST BEING CAREFUL, GOT IT? IF WE DON'T HANDLE THIS DELICATELY, YOU COULD FIND YOUR-SELF IN A TIGHT SPOT AS WELL.
ANYWAY, IF MY BOSS FINDS OUT ABOUT YOU, IT'LL BE TROUBLE. GET OUT OF HERE.

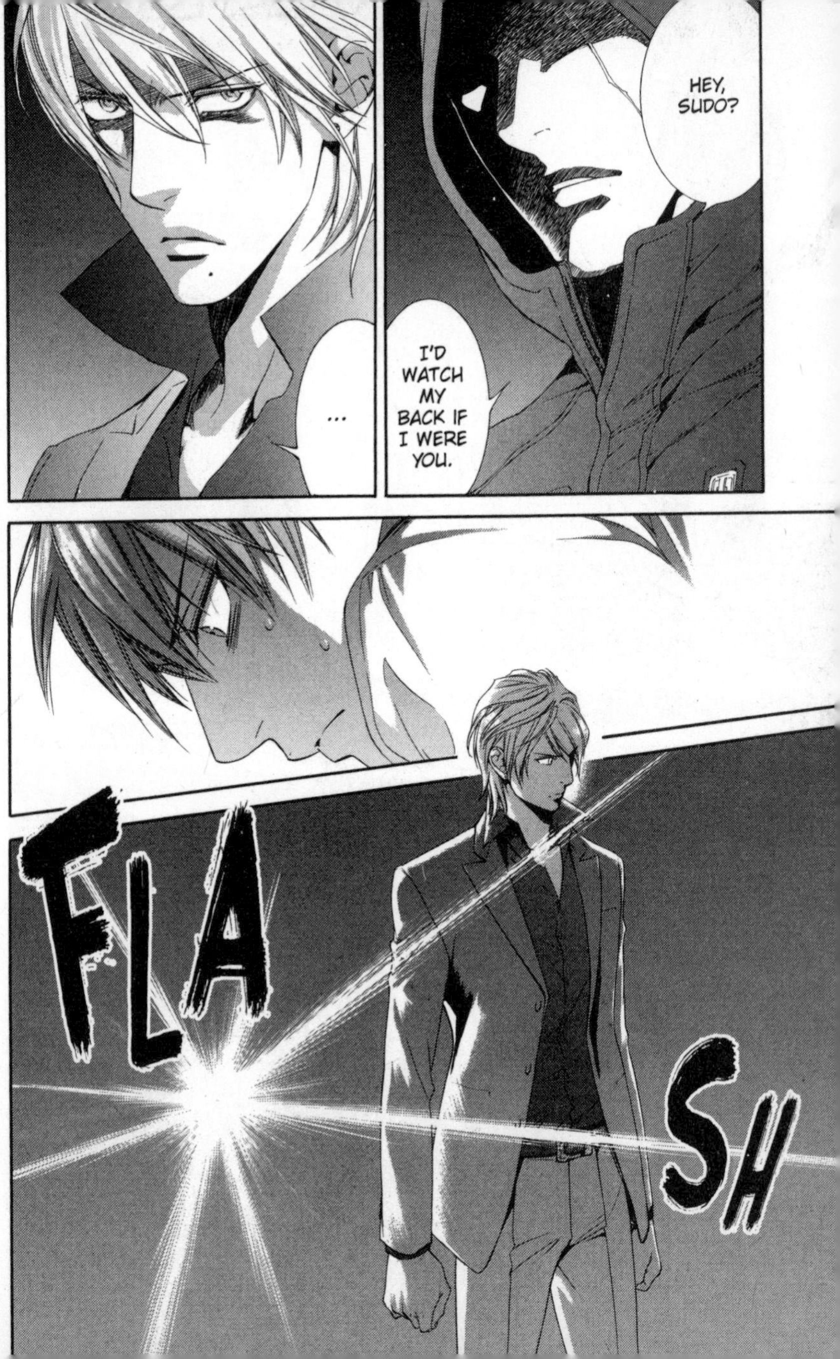
HEY, SUDO?
I'D WATCH MY BACK IF I WERE YOU.
...
FLASH

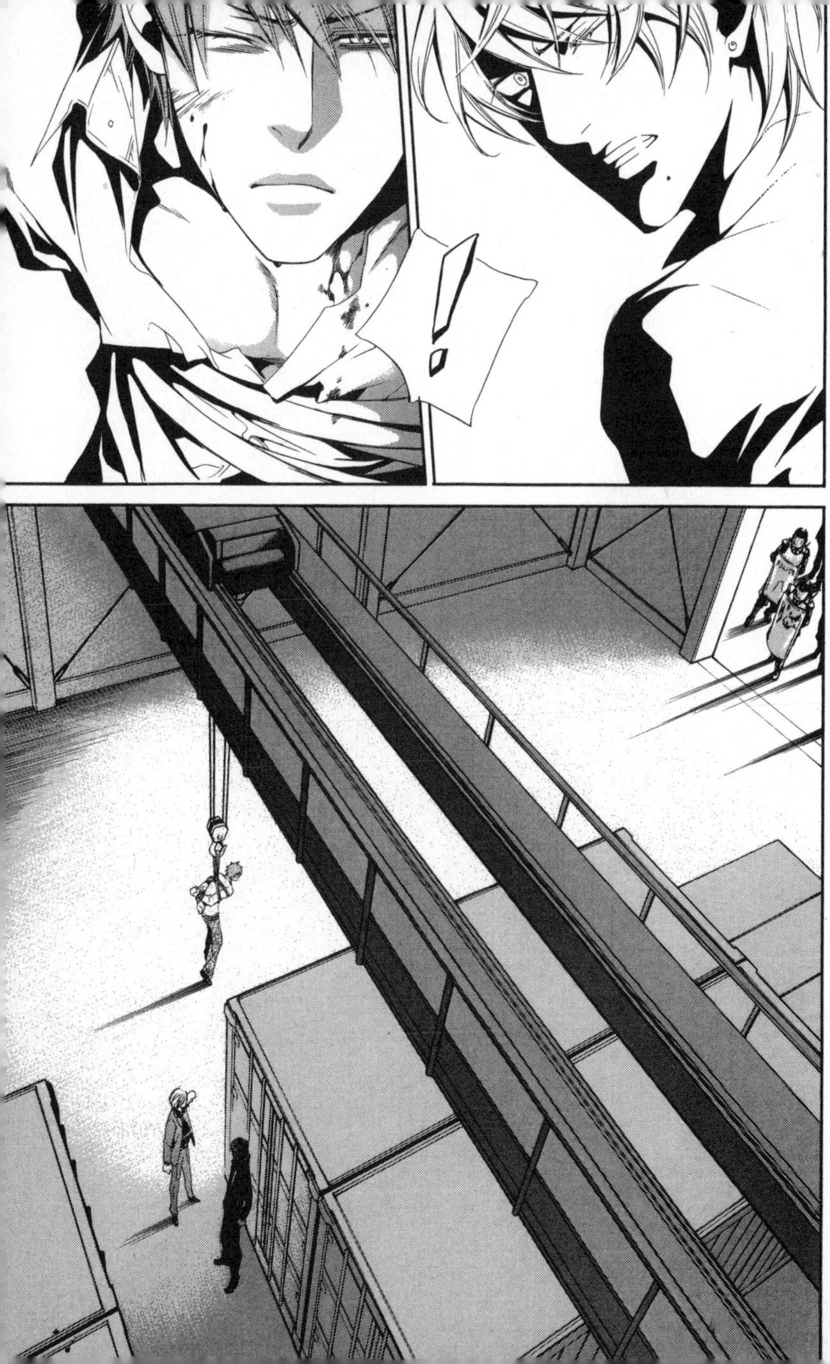
!

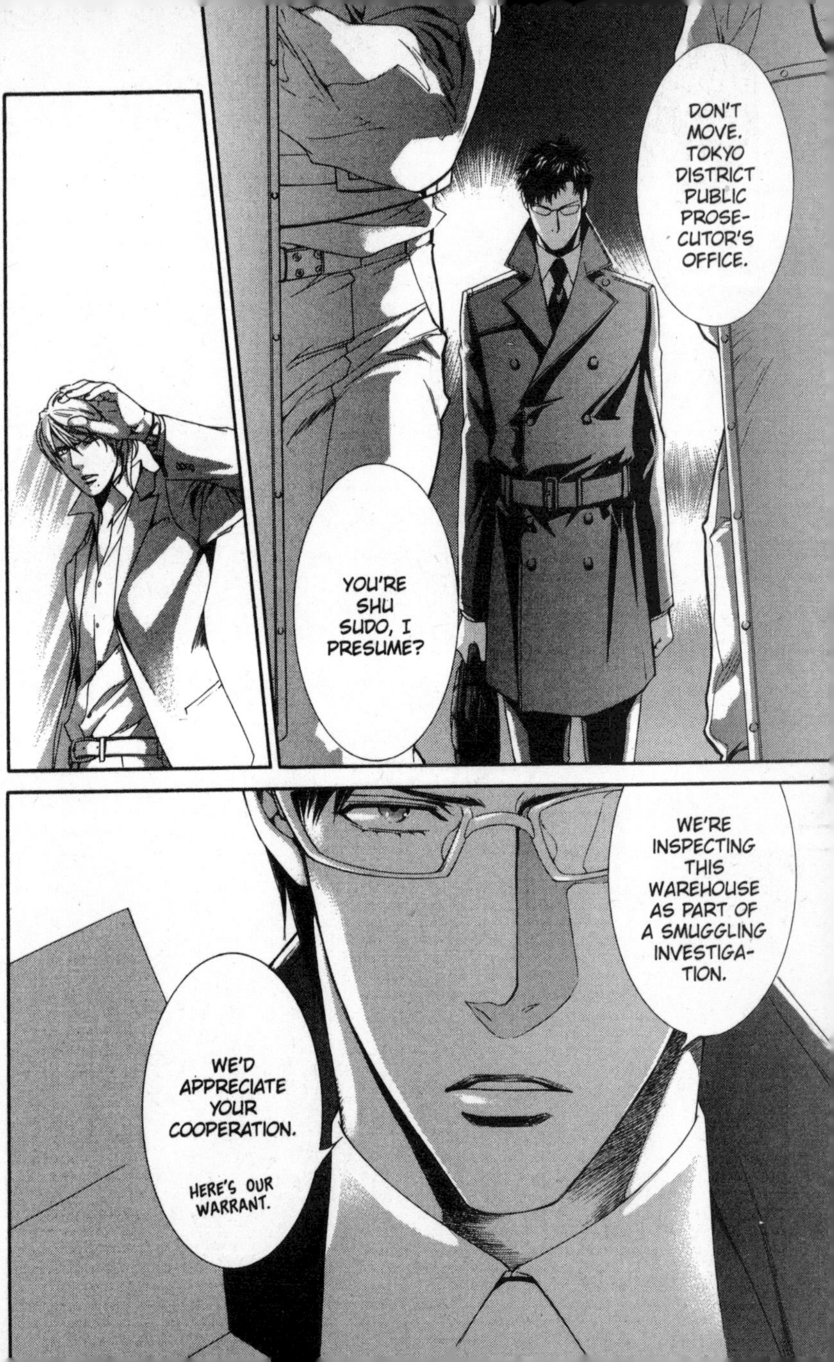
DON'T MOVE. TOKYO DISTRICT PUBLIC PROSE-CUTOR'S OFFICE.
YOU'RE SHU SUDO, I PRESUME?
WE'RE INSPECTING THIS WAREHOUSE AS PART OF A SMUGGLING INVESTIGA-TION.
WE'D APPRECIATE YOUR COOPERATION.
HERE'S OUR WARRANT.

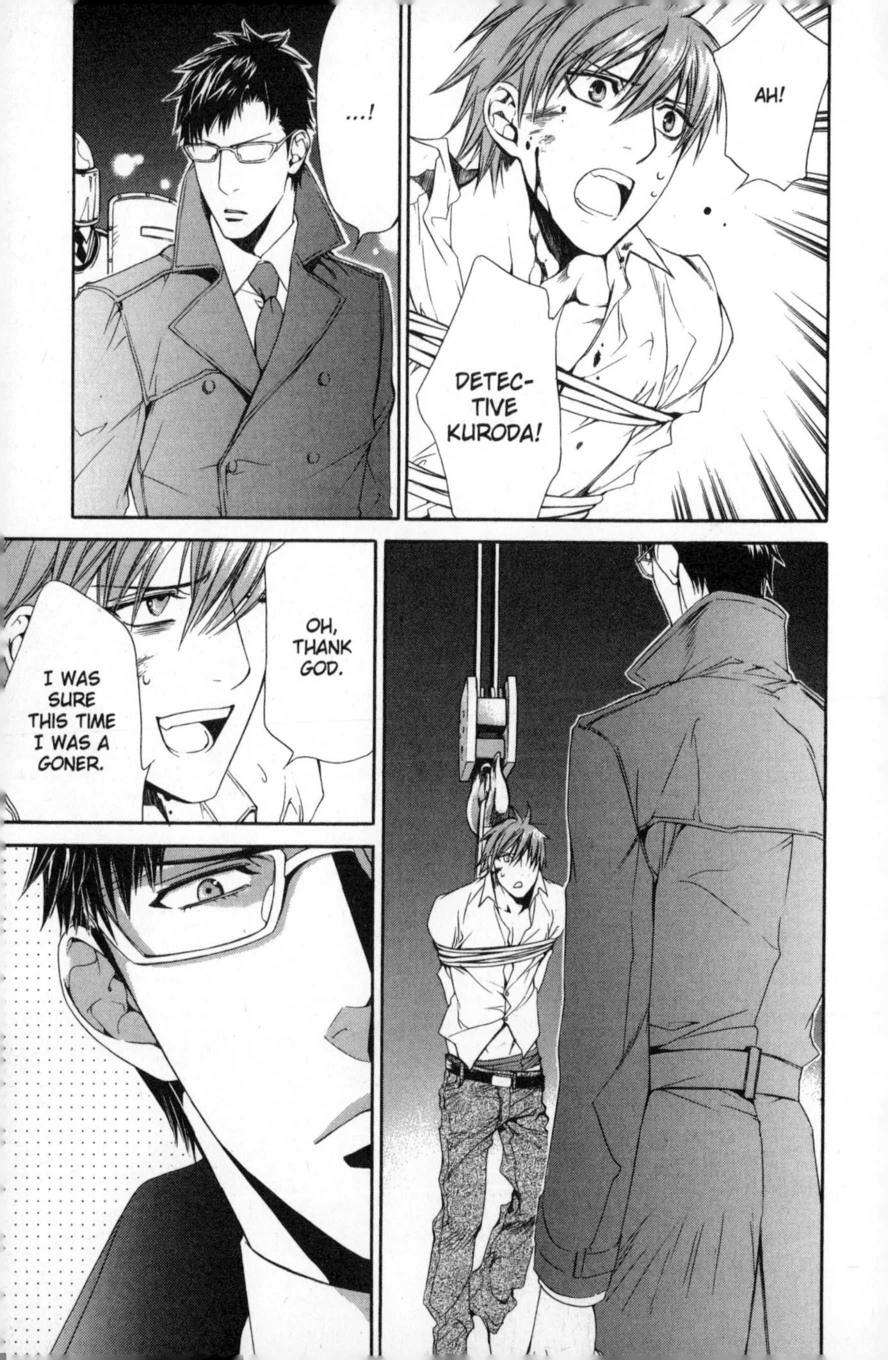
AH!
DETEC-TIVE KURODA!
...!
OH, THANK GOD.
I WAS SURE THIS TIME I WAS A GONER.

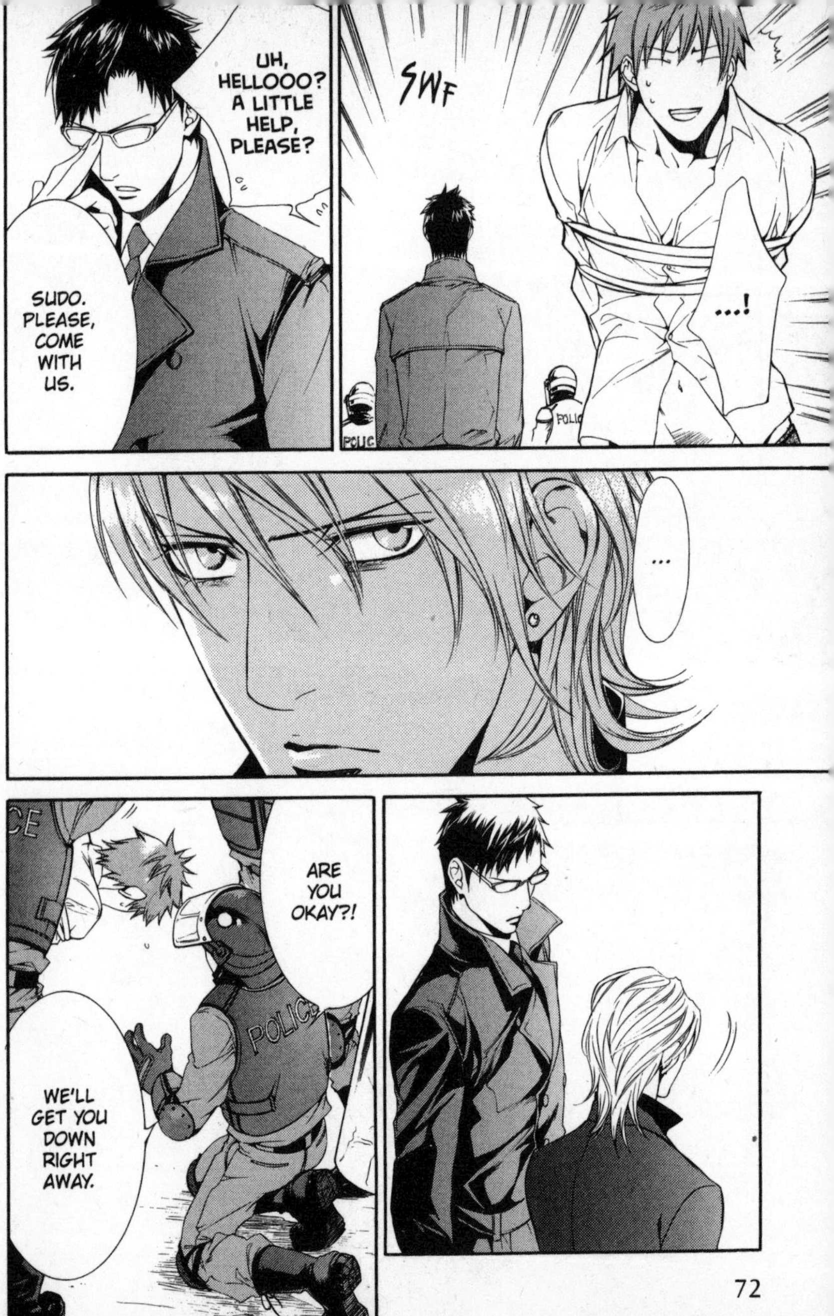
SWF
...!
UH, HELLOOO? A LITTLE HELP, PLEASE?
SUDO. PLEASE, COME WITH US.
...
ARE YOU OKAY?!
POLICE
WE'LL GET YOU DOWN RIGHT AWAY.

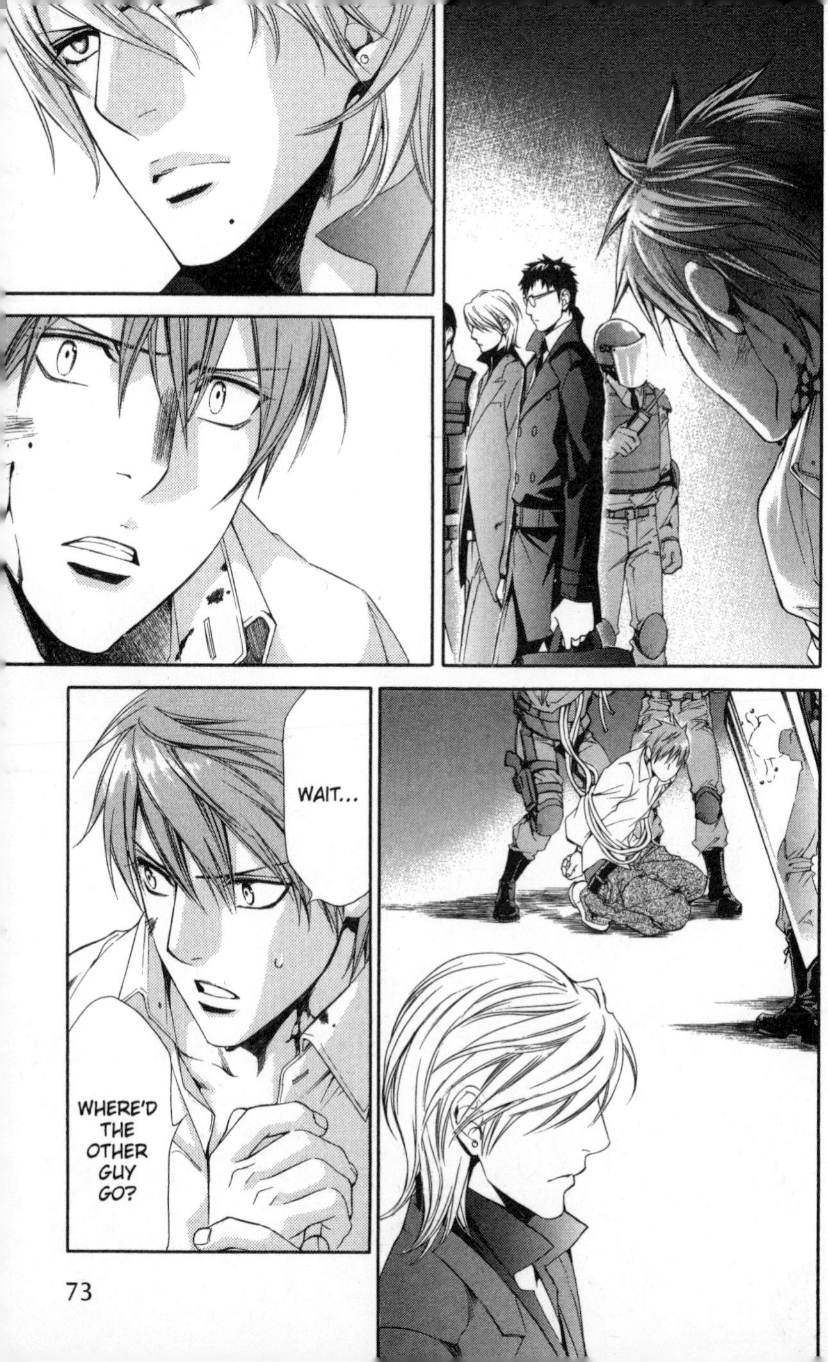
WAIT...
WHERE'D THE OTHER GUY GO?

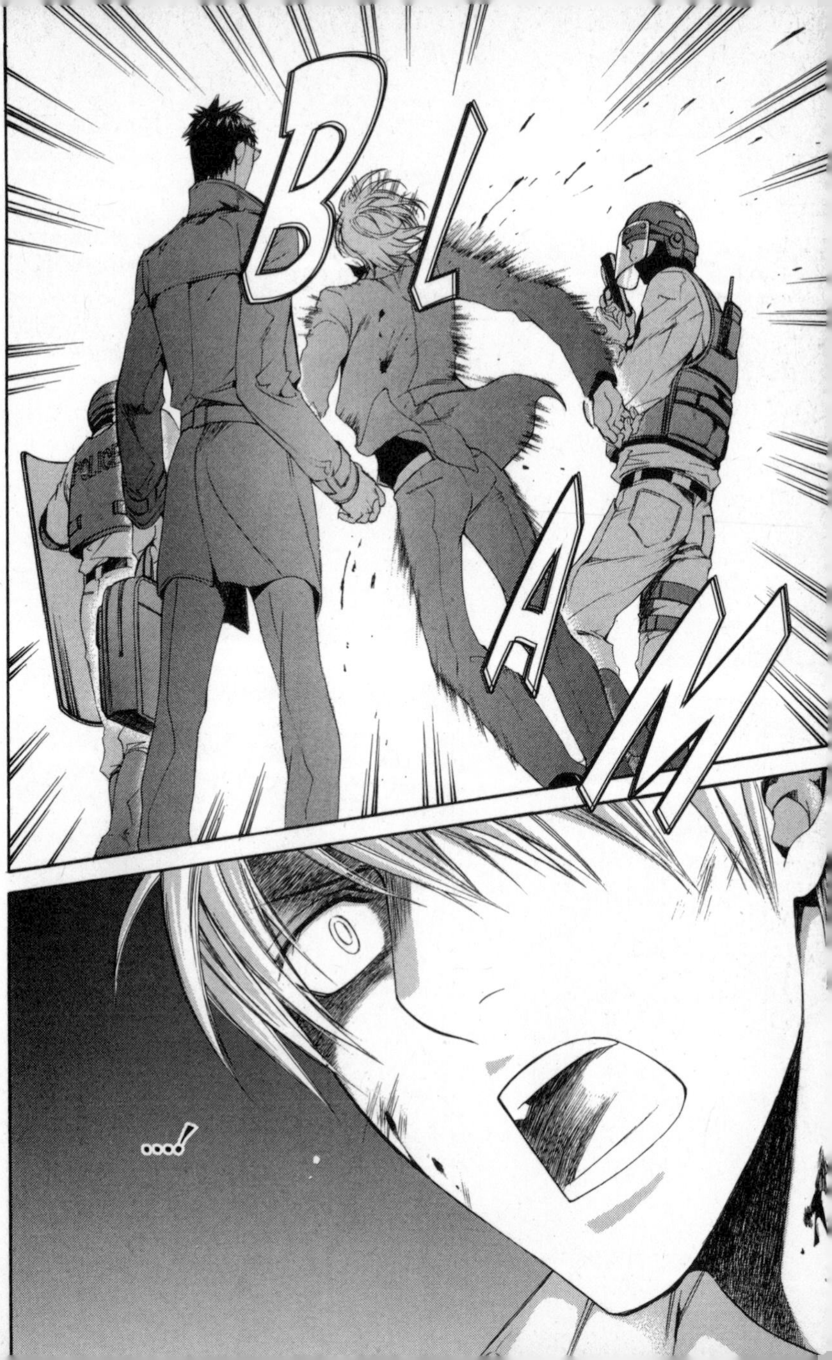
BLAM
POLICE
....!

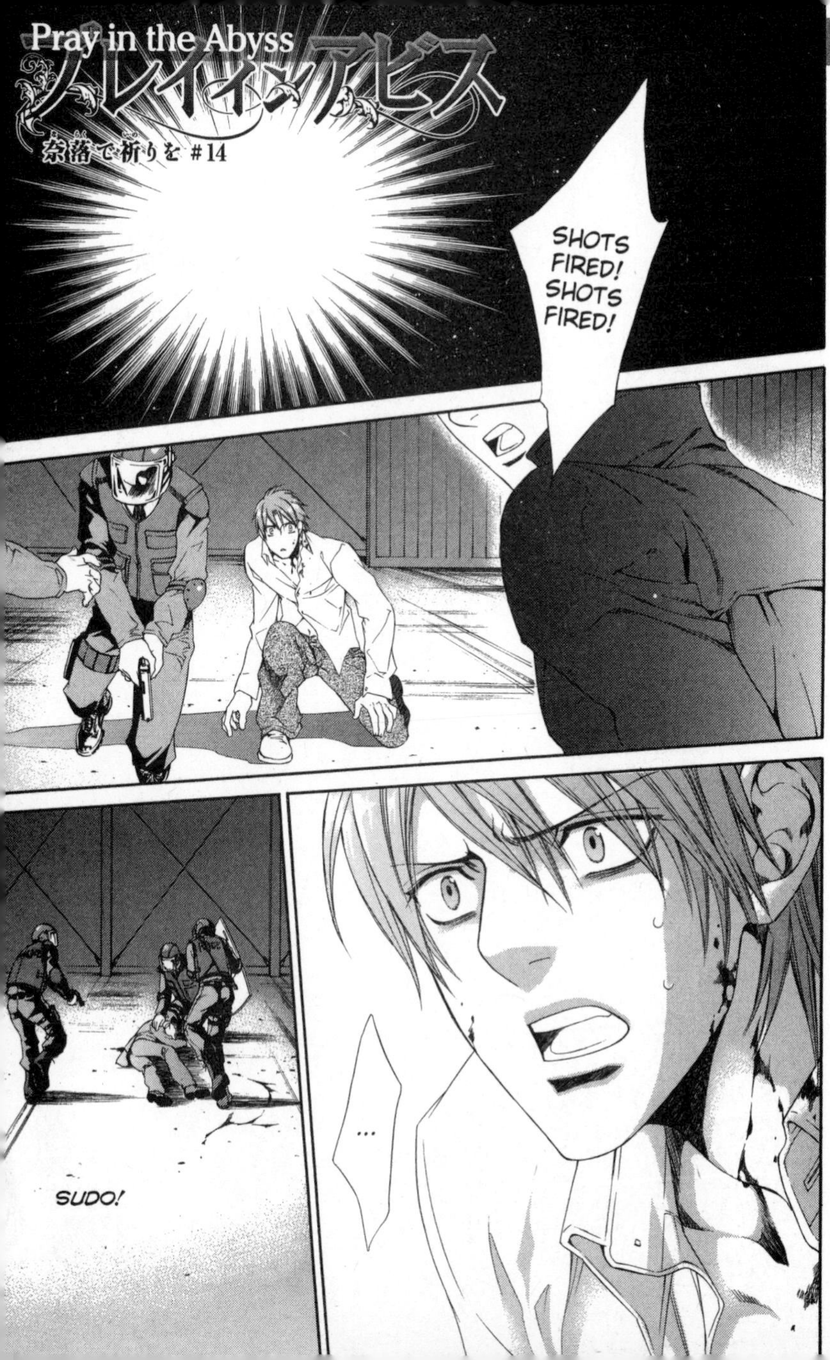
Pray in the Abyss
プレイインアビス
奈落で祈りを #14
SHOTS FIRED! SHOTS FIRED!
...
SUDO!

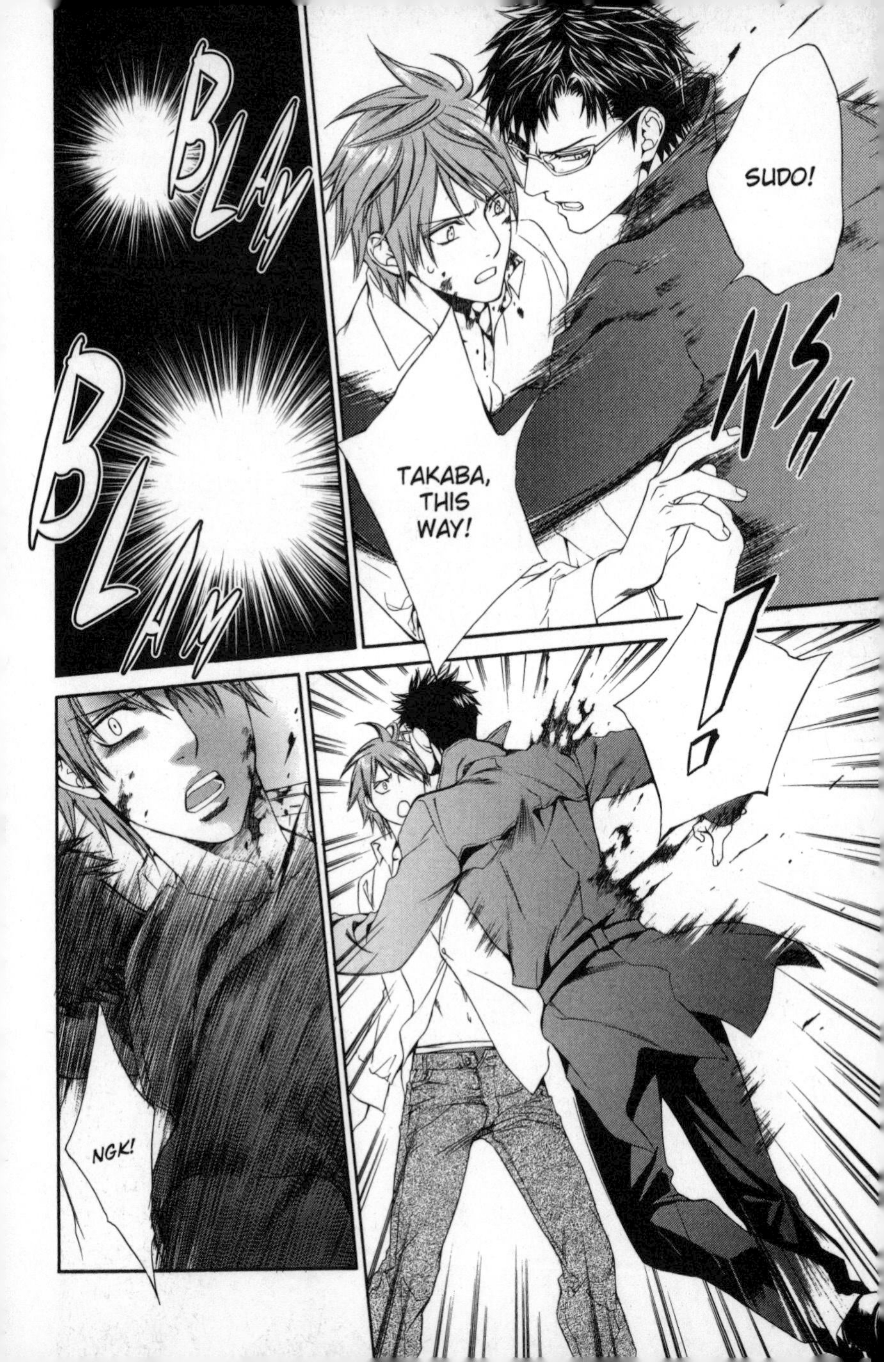
SUDO!
TAKABA, THIS WAY!
WSH
BLAM
BLAM
!
NGK!

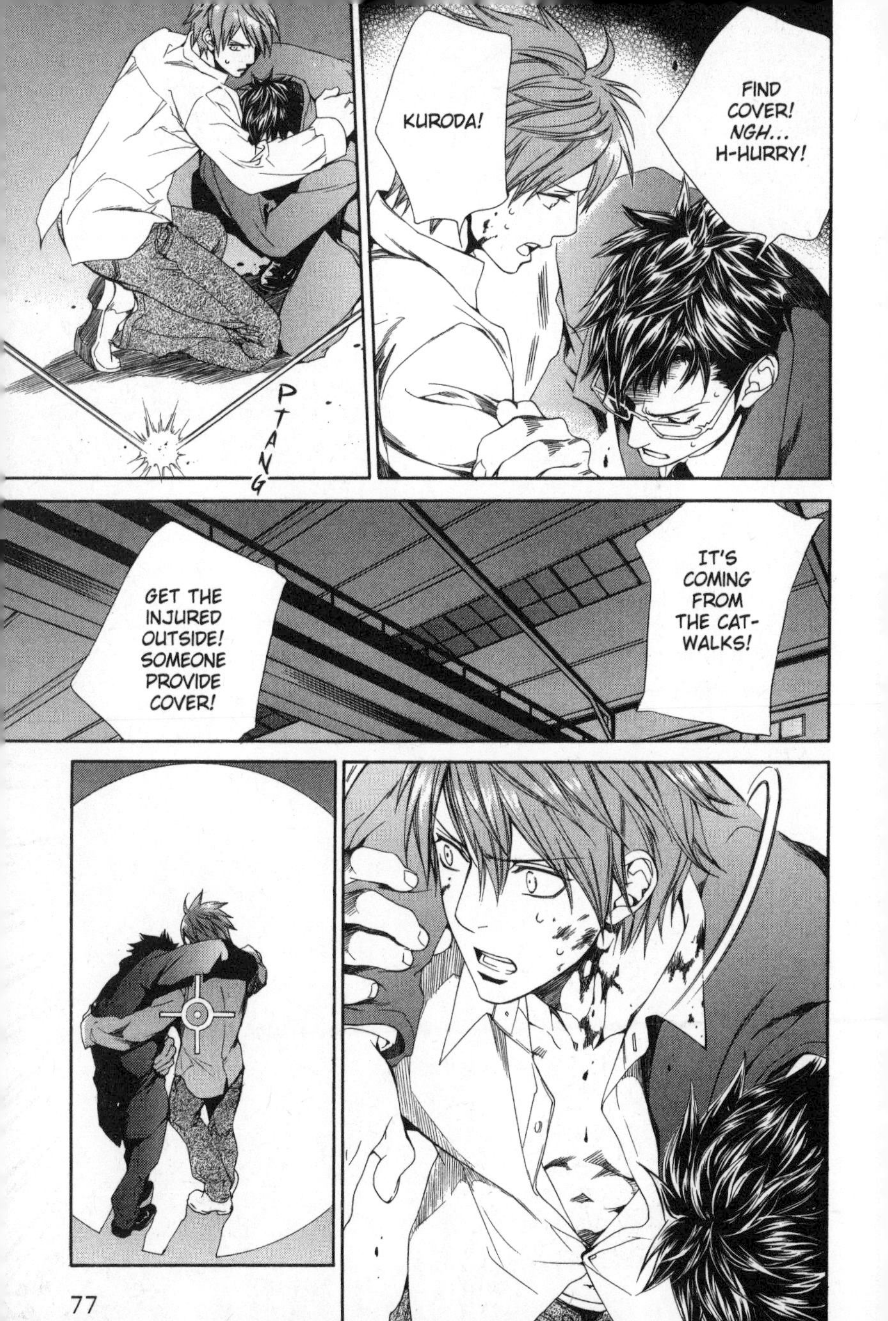
FIND COVER! NGH... H-HURRY!
KURODA!
PTANG
IT'S COMING FROM THE CAT-WALKS!
GET THE INJURED OUTSIDE! SOMEONE PROVIDE COVER!

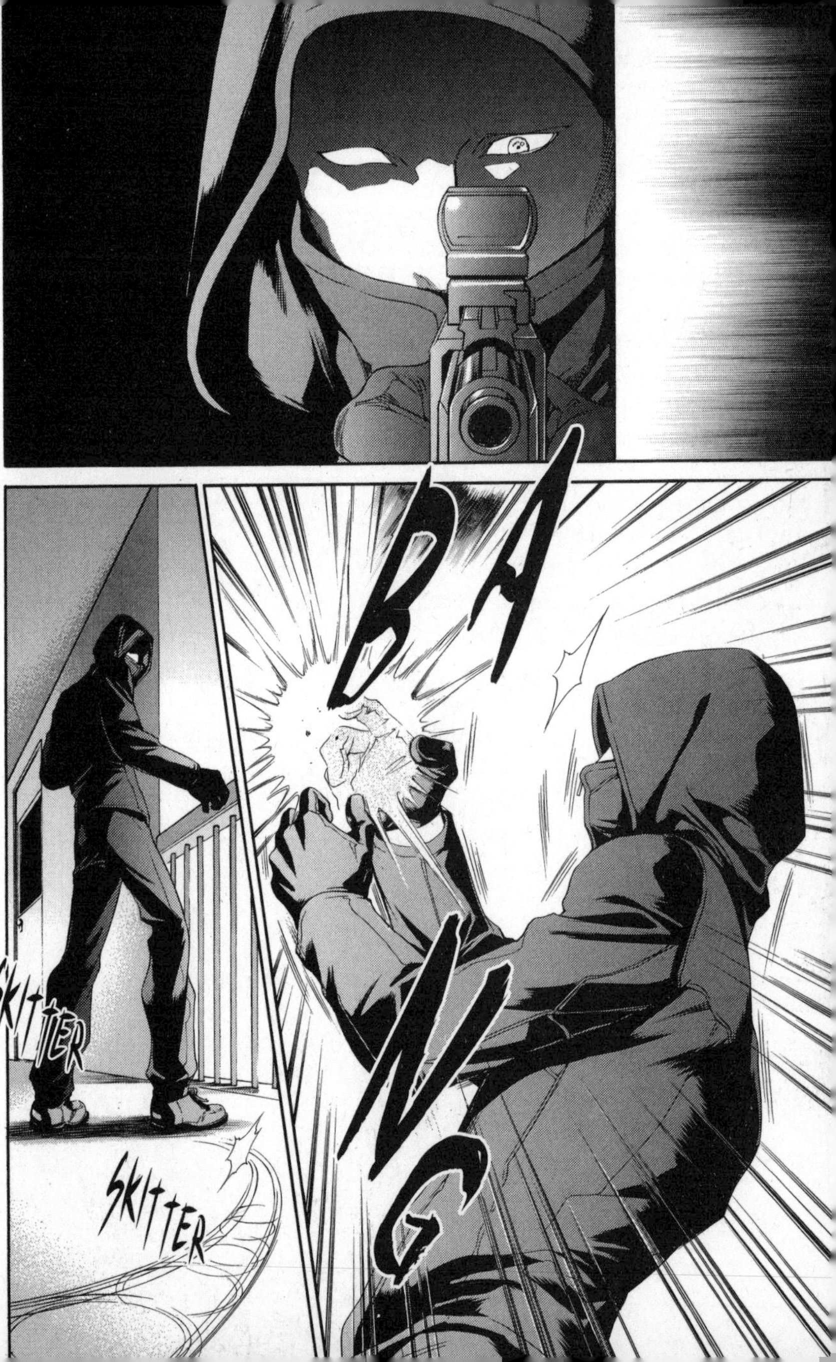
BANG
SKITTER
SKITTER

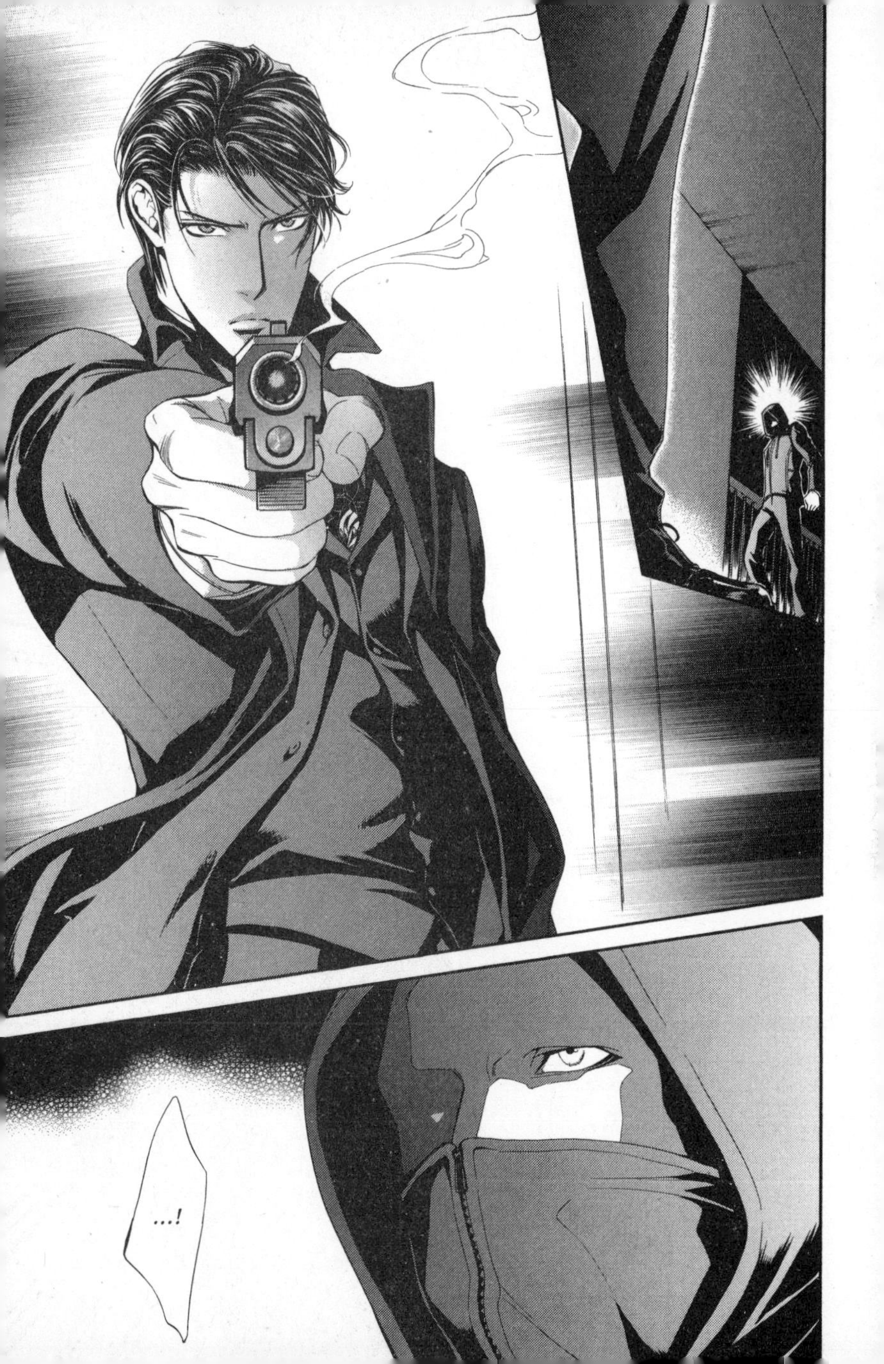
...!

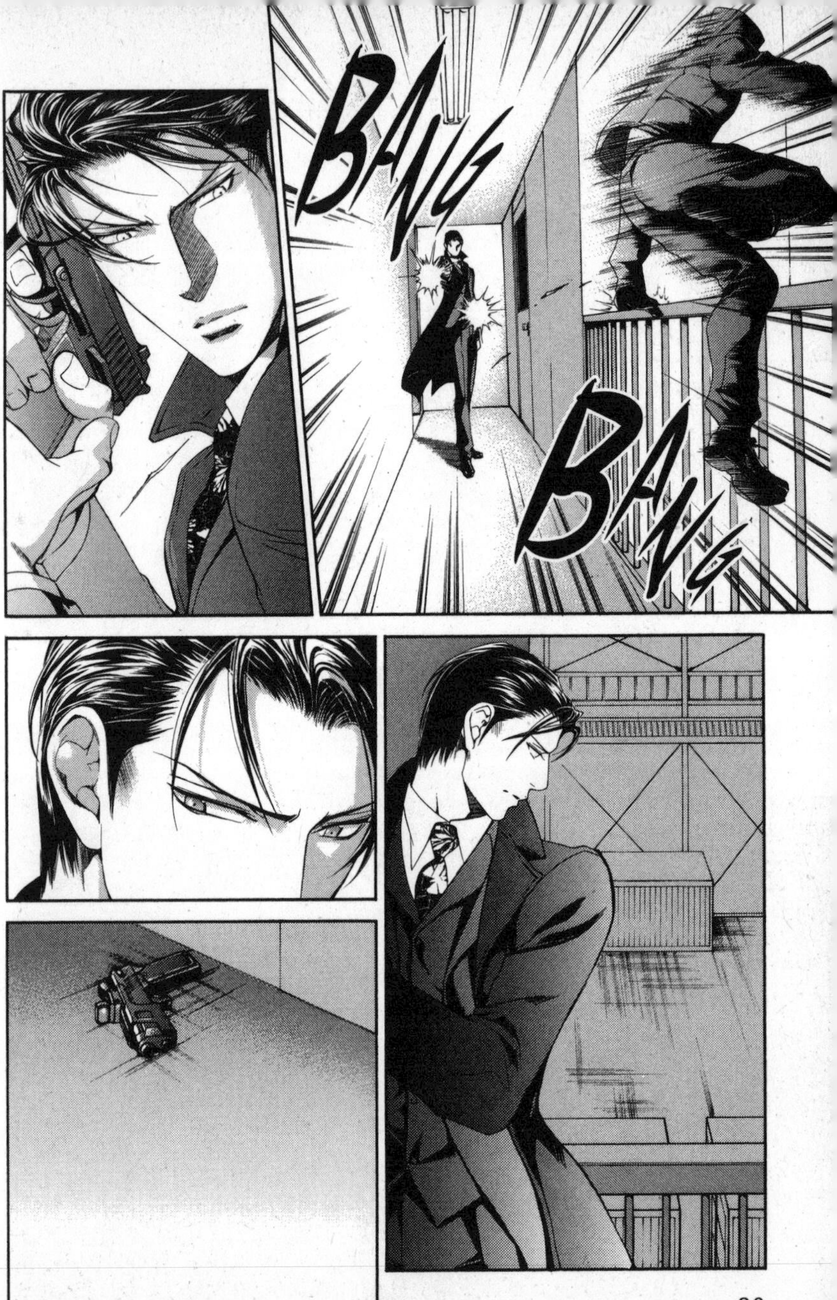
BANG
BANG

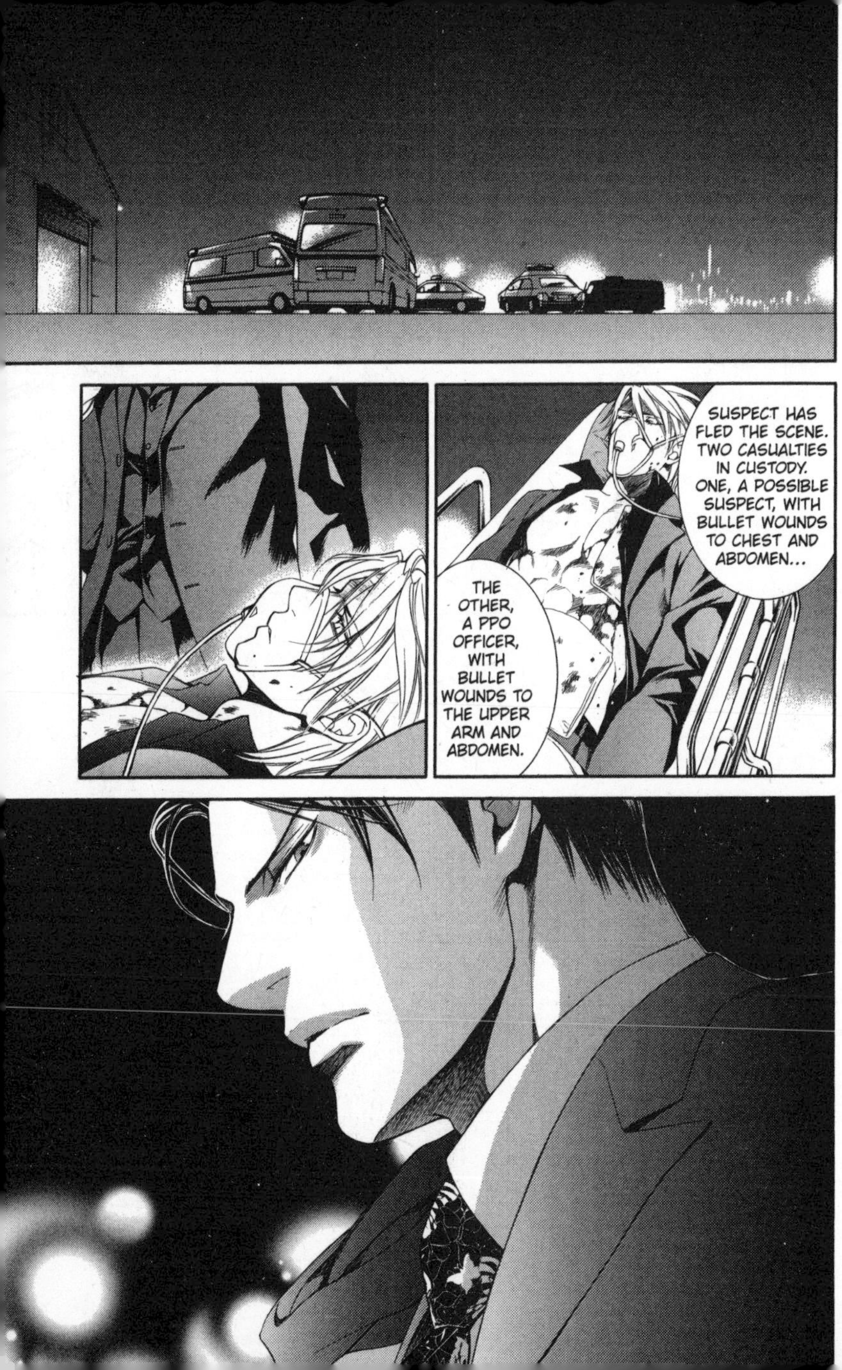
SUSPECT HAS FLED THE SCENE. TWO CASUALTIES IN CUSTODY. ONE, A POSSIBLE SUSPECT, WITH BULLET WOUNDS TO CHEST AND ABDOMEN...
THE OTHER, A PPO OFFICER, WITH BULLET WOUNDS TO THE UPPER ARM AND ABDOMEN.

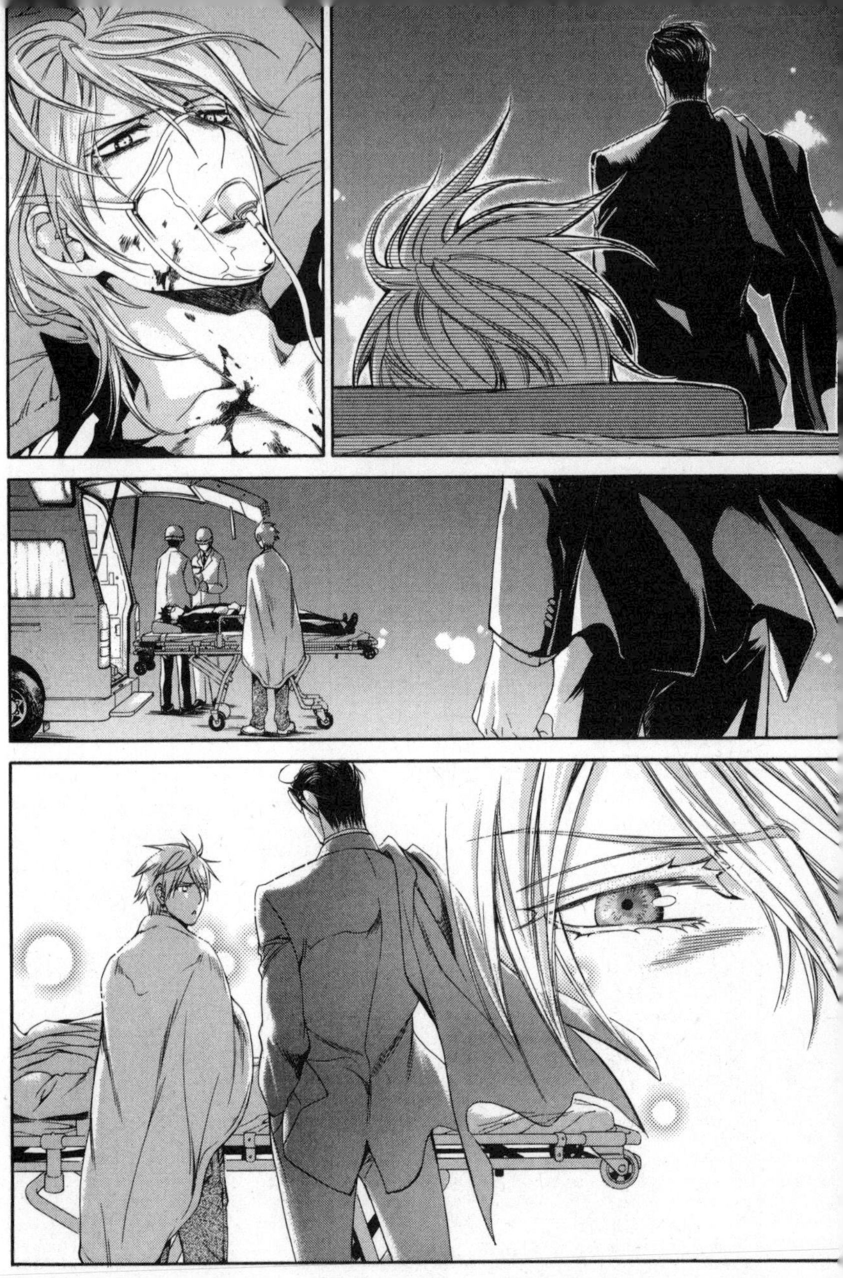

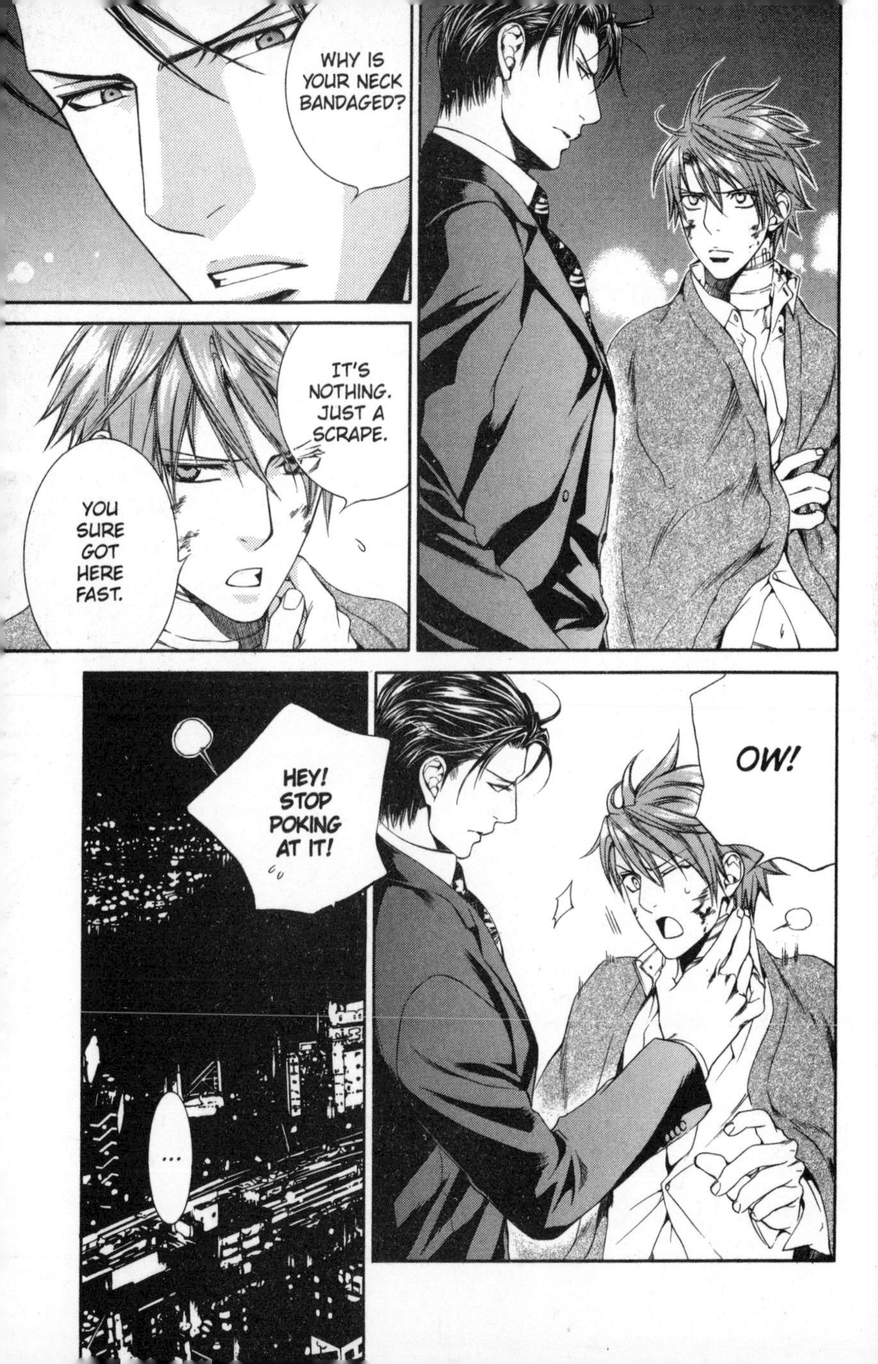
WHY IS YOUR NECK BANDAGED?
IT'S NOTHING. JUST A SCRAPE.
YOU SURE GOT HERE FAST.
OW!
HEY! STOP POKING AT IT!
...

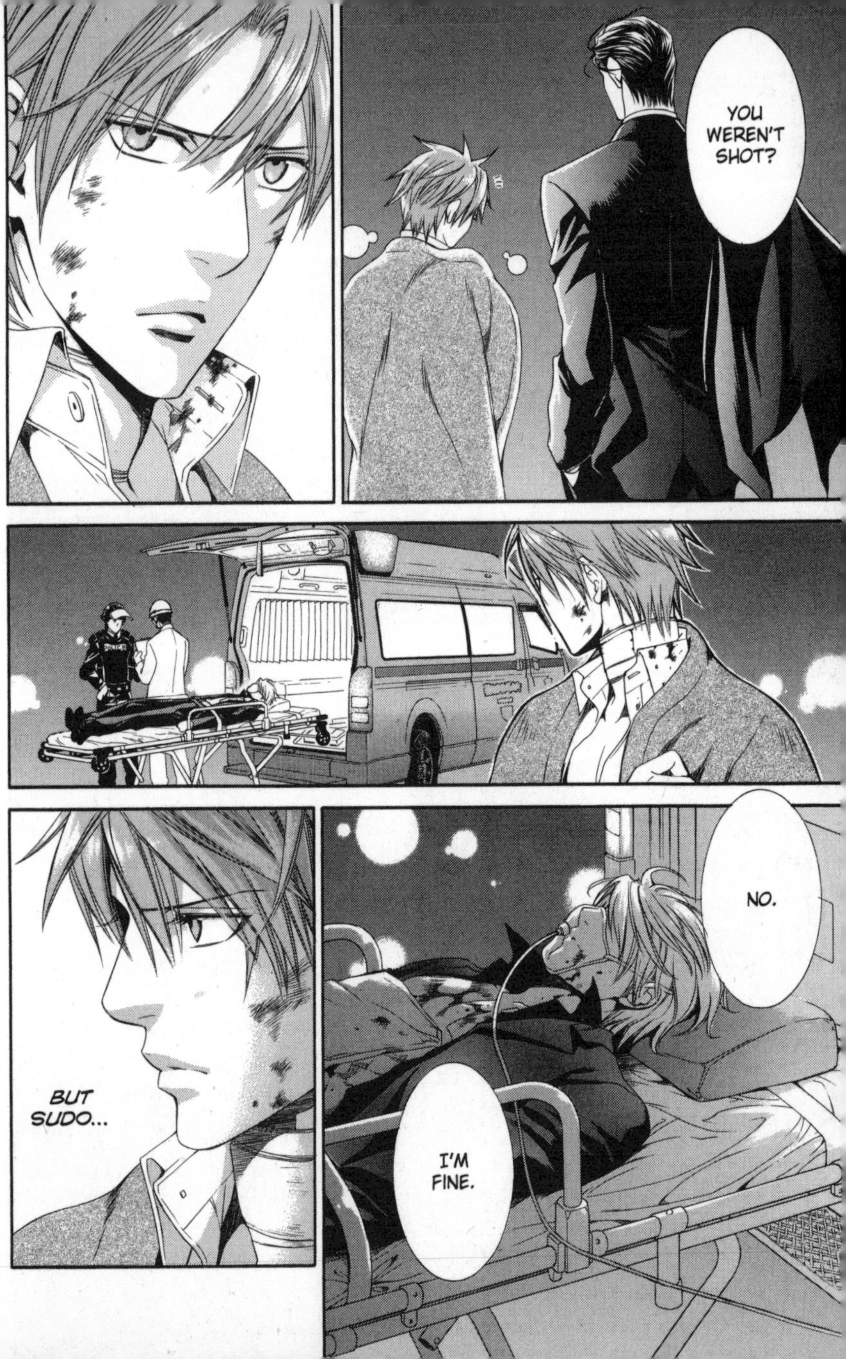
YOU WEREN'T SHOT?
NO.
I'M FINE.
BUT SUDO...

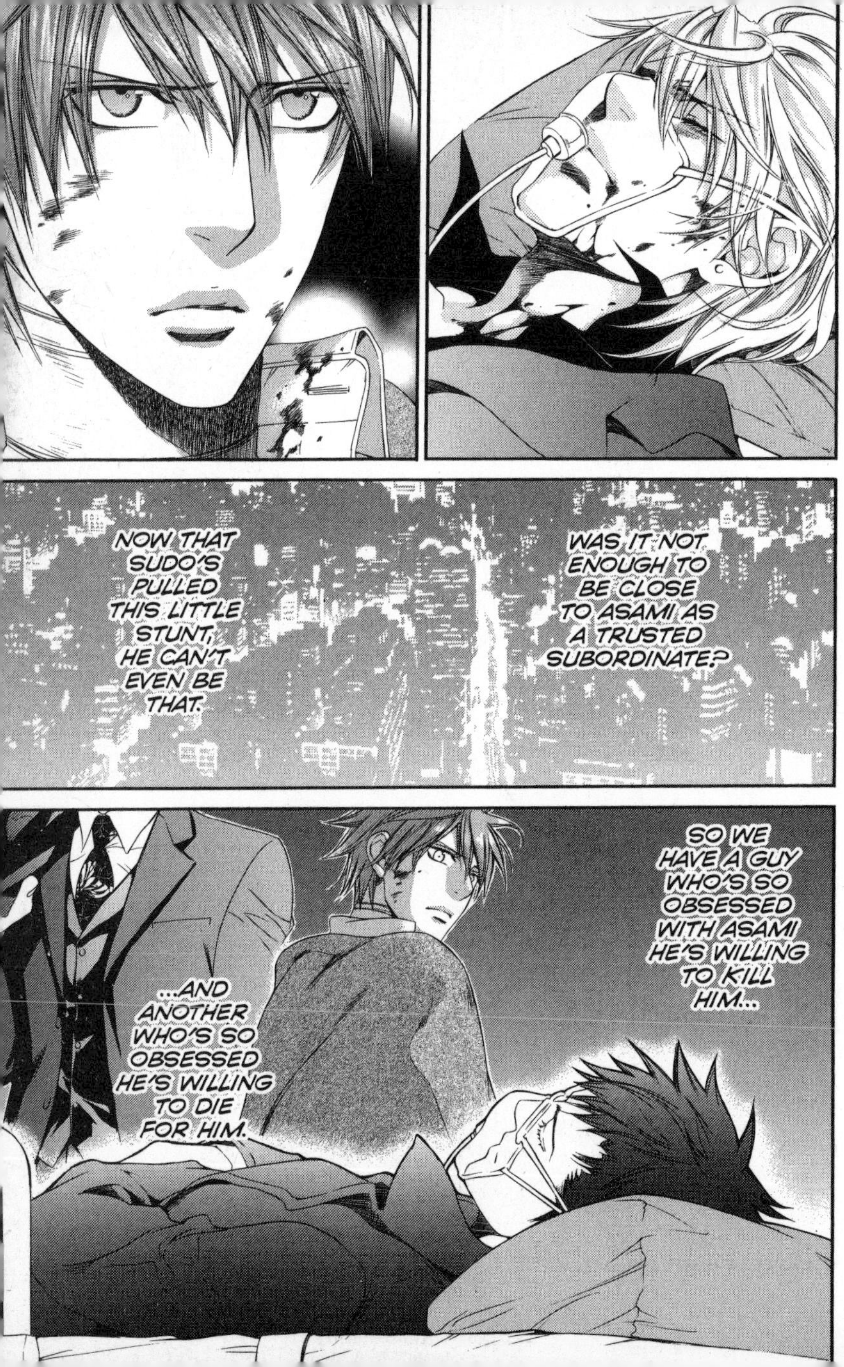
WAS IT NOT ENOUGH TO BE CLOSE TO ASAMI AS A TRUSTED SUBORDINATE?
NOW THAT SUDO'S PULLED THIS LITTLE STUNT, HE CAN'T EVEN BE THAT.
SO WE HAVE A GUY WHO'S SO OBSESSED WITH ASAMI HE'S WILLING TO KILL HIM...
...AND ANOTHER WHO'S SO OBSESSED HE'S WILLING TO DIE FOR HIM.

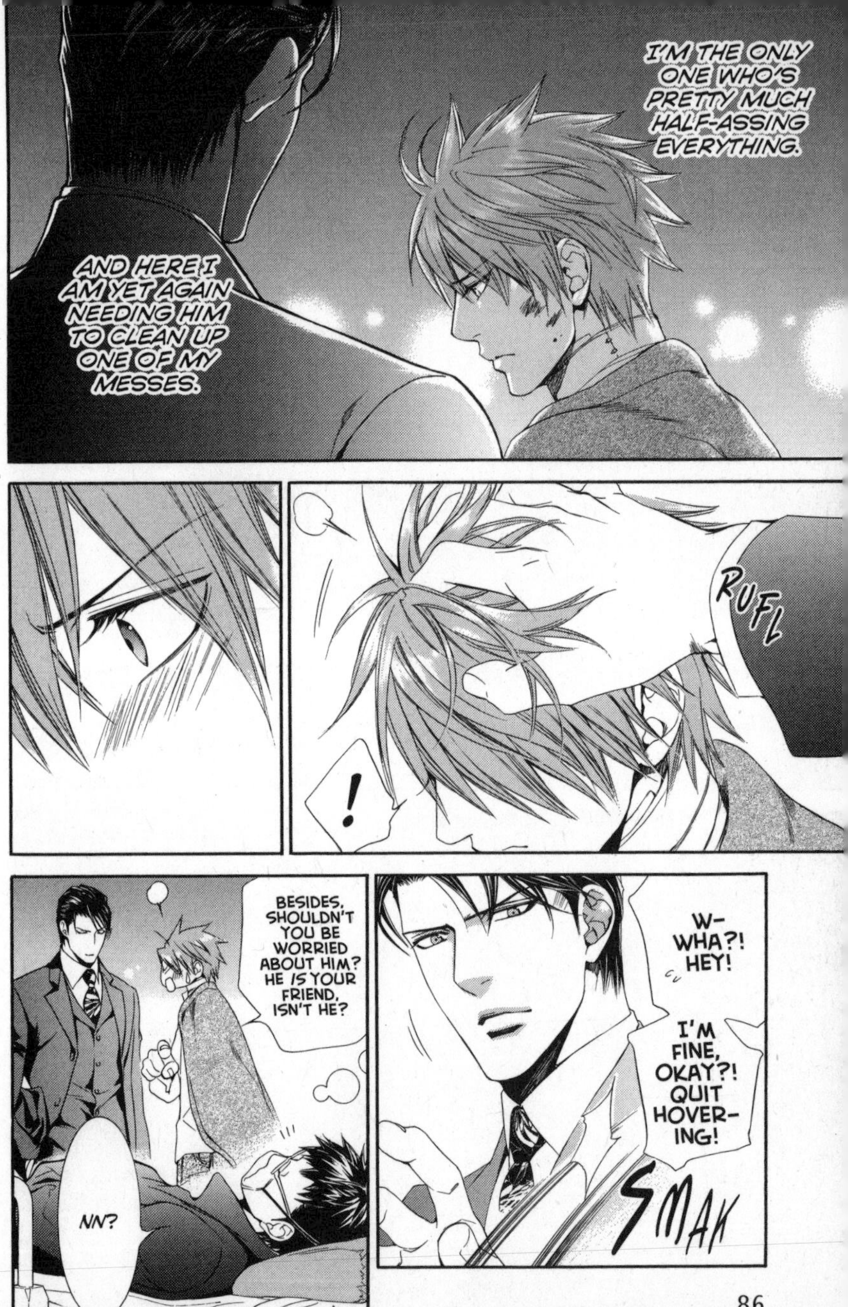
I'M THE ONLY ONE WHO'S PRETTY MUCH HALF-ASSING EVERYTHING.
AND HERE I AM YET AGAIN NEEDING HIM TO CLEAN UP ONE OF MY MESSES.
RUFL
!
W-WHA?! HEY!
I'M FINE, OKAY?! QUIT HOVERING!
SMAK
BESIDES, SHOULDN'T YOU BE WORRIED ABOUT HIM? HE IS YOUR FRIEND, ISN'T HE?
NN?

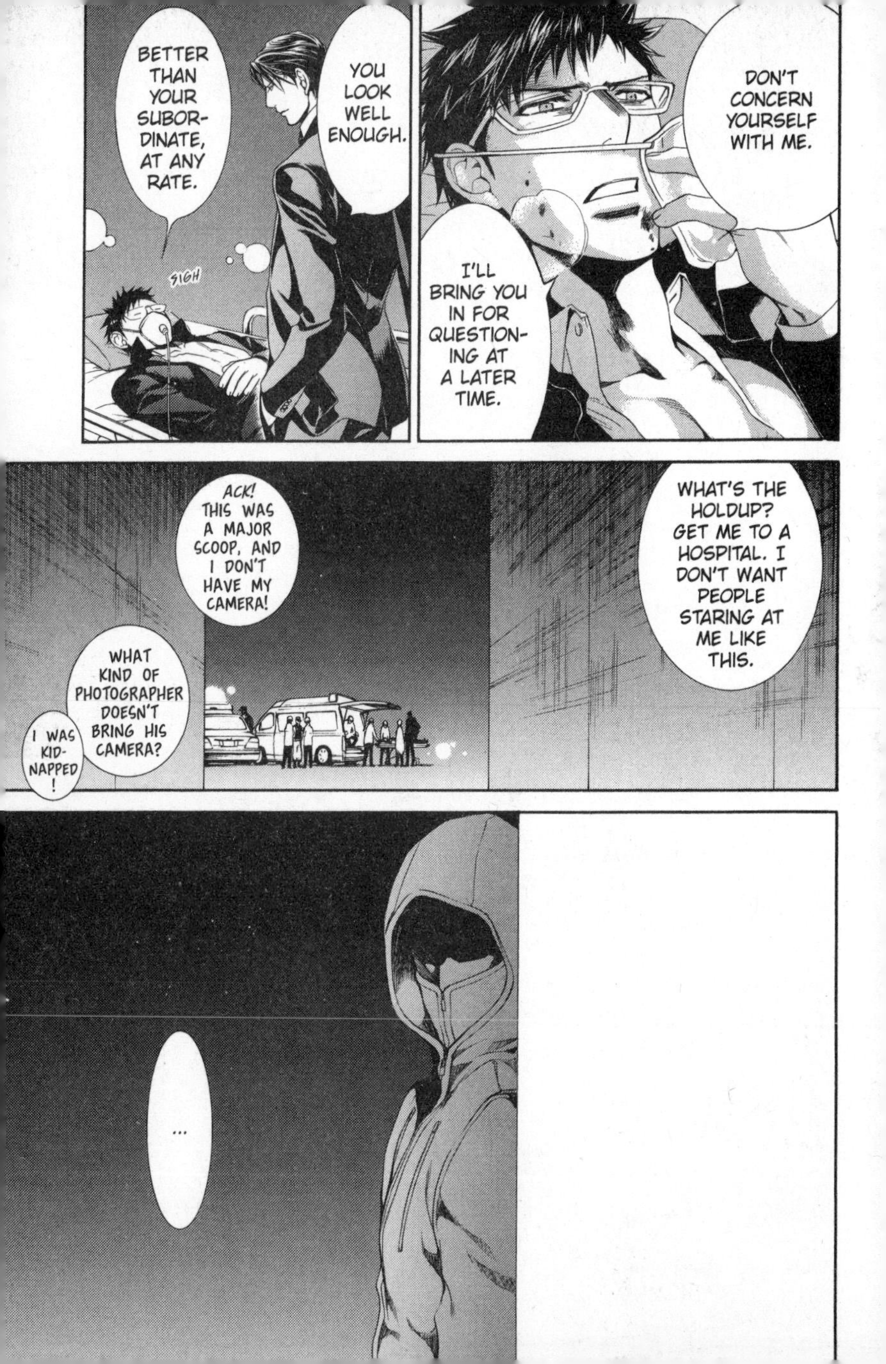
DON'T CONCERN YOURSELF WITH ME.
I'LL BRING YOU IN FOR QUESTIONING AT A LATER TIME.
YOU LOOK WELL ENOUGH.
BETTER THAN YOUR SUBORDINATE, AT ANY RATE.
SIGH
WHAT'S THE HOLDUP? GET ME TO A HOSPITAL. I DON'T WANT PEOPLE STARING AT ME LIKE THIS.
ACK! THIS WAS A MAJOR SCOOP, AND I DON'T HAVE MY CAMERA!
WHAT KIND OF PHOTOGRAPHER DOESN'T BRING HIS CAMERA?
I WAS KID-NAPPED!
...

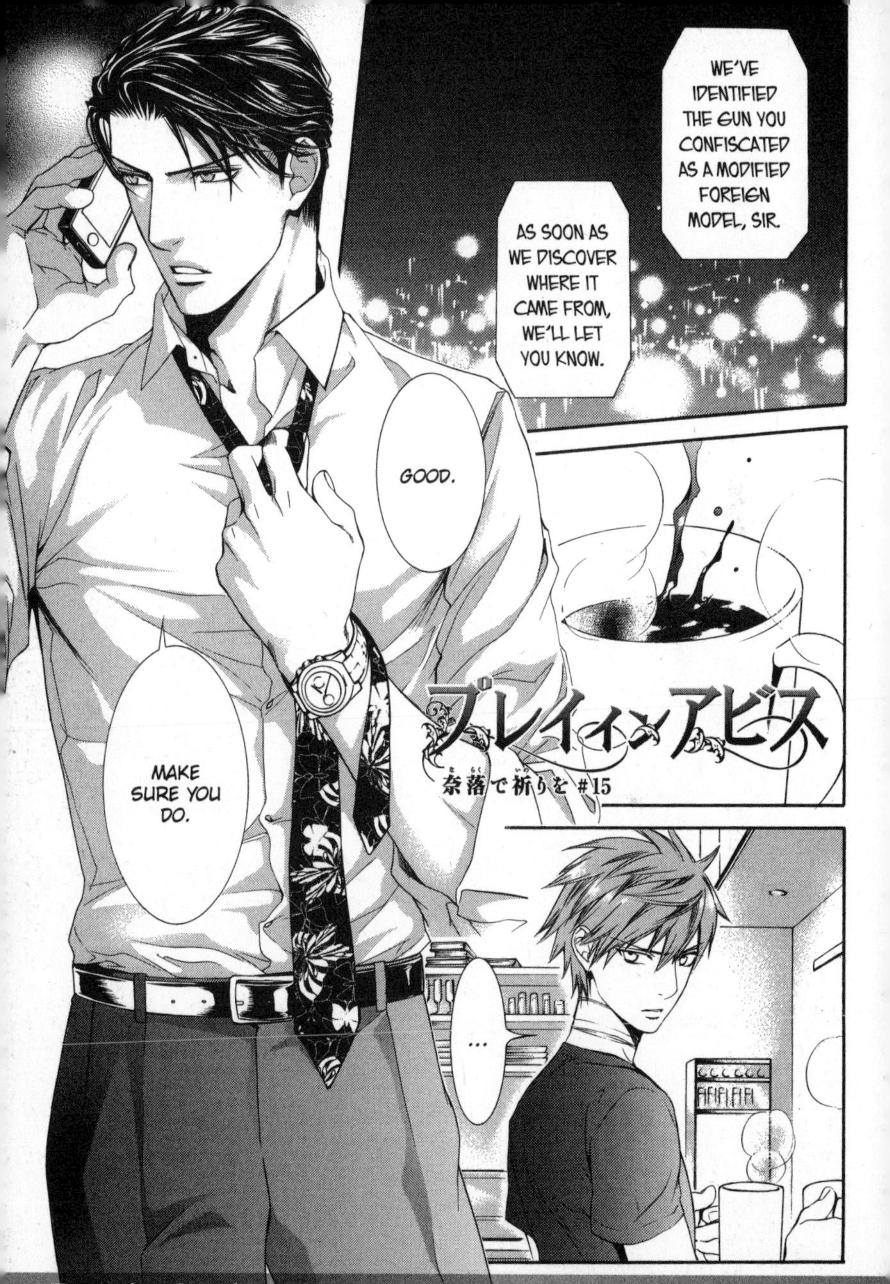
WE'VE IDENTIFIED THE GUN YOU CONFISCATED AS A MODIFIED FOREIGN MODEL, SIR.
AS SOON AS WE DISCOVER WHERE IT CAME FROM, WE'LL LET YOU KNOW.
GOOD.
MAKE SURE YOU DO.
プレイ・イン・アビス
奈落で祈りを #15
...

Pray in the Abyss

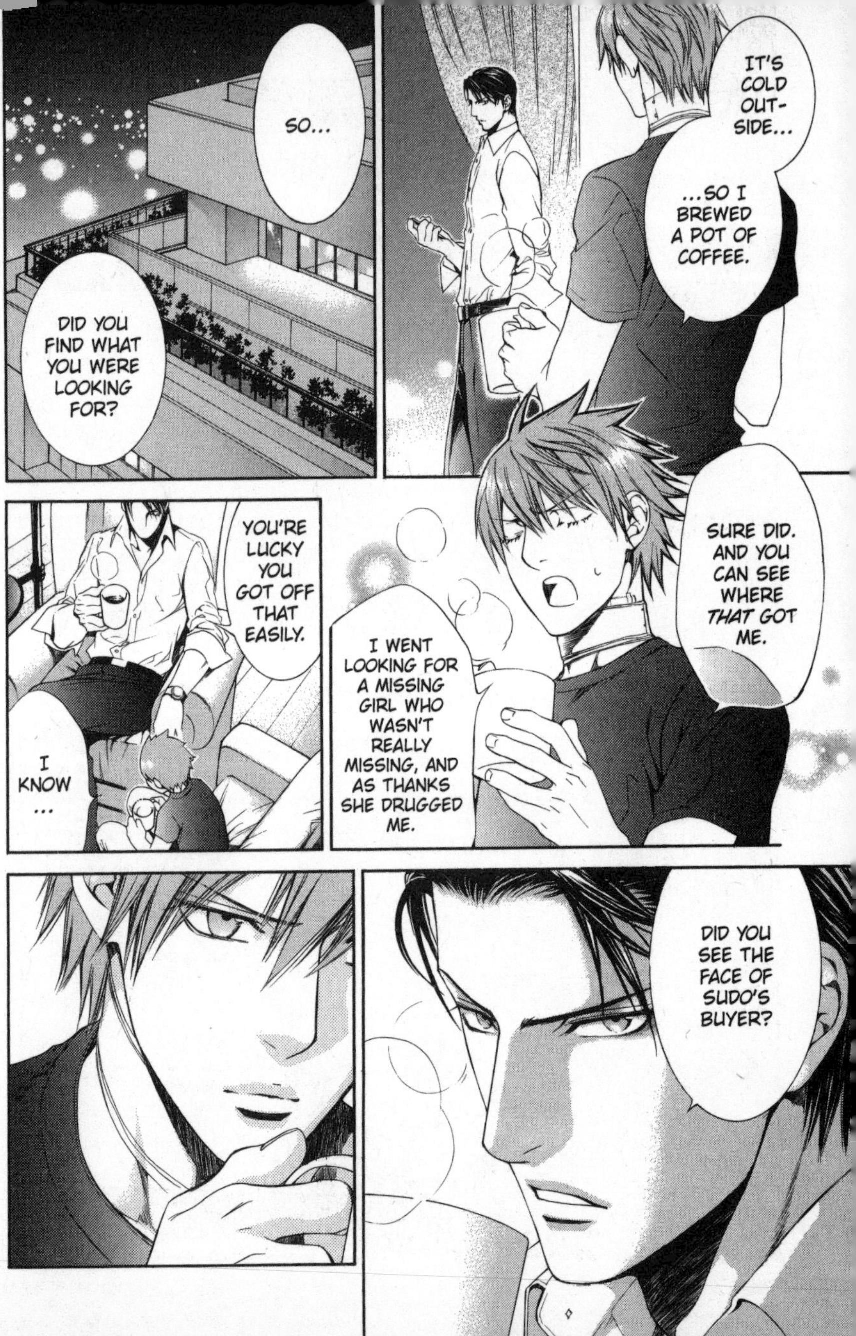
IT'S COLD OUT-SIDE...
...SO I BREWED A POT OF COFFEE.
SO...
DID YOU FIND WHAT YOU WERE LOOKING FOR?
SURE DID. AND YOU CAN SEE WHERE *THAT* GOT ME.
I WENT LOOKING FOR A MISSING GIRL WHO WASN'T REALLY MISSING, AND AS THANKS SHE DRUGGED ME.
YOU'RE LUCKY YOU GOT OFF THAT EASILY.
I KNOW...
DID YOU SEE THE FACE OF SUDO'S BUYER?

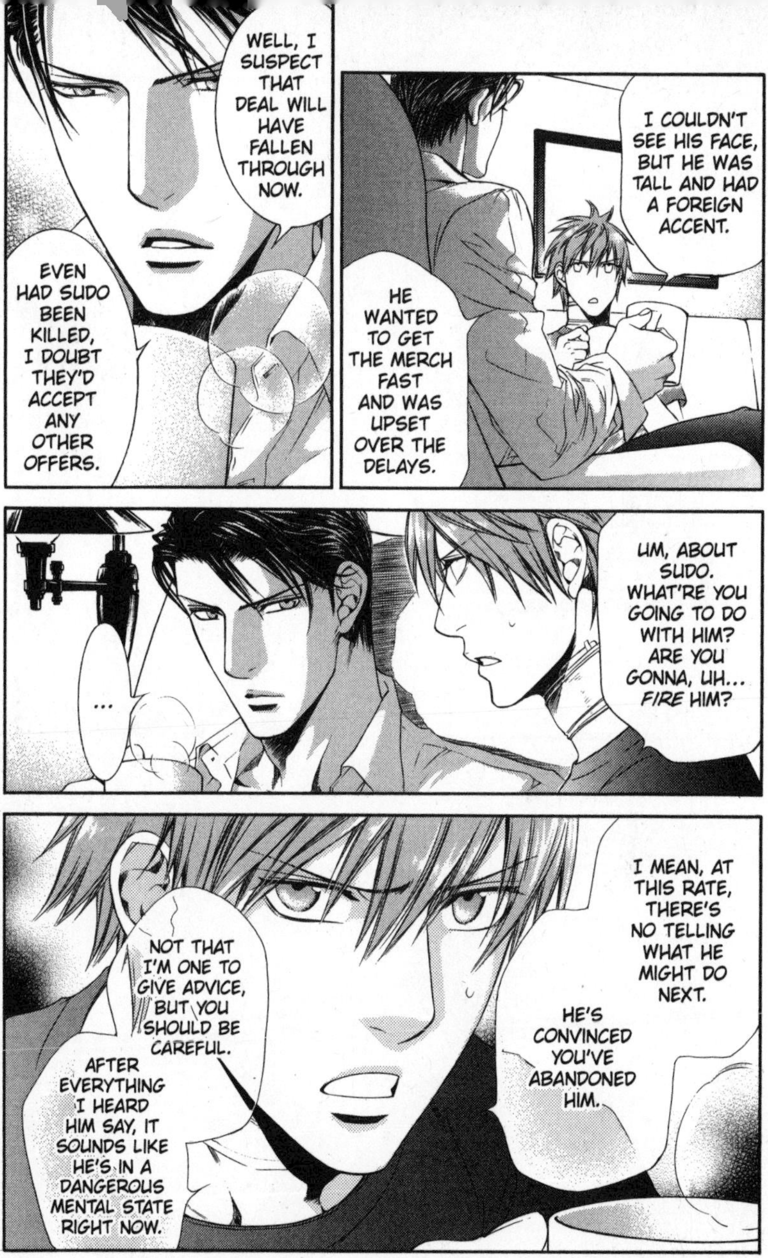

I COULDN'T SEE HIS FACE, BUT HE WAS TALL AND HAD A FOREIGN ACCENT.
HE WANTED TO GET THE MERCH FAST AND WAS UPSET OVER THE DELAYS.
WELL, I SUSPECT THAT DEAL WILL HAVE FALLEN THROUGH NOW.
EVEN HAD SUDO BEEN KILLED, I DOUBT THEY'D ACCEPT ANY OTHER OFFERS.
UM, ABOUT SUDO. WHAT'RE YOU GOING TO DO WITH HIM? ARE YOU GONNA, UH... *FIRE* HIM?
...
I MEAN, AT THIS RATE, THERE'S NO TELLING WHAT HE MIGHT DO NEXT.
HE'S CONVINCED YOU'VE ABANDONED HIM.
NOT THAT I'M ONE TO GIVE ADVICE, BUT YOU SHOULD BE CAREFUL.
AFTER EVERYTHING I HEARD HIM SAY, IT SOUNDS LIKE HE'S IN A DANGEROUS MENTAL STATE RIGHT NOW.

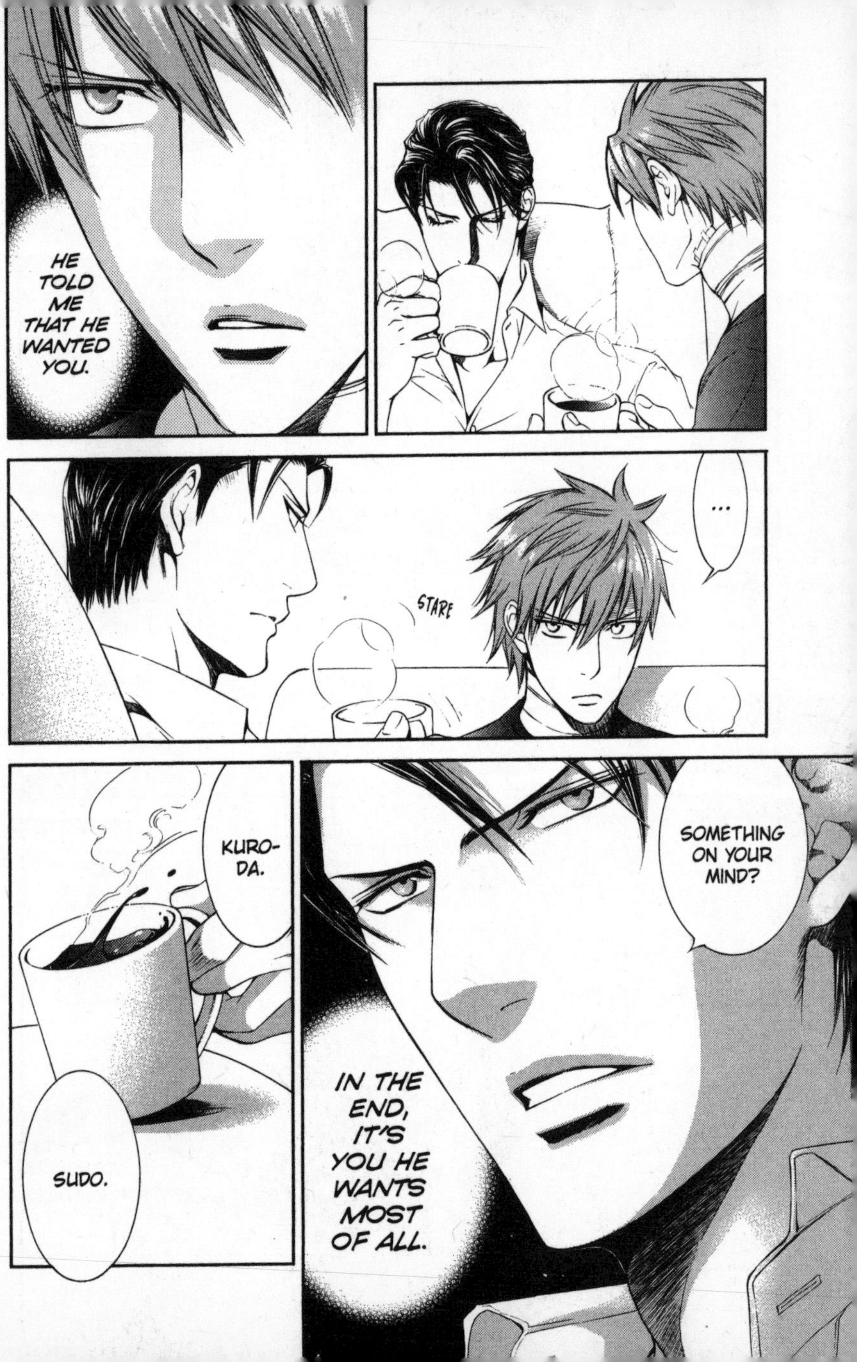
HE TOLD ME THAT HE WANTED YOU.
...
STARE
SOMETHING ON YOUR MIND?
IN THE END, IT'S YOU HE WANTS MOST OF ALL.
KURO-DA.
SUDO.

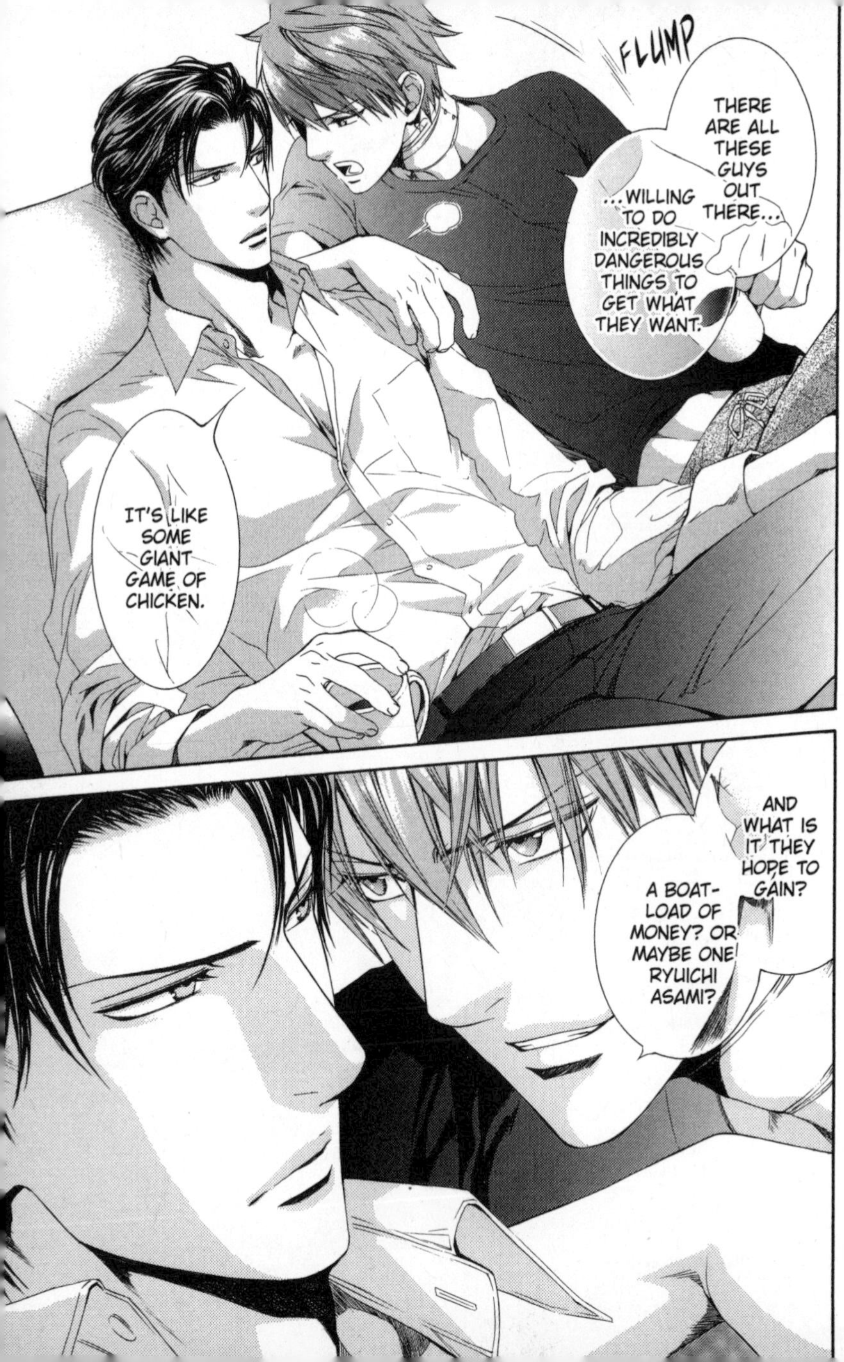
FLUMP
THERE ARE ALL THESE GUYS OUT THERE...
...WILLING TO DO INCREDIBLY DANGEROUS THINGS TO GET WHAT THEY WANT.
IT'S LIKE SOME GIANT GAME OF CHICKEN.
AND WHAT IS IT THEY HOPE TO GAIN?
A BOAT-LOAD OF MONEY? OR MAYBE ONE RYUICHI ASAMI?

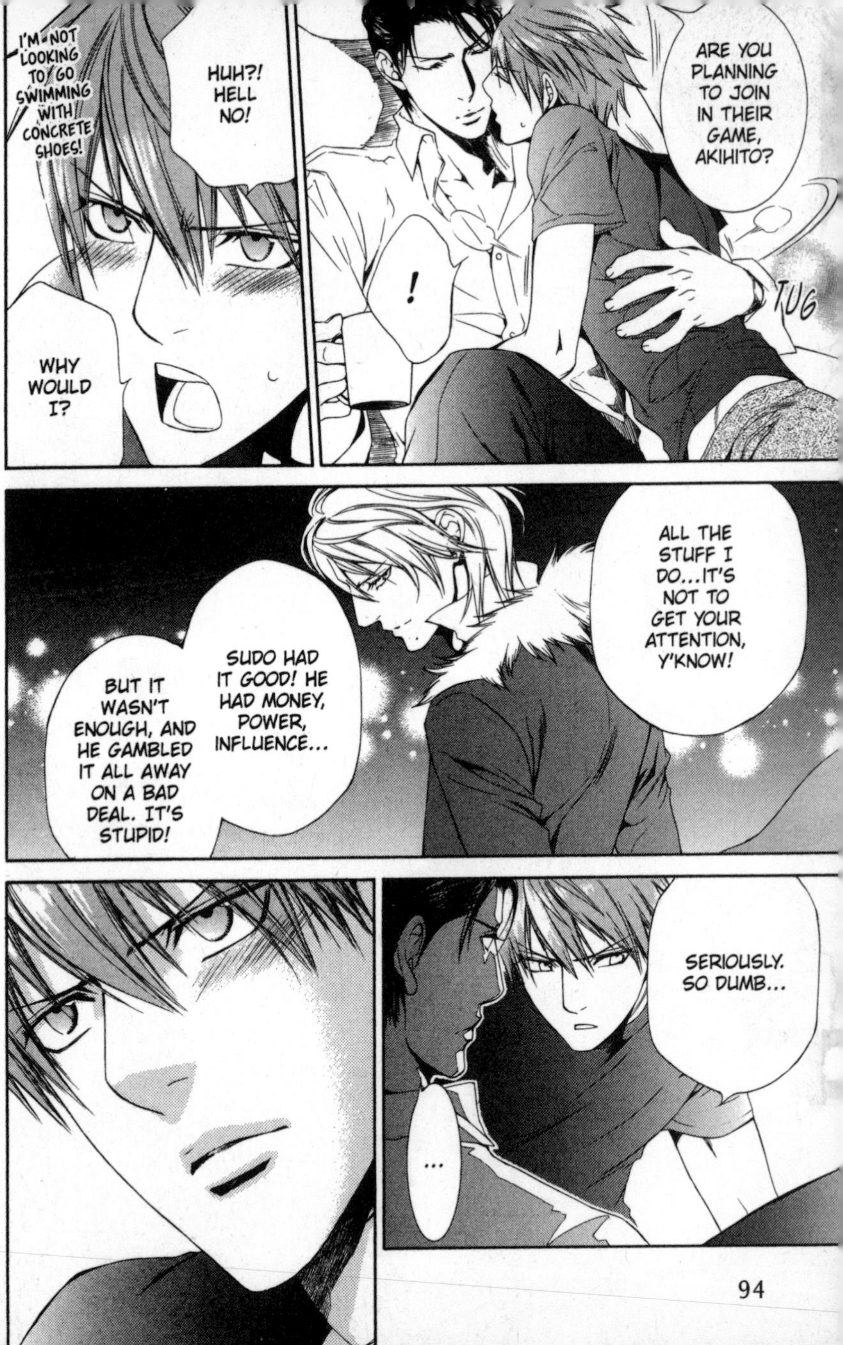
ARE YOU PLANNING TO JOIN IN THEIR GAME, AKIHITO?
!
TUG
HUH?! HELL NO!
I'M NOT LOOKING TO GO SWIMMING WITH CONCRETE SHOES!
WHY WOULD I?
ALL THE STUFF I DO...IT'S NOT TO GET YOUR ATTENTION, Y'KNOW!
SUDO HAD IT GOOD! HE HAD MONEY, POWER, INFLUENCE...
BUT IT WASN'T ENOUGH, AND HE GAMBLED IT ALL AWAY ON A BAD DEAL. IT'S STUPID!
SERIOUSLY. SO DUMB...
...

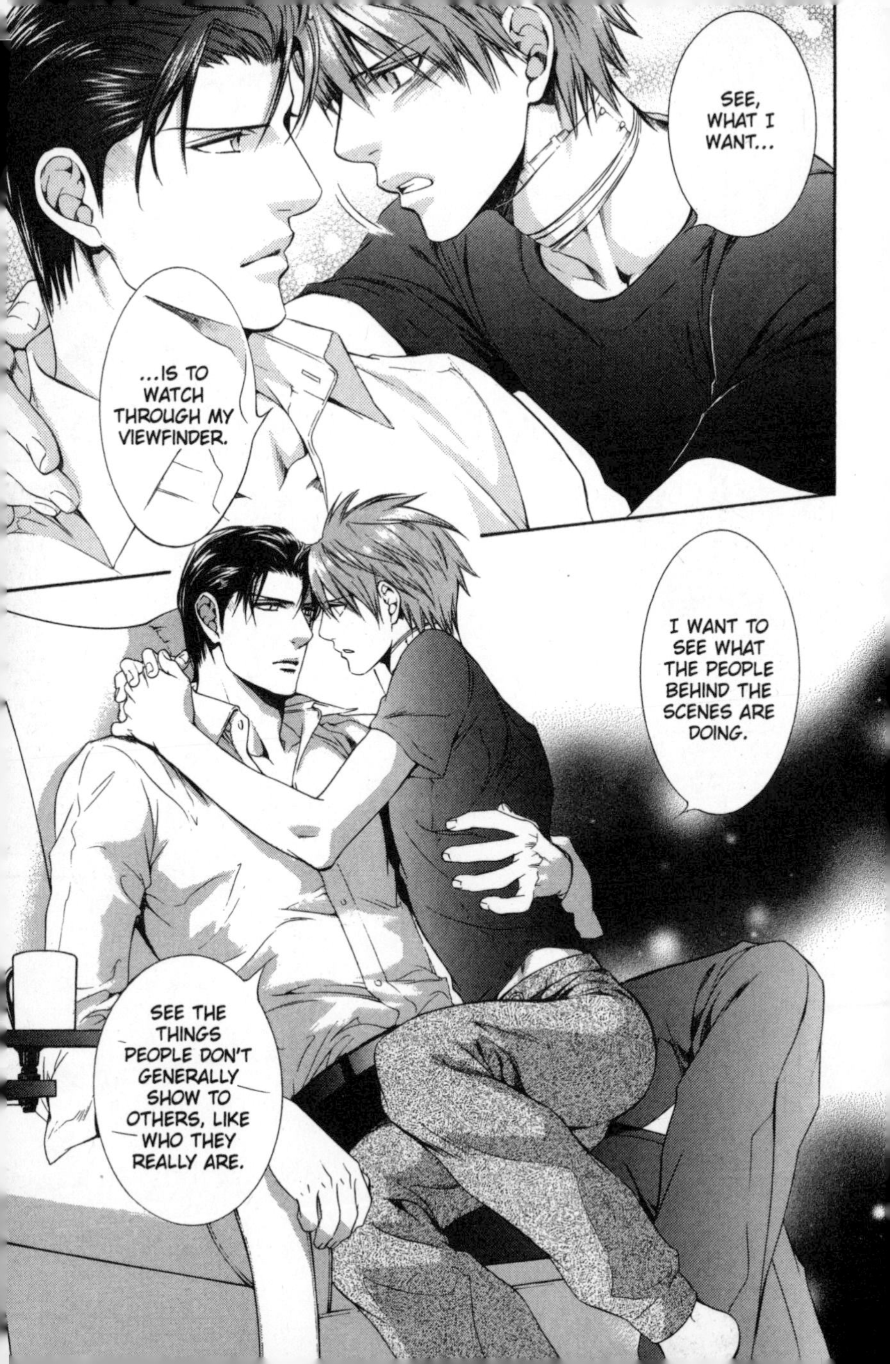
SEE, WHAT I WANT...
...IS TO WATCH THROUGH MY VIEWFINDER.
I WANT TO SEE WHAT THE PEOPLE BEHIND THE SCENES ARE DOING.
SEE THE THINGS PEOPLE DON'T GENERALLY SHOW TO OTHERS, LIKE WHO THEY REALLY ARE.

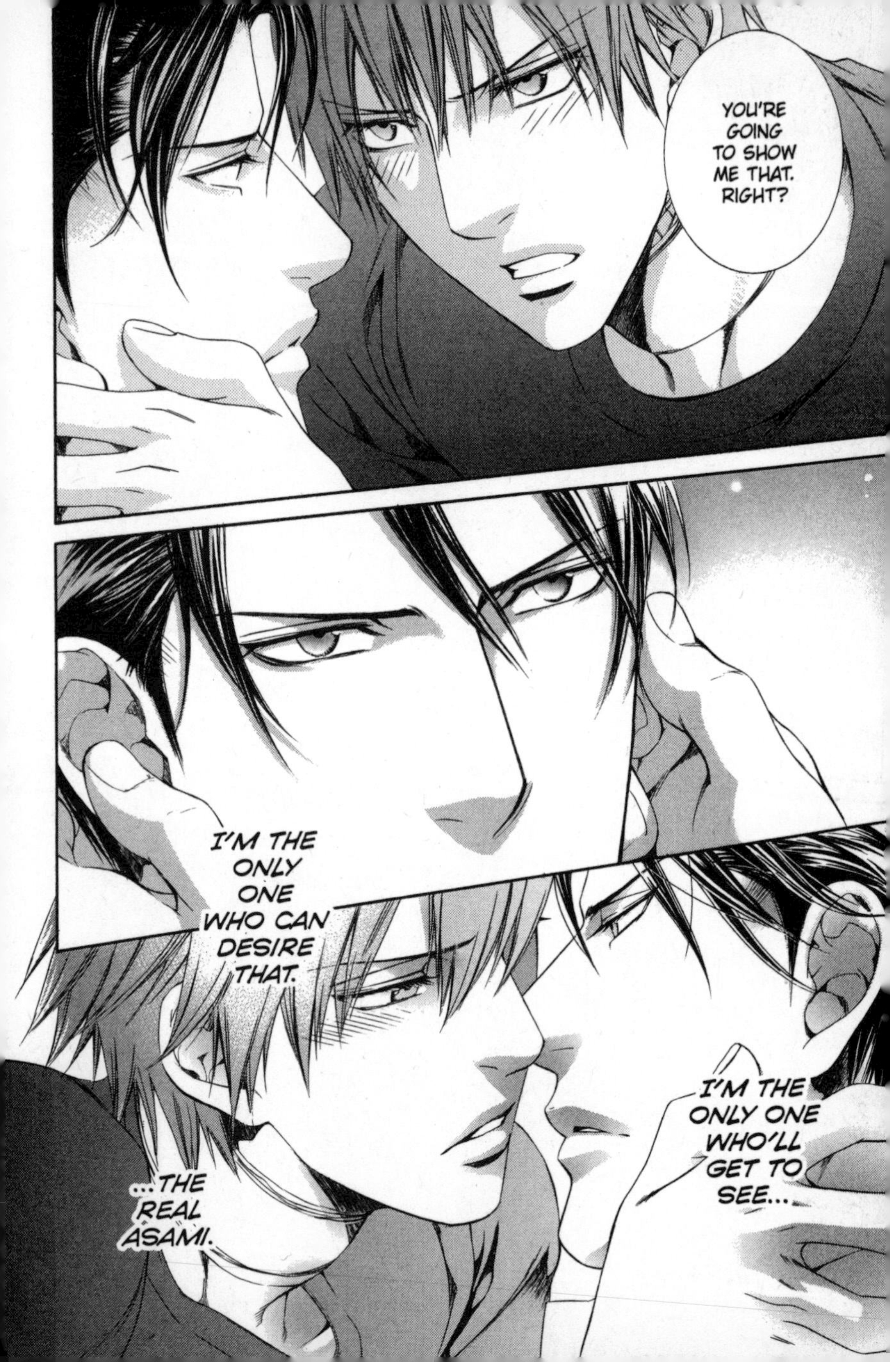
YOU'RE GOING TO SHOW ME THAT. RIGHT?
I'M THE ONLY ONE WHO CAN DESIRE THAT.
I'M THE ONLY ONE WHO'LL GET TO SEE...
...THE REAL ASAMI.

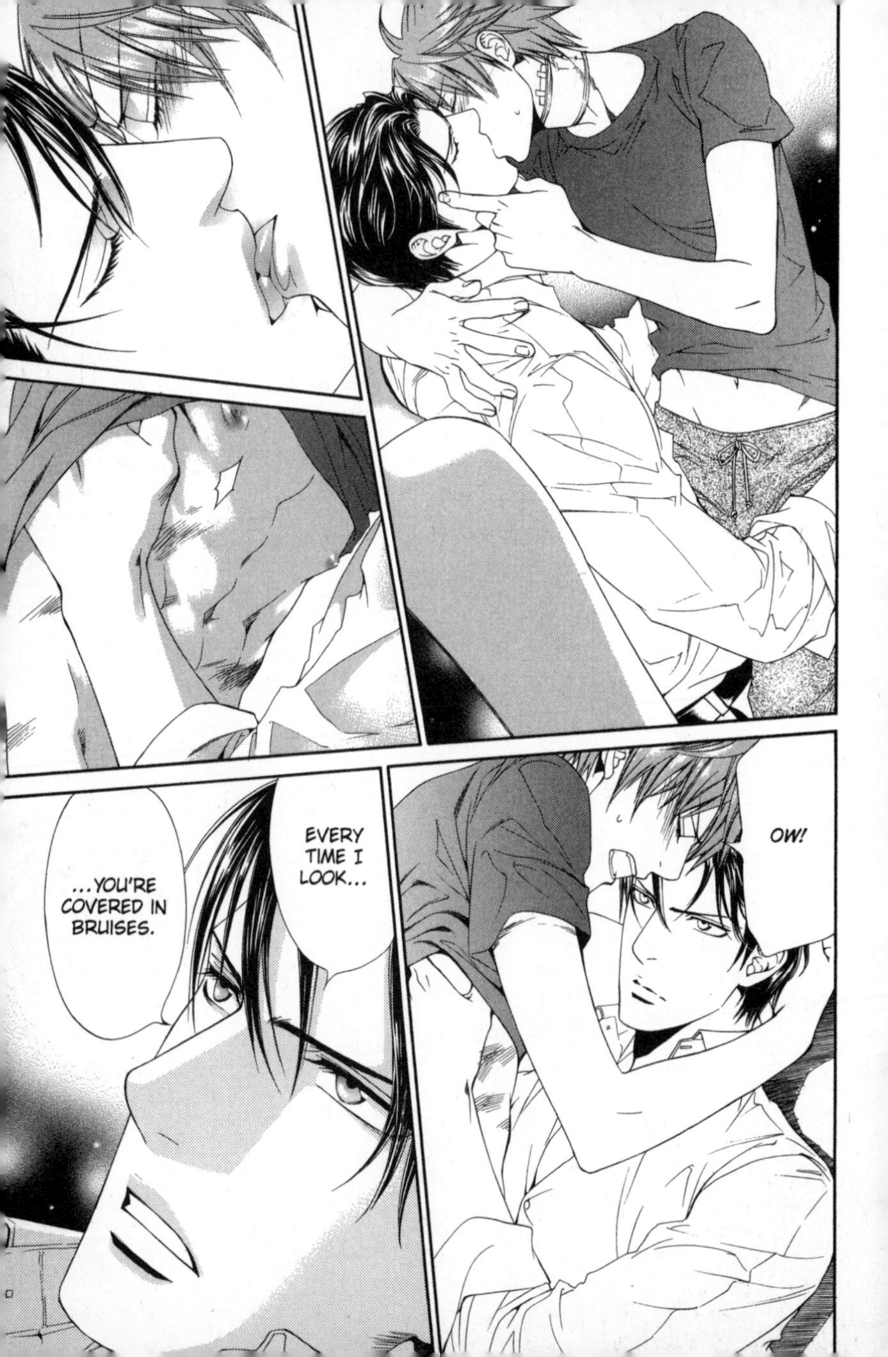
OW!
EVERY TIME I LOOK...
...YOU'RE COVERED IN BRUISES.

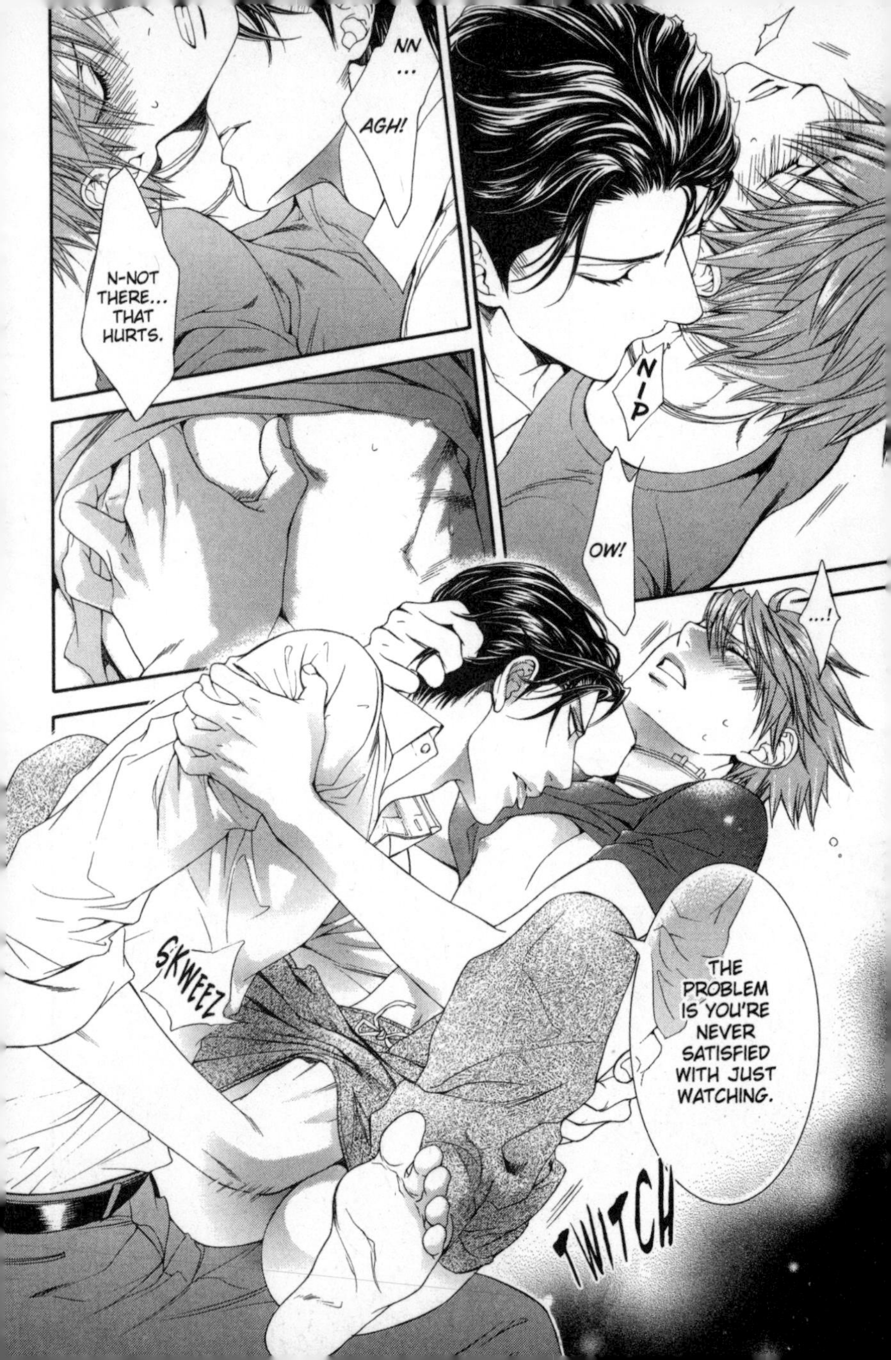
NIP
OW!
NN... AGH!
N-NOT THERE... THAT HURTS.
...!
THE PROBLEM IS YOU'RE NEVER SATISFIED WITH JUST WATCHING.
SKWEEZ
TWITCH

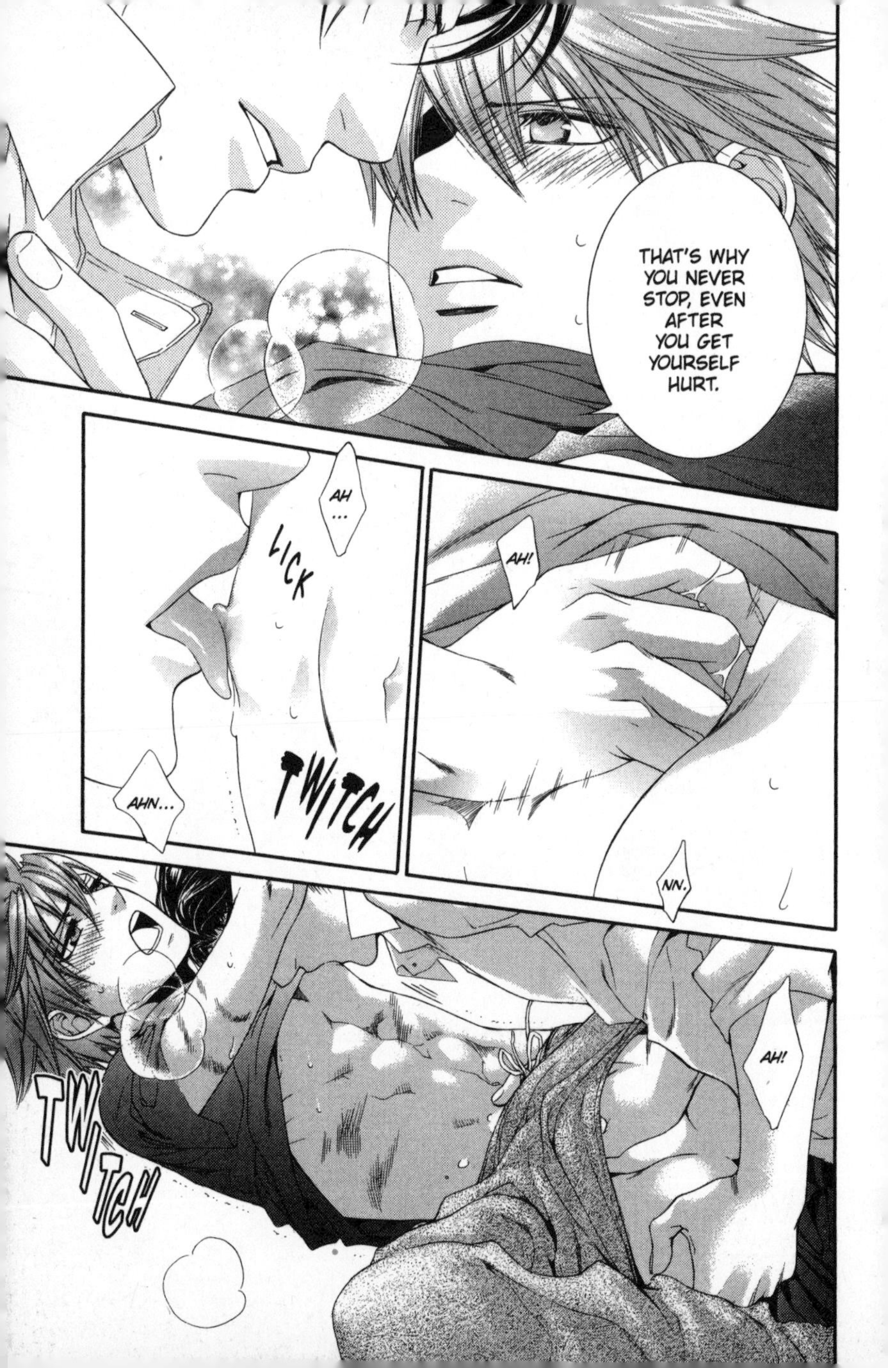
THAT'S WHY YOU NEVER STOP, EVEN AFTER YOU GET YOURSELF HURT.
AH!
NN.
AH ...
LICK
TWITCH
AHN...
AH!
TWITCH

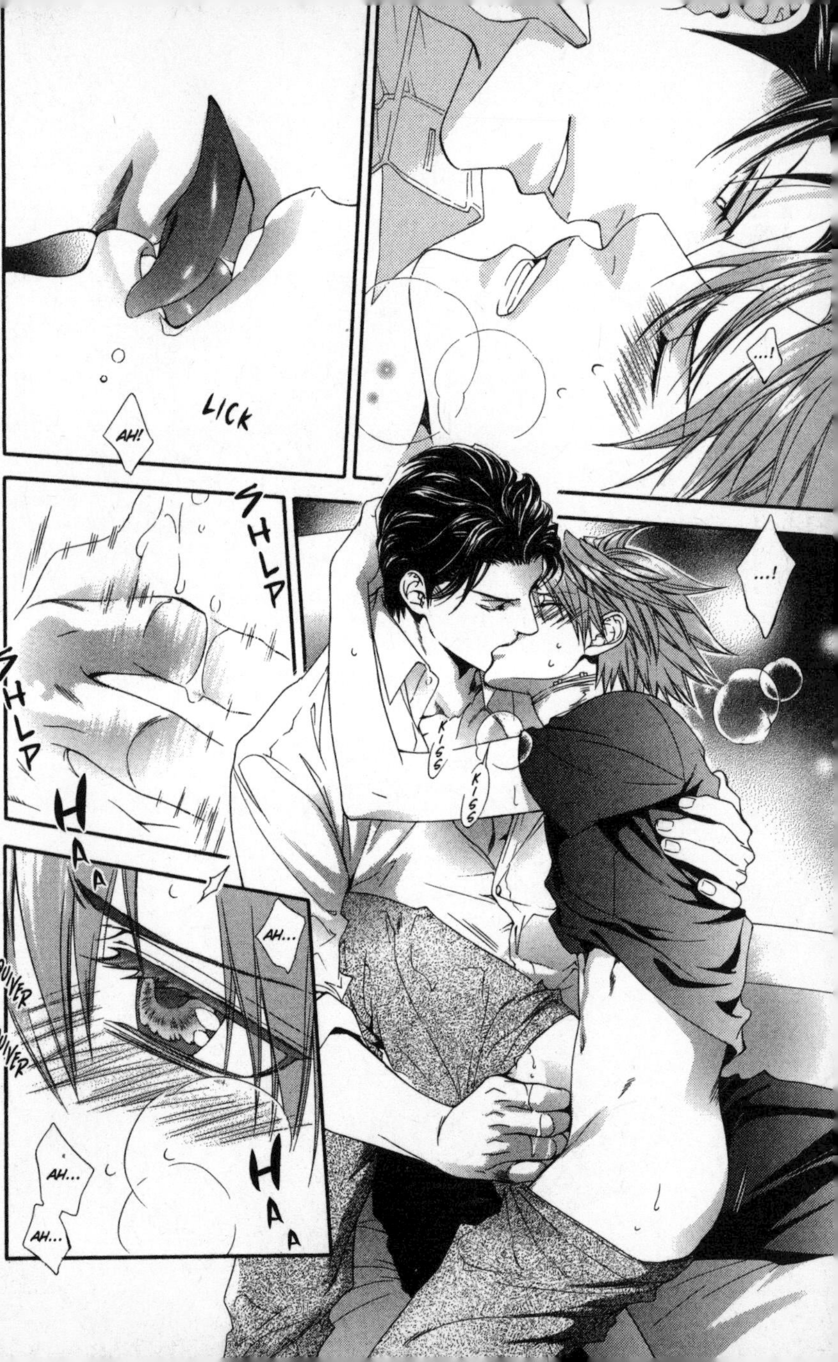
...!
LICK
AH!
...!
KISS
KISS
SHLP
SHLP
HAA
AH...
QUIVER
QUIVER
AH...
AH...
HAA

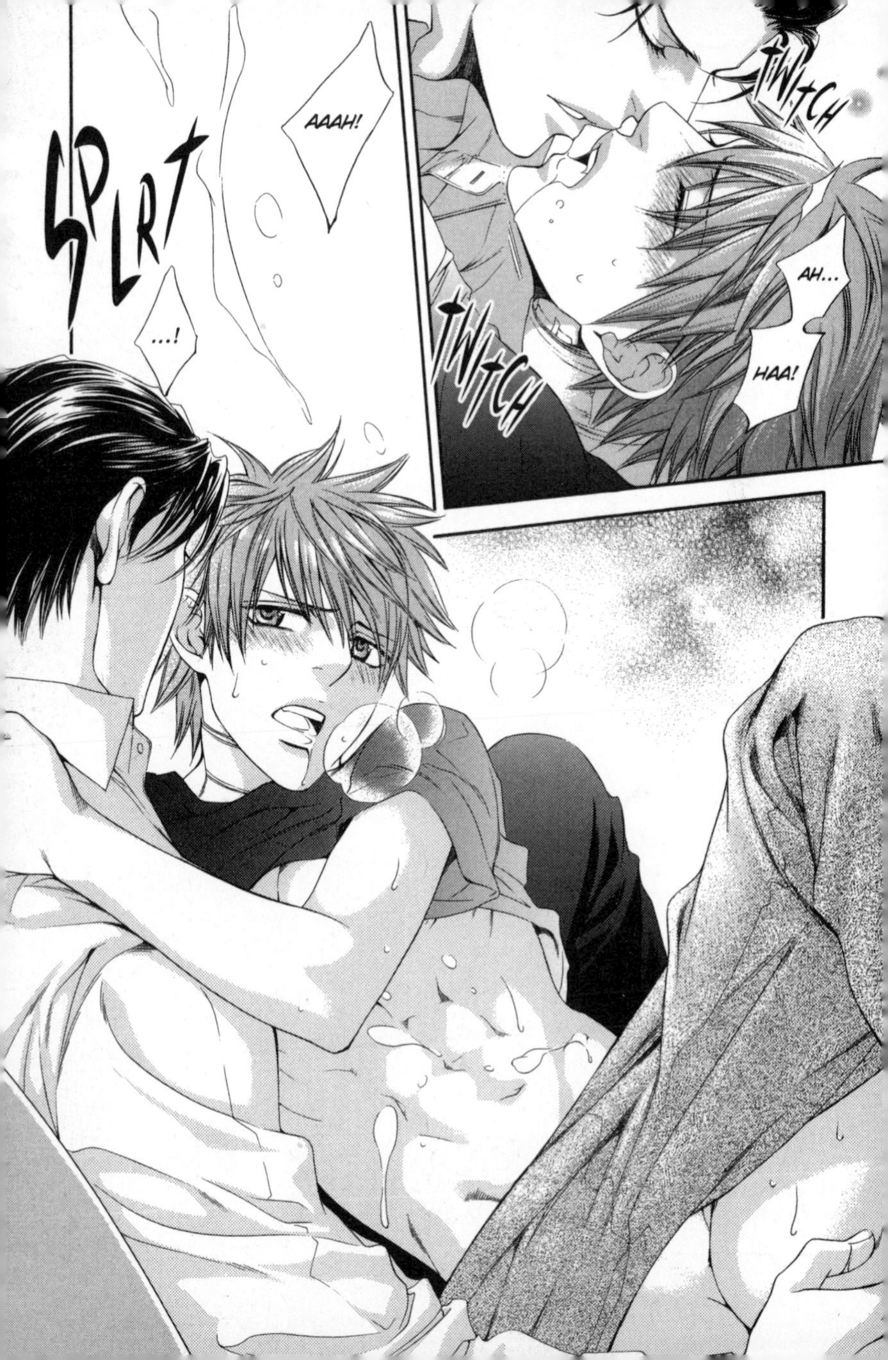
TWITCH
AH...
HAA!
TWITCH
AAAH!
SPLRT
...!

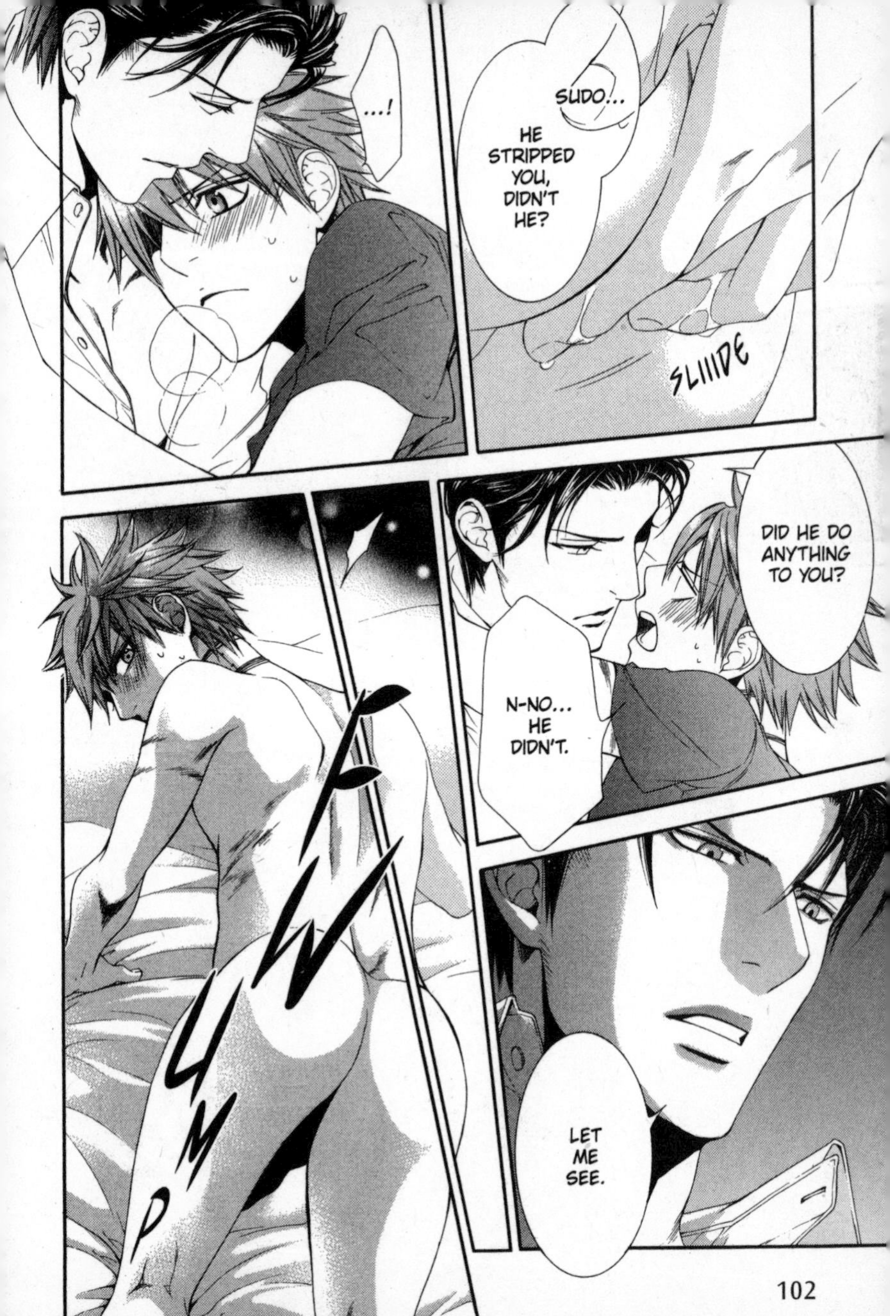
SUDO...
HE STRIPPED YOU, DIDN'T HE?
SLIIIDE
...!
DID HE DO ANYTHING TO YOU?
N-NO... HE DIDN'T.
LET ME SEE.
FWUMP

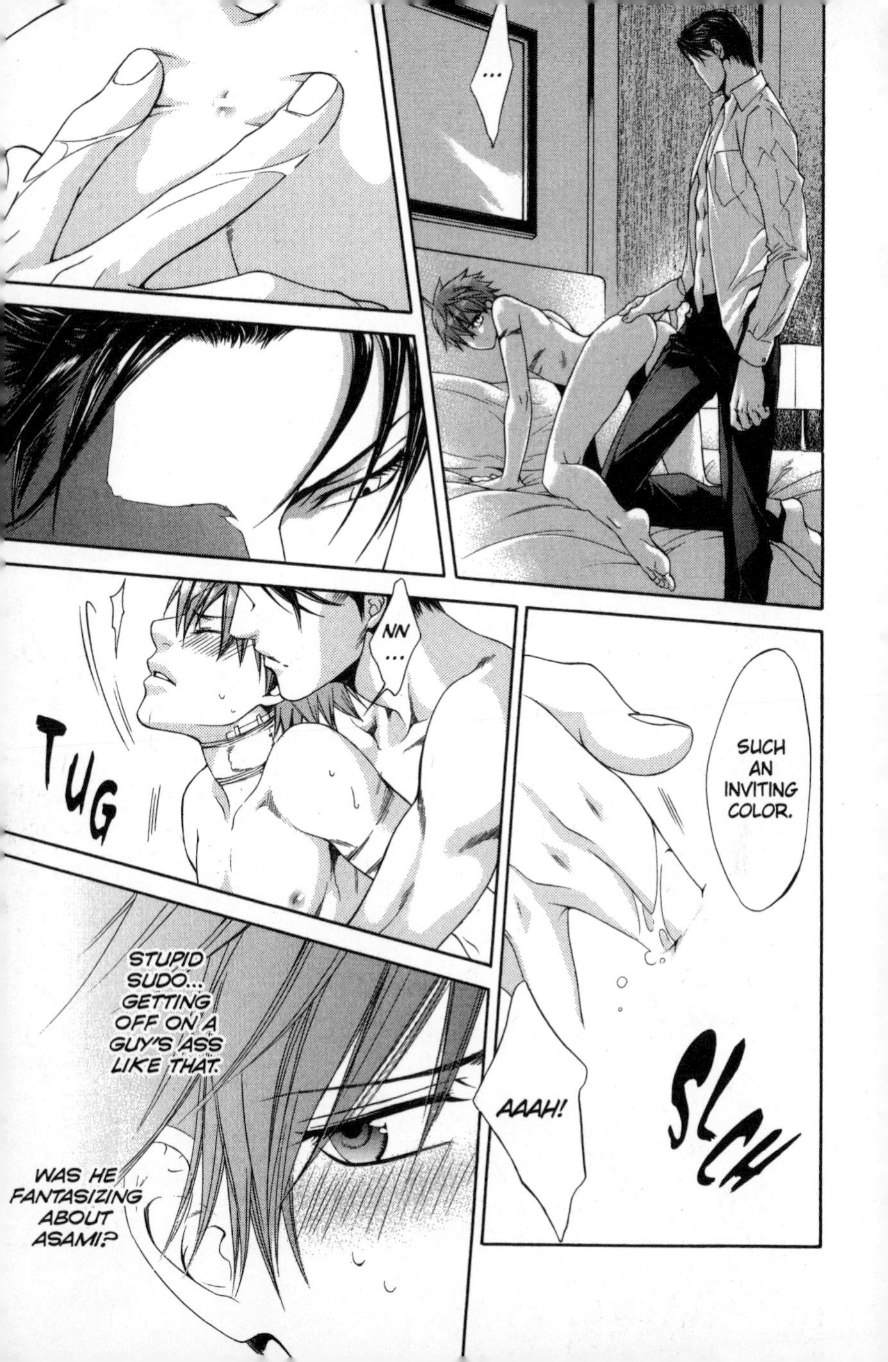
...
SUCH AN INVITING COLOR.
SLCH
AAAH!
NN ...
TUG
STUPID SUDO... GETTING OFF ON A GUY'S ASS LIKE THAT.
WAS HE FANTASIZING ABOUT ASAMI?

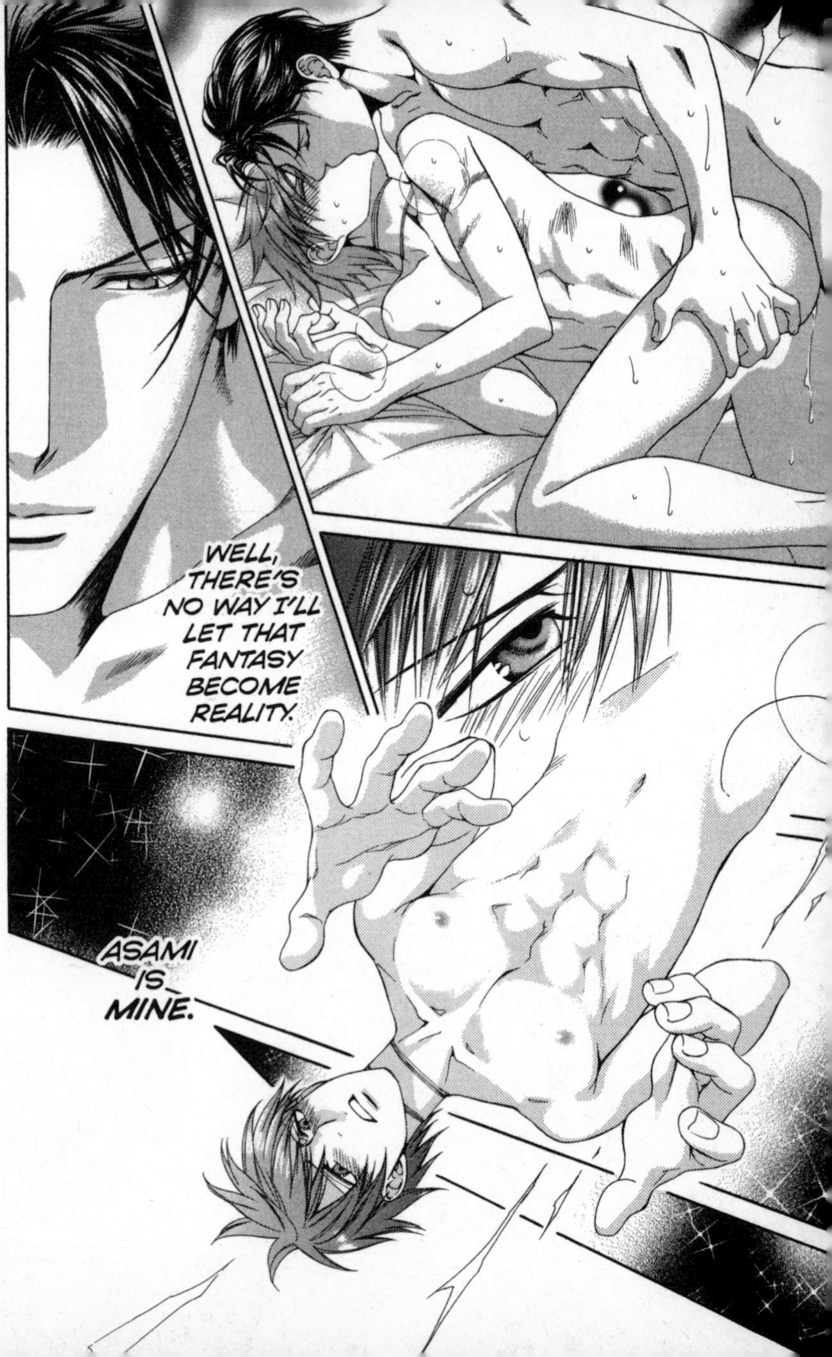
WELL, THERE'S NO WAY I'LL LET THAT FANTASY BECOME REALITY.
ASAMI IS MINE.

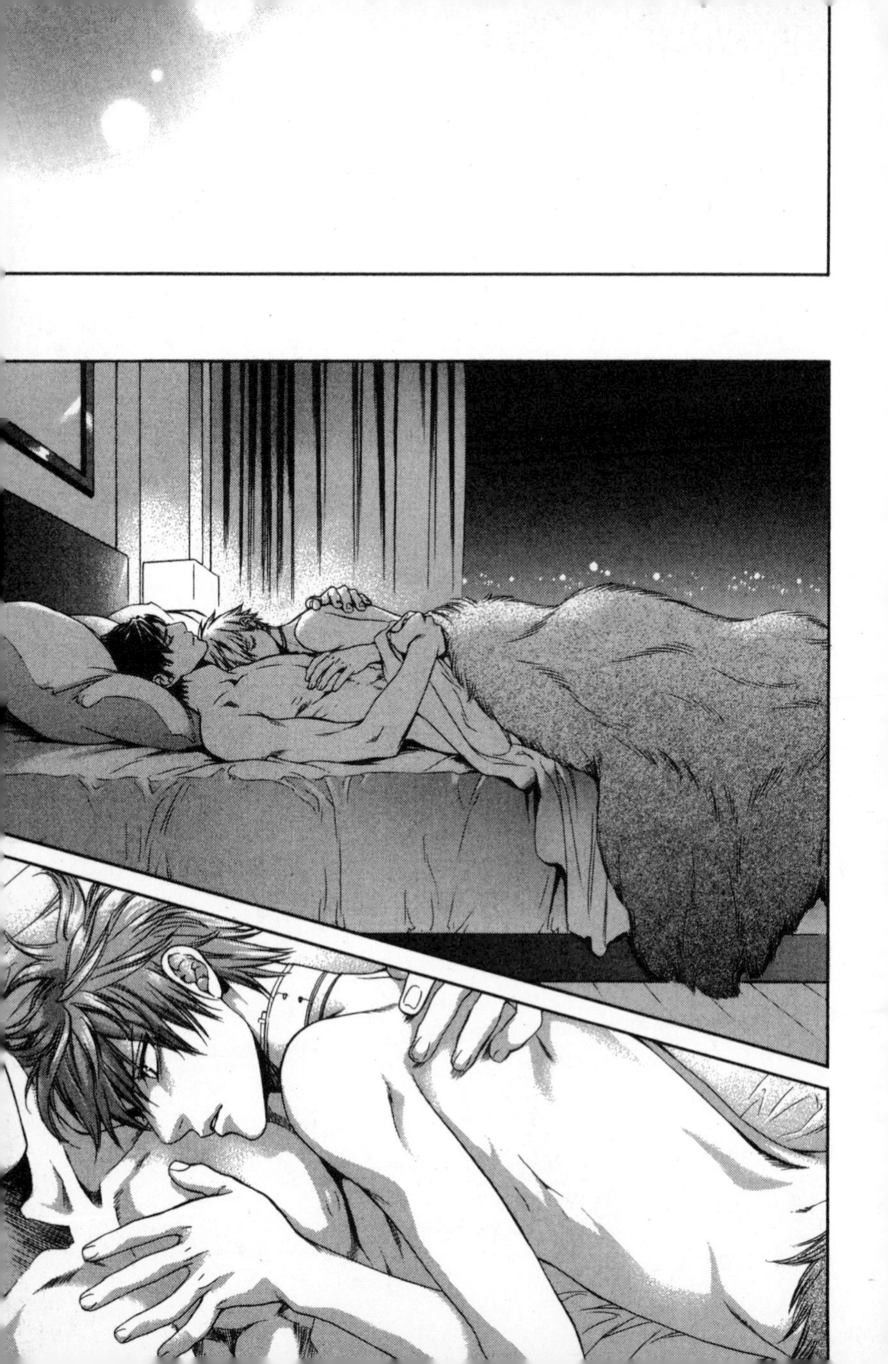

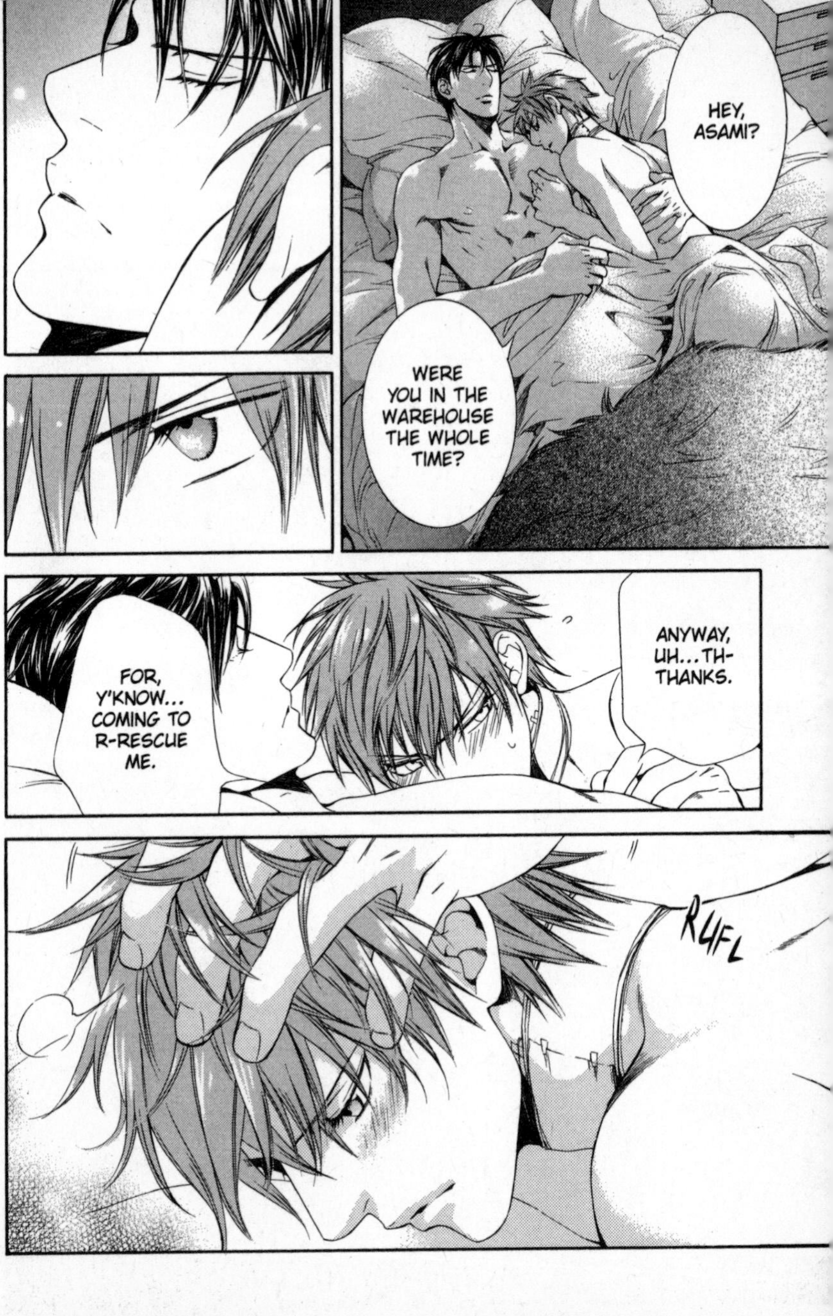
HEY, ASAMI?
WERE YOU IN THE WAREHOUSE THE WHOLE TIME?
ANYWAY, UH...TH-THANKS.
FOR, Y'KNOW... COMING TO R-RESCUE ME.
RUFL

ブレイ・インアビス

Pray in the Abyss

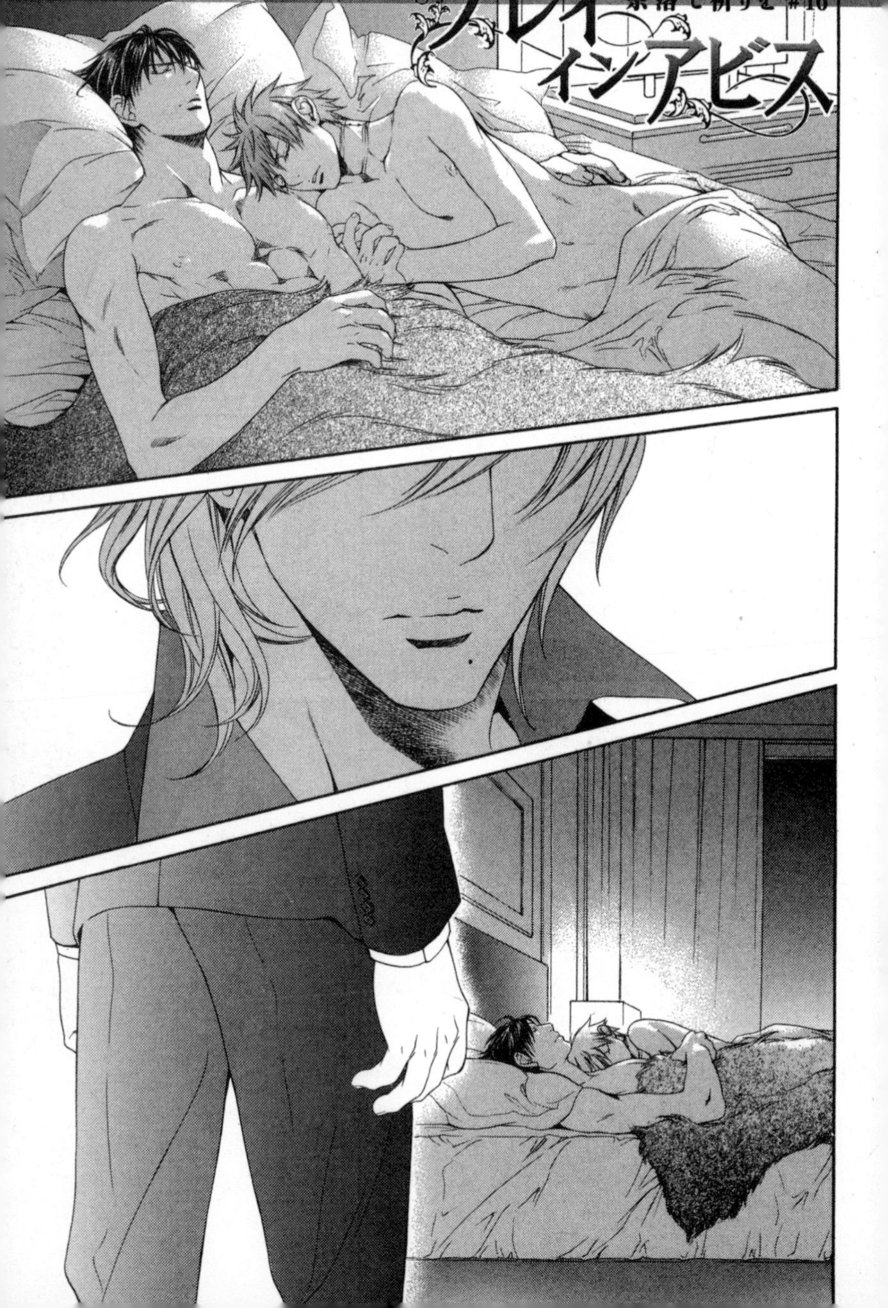
プレイ イン アビス
奈落で祈りを #16

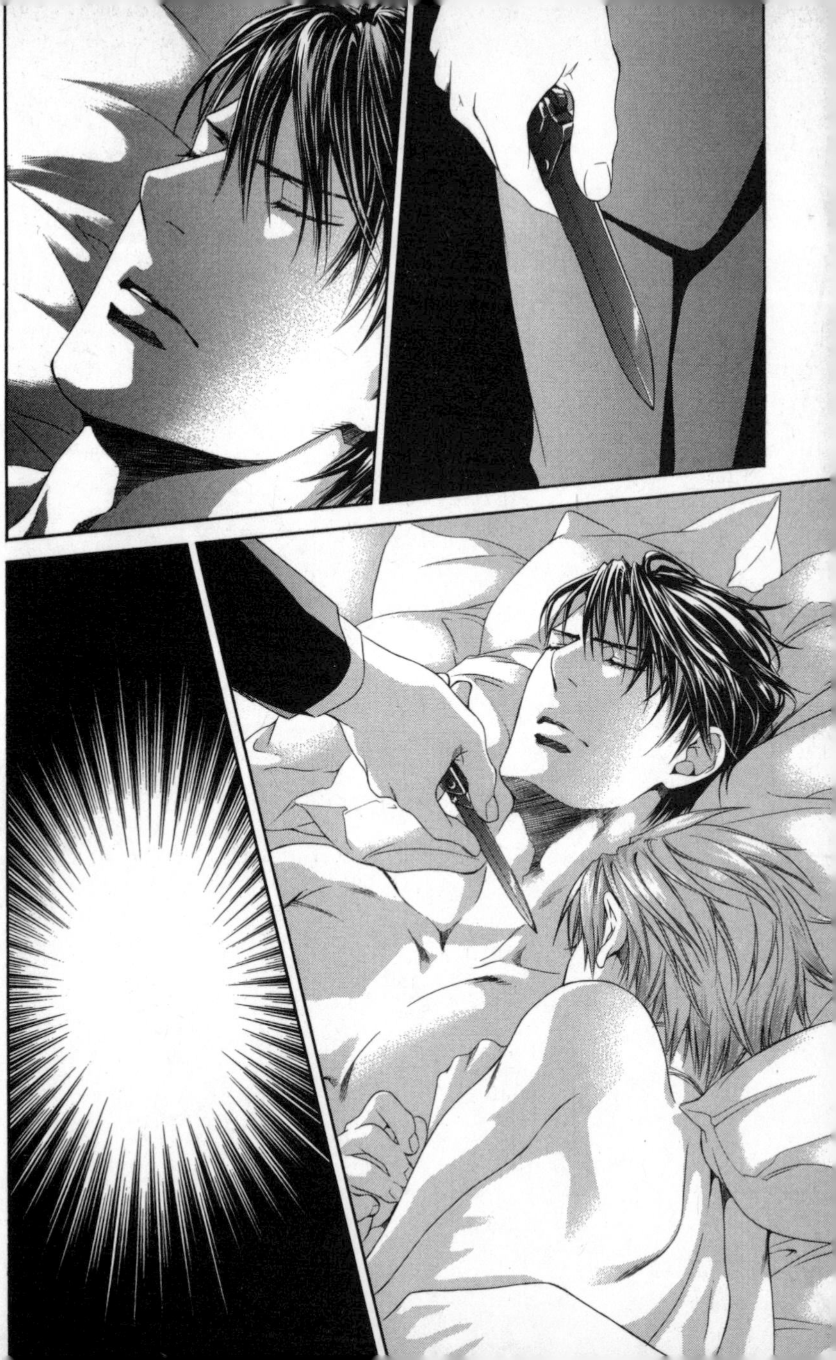

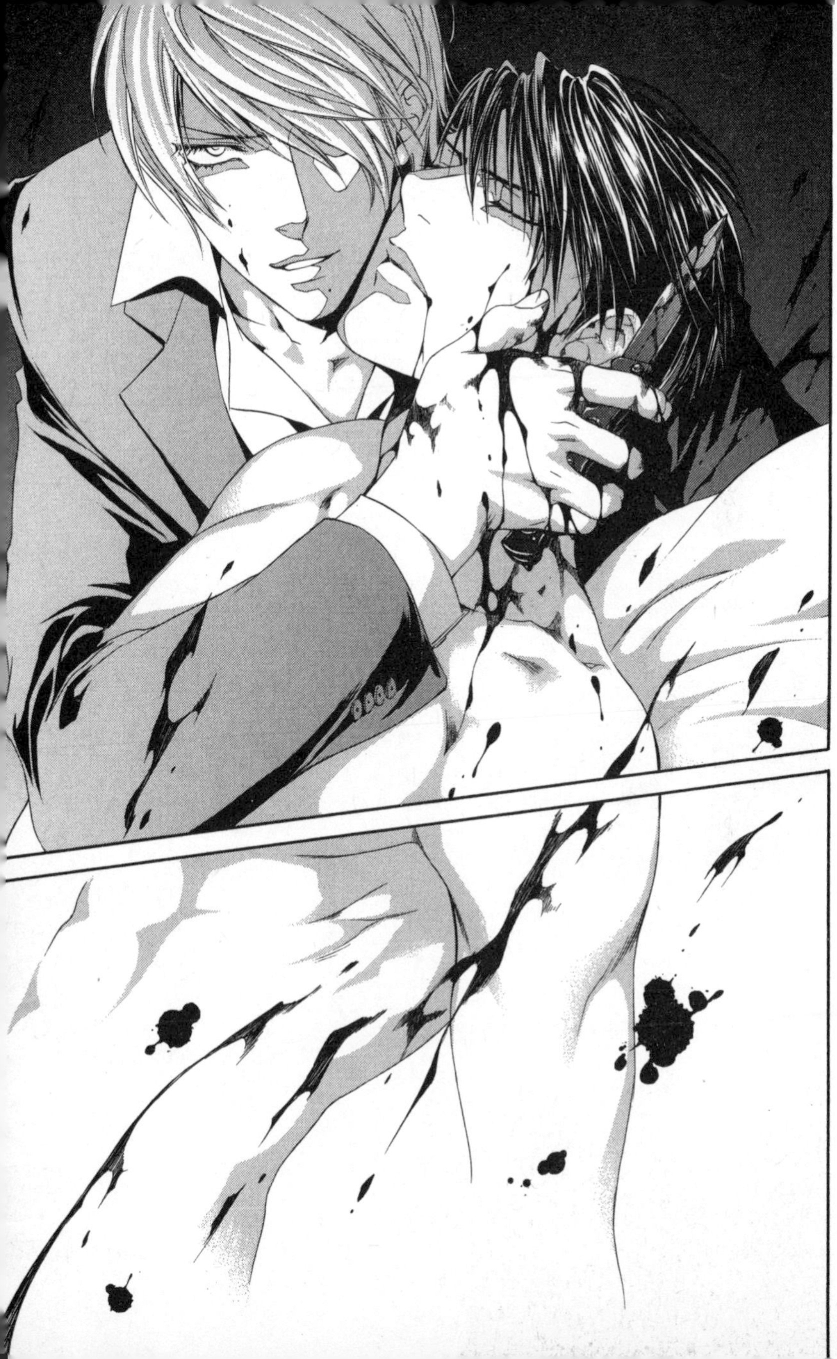

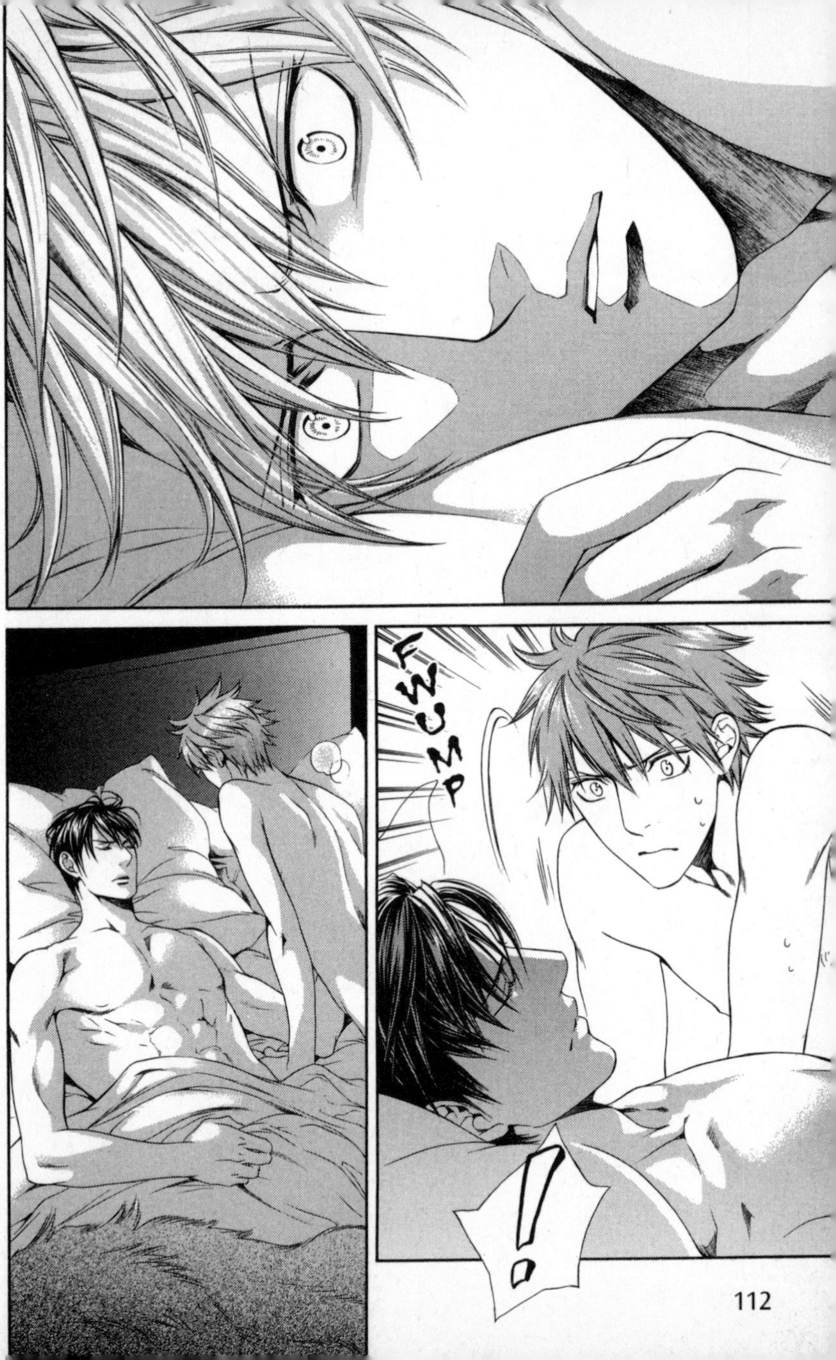
FWUMP
!

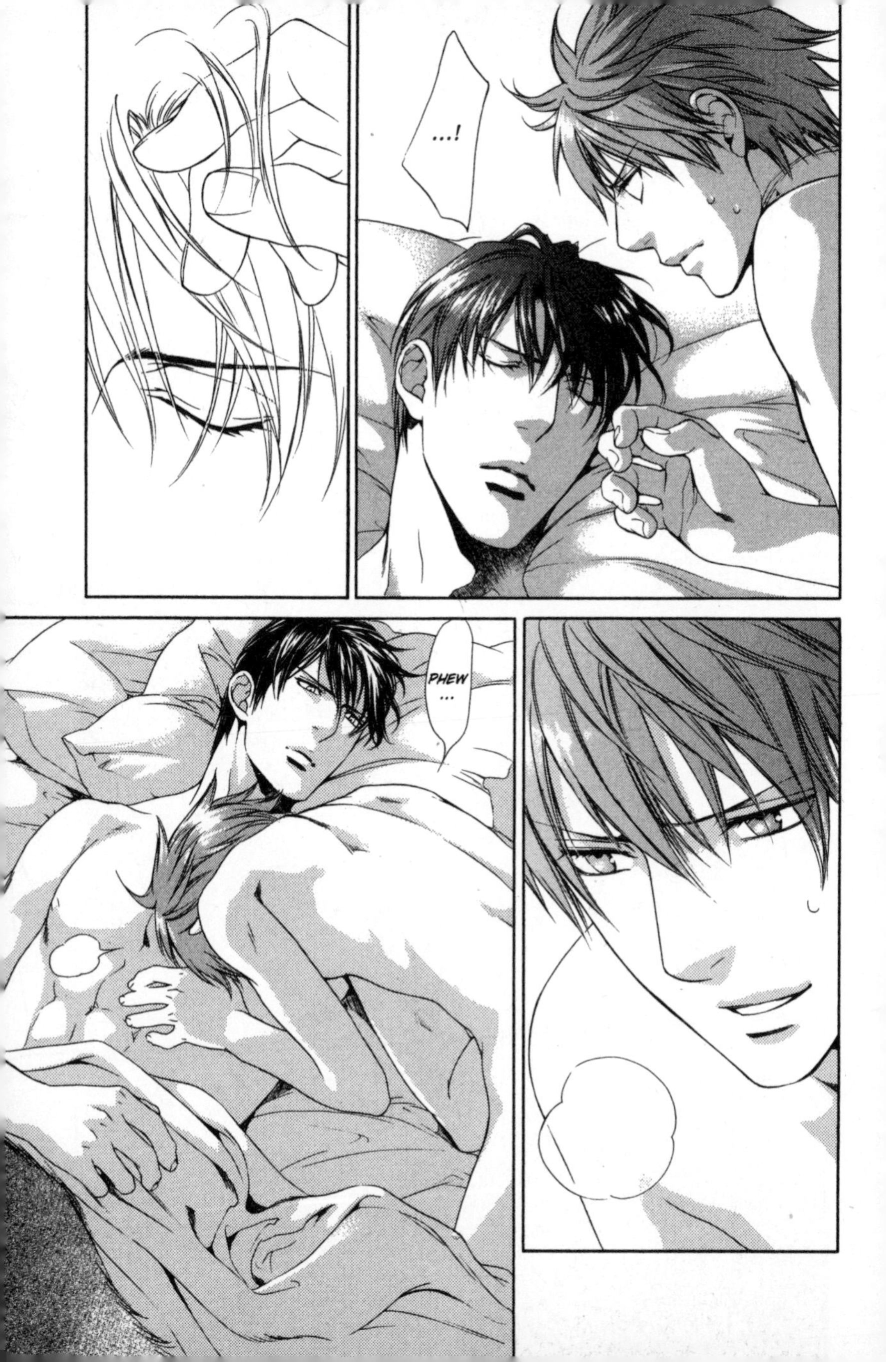
...!
PHEW ...

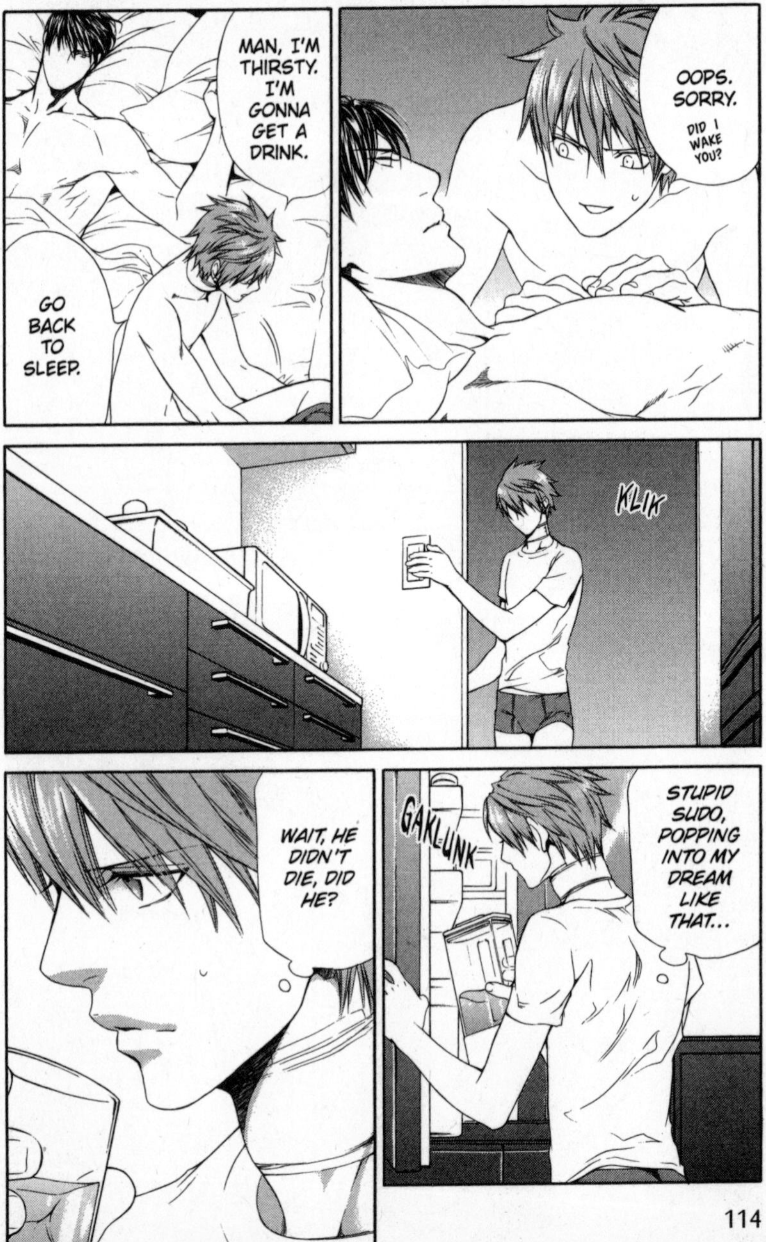
OOPS. SORRY.
DID I WAKE YOU?
MAN, I'M THIRSTY. I'M GONNA GET A DRINK.
GO BACK TO SLEEP.
KLIK
GAKLUNK
STUPID SUDO, POPPING INTO MY DREAM LIKE THAT...
WAIT, HE DIDN'T DIE, DID HE?

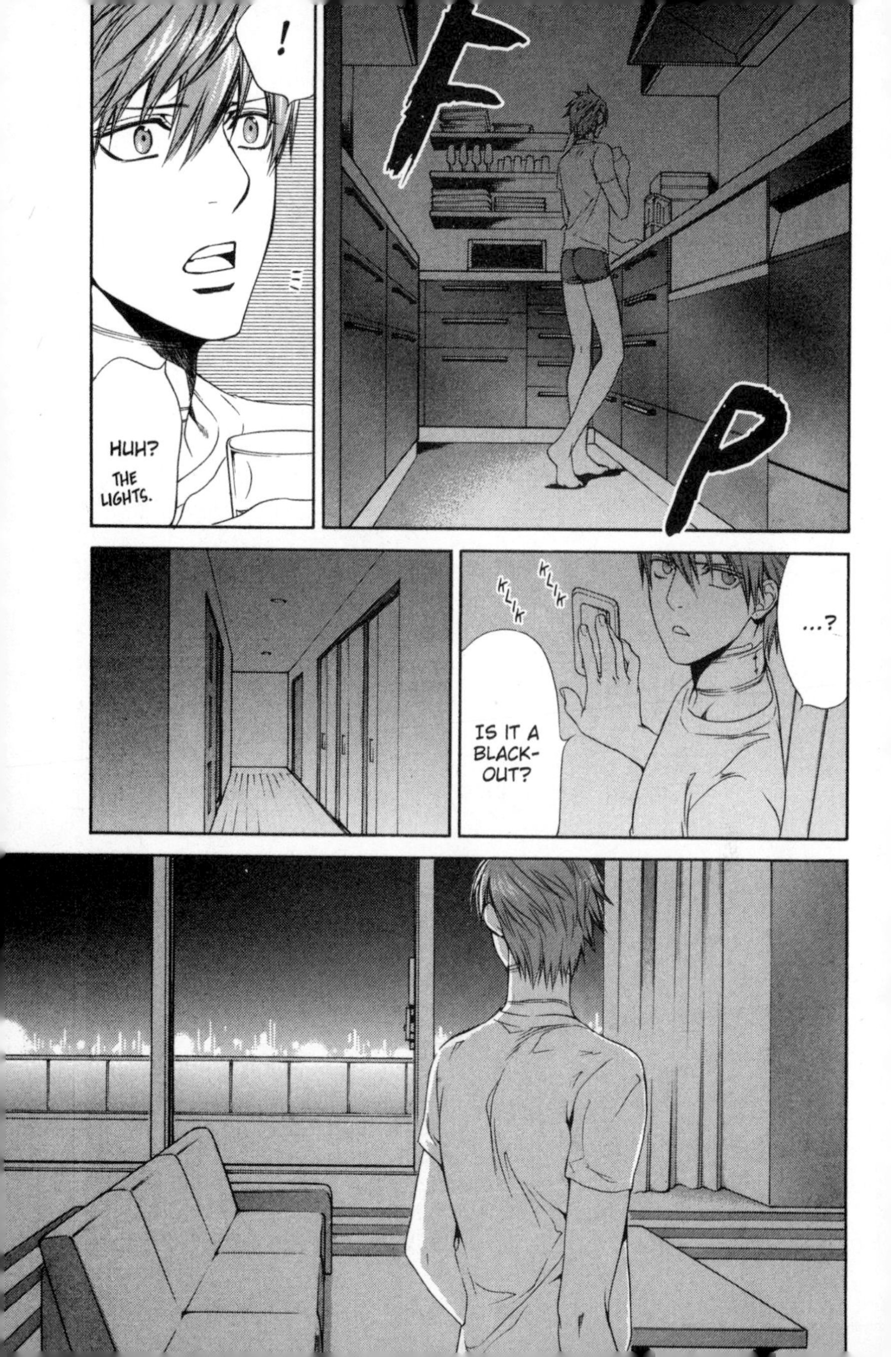
FP
!
HUH?
THE LIGHTS.
KLIK KLIK
...?
IS IT A BLACK-OUT?

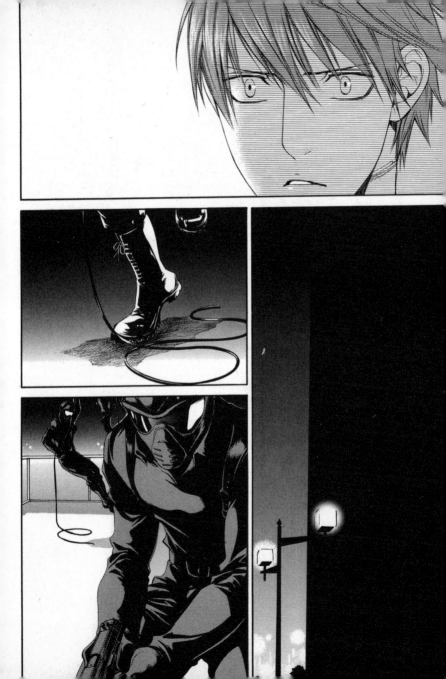

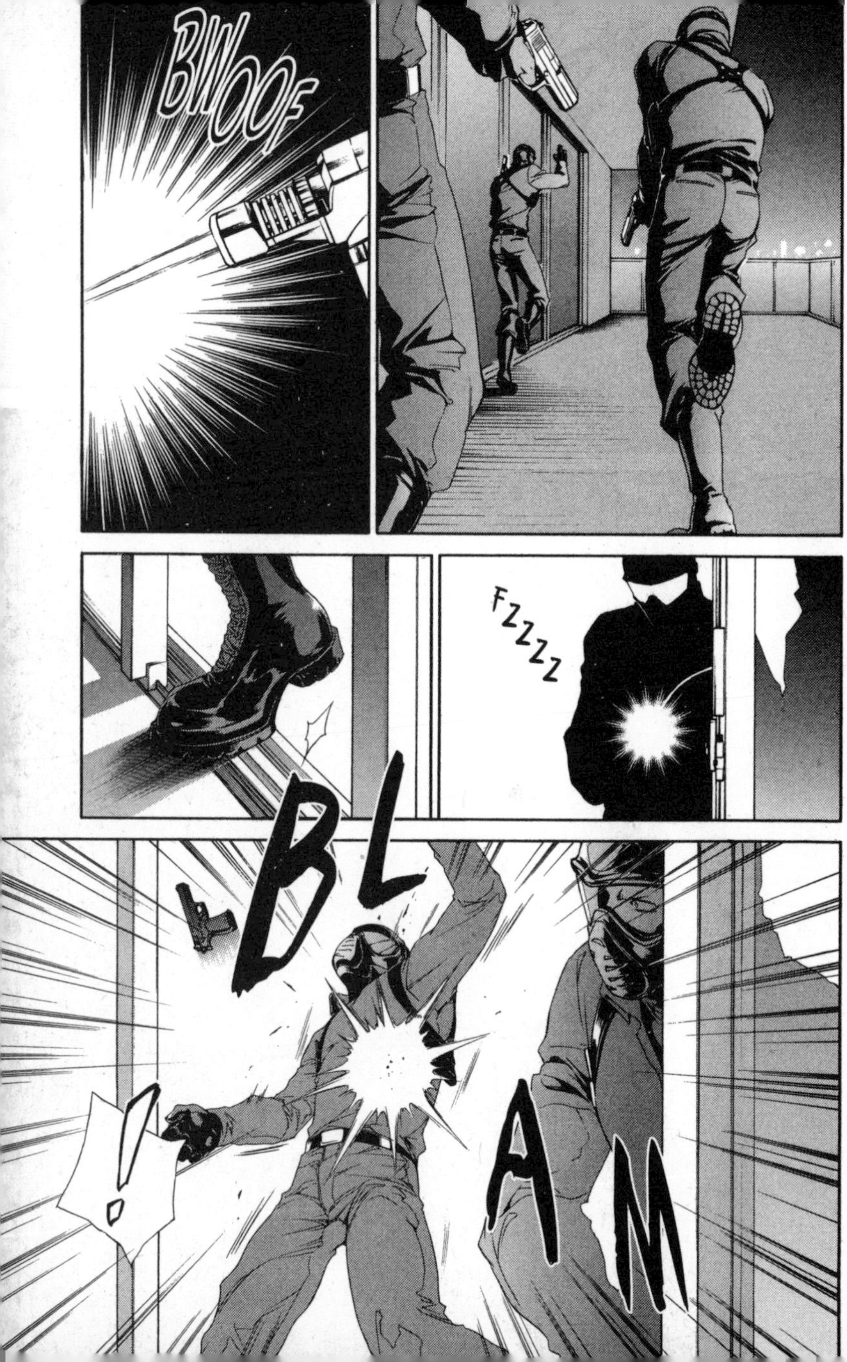
BWOOF
FZZZZ
BLAM
!

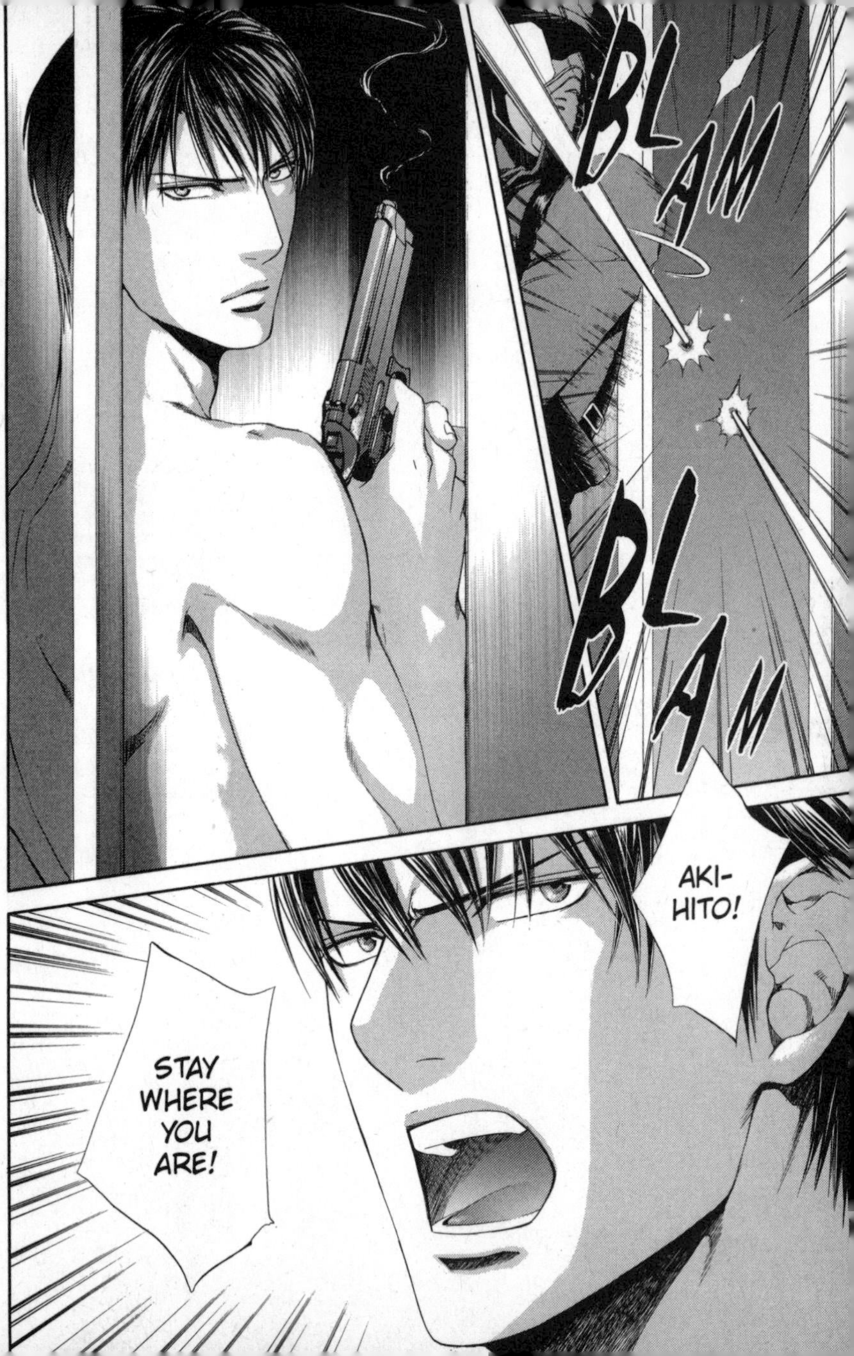
BLAM
BLAM
AKI-HITO!
STAY WHERE YOU ARE!

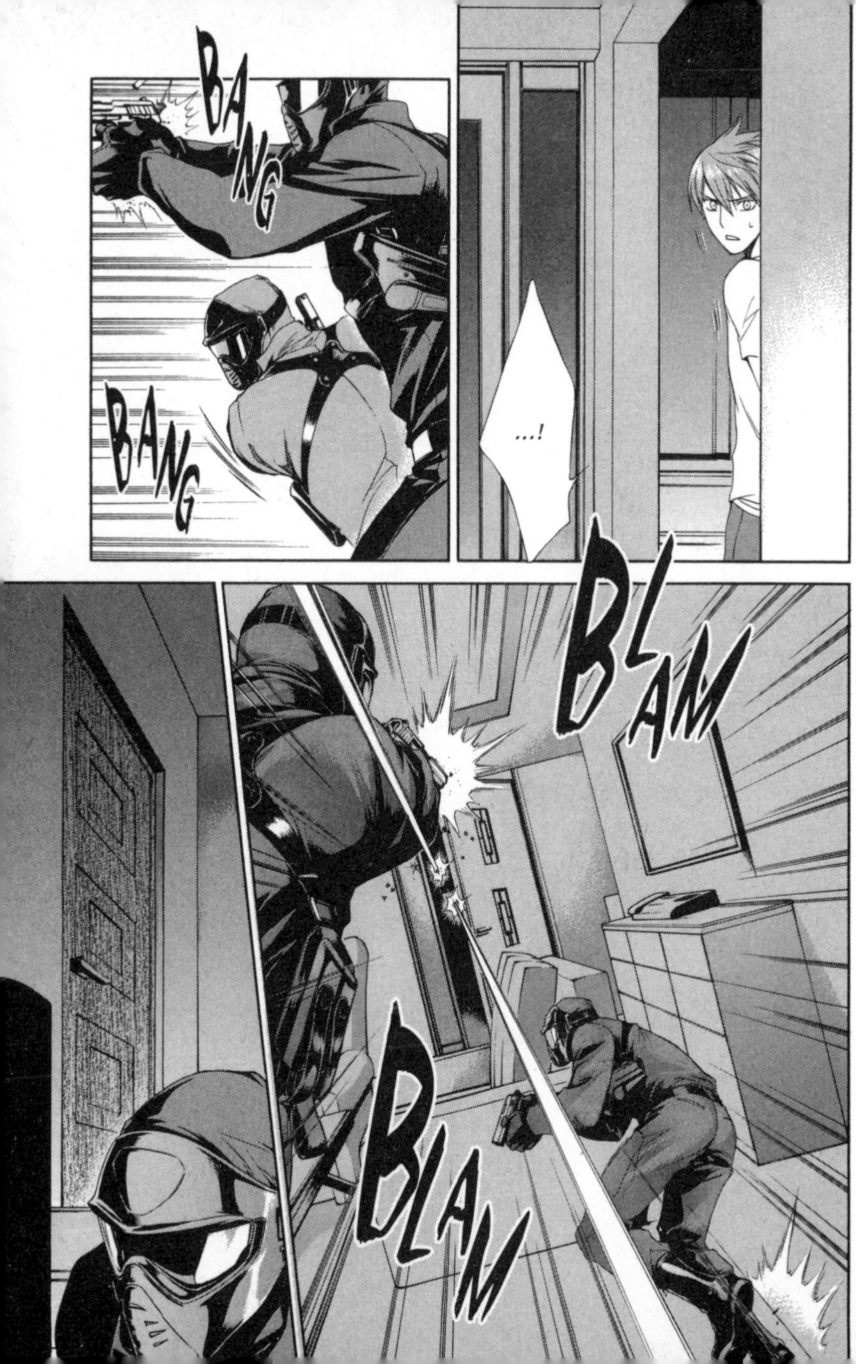
...!
BANG
BANG
BLAM
BLAM

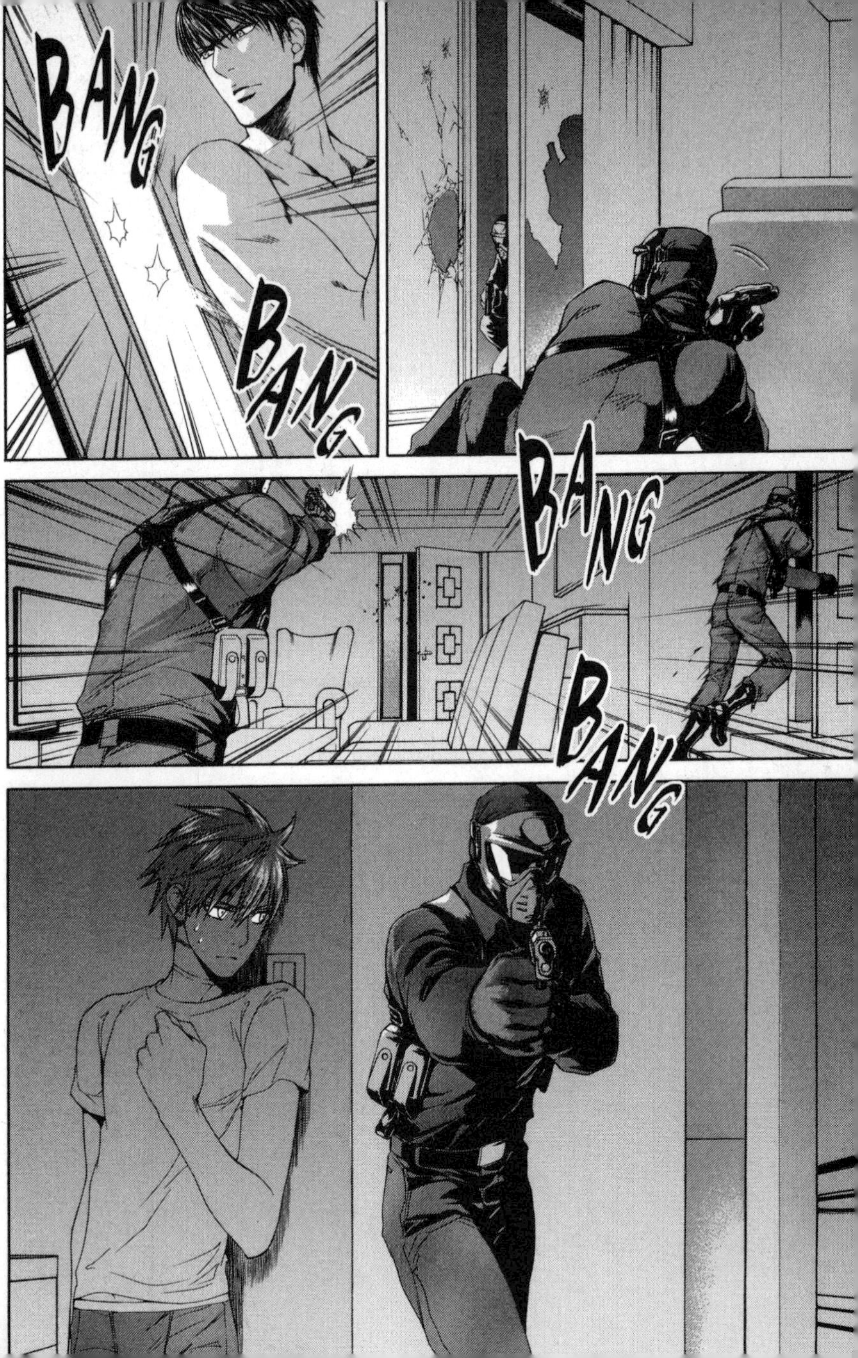
BANG
BANG
BANG
BANG

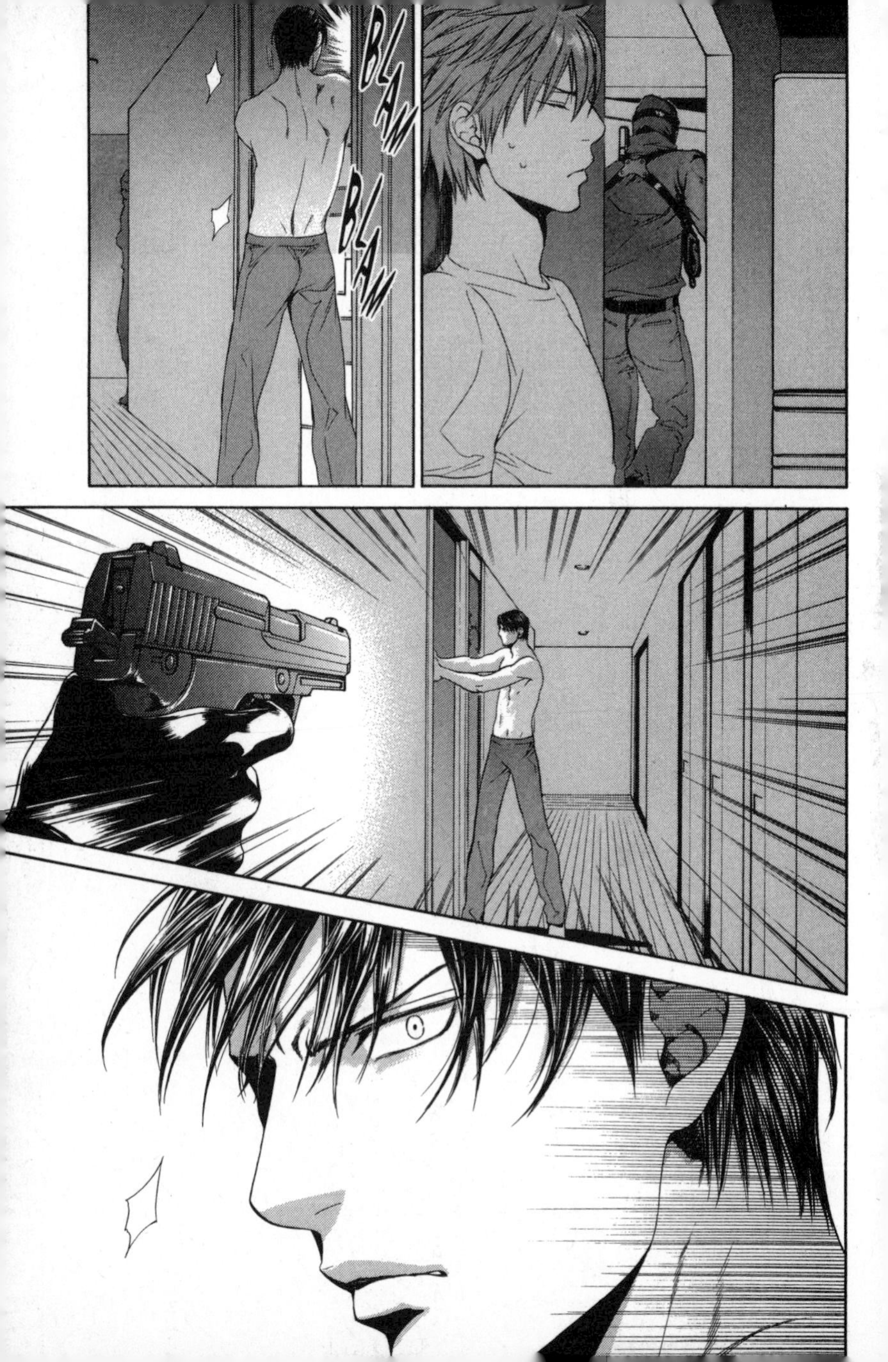
BLAM
BLAM
BLAM

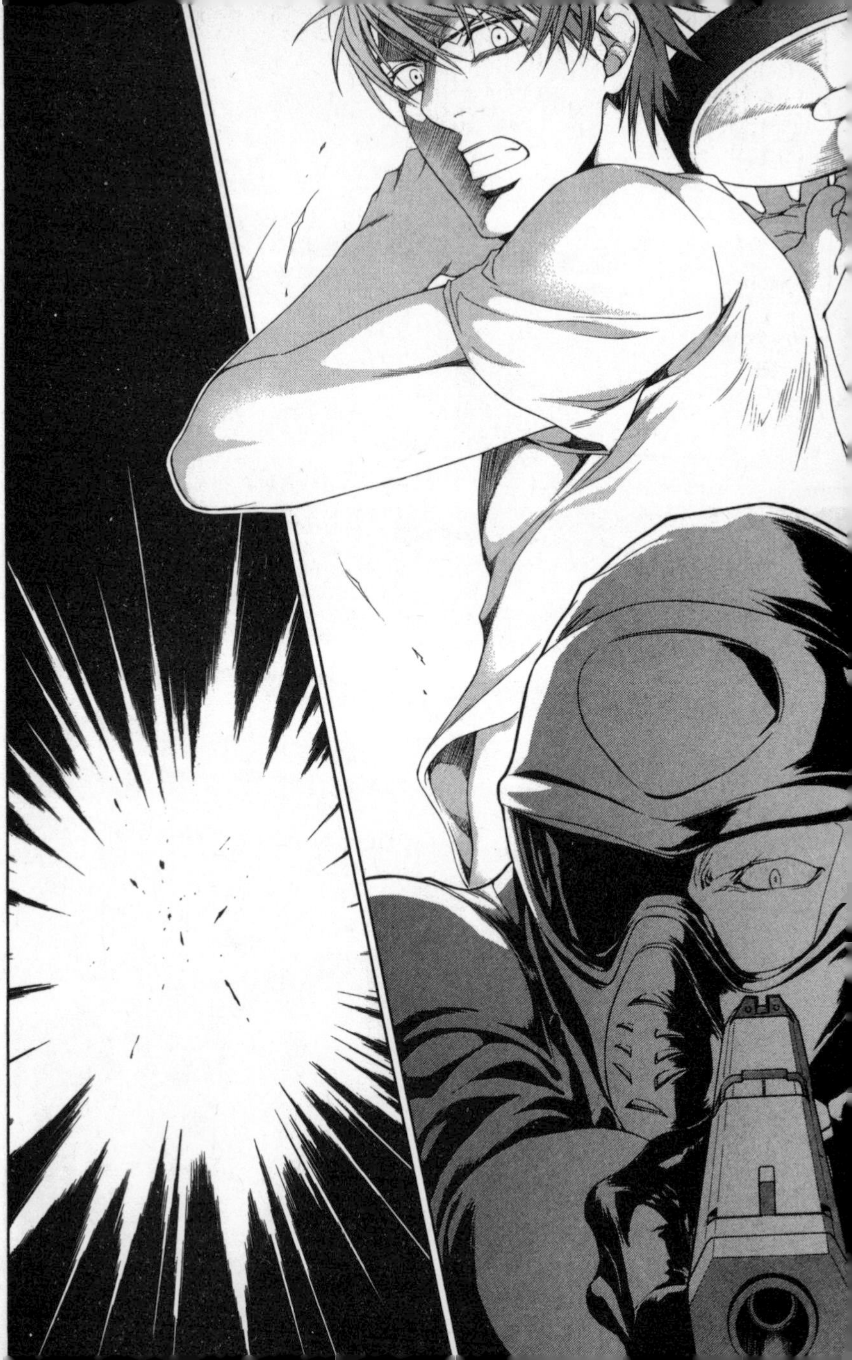

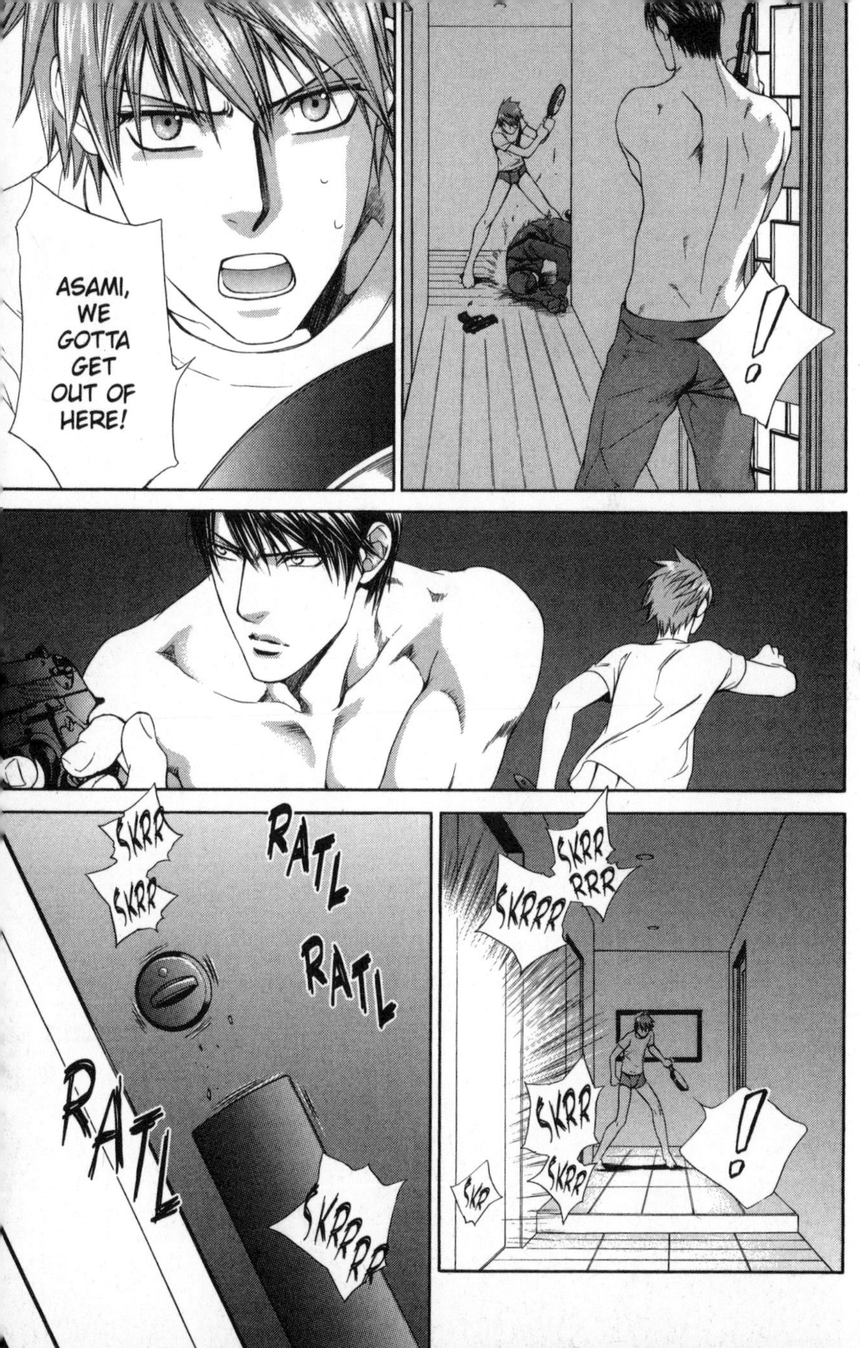
!
ASAMI, WE GOTTA GET OUT OF HERE!
SKRR RRR
SKRRR
SKRR
!
SKRR
SKR
SKRR
SKRR
RATL
RATL
RATL
SKRRRR

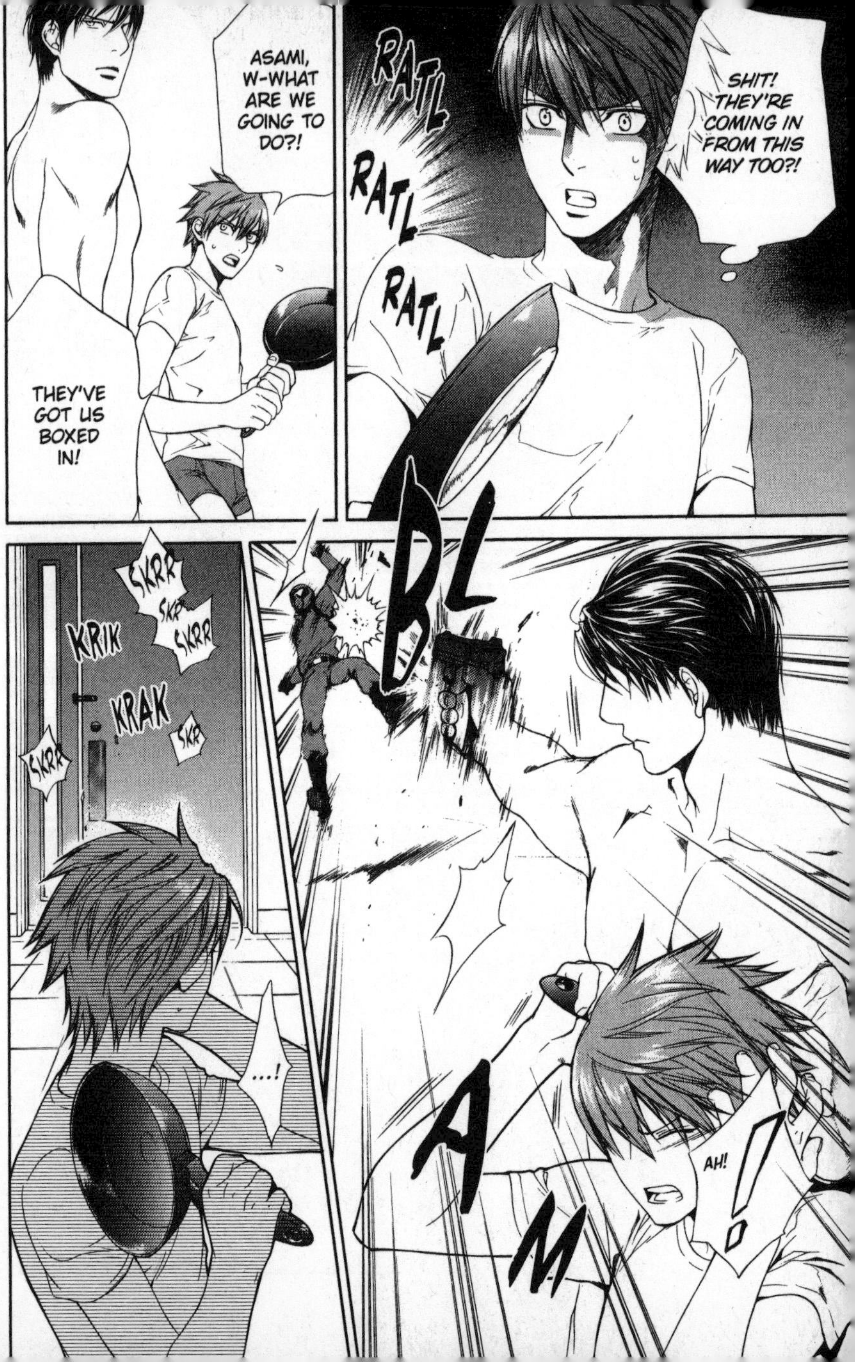
RATL
RATL
RATL
SHIT! THEY'RE COMING IN FROM THIS WAY TOO?!
ASAMI, W-WHAT ARE WE GOING TO DO?!
THEY'VE GOT US BOXED IN!
BLAM
AH!
SKRR
SKR
SKRR
KRIK
KRAK
SKR
SKRR
...!

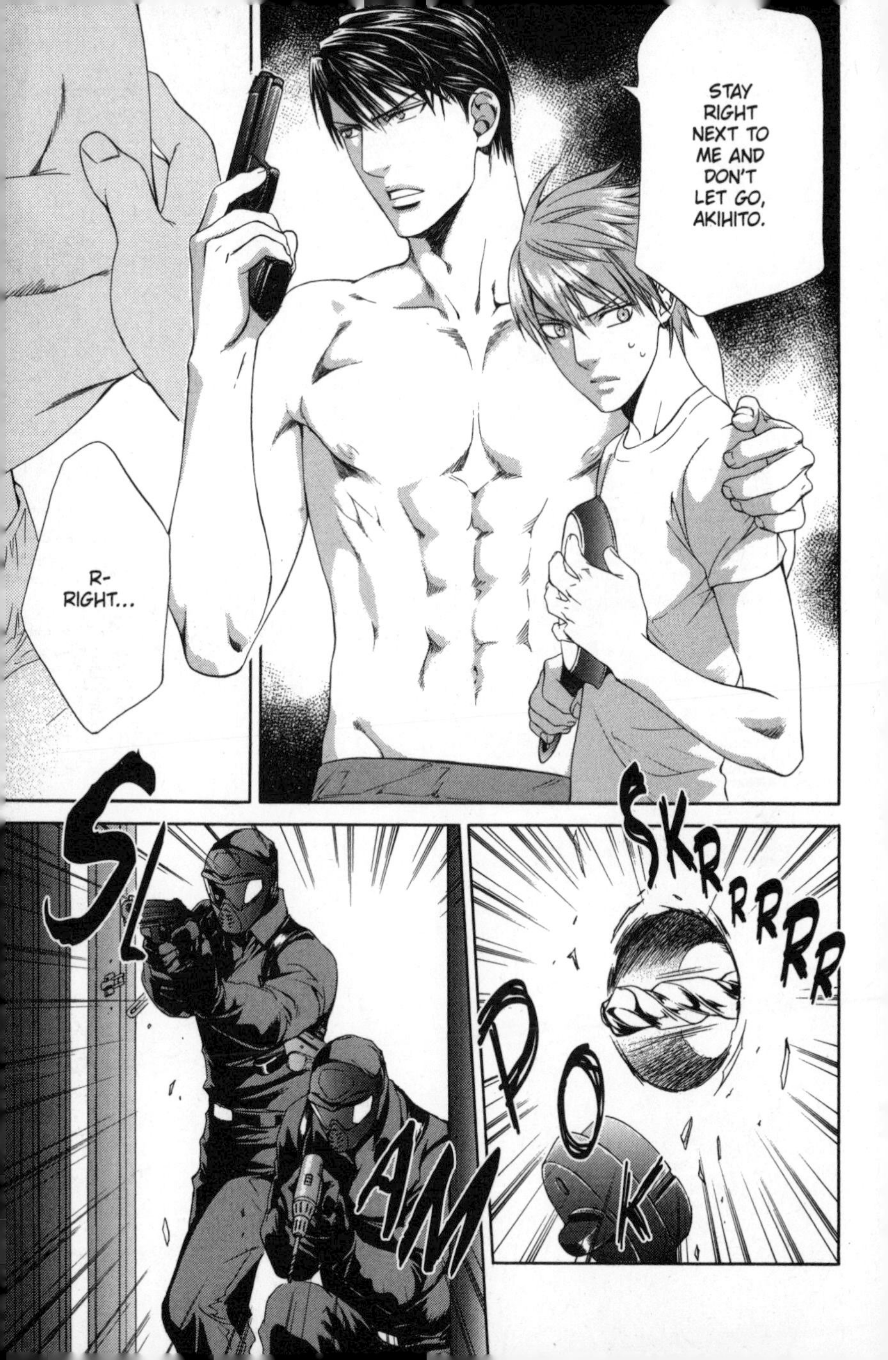
STAY RIGHT NEXT TO ME AND DON'T LET GO, AKIHITO.
R-RIGHT...
SKRRRRRRR
POK
SLAM

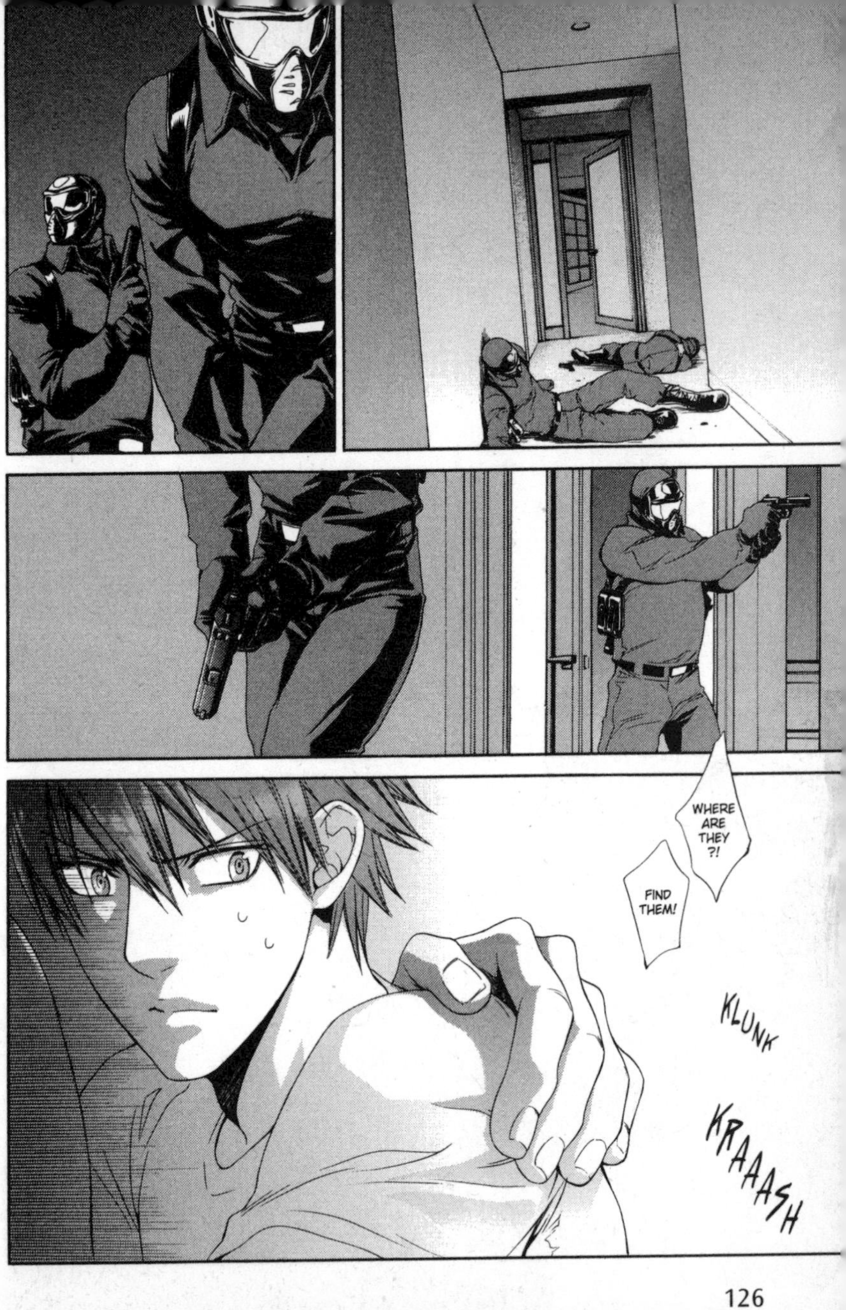
WHERE ARE THEY ?!
FIND THEM!
KLUNK
KRAAASH

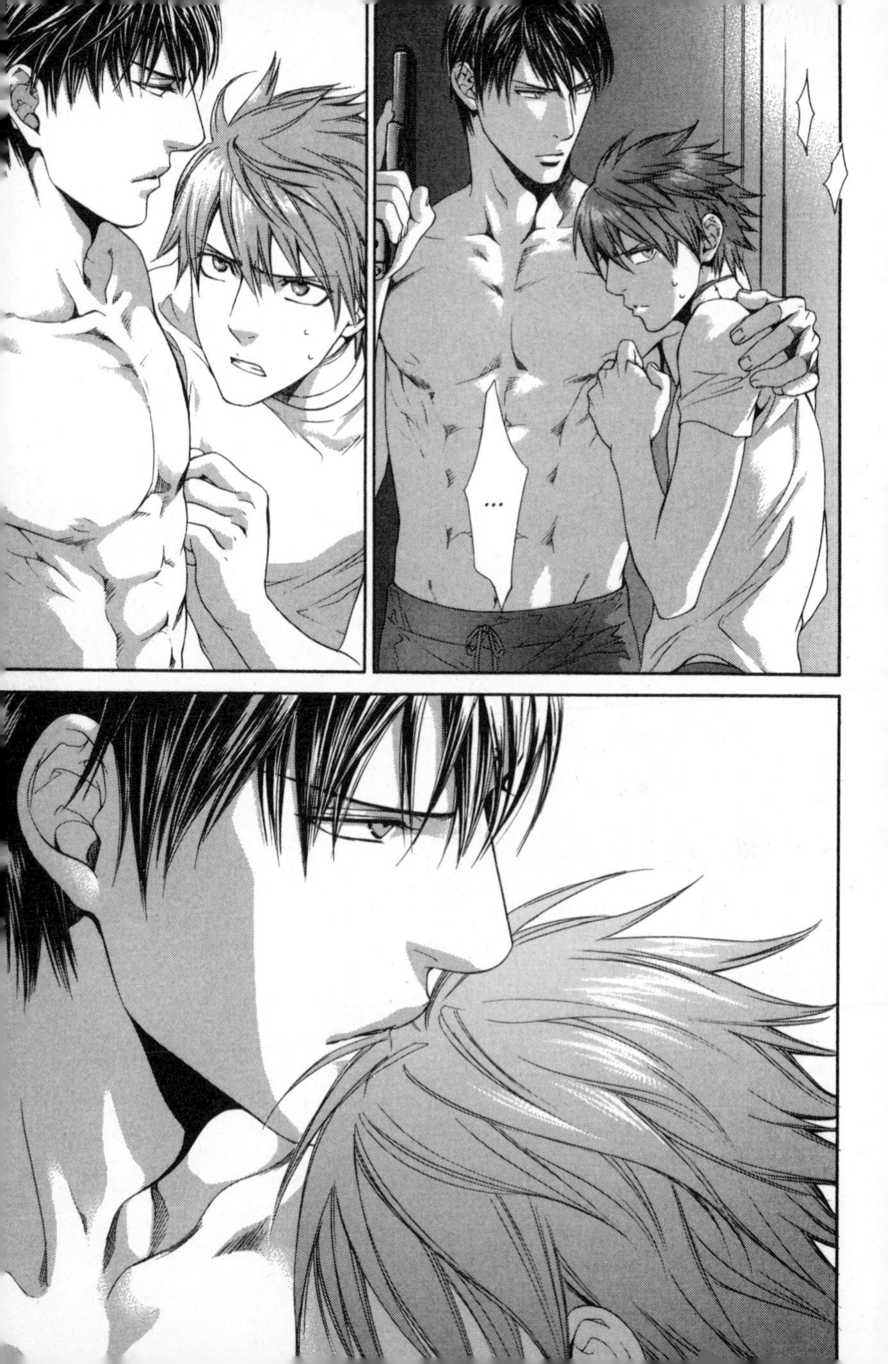
...

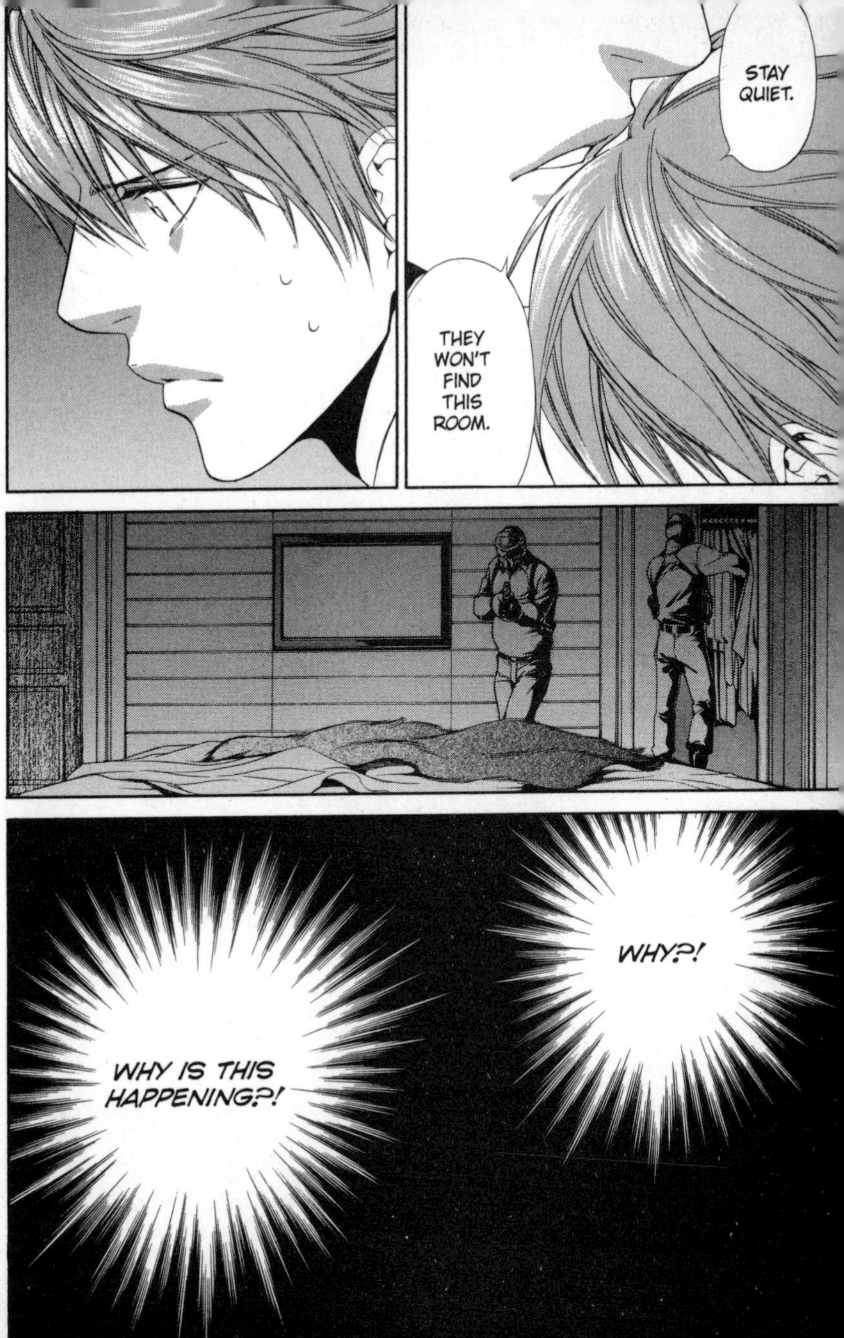
STAY QUIET.
THEY WON'T FIND THIS ROOM.
WHY?!
WHY IS THIS HAPPENING?!

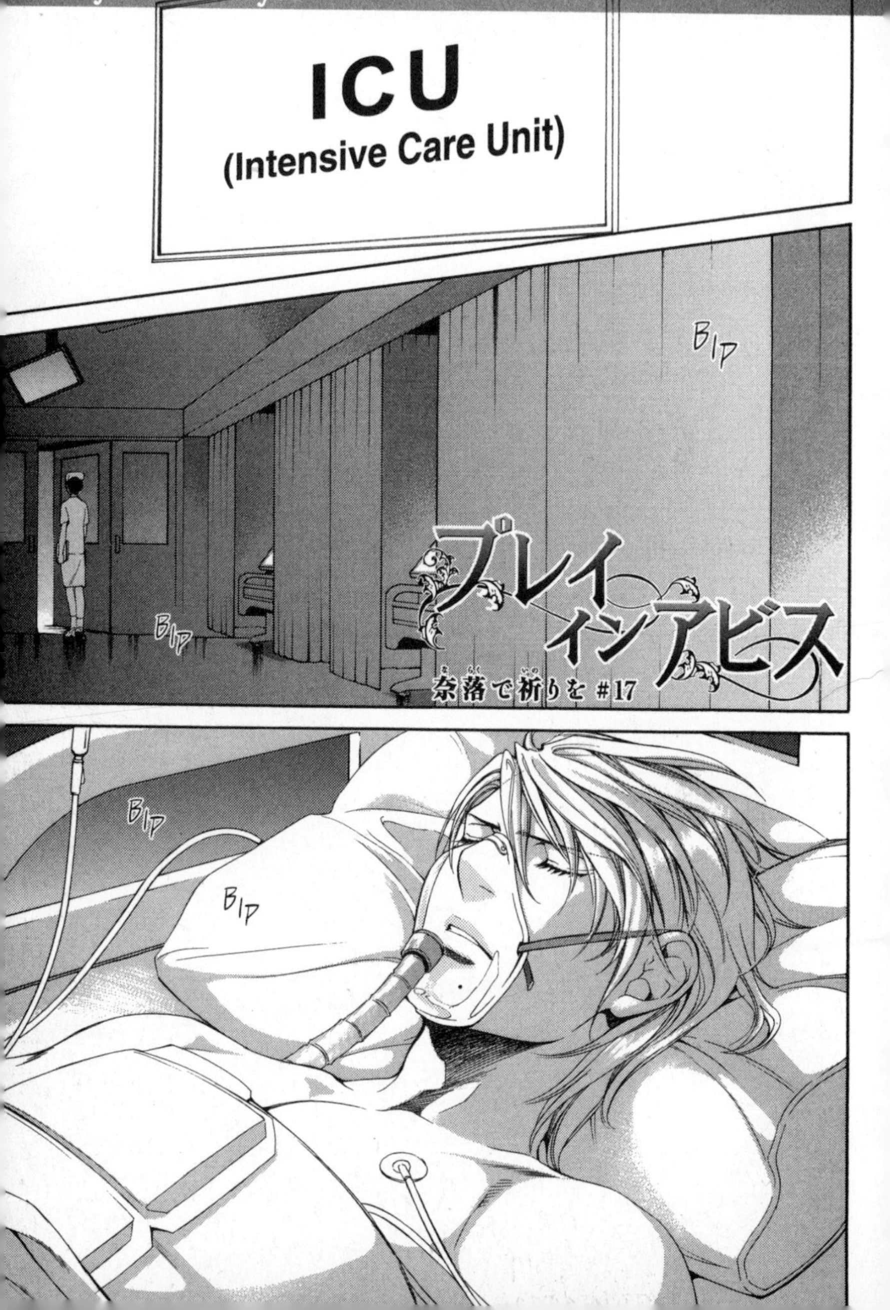
ICU
(Intensive Care Unit)
Bip
プレイインアビス
奈落で祈りを #17
Bip
Bip
Bip

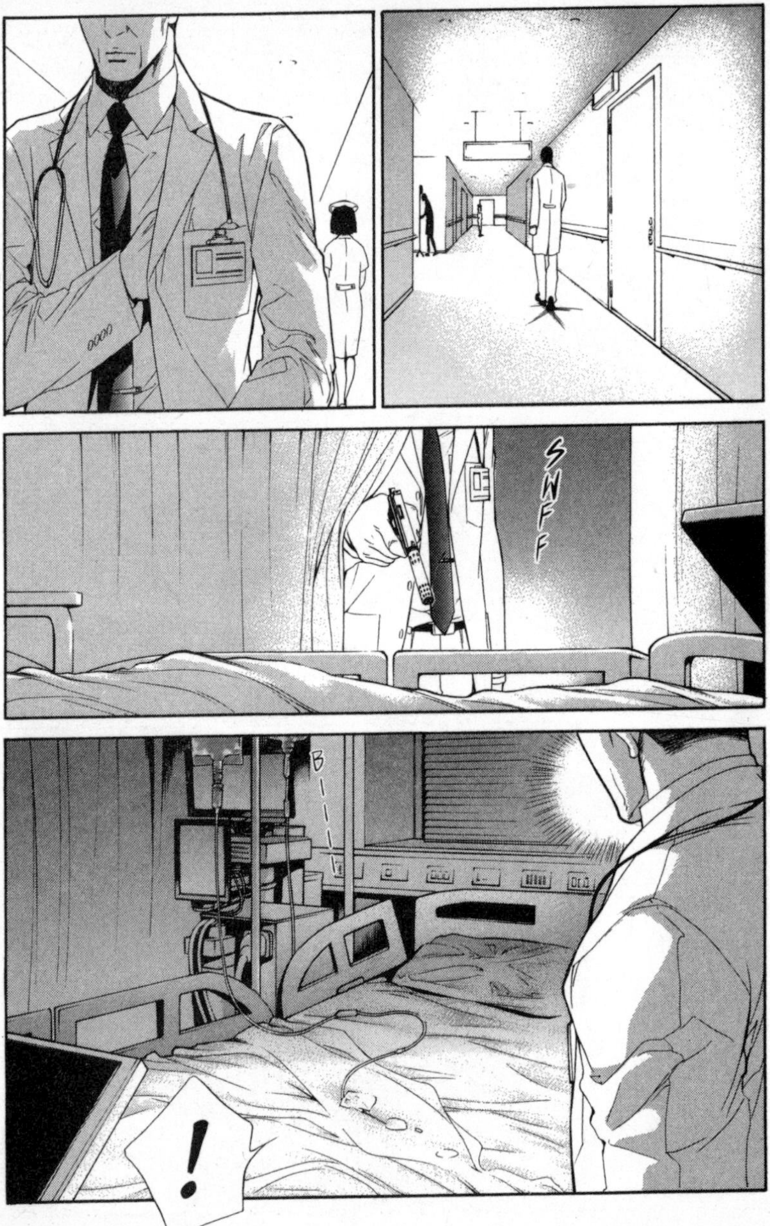
SNFF
B
!

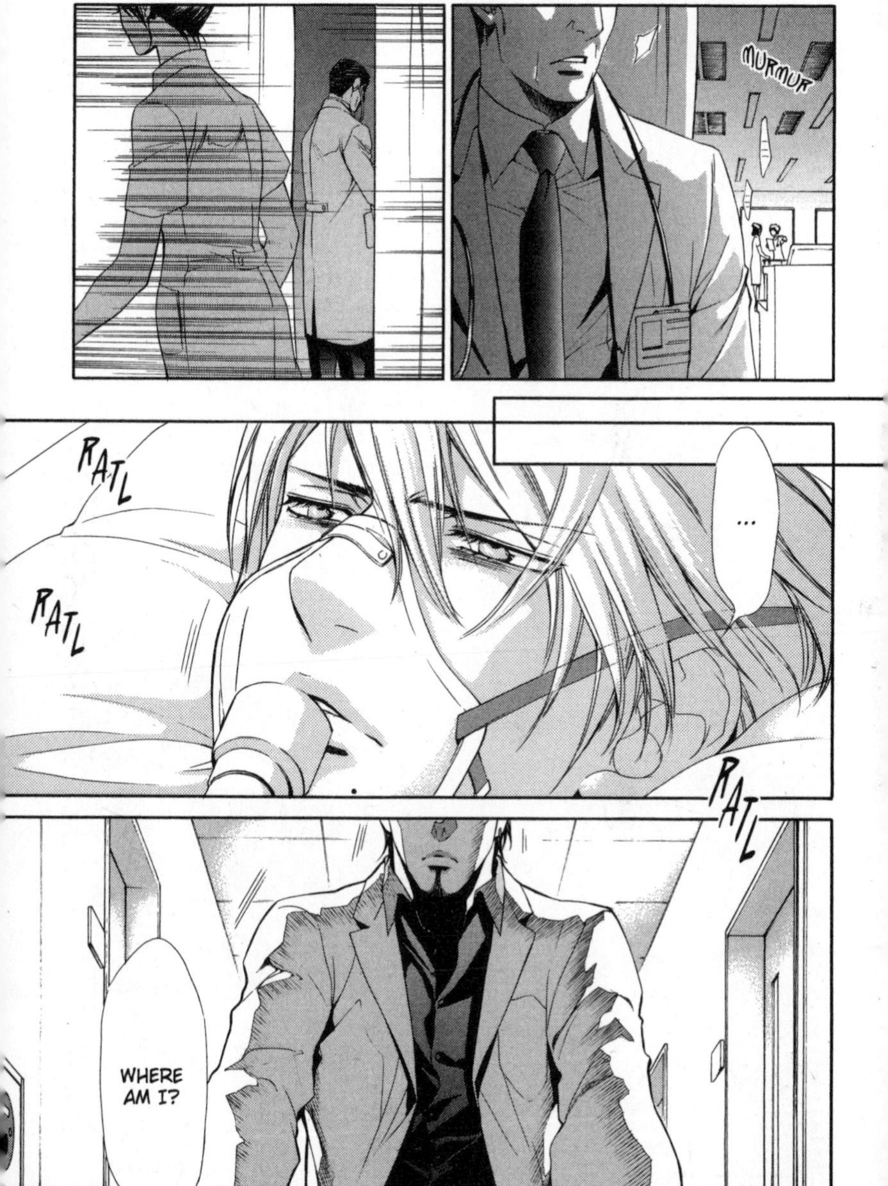
MURMUR
…
RATL
RATL
RATL
WHERE AM I?

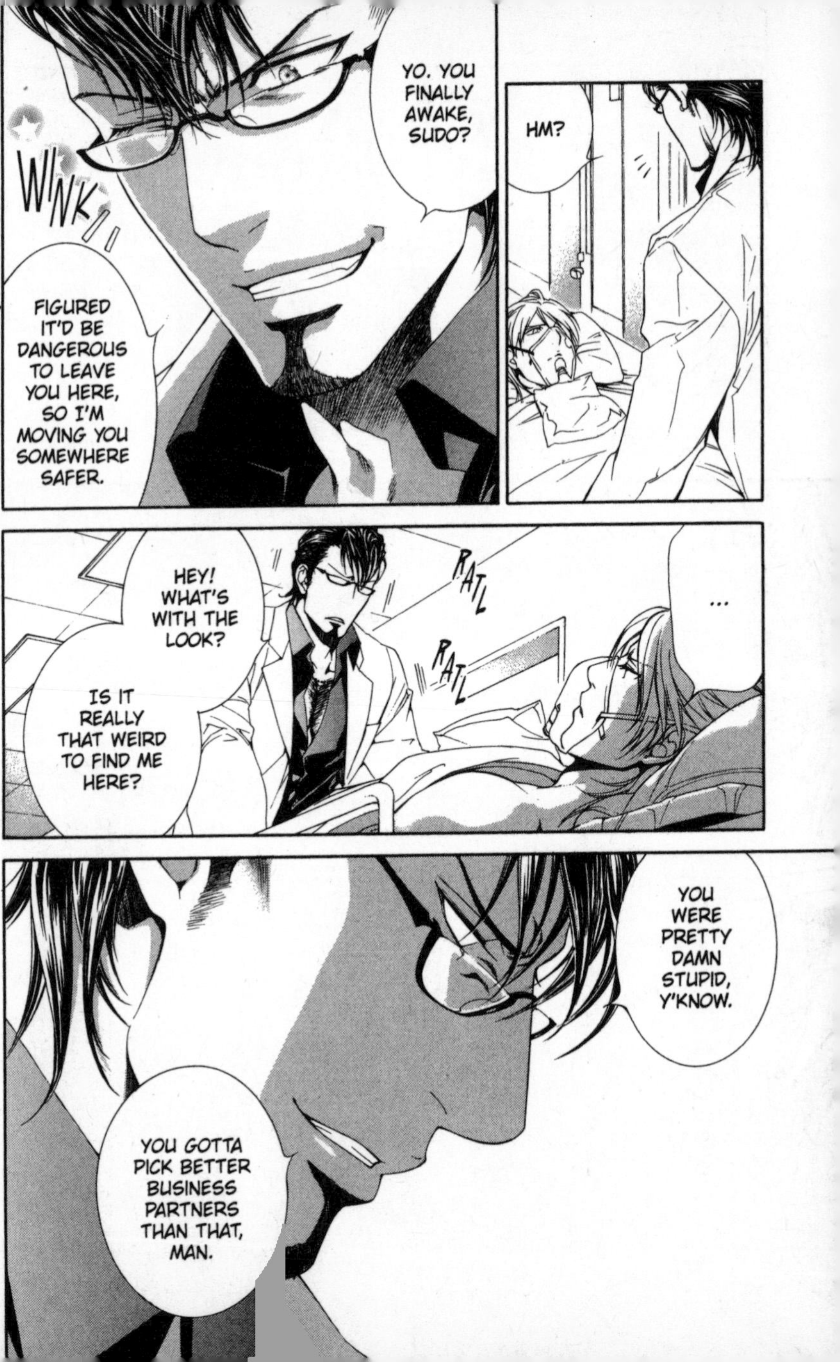
HM?
YO. YOU FINALLY AWAKE, SUDO?
WINK
FIGURED IT'D BE DANGEROUS TO LEAVE YOU HERE, SO I'M MOVING YOU SOMEWHERE SAFER.
...
RATL
RATL
HEY! WHAT'S WITH THE LOOK?
IS IT REALLY THAT WEIRD TO FIND ME HERE?
YOU WERE PRETTY DAMN STUPID, Y'KNOW.
YOU GOTTA PICK BETTER BUSINESS PARTNERS THAN THAT, MAN.

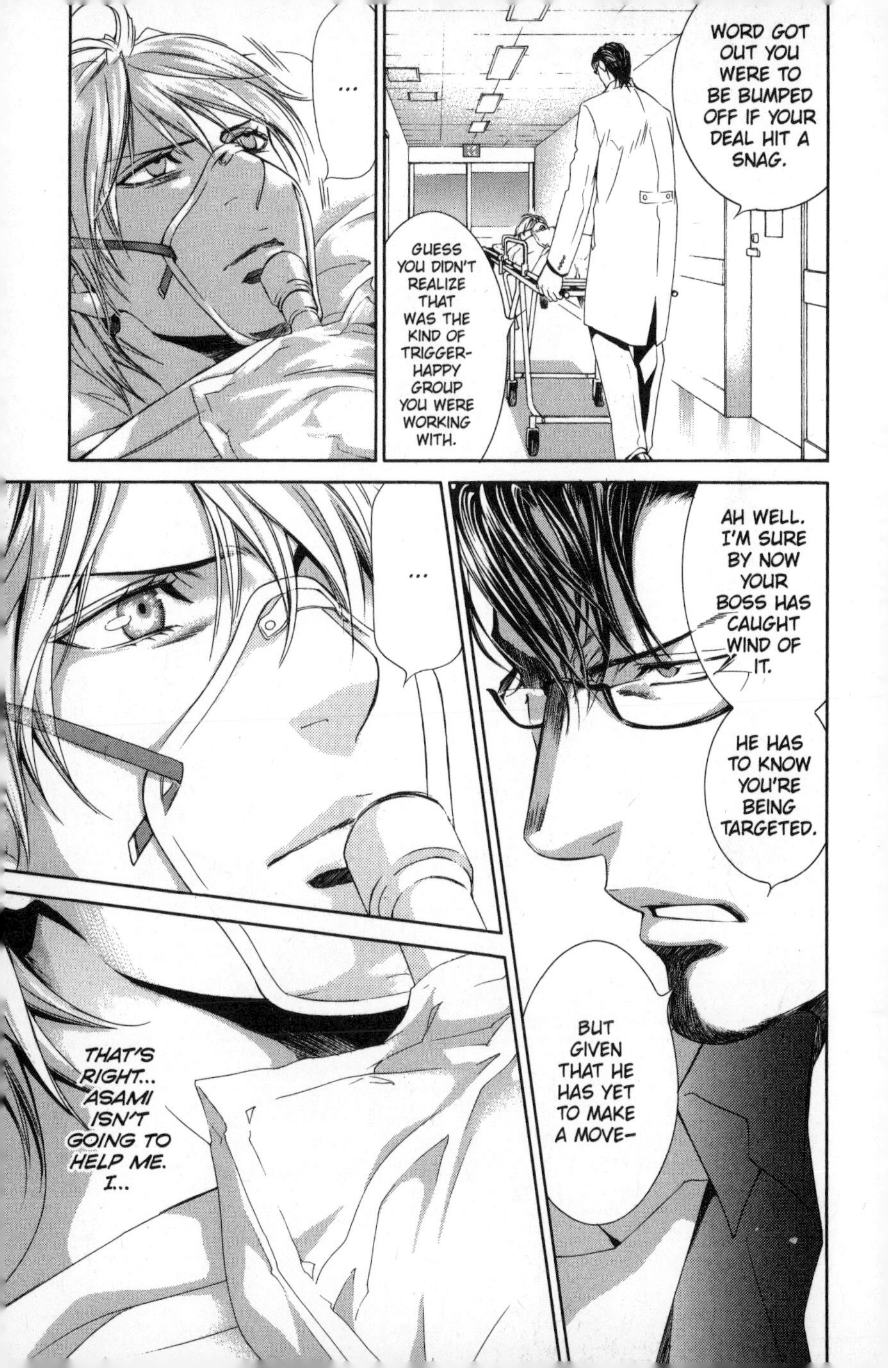
WORD GOT OUT YOU WERE TO BE BUMPED OFF IF YOUR DEAL HIT A SNAG.
GUESS YOU DIDN'T REALIZE THAT WAS THE KIND OF TRIGGER-HAPPY GROUP YOU WERE WORKING WITH.
...
AH WELL. I'M SURE BY NOW YOUR BOSS HAS CAUGHT WIND OF IT.
HE HAS TO KNOW YOU'RE BEING TARGETED.
BUT GIVEN THAT HE HAS YET TO MAKE A MOVE—
...
THAT'S RIGHT... ASAMI ISN'T GOING TO HELP ME. I...

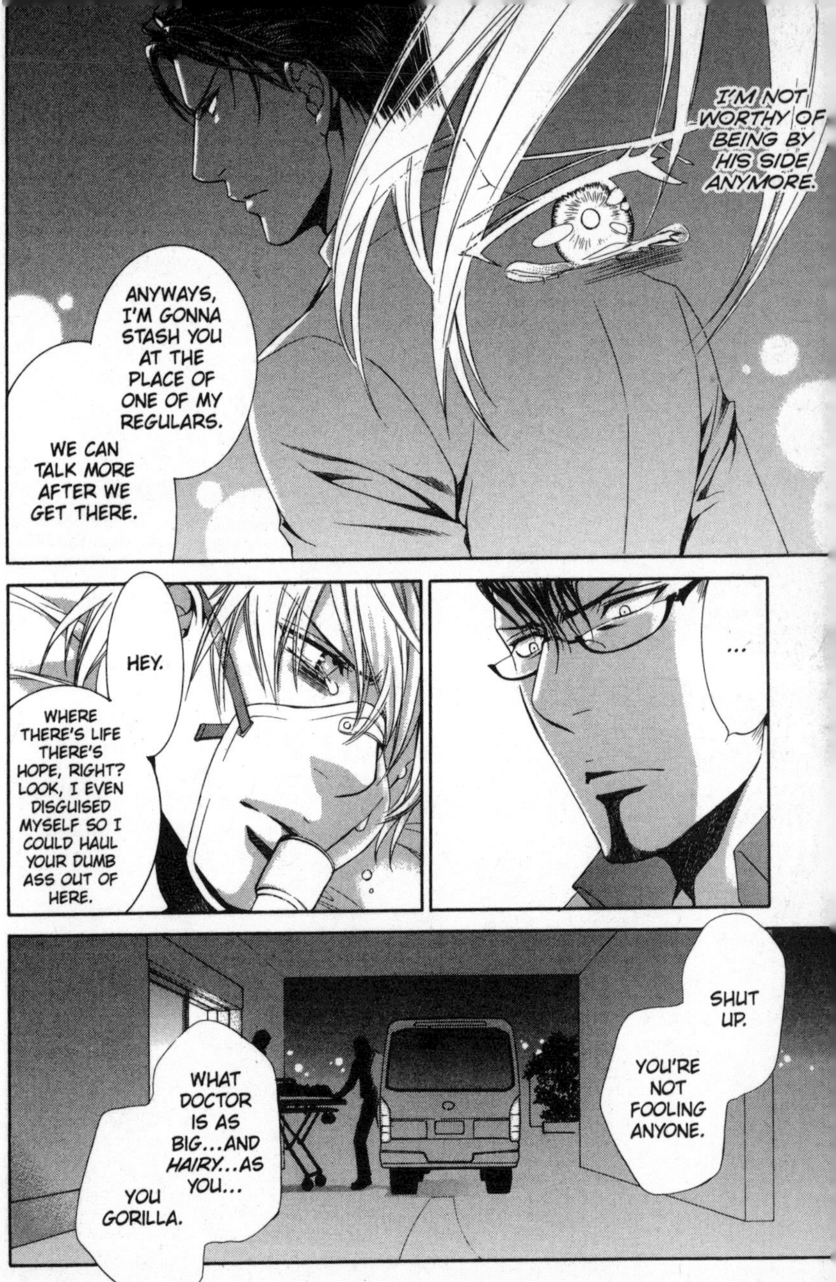
I'M NOT WORTHY OF BEING BY HIS SIDE ANYMORE.
ANYWAYS, I'M GONNA STASH YOU AT THE PLACE OF ONE OF MY REGULARS.
WE CAN TALK MORE AFTER WE GET THERE.
...
HEY.
WHERE THERE'S LIFE THERE'S HOPE, RIGHT? LOOK, I EVEN DISGUISED MYSELF SO I COULD HAUL YOUR DUMB ASS OUT OF HERE.
SHUT UP.
YOU'RE NOT FOOLING ANYONE.
WHAT DOCTOR IS AS BIG...AND *HAIRY*...AS YOU...
YOU GORILLA.

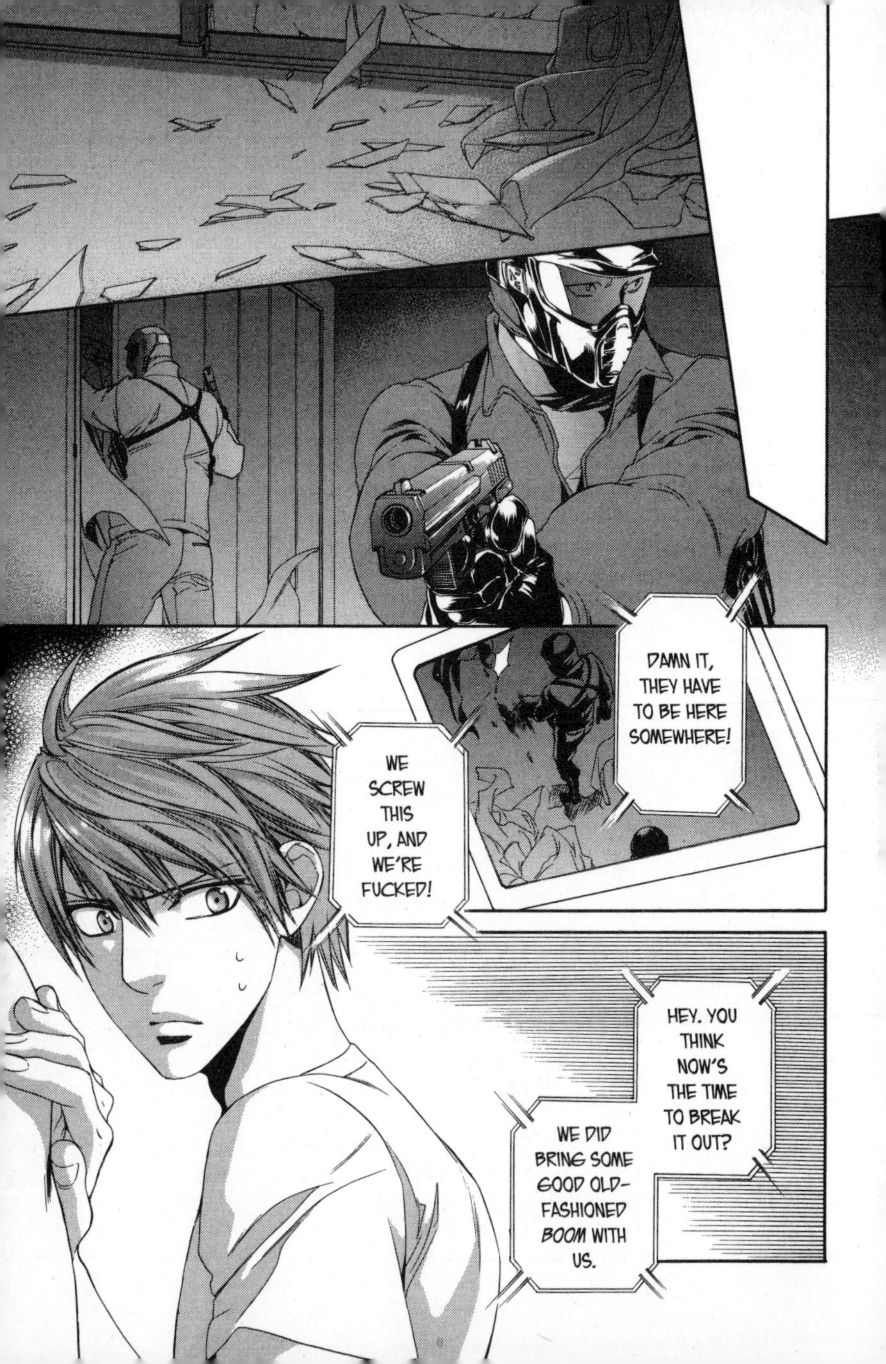
DAMN IT, THEY HAVE TO BE HERE SOMEWHERE!
WE SCREW THIS UP, AND WE'RE FUCKED!
HEY. YOU THINK NOW'S THE TIME TO BREAK IT OUT?
WE DID BRING SOME GOOD OLD-FASHIONED *BOOM* WITH US.

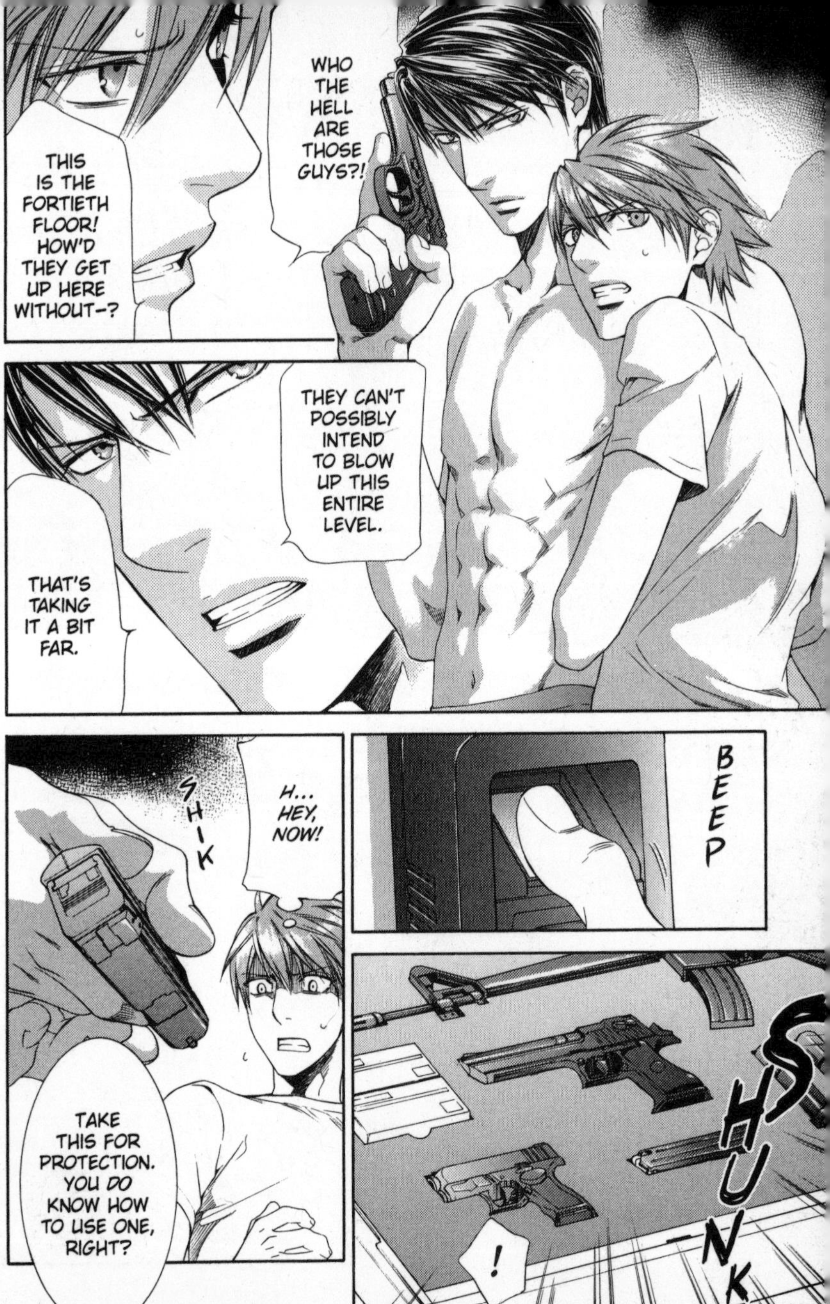
WHO THE HELL ARE THOSE GUYS?!
THIS IS THE FORTIETH FLOOR! HOW'D THEY GET UP HERE WITHOUT-?
THEY CAN'T POSSIBLY INTEND TO BLOW UP THIS ENTIRE LEVEL.
THAT'S TAKING IT A BIT FAR.
BEEP
SHUNK
!
SHIK
H... HEY, NOW!
TAKE THIS FOR PROTECTION. YOU DO KNOW HOW TO USE ONE, RIGHT?

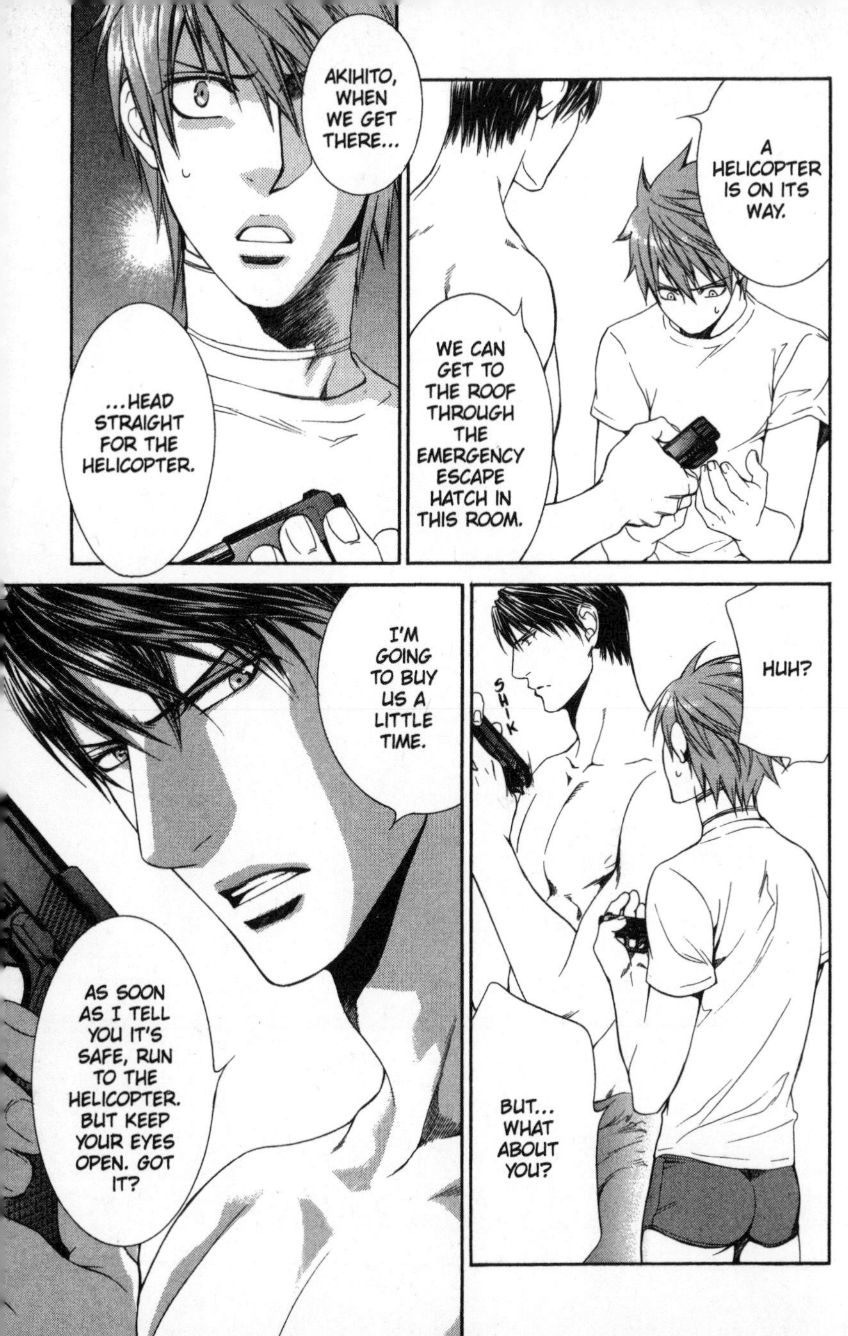
A HELICOPTER IS ON ITS WAY.
WE CAN GET TO THE ROOF THROUGH THE EMERGENCY ESCAPE HATCH IN THIS ROOM.
AKIHITO, WHEN WE GET THERE...
...HEAD STRAIGHT FOR THE HELICOPTER.
HUH?
SHIK
BUT... WHAT ABOUT YOU?
I'M GOING TO BUY US A LITTLE TIME.
AS SOON AS I TELL YOU IT'S SAFE, RUN TO THE HELICOPTER. BUT KEEP YOUR EYES OPEN. GOT IT?

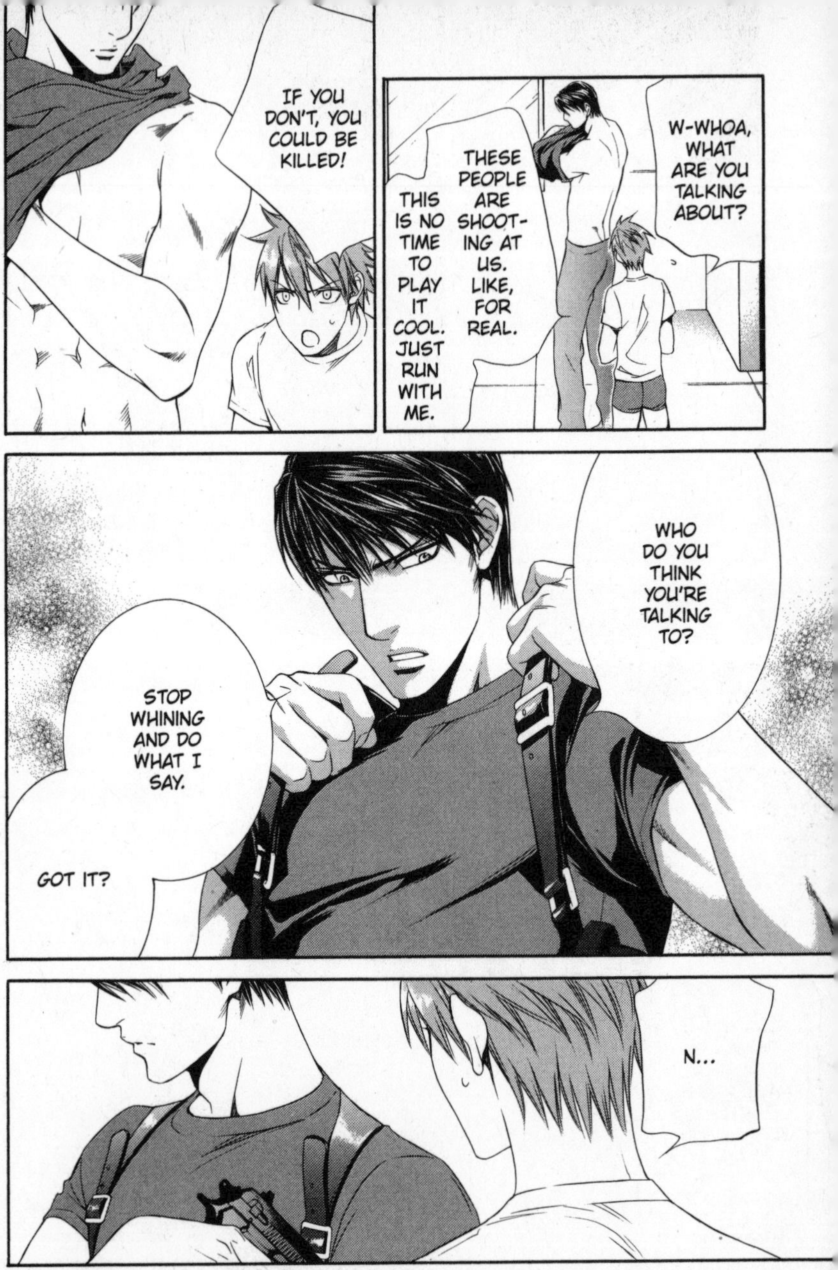
W-WHOA, WHAT ARE YOU TALKING ABOUT?
THESE PEOPLE ARE SHOOTING AT US. LIKE, FOR REAL.
THIS IS NO TIME TO PLAY IT COOL. JUST RUN WITH ME.
IF YOU DON'T, YOU COULD BE KILLED!
WHO DO YOU THINK YOU'RE TALKING TO?
STOP WHINING AND DO WHAT I SAY.
GOT IT?
N...

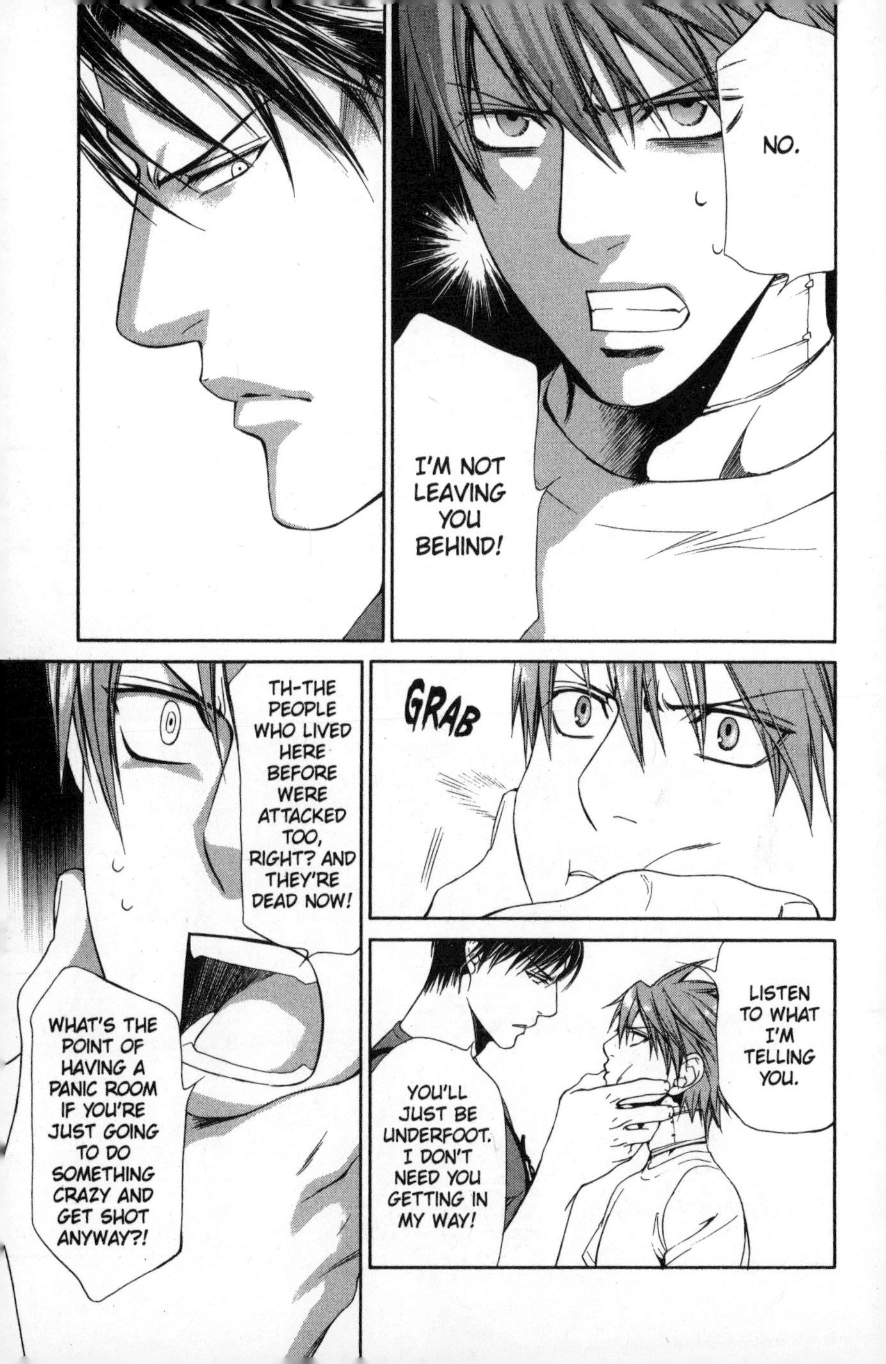
NO.
I'M NOT LEAVING YOU BEHIND!
GRAB
LISTEN TO WHAT I'M TELLING YOU.
YOU'LL JUST BE UNDERFOOT. I DON'T NEED YOU GETTING IN MY WAY!
TH-THE PEOPLE WHO LIVED HERE BEFORE WERE ATTACKED TOO, RIGHT? AND THEY'RE DEAD NOW!
WHAT'S THE POINT OF HAVING A PANIC ROOM IF YOU'RE JUST GOING TO DO SOMETHING CRAZY AND GET SHOT ANYWAY?!

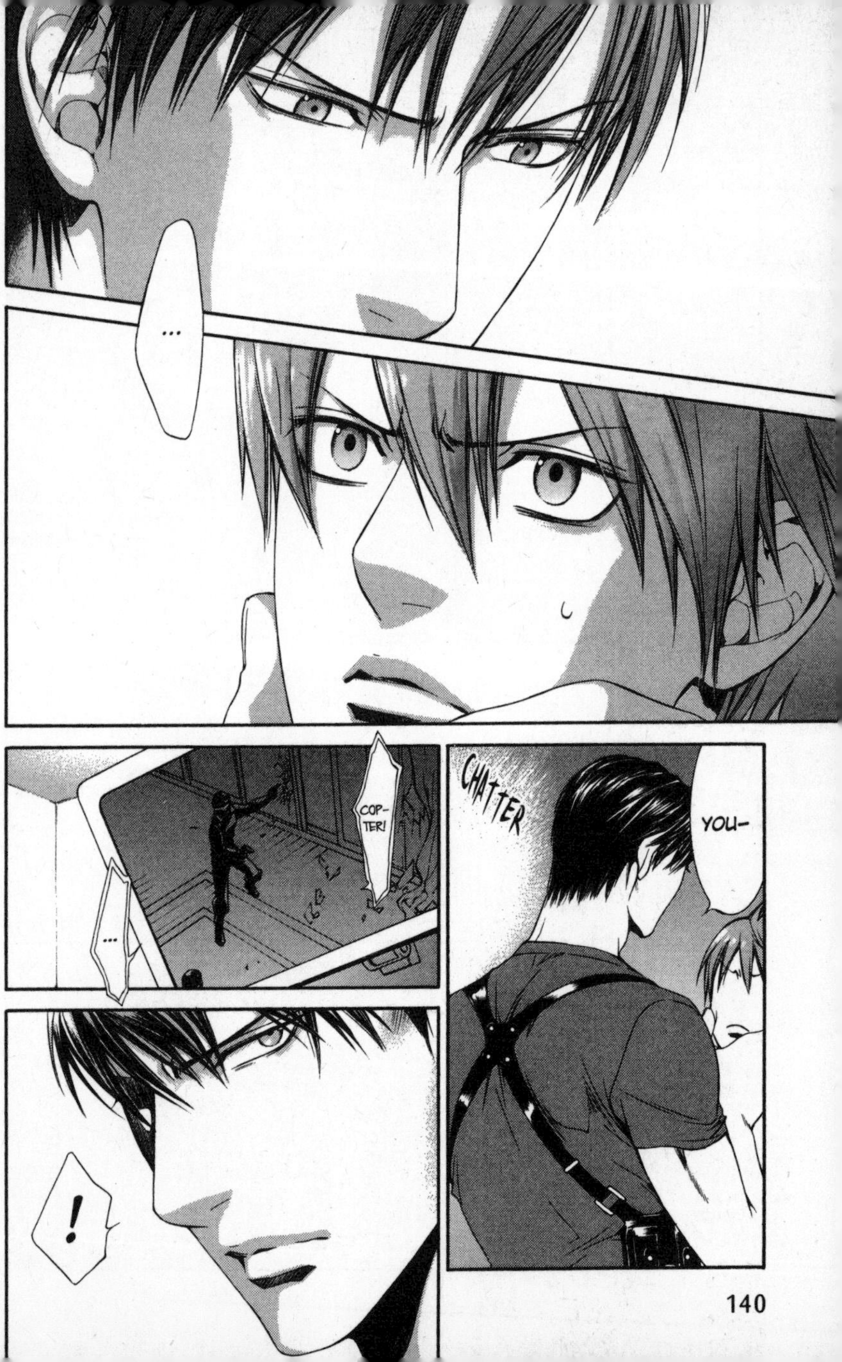
...
CHATTER
YOU-
COP-
TER!
...
!

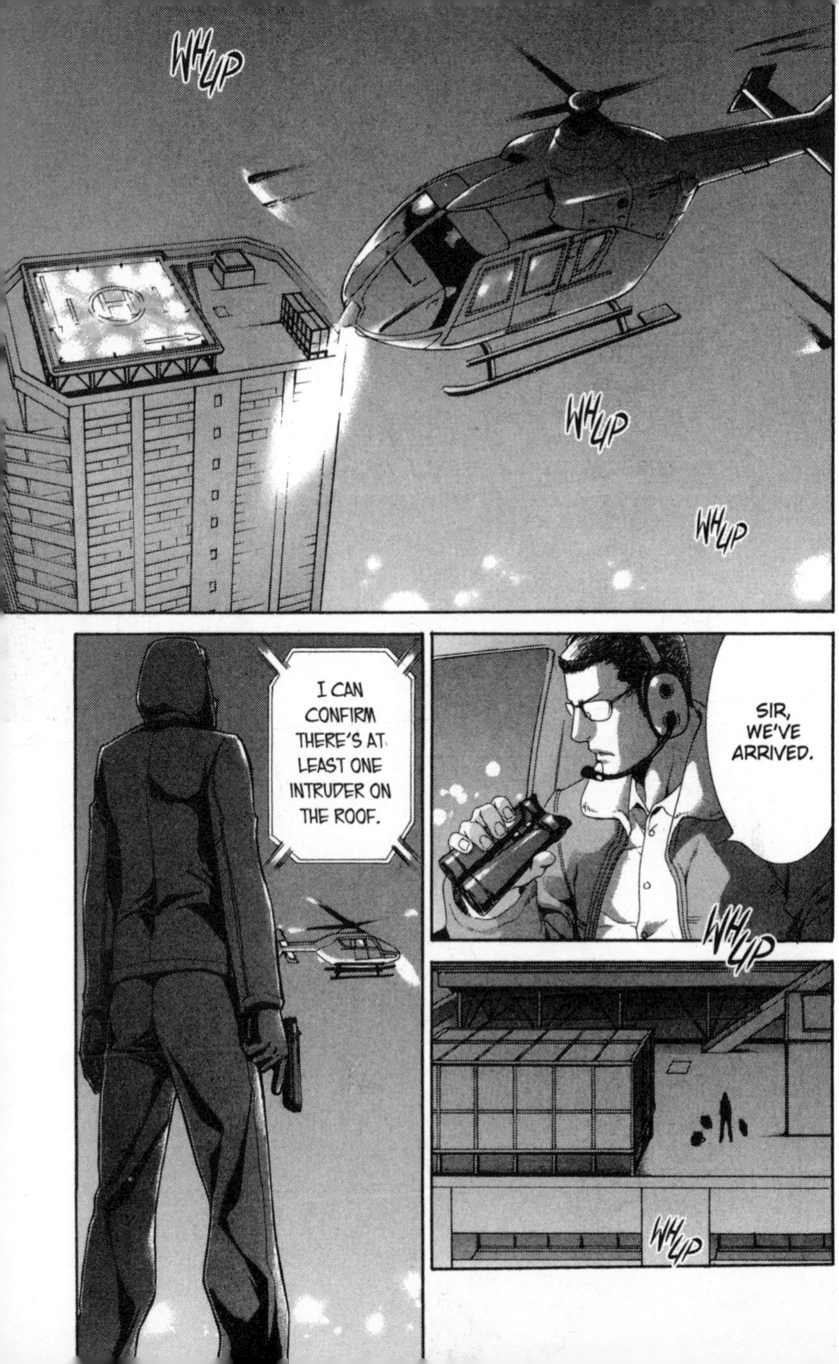
WHUP
WHUP
WHUP
SIR, WE'VE ARRIVED.
WHUP
WHUP
I CAN CONFIRM THERE'S AT LEAST ONE INTRUDER ON THE ROOF.

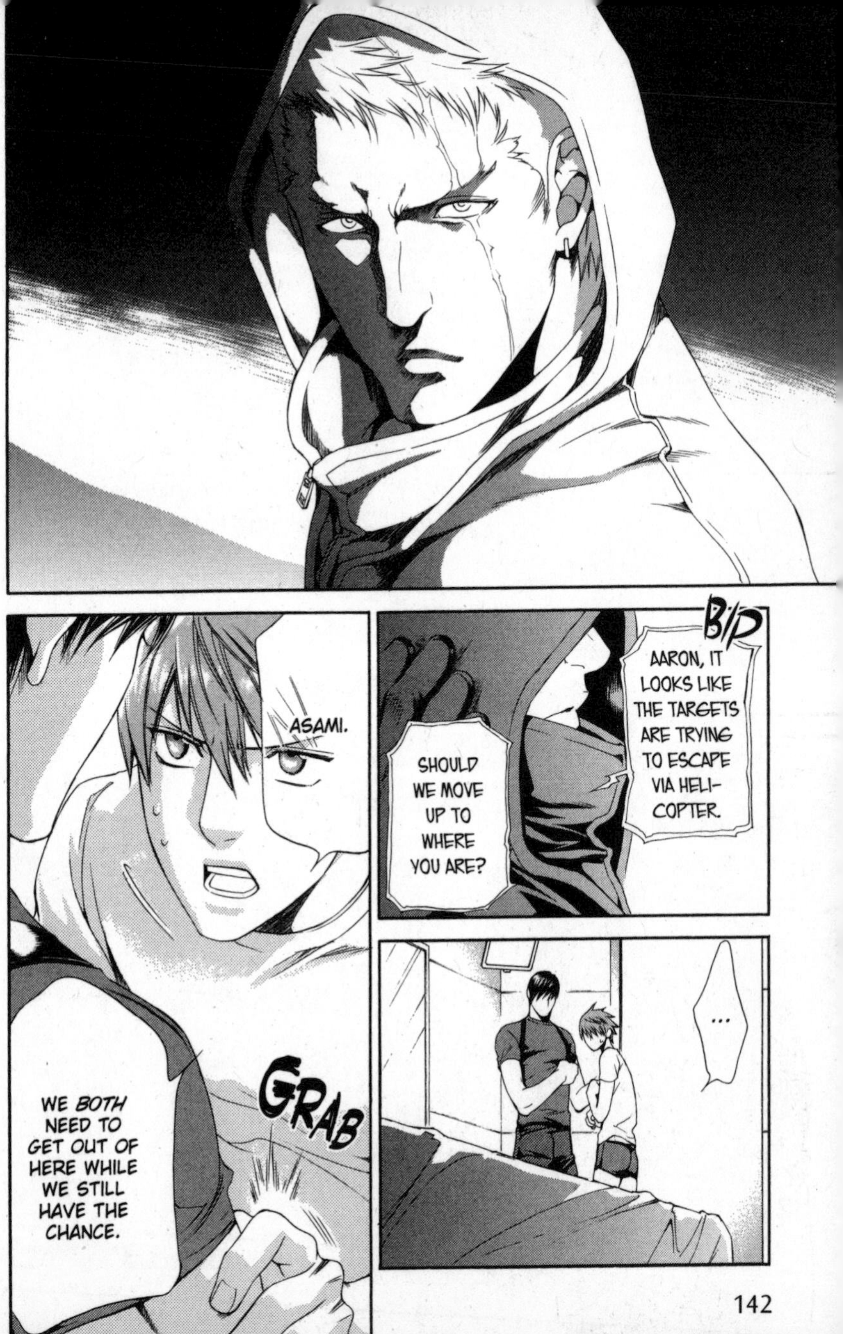
BIP
AARON, IT LOOKS LIKE THE TARGETS ARE TRYING TO ESCAPE VIA HELI-COPTER.
SHOULD WE MOVE UP TO WHERE YOU ARE?
...
ASAMI.
GRAB
WE *BOTH* NEED TO GET OUT OF HERE WHILE WE STILL HAVE THE CHANCE.

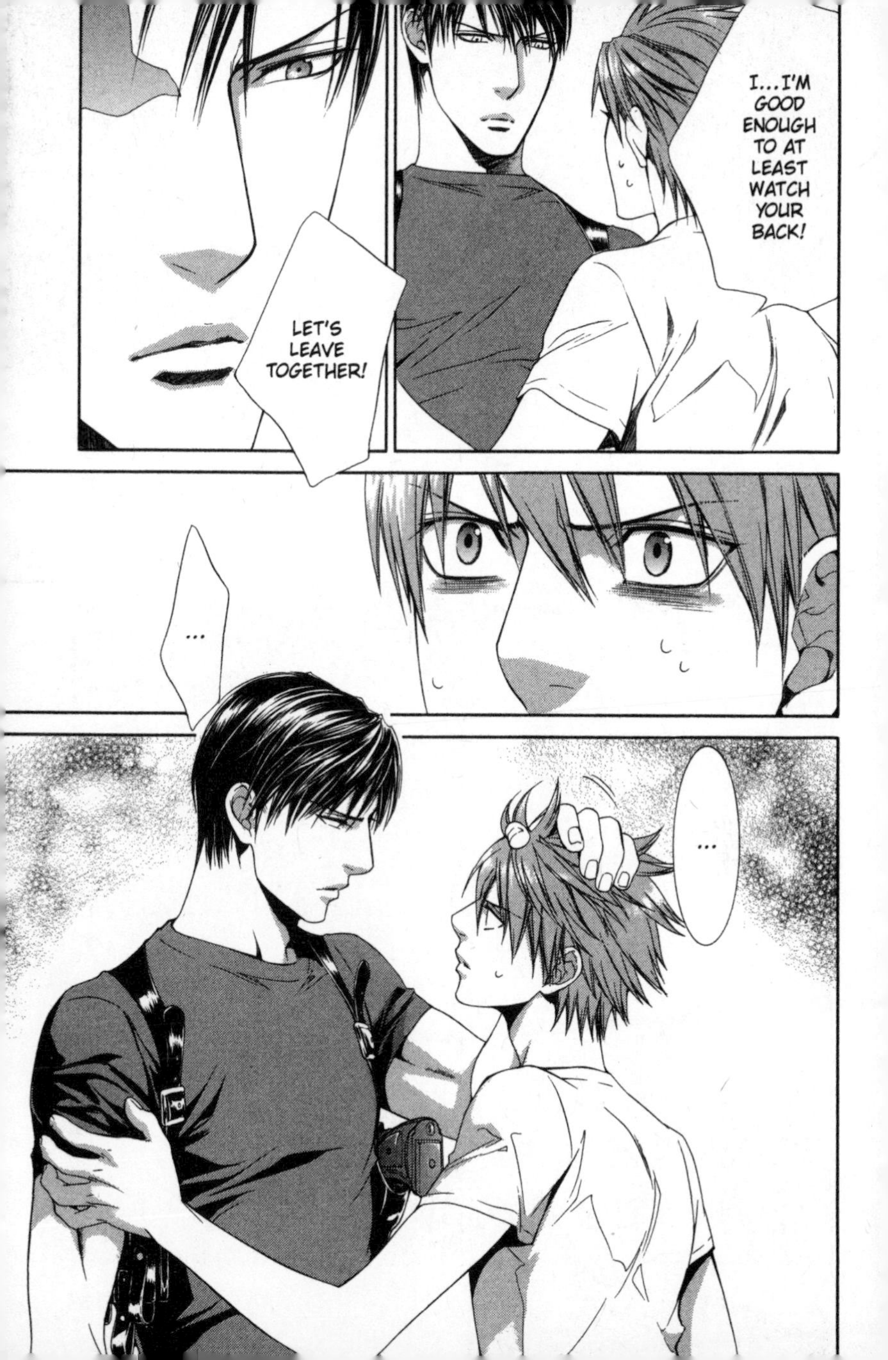
I...I'M GOOD ENOUGH TO AT LEAST WATCH YOUR BACK!
LET'S LEAVE TOGETHER!
...
...

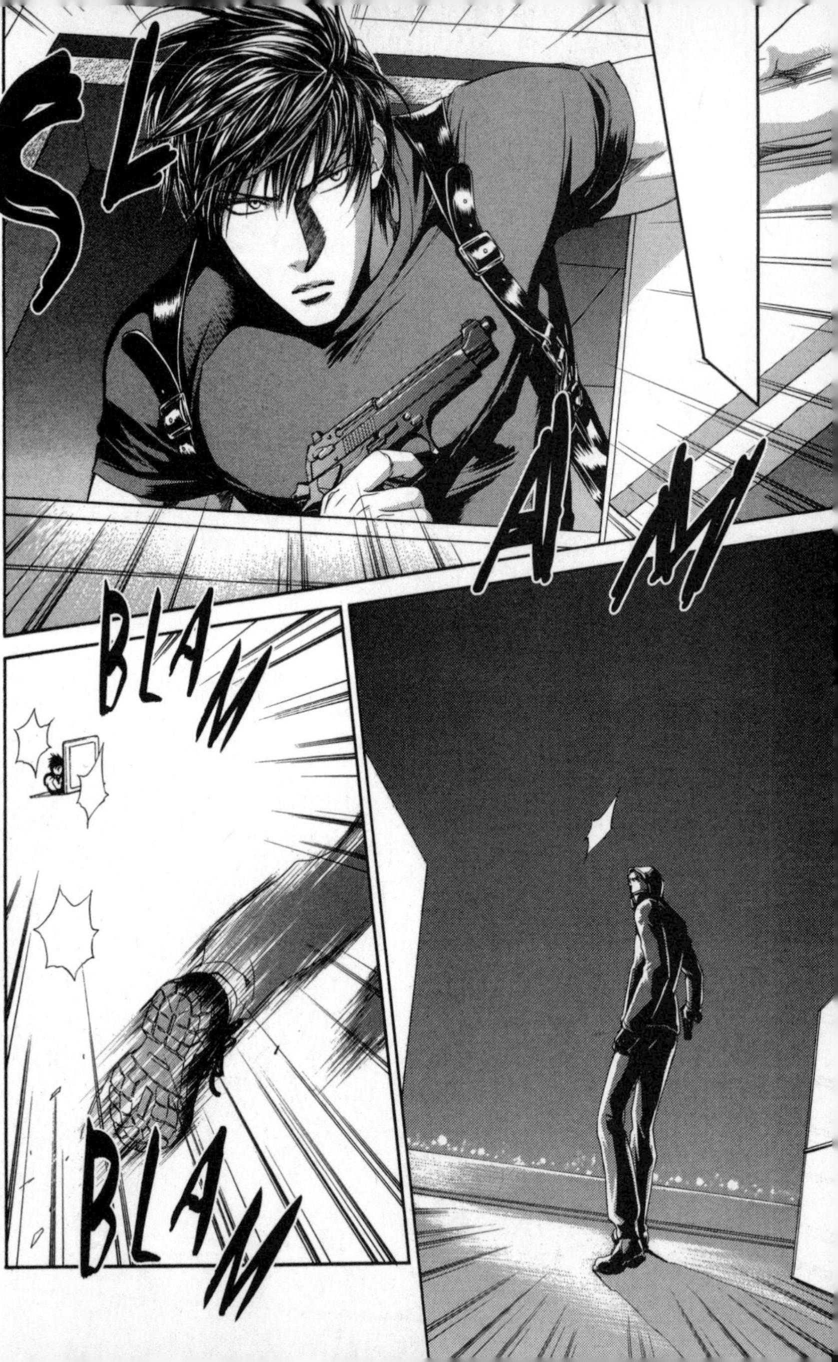
SLAM
BLAM
BLAM

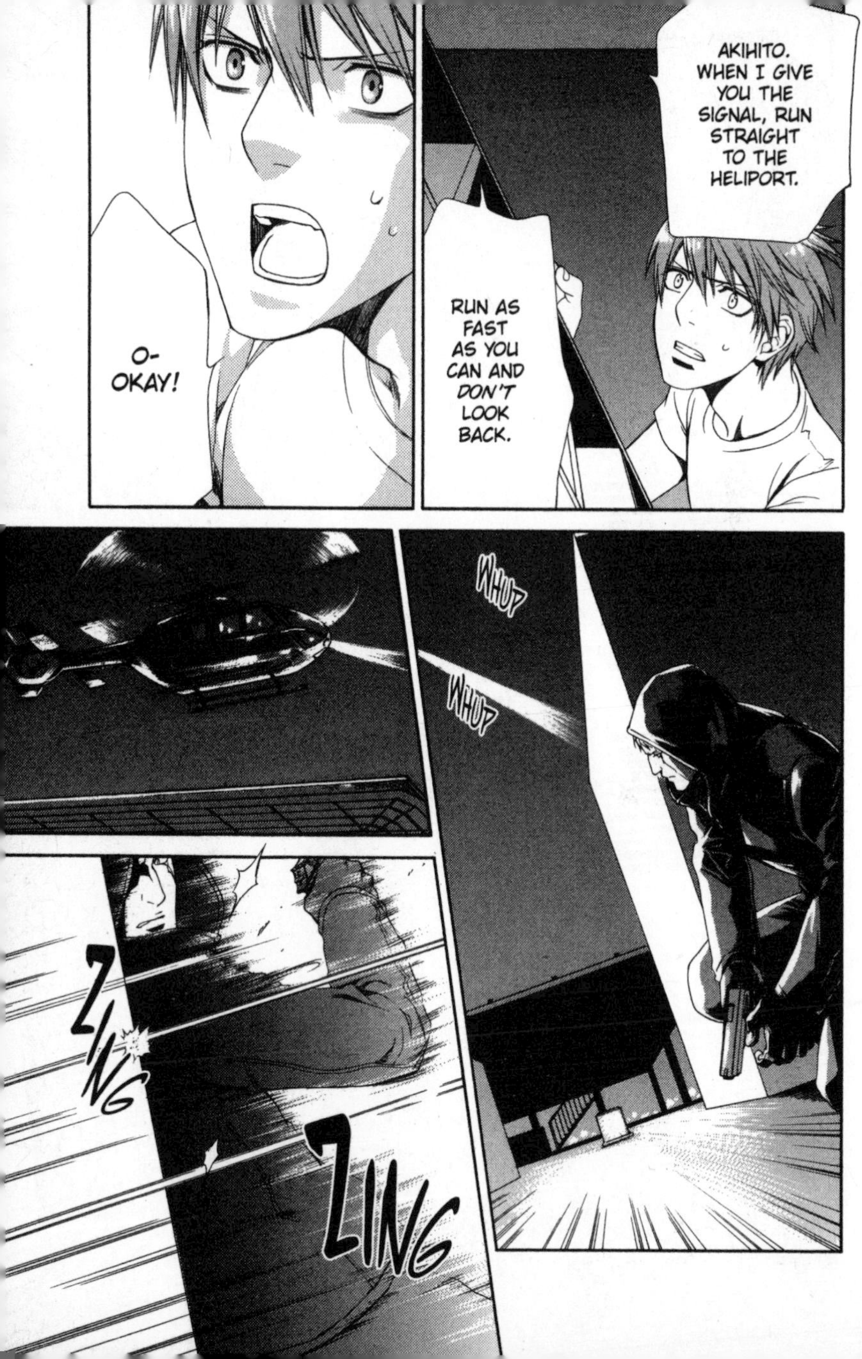
AKIHITO. WHEN I GIVE YOU THE SIGNAL, RUN STRAIGHT TO THE HELIPORT.
RUN AS FAST AS YOU CAN AND *DON'T* LOOK BACK.
O-OKAY!
WHUP
WHUP
ZING
ZING

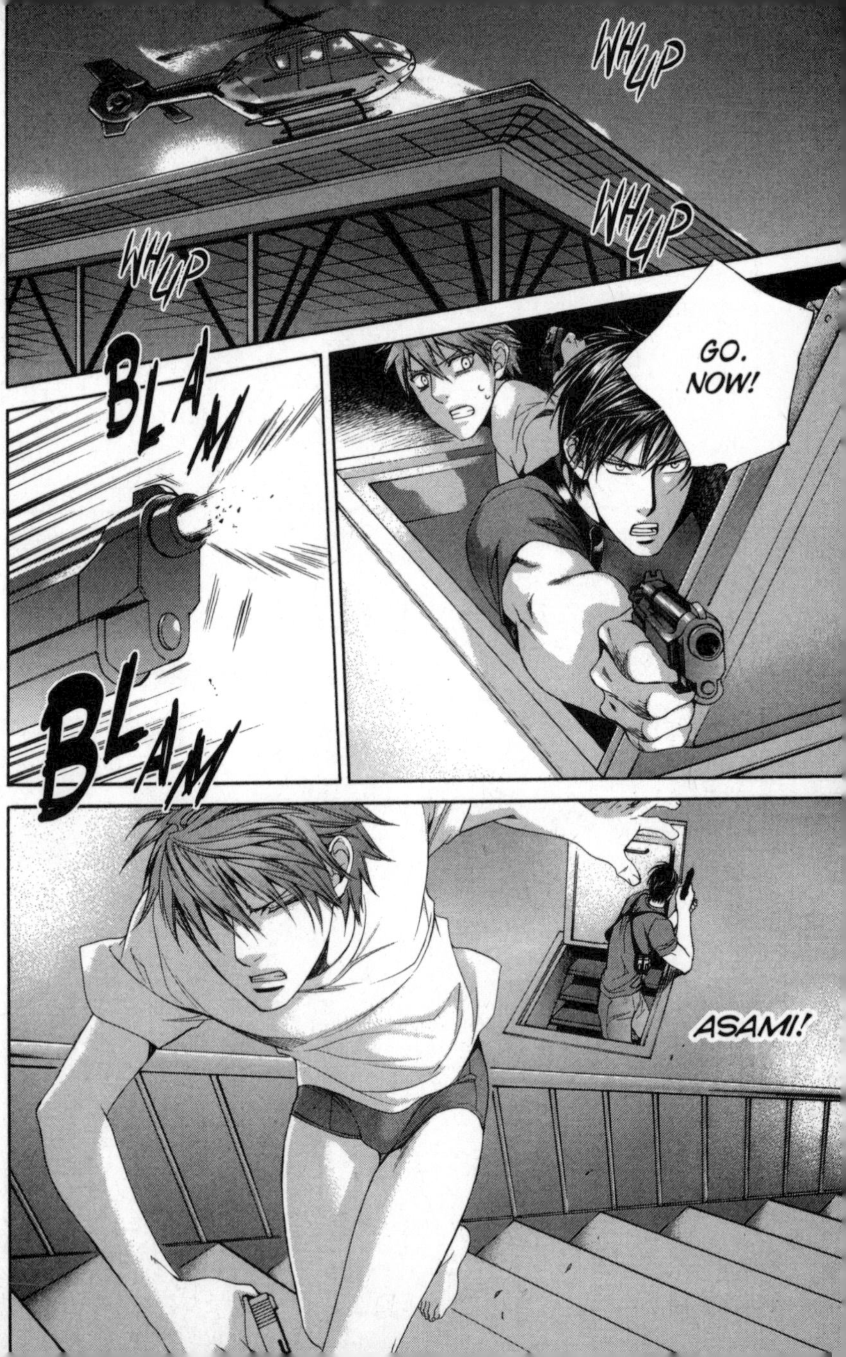
WHUP
WHUP
WHUP
GO. NOW!
BLAM
BLAM
ASAMI!

プレイ
イン アビス

Pray in the Abyss

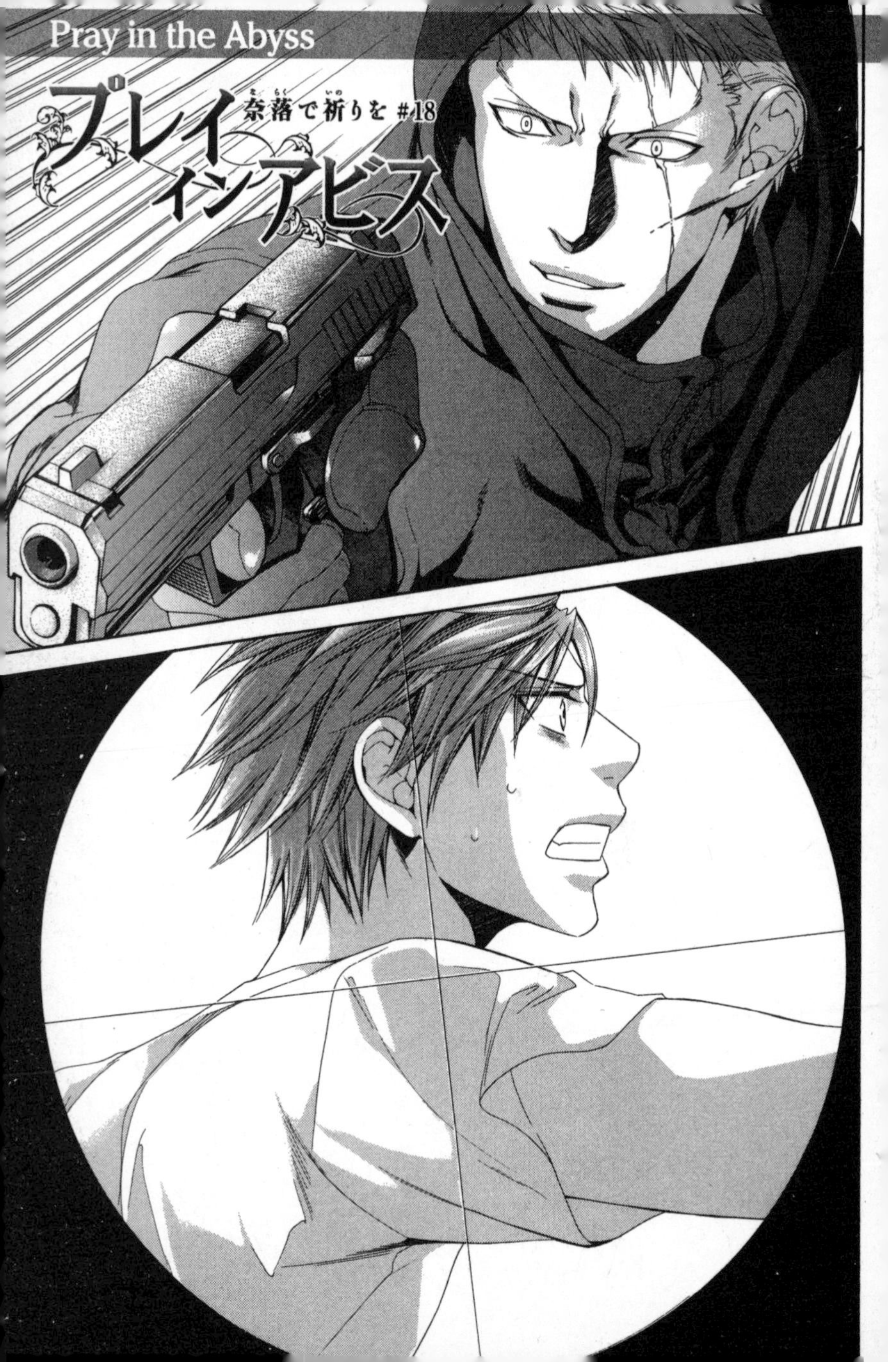
Pray in the Abyss
プレイ・イン・アビス
奈落で祈りを #18

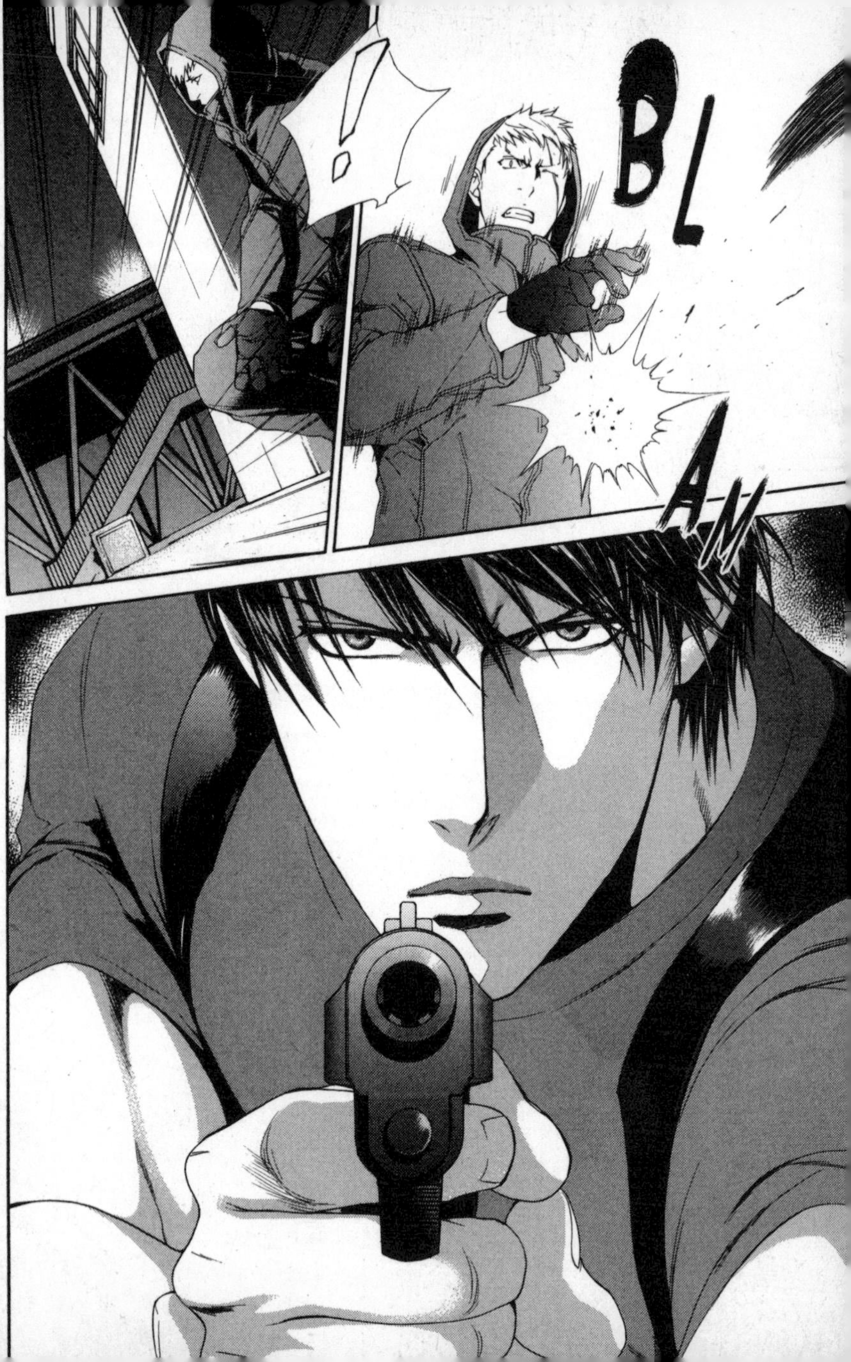
!
BLAM

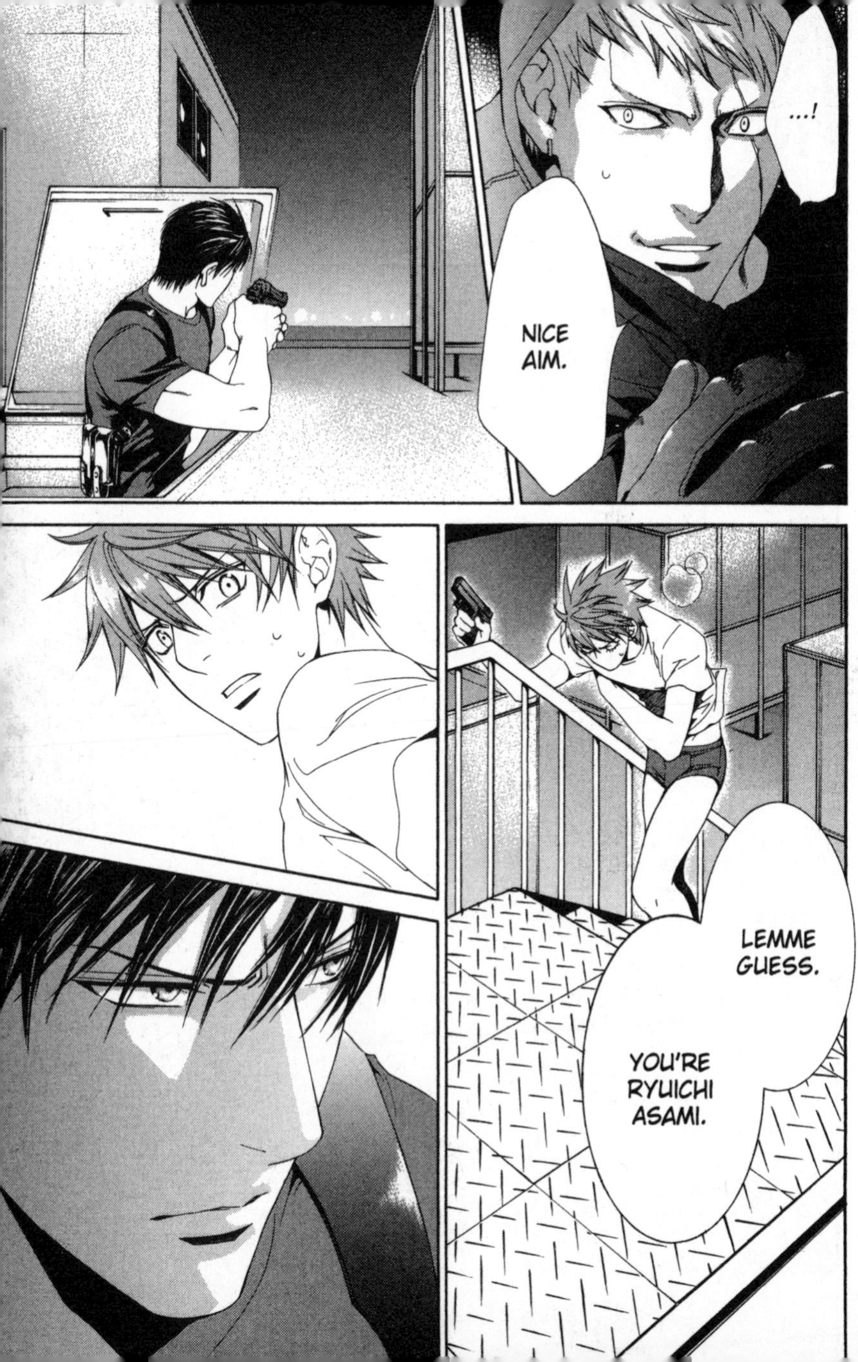
...!
NICE AIM.
LEMME GUESS.
YOU'RE RYUICHI ASAMI.

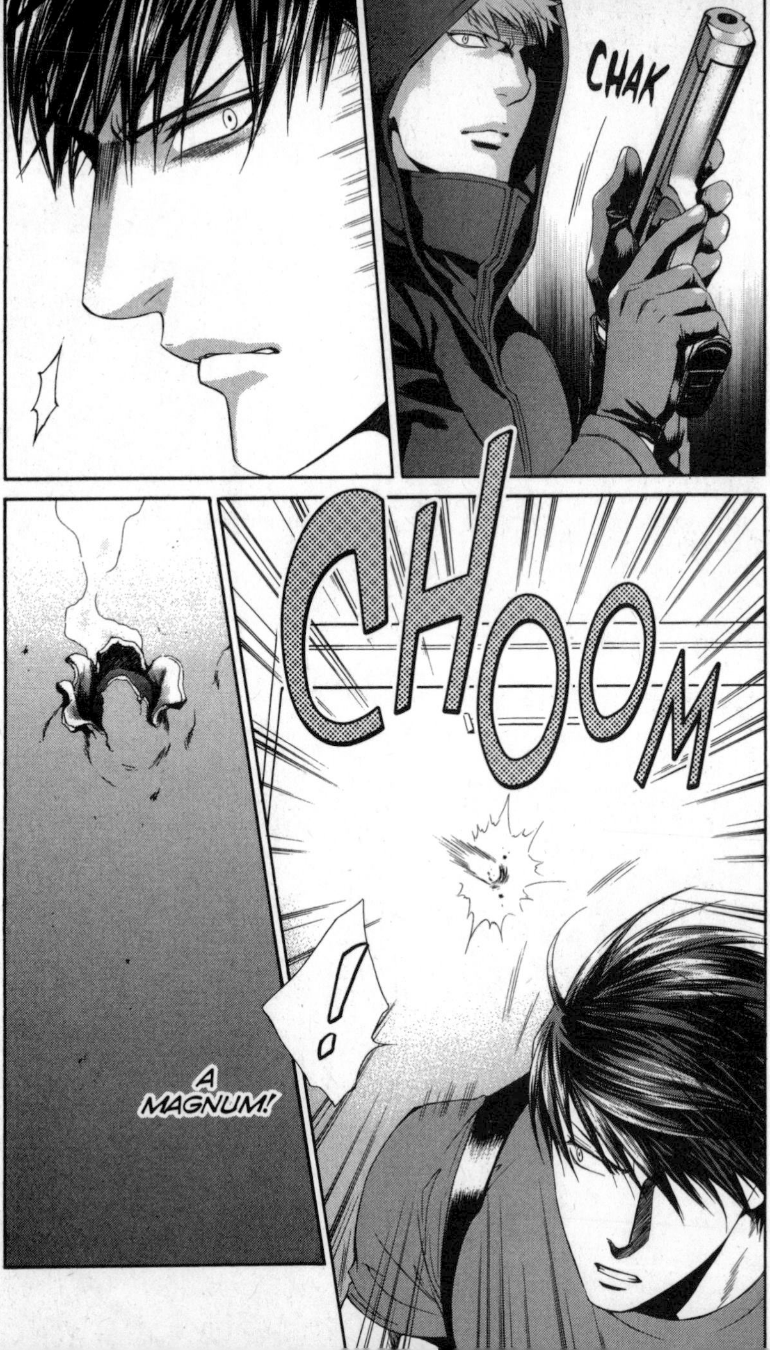
CHAK
CHOOM
A MAGNUM!

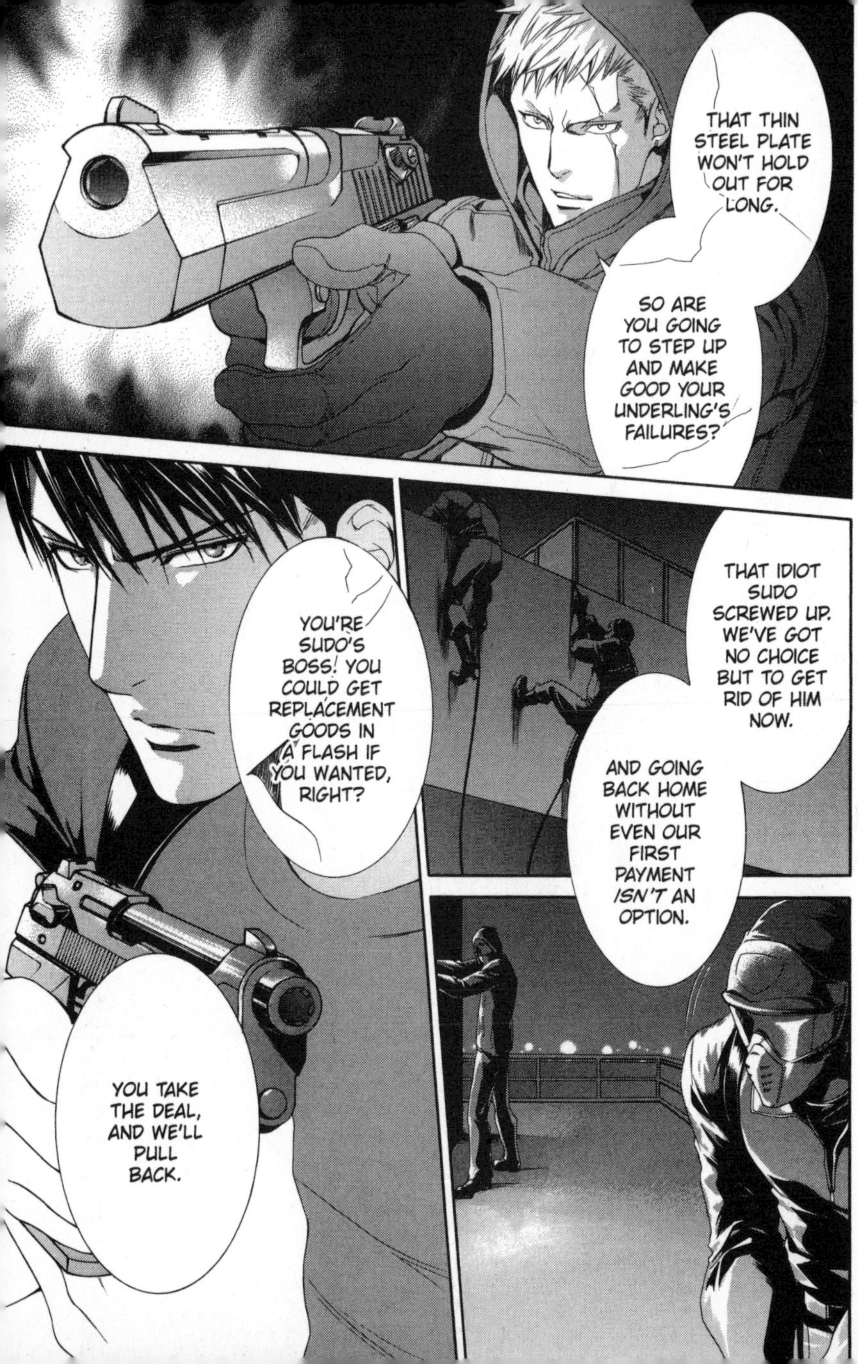
THAT THIN STEEL PLATE WON'T HOLD OUT FOR LONG.
SO ARE YOU GOING TO STEP UP AND MAKE GOOD YOUR UNDERLING'S FAILURES?
THAT IDIOT SUDO SCREWED UP. WE'VE GOT NO CHOICE BUT TO GET RID OF HIM NOW.
AND GOING BACK HOME WITHOUT EVEN OUR FIRST PAYMENT *ISN'T* AN OPTION.
YOU'RE SUDO'S BOSS! YOU COULD GET REPLACEMENT GOODS IN A FLASH IF YOU WANTED, RIGHT?
YOU TAKE THE DEAL, AND WE'LL PULL BACK.

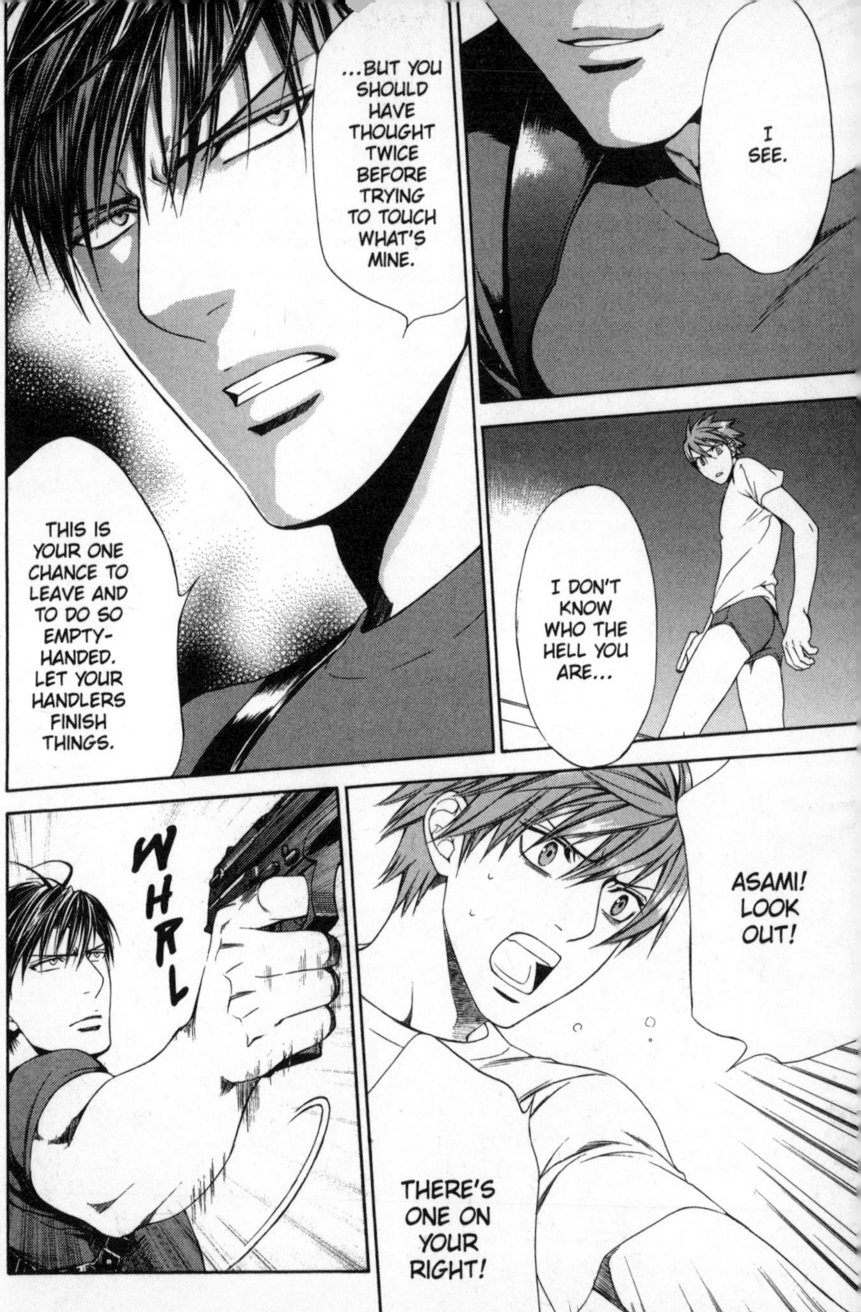
I SEE.
I DON'T KNOW WHO THE HELL YOU ARE...
...BUT YOU SHOULD HAVE THOUGHT TWICE BEFORE TRYING TO TOUCH WHAT'S MINE.
THIS IS YOUR ONE CHANCE TO LEAVE AND TO DO SO EMPTY-HANDED. LET YOUR HANDLERS FINISH THINGS.
ASAMI! LOOK OUT!
THERE'S ONE ON YOUR RIGHT!
WHRL

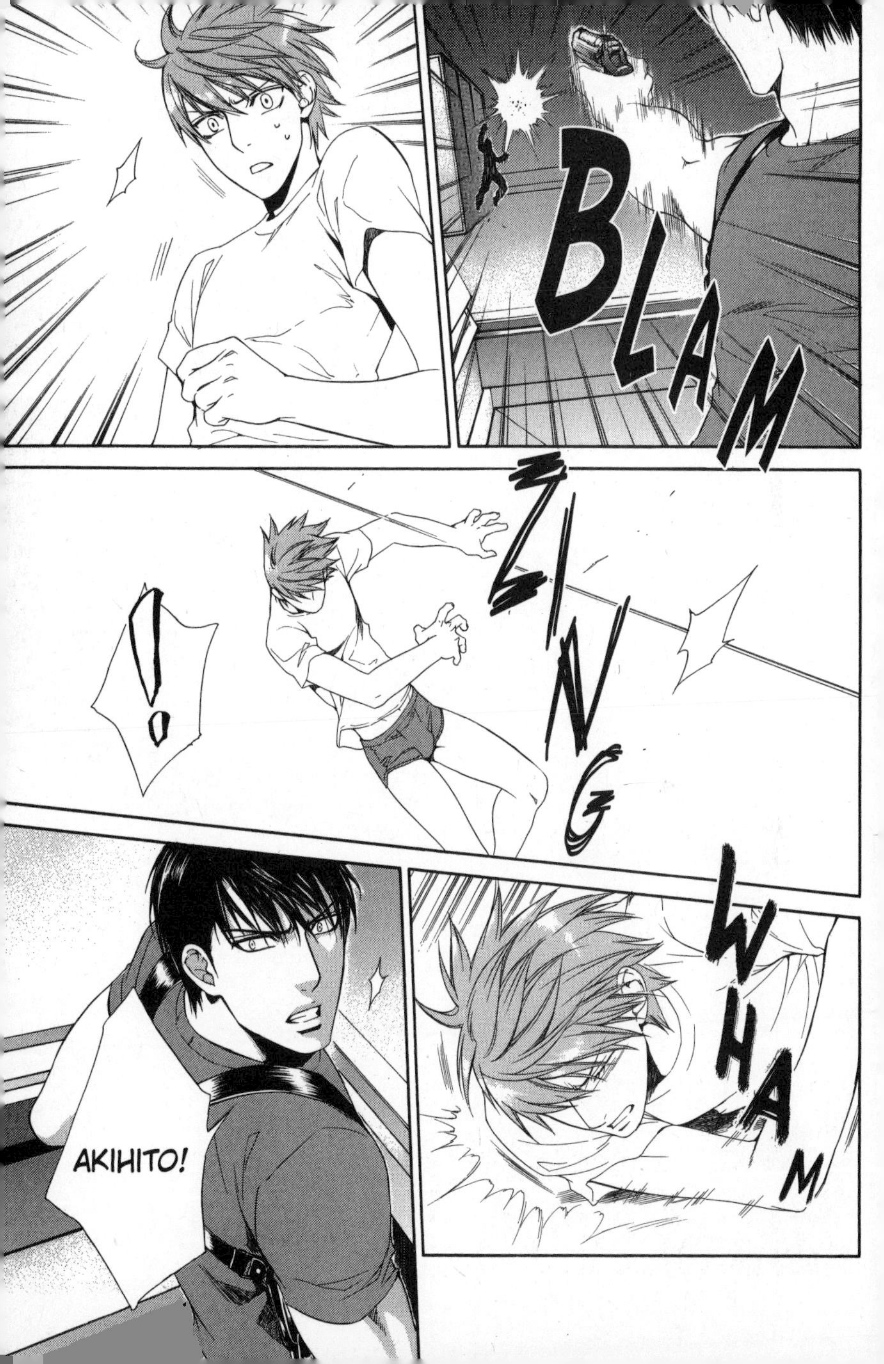
BLAM
ZING
!
WHAM
AKIHITO!

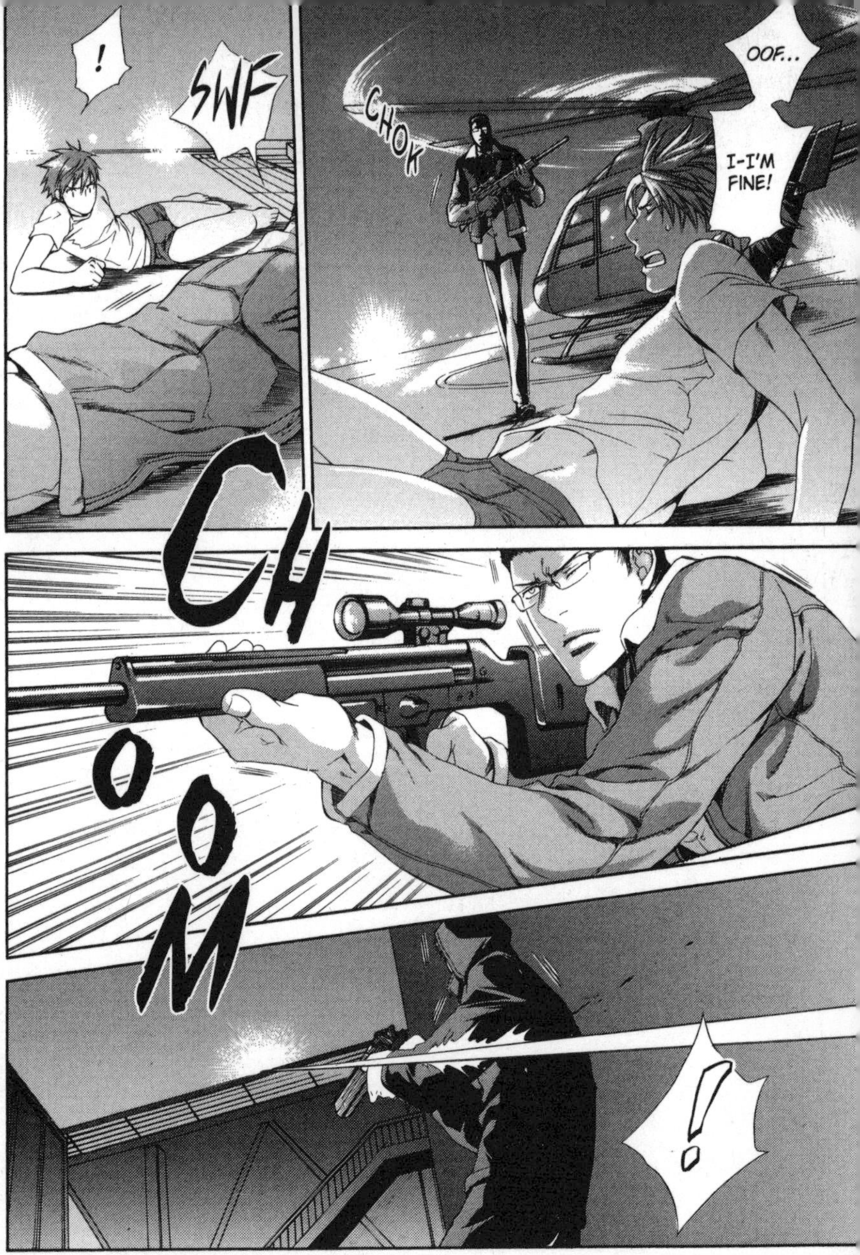
OOF...
I-I'M FINE!
CHOK
!
SWF
CHOOOM
!

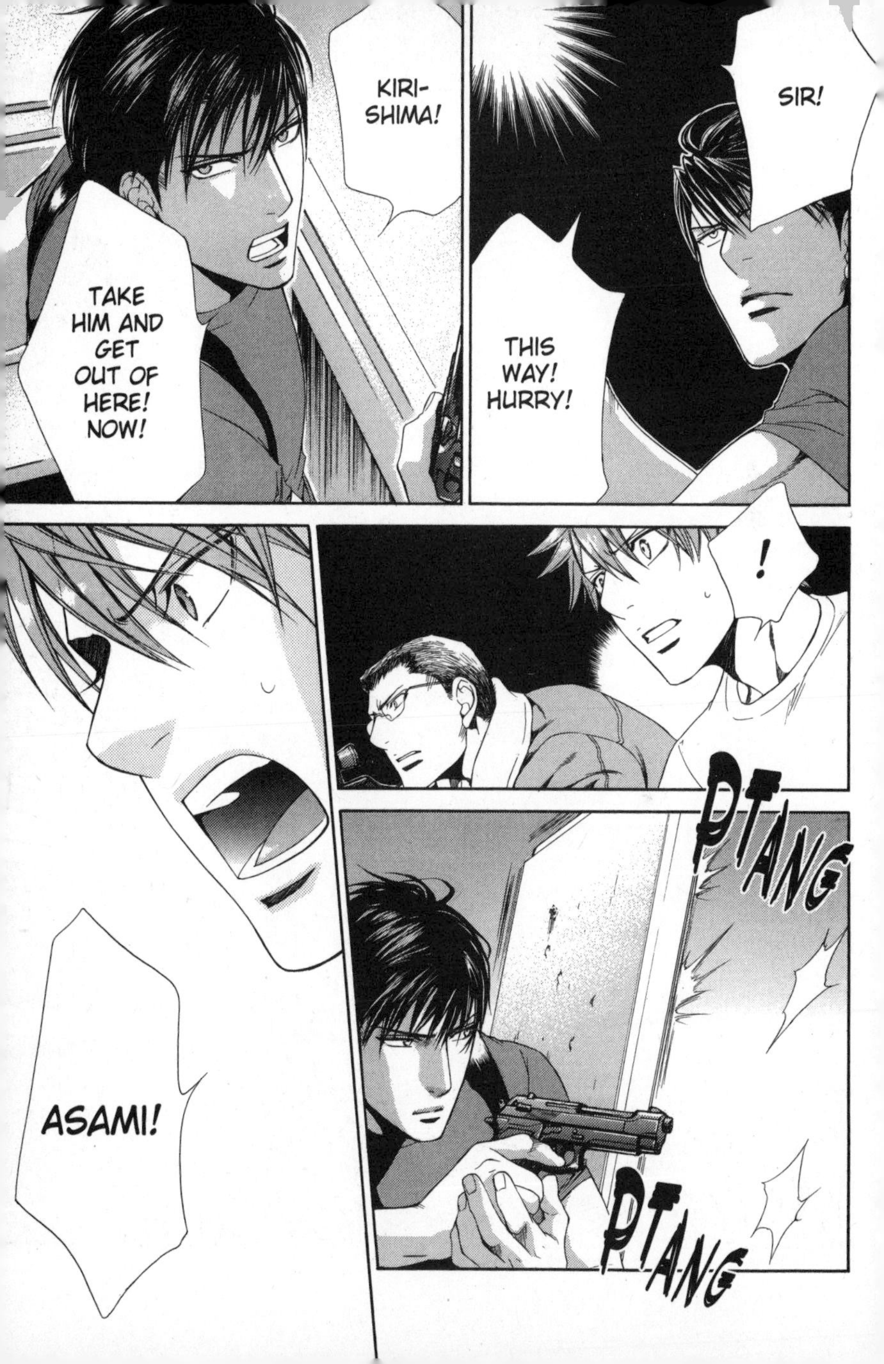
SIR!
THIS WAY! HURRY!
KIRI-SHIMA!
TAKE HIM AND GET OUT OF HERE! NOW!
!
PTANG
PTANG
ASAMI!

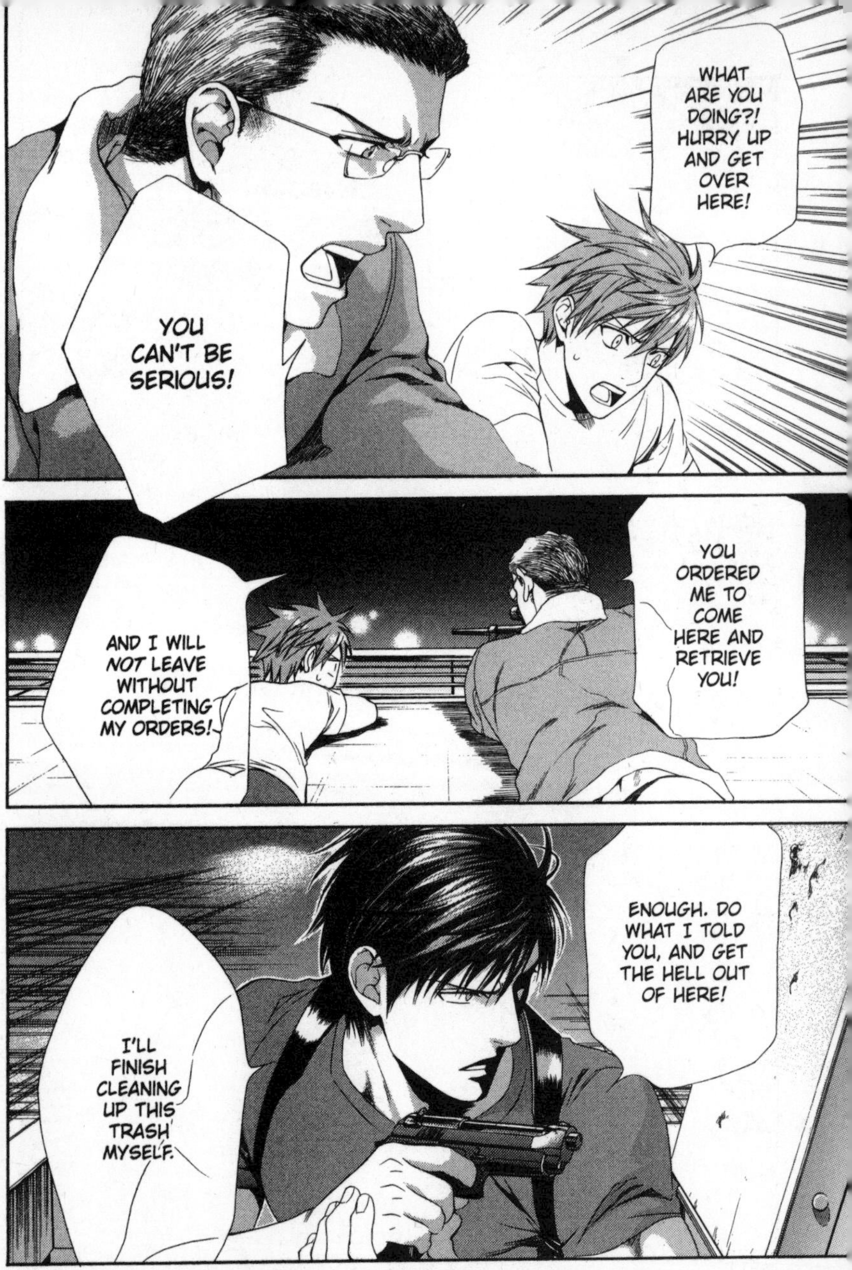
WHAT ARE YOU DOING?! HURRY UP AND GET OVER HERE!
YOU CAN'T BE SERIOUS!
YOU ORDERED ME TO COME HERE AND RETRIEVE YOU!
AND I WILL *NOT* LEAVE WITHOUT COMPLETING MY ORDERS!
ENOUGH. DO WHAT I TOLD YOU, AND GET THE HELL OUT OF HERE!
I'LL FINISH CLEANING UP THIS TRASH MYSELF.

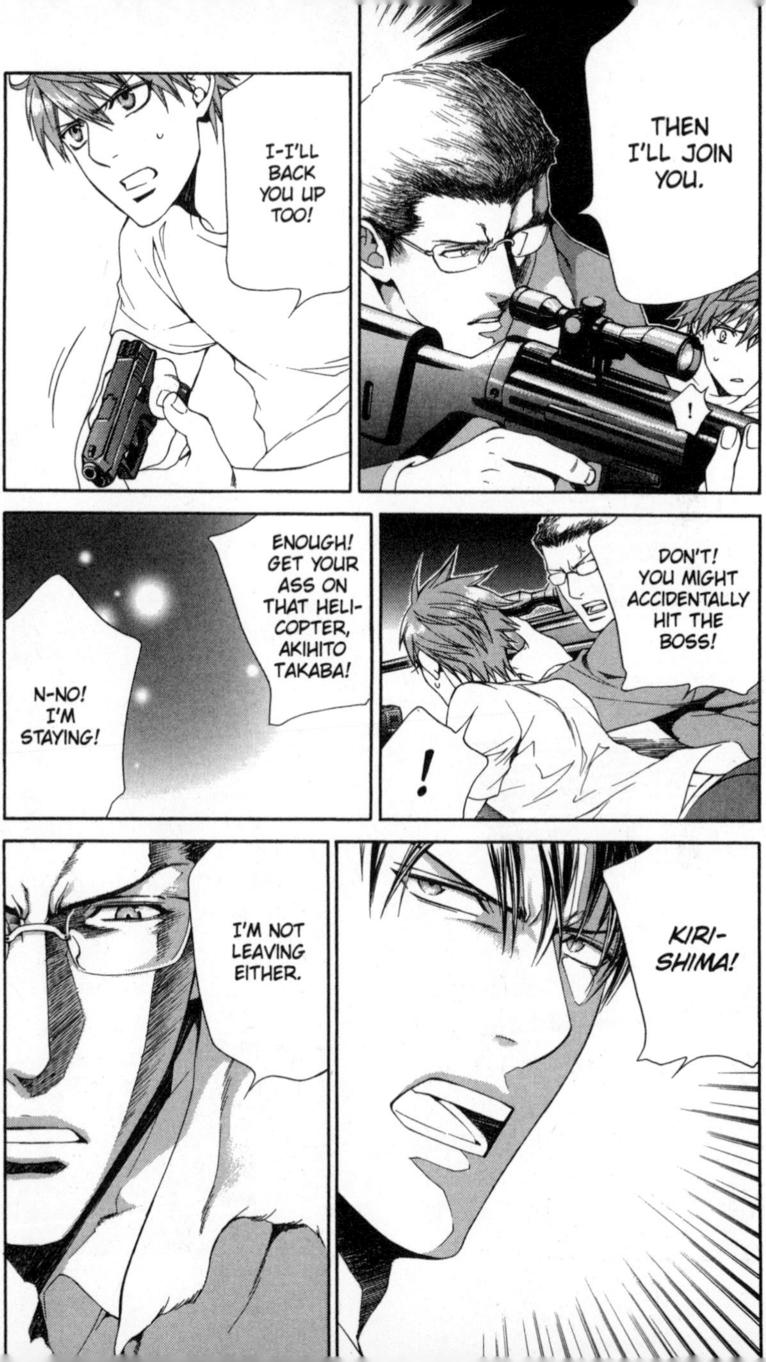
THEN I'LL JOIN YOU.
!
I-I'LL BACK YOU UP TOO!
DON'T! YOU MIGHT ACCIDENTALLY HIT THE BOSS!
!
ENOUGH! GET YOUR ASS ON THAT HELI-COPTER, AKIHITO TAKABA!
N-NO! I'M STAYING!
KIRI-SHIMA!
I'M NOT LEAVING EITHER.

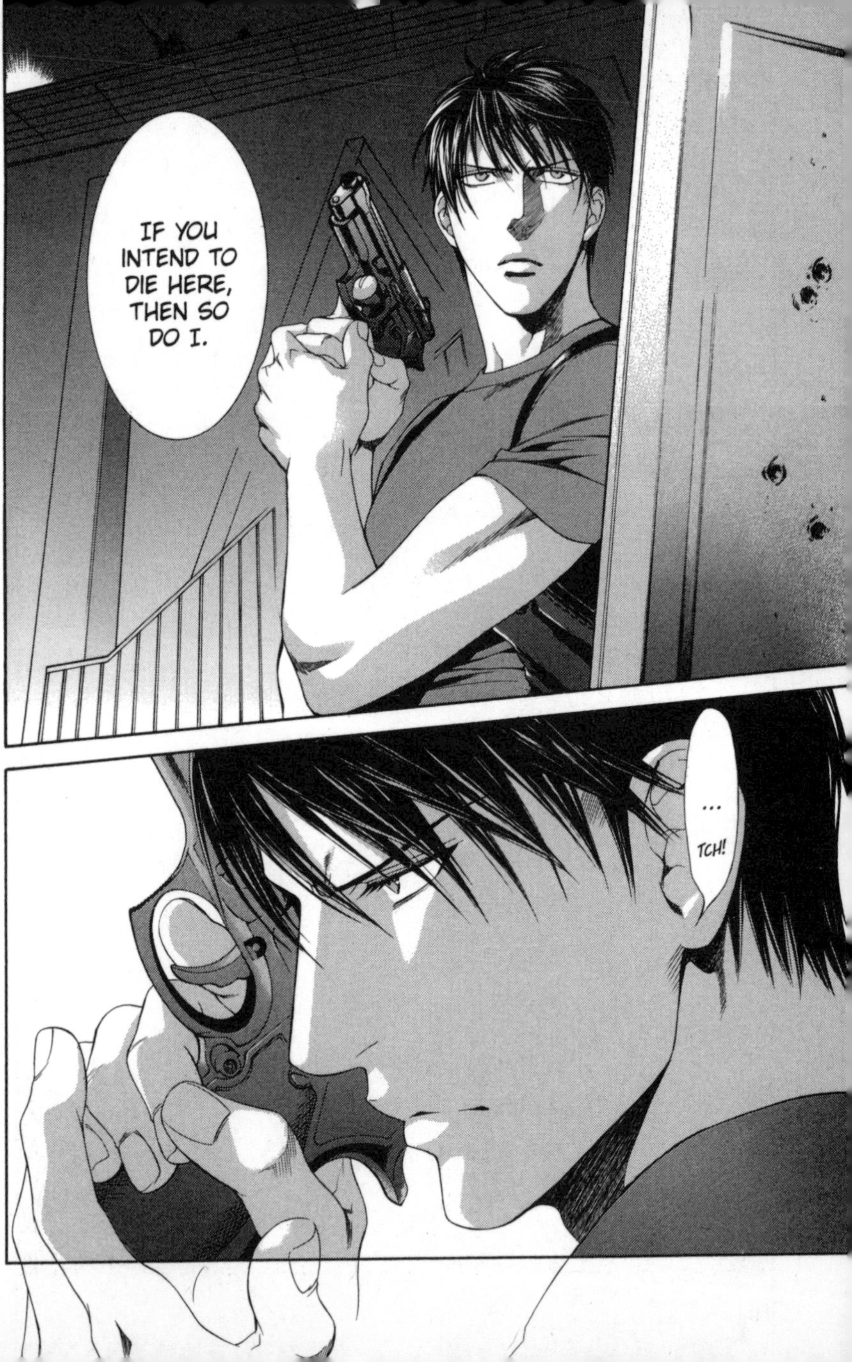
IF YOU INTEND TO DIE HERE, THEN SO DO I.
...
TCH!

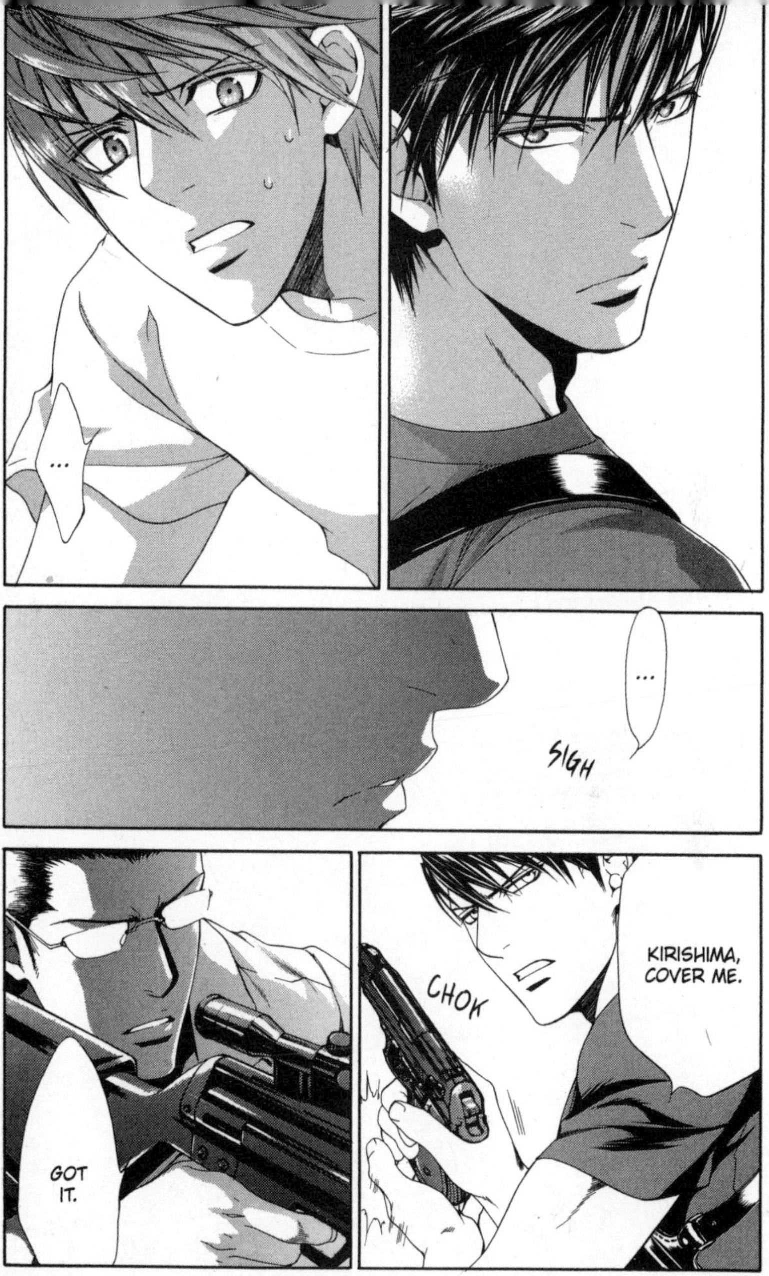
...
...
SIGH
KIRISHIMA, COVER ME.
CHOK
GOT IT.

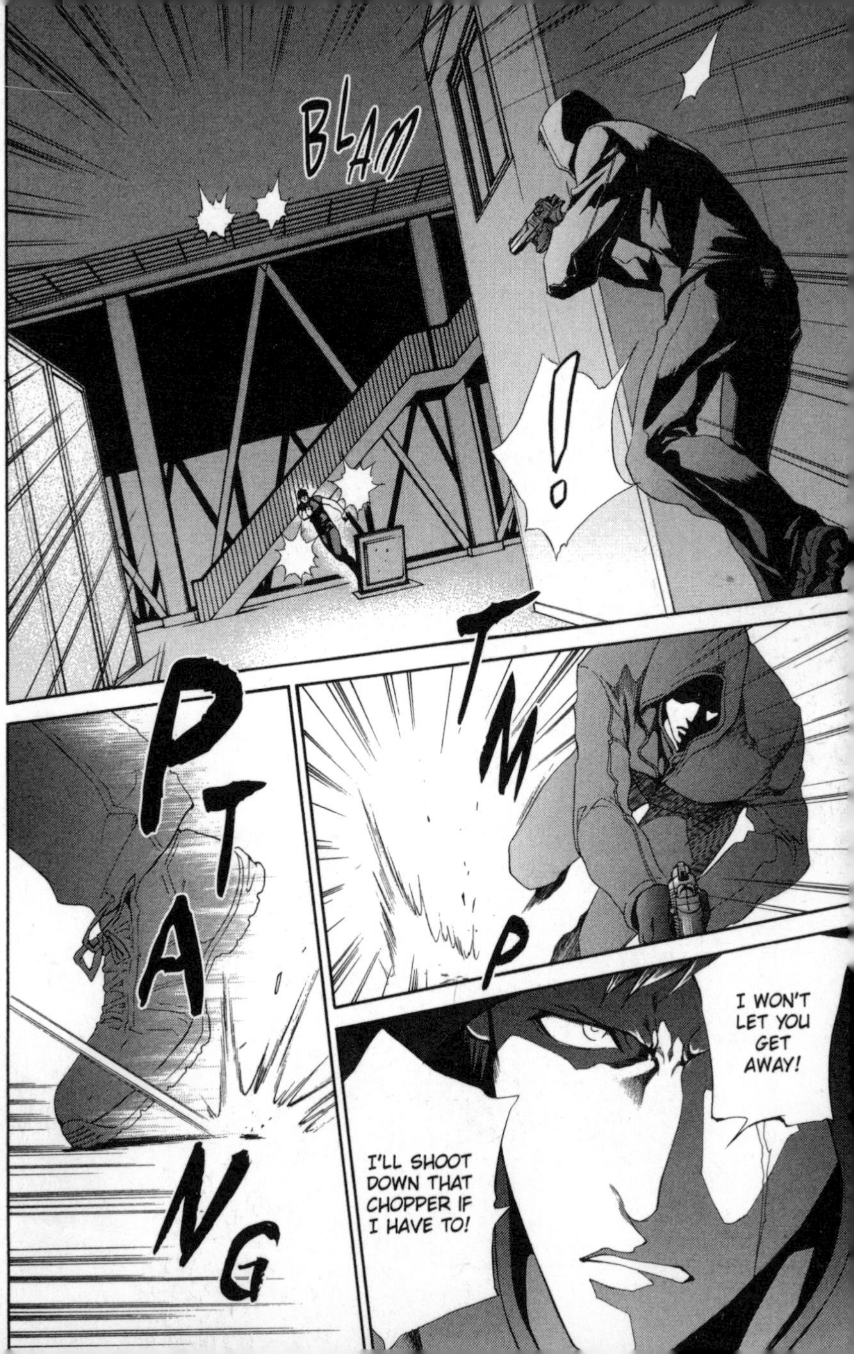
BLAM
!
TMP
PTANG
I WON'T LET YOU GET AWAY!
I'LL SHOOT DOWN THAT CHOPPER IF I HAVE TO!

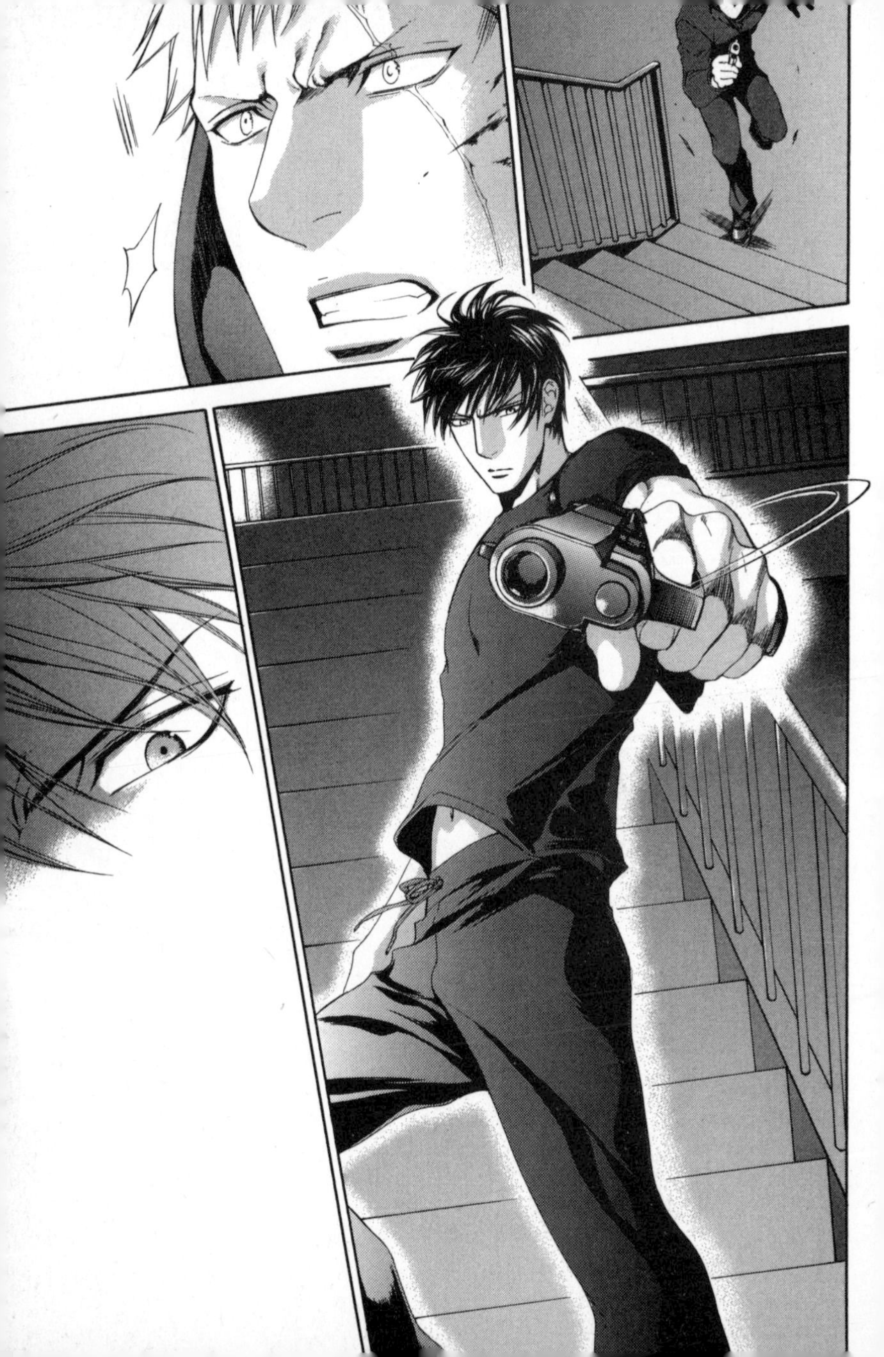

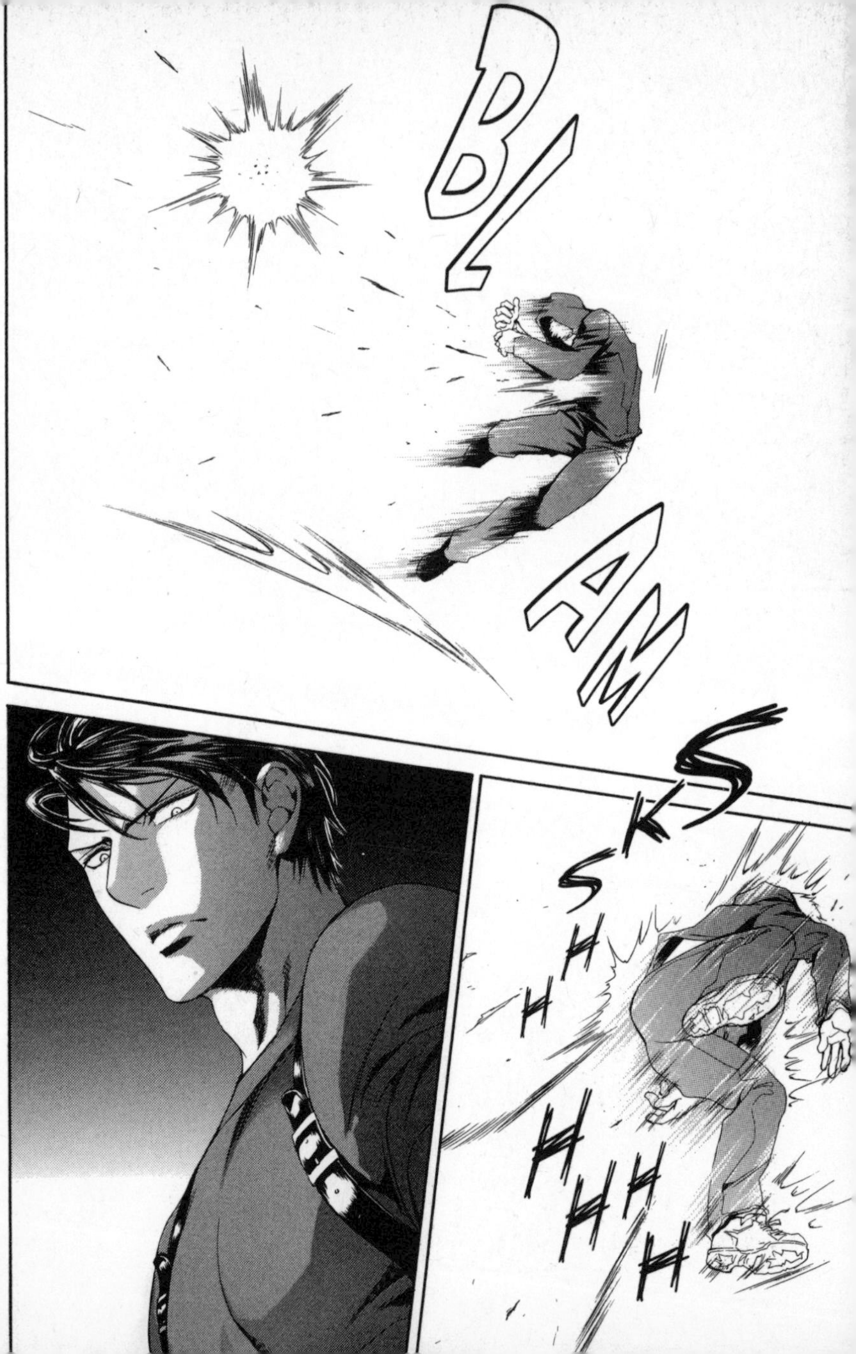
BLAM
SKSHHHHHH

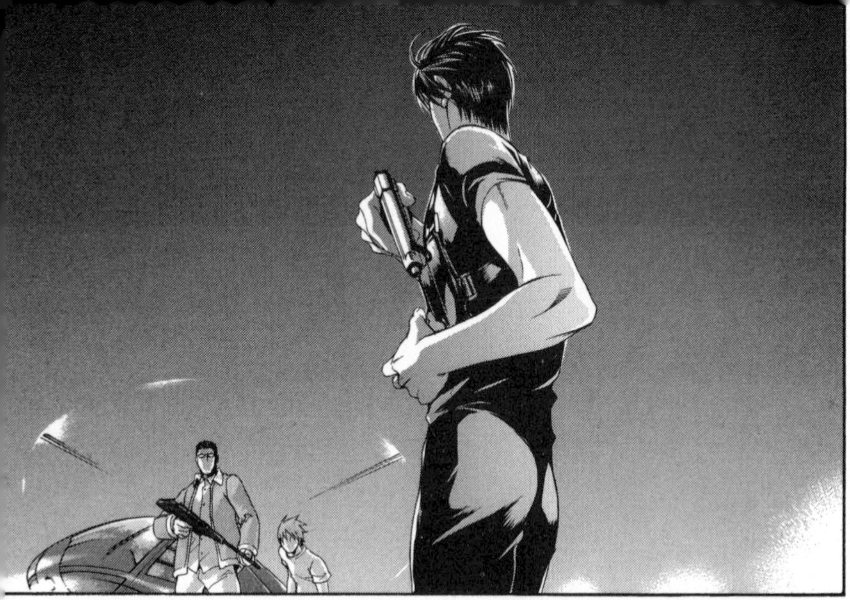
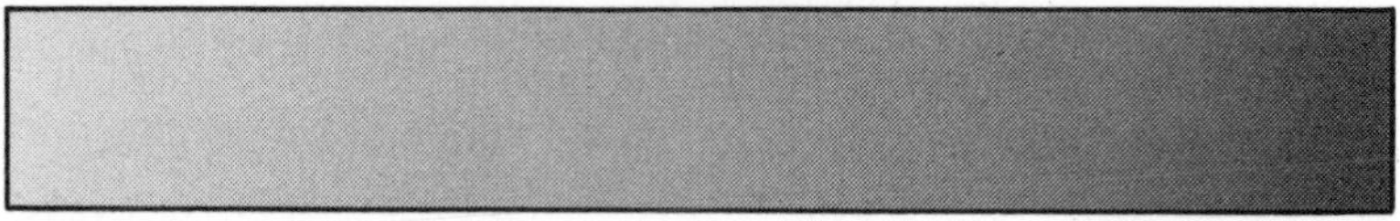
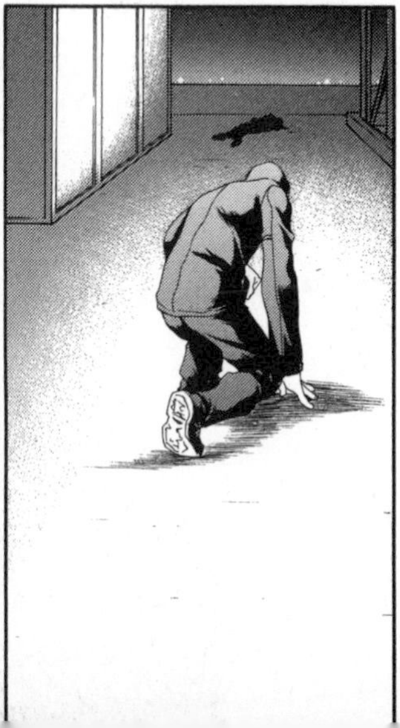
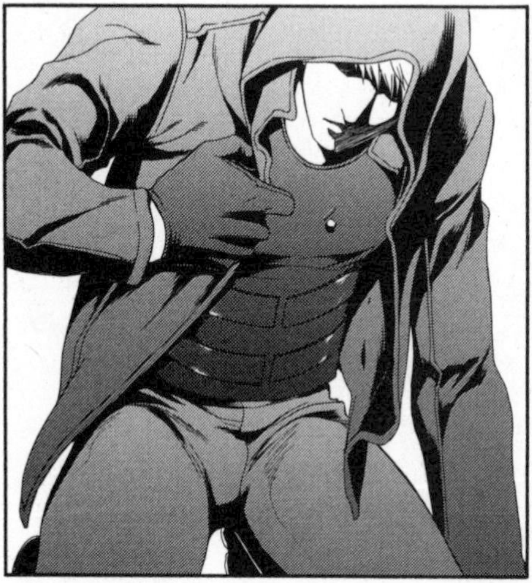

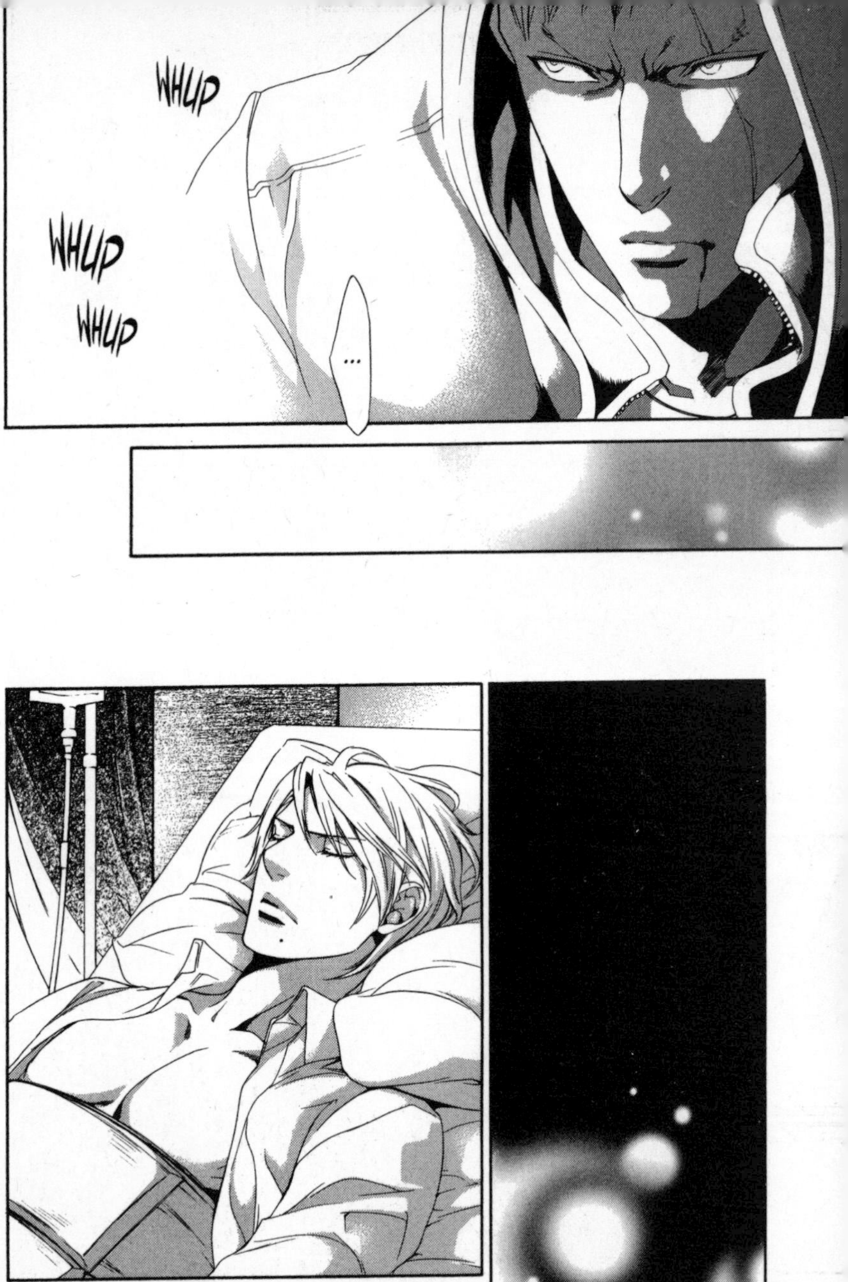
WHUP
...
WHUP
WHUP

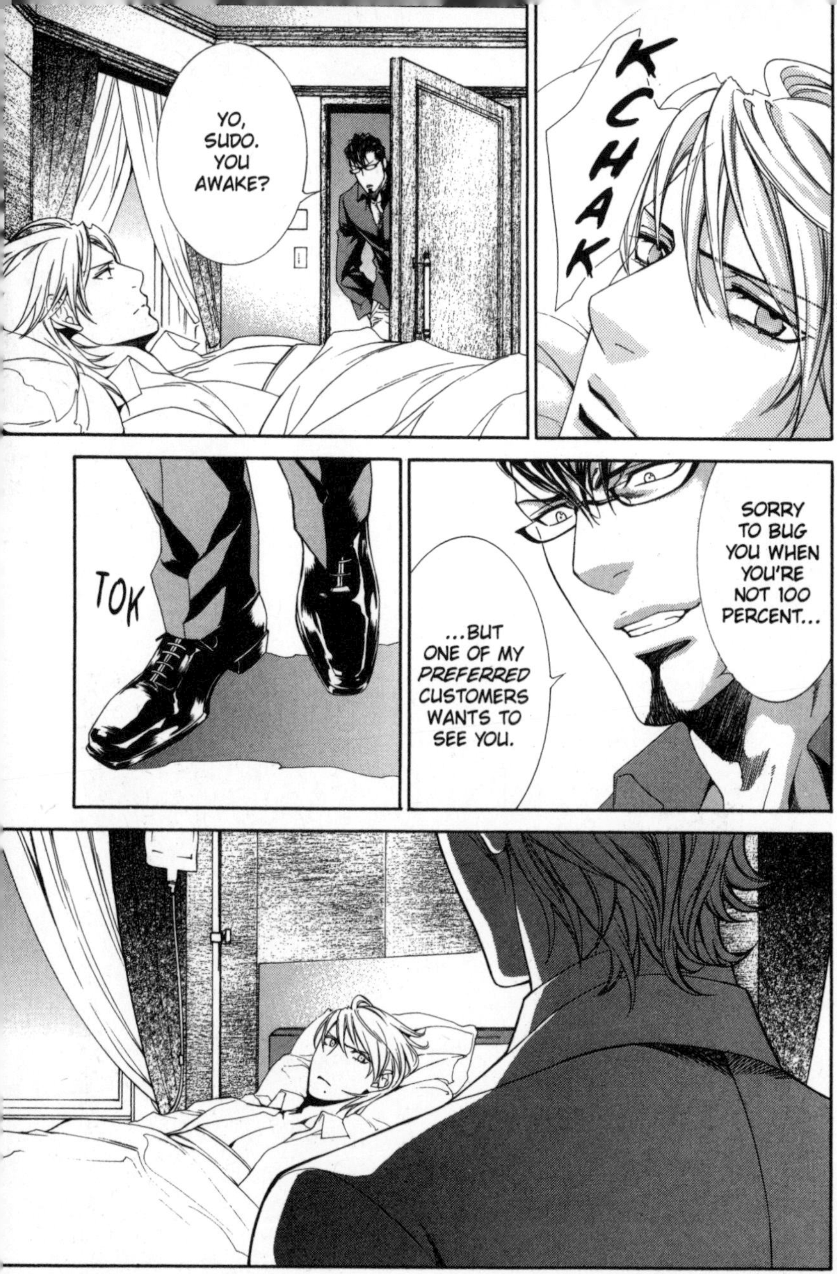
KCHAK
YO, SUDO. YOU AWAKE?
SORRY TO BUG YOU WHEN YOU'RE NOT 100 PERCENT...
...BUT ONE OF MY *PREFERRED* CUSTOMERS WANTS TO SEE YOU.
TOK

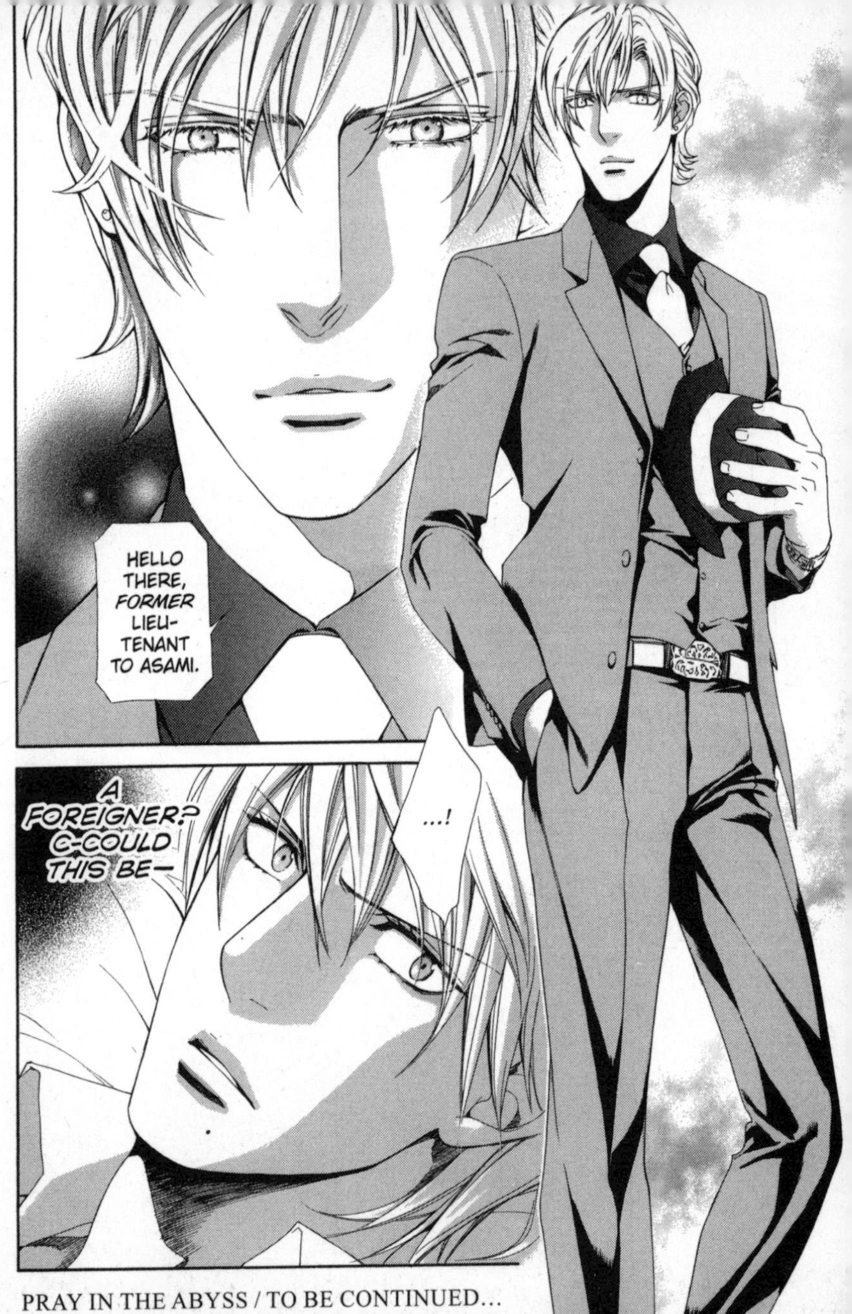
HELLO THERE, FORMER LIEU-TENANT TO ASAMI.
...!
A FOREIGNER? C-COULD THIS BE—

PRAY IN THE ABYSS / TO BE CONTINUED…

ブレイ
インアビス

Pray in the Abyss

Be Boy Gold, August 2015 Issue
20th Anniversary Congratulatory Message ▼

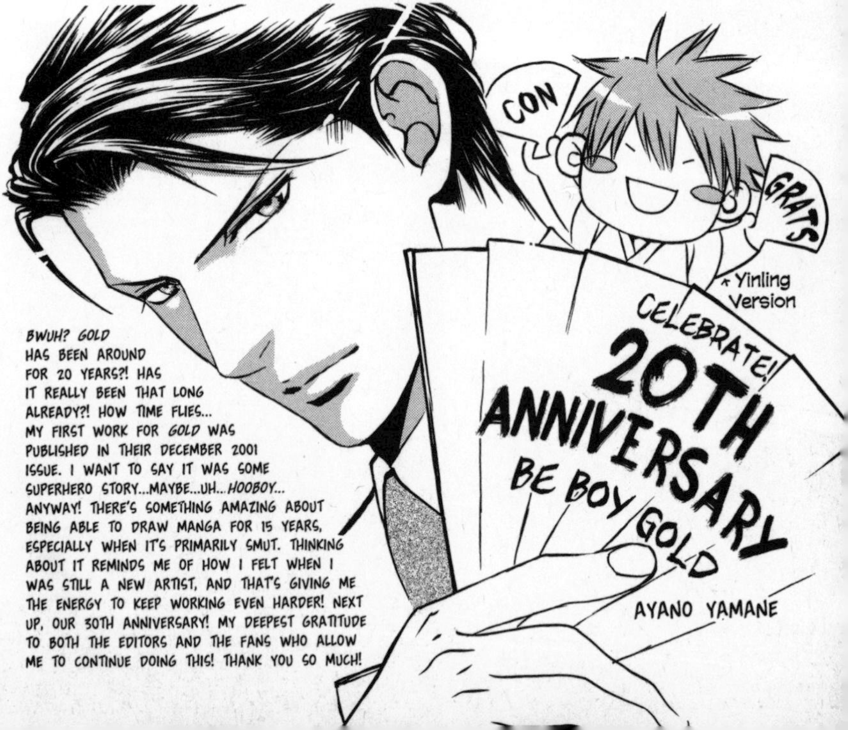
CON
GRATS
Yinling Version
CELEBRATE!
20TH ANNIVERSARY
BE BOY GOLD
BWUH? *GOLD* HAS BEEN AROUND FOR 20 YEARS?! HAS IT REALLY BEEN THAT LONG ALREADY?! HOW TIME FLIES... MY FIRST WORK FOR *GOLD* WAS PUBLISHED IN THEIR DECEMBER 2001 ISSUE. I WANT TO SAY IT WAS SOME SUPERHERO STORY...MAYBE...UH...*HOOBOY*... ANYWAY! THERE'S SOMETHING AMAZING ABOUT BEING ABLE TO DRAW MANGA FOR 15 YEARS, ESPECIALLY WHEN IT'S PRIMARILY SMUT. THINKING ABOUT IT REMINDS ME OF HOW I FELT WHEN I WAS STILL A NEW ARTIST, AND THAT'S GIVING ME THE ENERGY TO KEEP WORKING EVEN HARDER! NEXT UP, OUR 30TH ANNIVERSARY! MY DEEPEST GRATITUDE TO BOTH THE EDITORS AND THE FANS WHO ALLOW ME TO CONTINUE DOING THIS! THANK YOU SO MUCH!
AYANO YAMANE

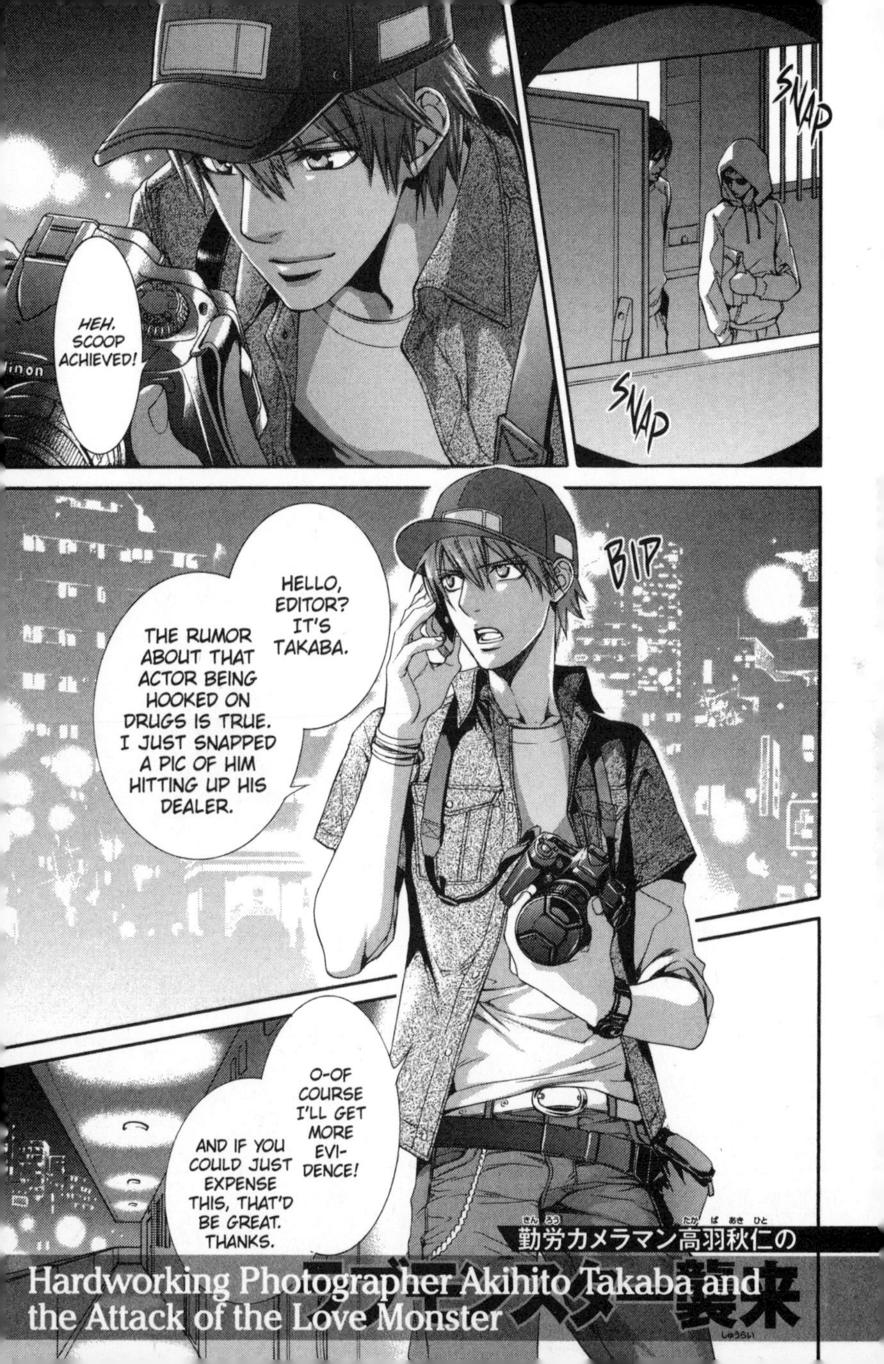
SNAP
SNAP
HEH. SCOOP ACHIEVED!
inon
BIP
HELLO, EDITOR? IT'S TAKABA.
THE RUMOR ABOUT THAT ACTOR BEING HOOKED ON DRUGS IS TRUE. I JUST SNAPPED A PIC OF HIM HITTING UP HIS DEALER.
O-OF COURSE I'LL GET MORE EVI-DENCE!
AND IF YOU COULD JUST EXPENSE THIS, THAT'D BE GREAT. THANKS.
勤労カメラマン高羽秋仁の
襲来
Hardworking Photographer Akihito Takaba and the Attack of the Love Monster

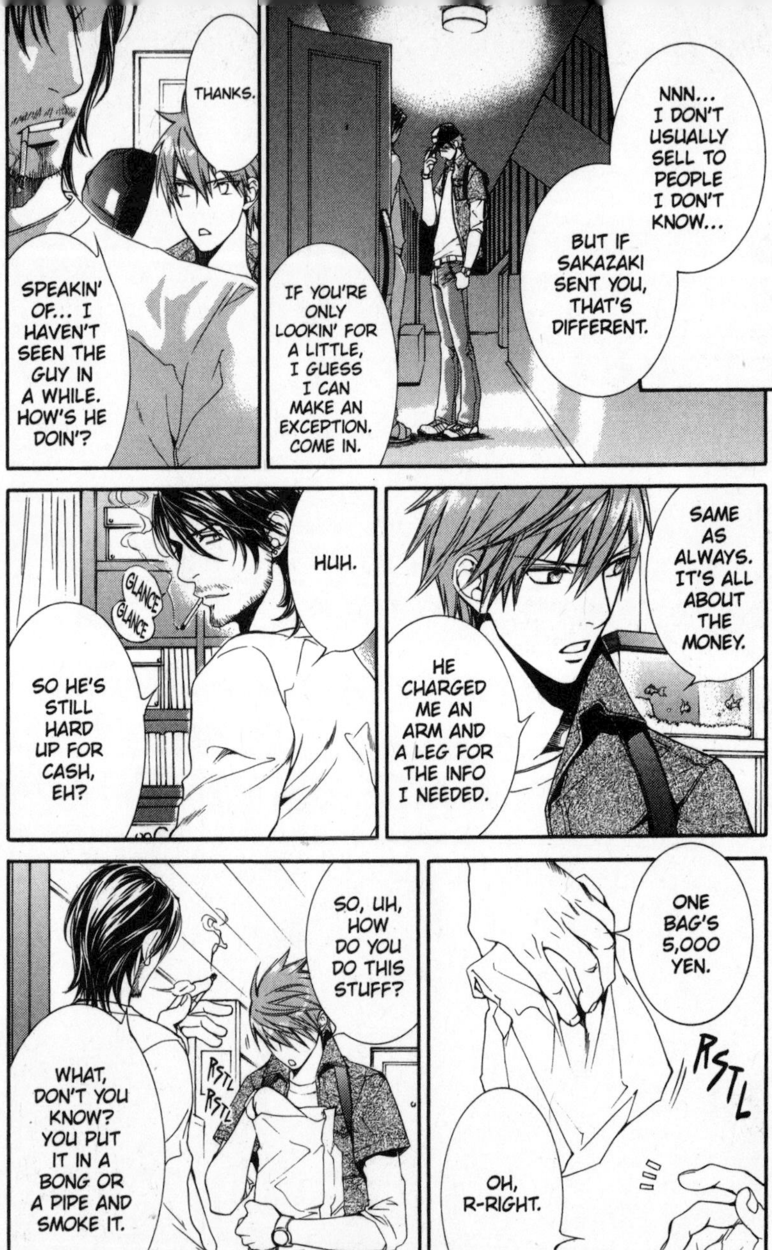
NNN... I DON'T USUALLY SELL TO PEOPLE I DON'T KNOW...
BUT IF SAKAZAKI SENT YOU, THAT'S DIFFERENT.
IF YOU'RE ONLY LOOKIN' FOR A LITTLE, I GUESS I CAN MAKE AN EXCEPTION. COME IN.
THANKS.
SPEAKIN' OF... I HAVEN'T SEEN THE GUY IN A WHILE. HOW'S HE DOIN'?
SAME AS ALWAYS. IT'S ALL ABOUT THE MONEY.
HE CHARGED ME AN ARM AND A LEG FOR THE INFO I NEEDED.
HUH.
GLANCE GLANCE
SO HE'S STILL HARD UP FOR CASH, EH?
ONE BAG'S 5,000 YEN.
RSTL
OH, R-RIGHT.
SO, UH, HOW DO YOU DO THIS STUFF?
RSTL RSTL
WHAT, DON'T YOU KNOW? YOU PUT IT IN A BONG OR A PIPE AND SMOKE IT.

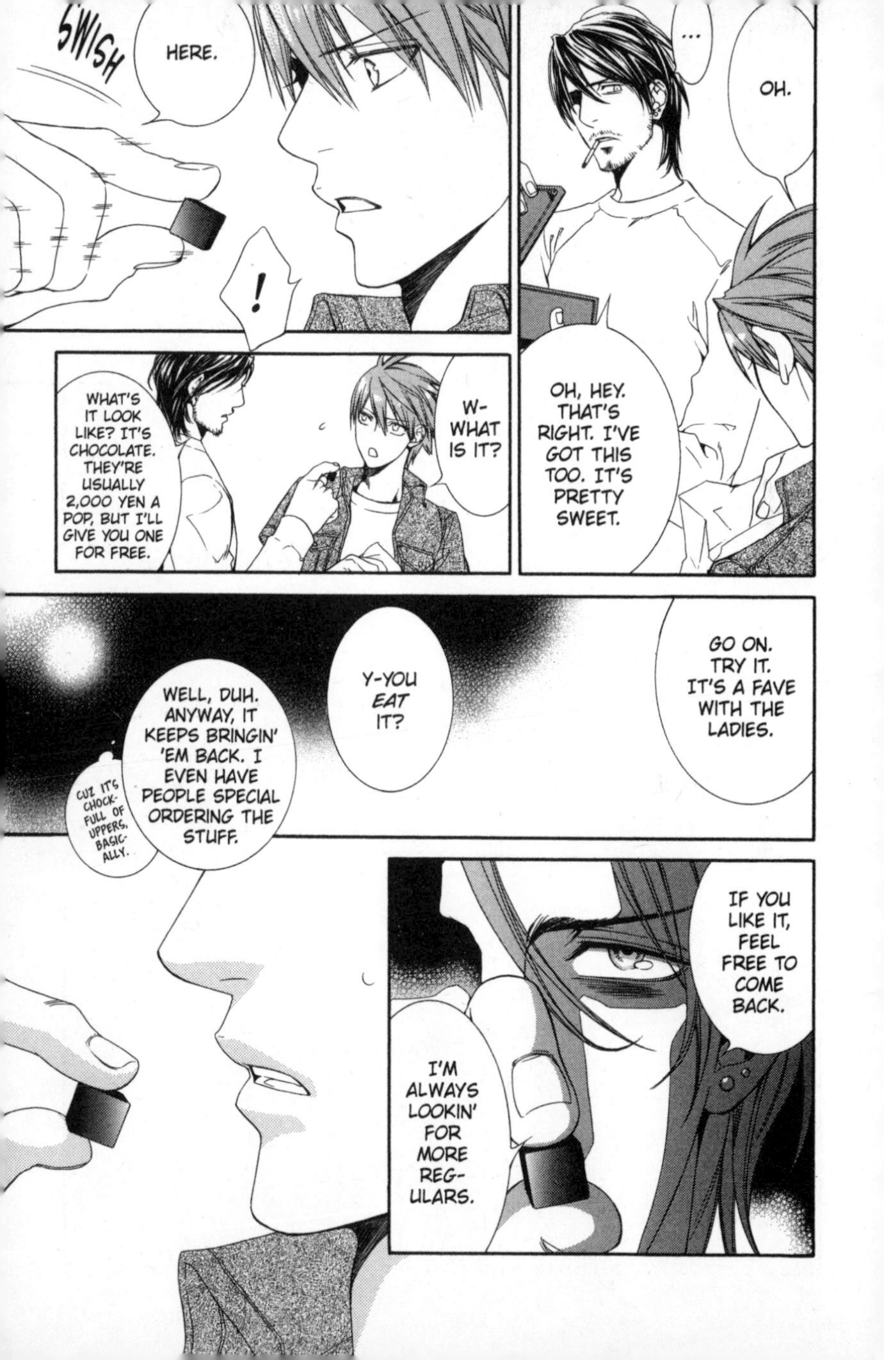
...
OH.
OH, HEY. THAT'S RIGHT. I'VE GOT THIS TOO. IT'S PRETTY SWEET.
HERE.
SWISH
!
W-WHAT IS IT?
WHAT'S IT LOOK LIKE? IT'S CHOCOLATE. THEY'RE USUALLY 2,000 YEN A POP, BUT I'LL GIVE YOU ONE FOR FREE.
GO ON. TRY IT. IT'S A FAVE WITH THE LADIES.
Y-YOU *EAT* IT?
WELL, DUH. ANYWAY, IT KEEPS BRINGIN' 'EM BACK. I EVEN HAVE PEOPLE SPECIAL ORDERING THE STUFF.
CUZ IT'S CHOCK-FULL OF UPPERS, BASIC-ALLY.
IF YOU LIKE IT, FEEL FREE TO COME BACK.
I'M ALWAYS LOOKIN' FOR MORE REG-ULARS.

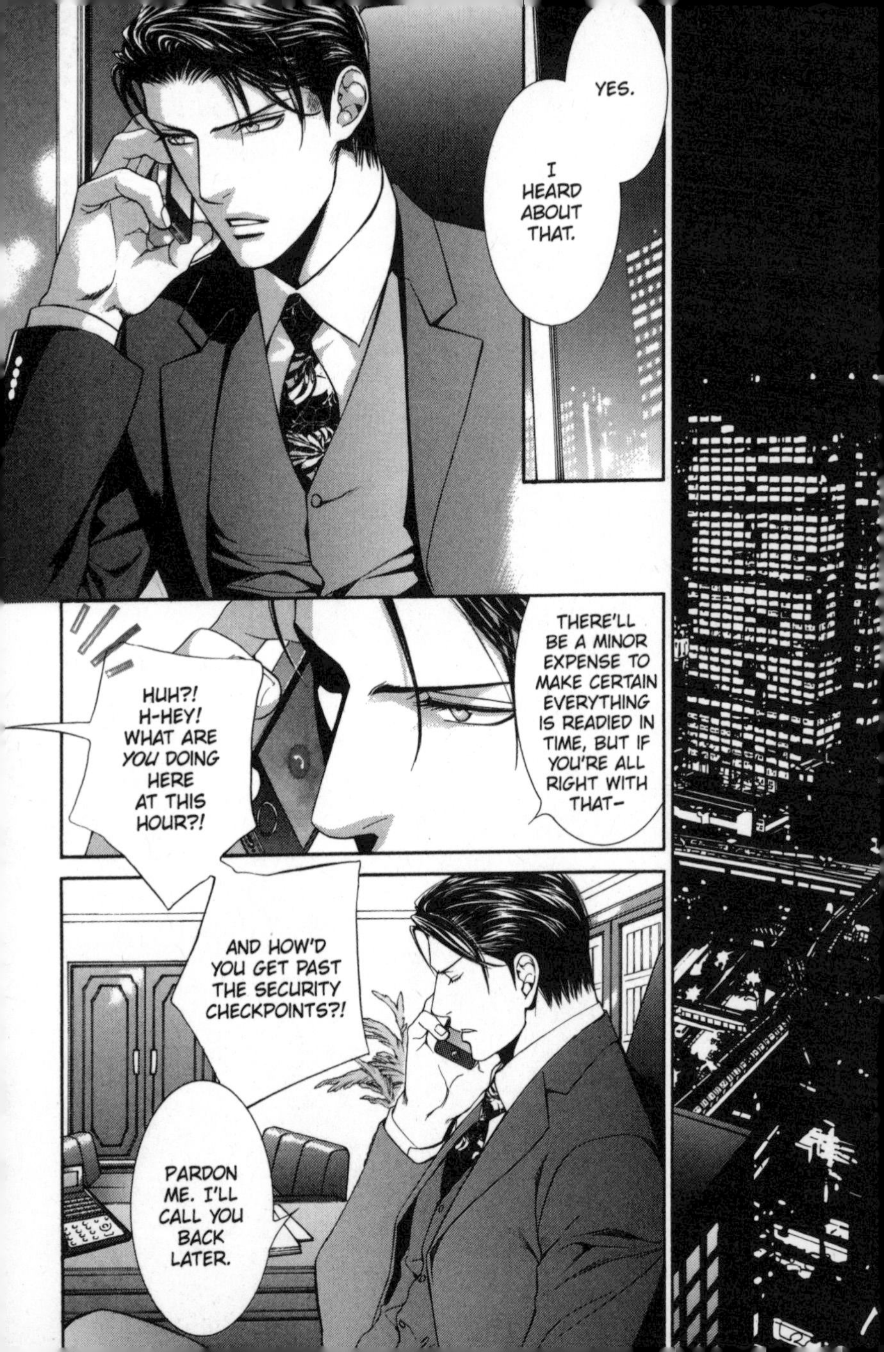
YES.
I HEARD ABOUT THAT.
THERE'LL BE A MINOR EXPENSE TO MAKE CERTAIN EVERYTHING IS READIED IN TIME, BUT IF YOU'RE ALL RIGHT WITH THAT–
HUH?! H-HEY! WHAT ARE *YOU* DOING HERE AT THIS HOUR?!
AND HOW'D YOU GET PAST THE SECURITY CHECKPOINTS?!
PARDON ME. I'LL CALL YOU BACK LATER.

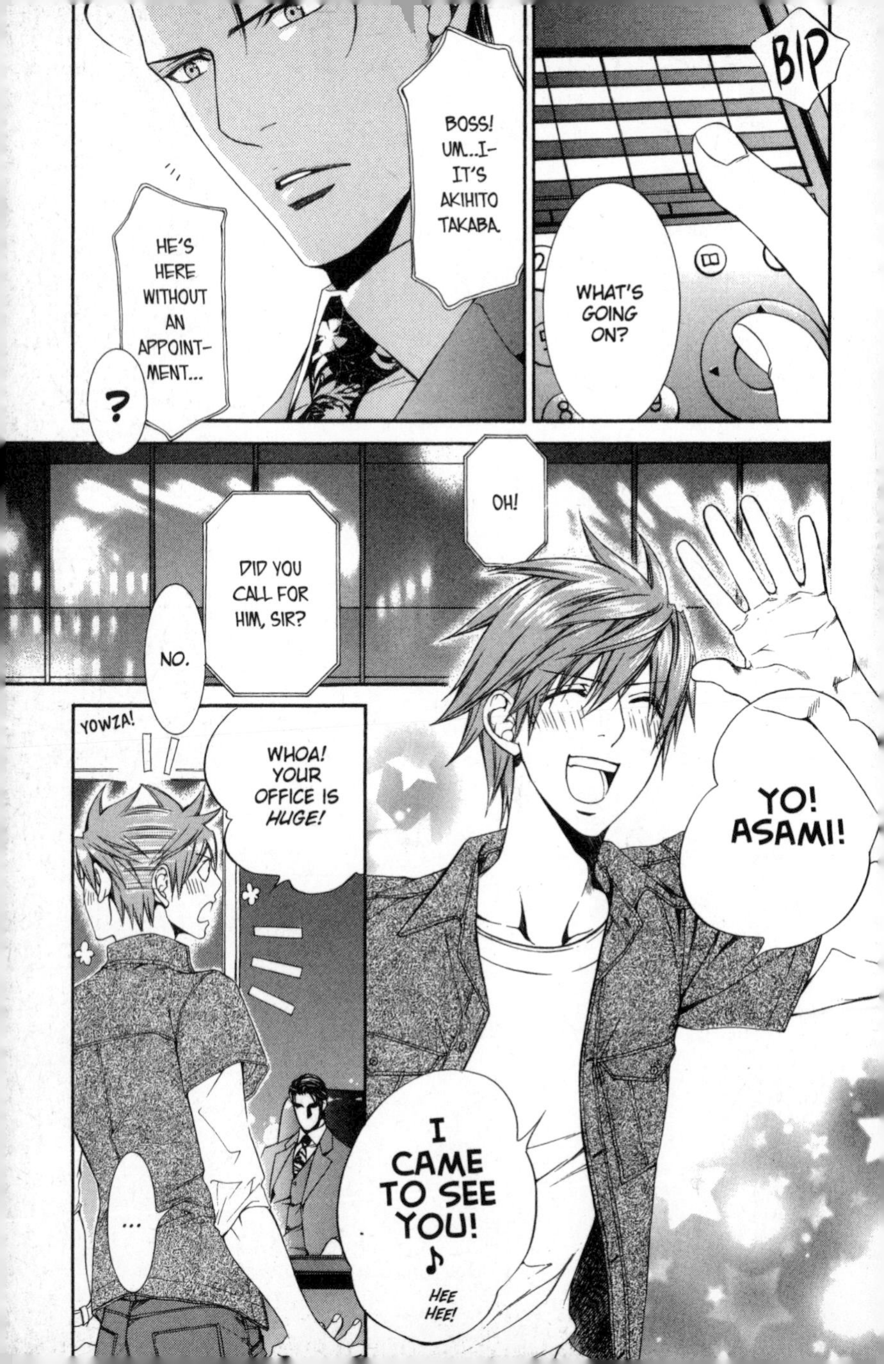
BIP
WHAT'S GOING ON?
BOSS! UM...I-IT'S AKIHITO TAKABA.
HE'S HERE WITHOUT AN APPOINT-MENT...
?
OH!
DID YOU CALL FOR HIM, SIR?
NO.
YO! ASAMI!
I CAME TO SEE YOU! ♪
HEE HEE!
YOWZA!
WHOA! YOUR OFFICE IS HUGE!
...

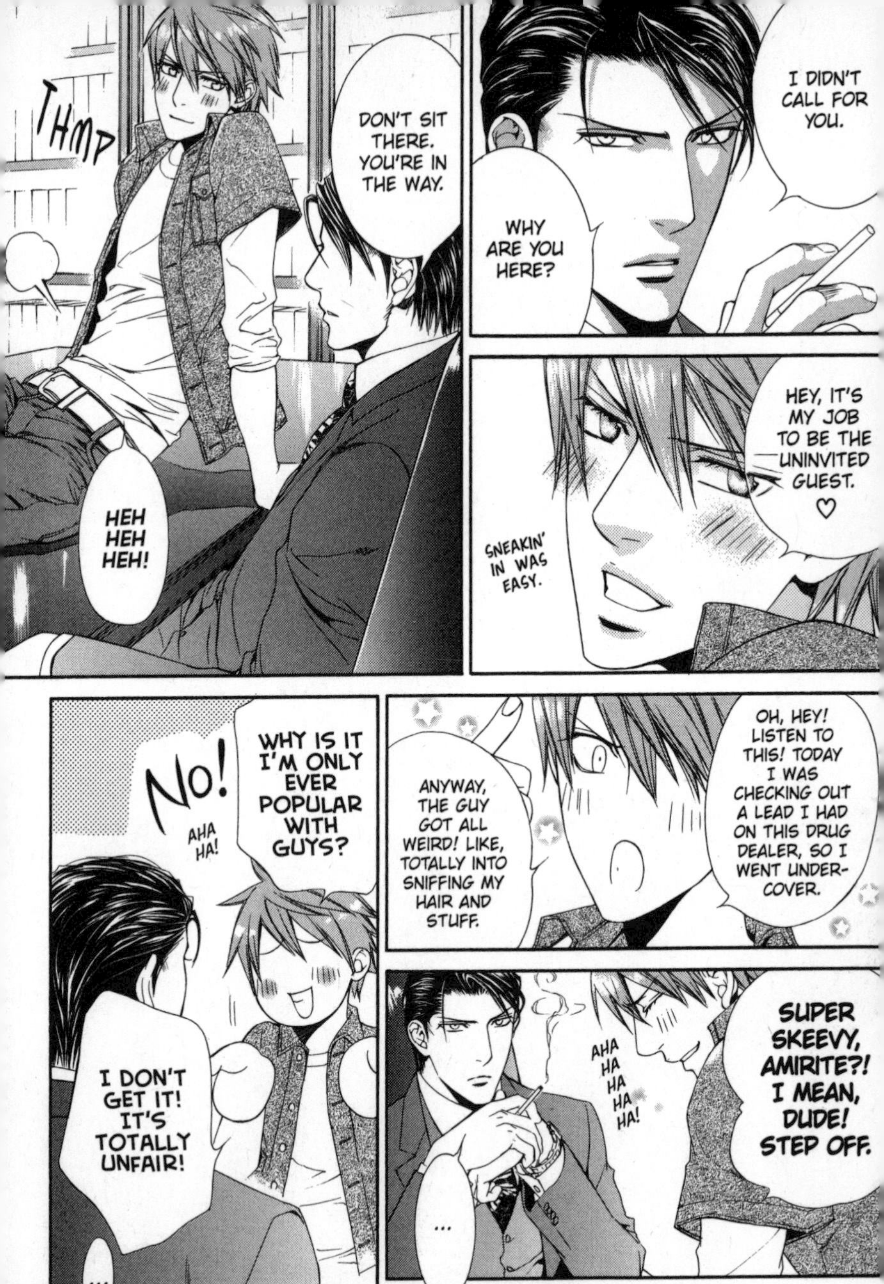
I DIDN'T CALL FOR YOU.
WHY ARE YOU HERE?
HEY, IT'S MY JOB TO BE THE UNINVITED GUEST. ♡
SNEAKIN' IN WAS EASY.
THMP
DON'T SIT THERE. YOU'RE IN THE WAY.
HEH HEH HEH!
OH, HEY! LISTEN TO THIS! TODAY I WAS CHECKING OUT A LEAD I HAD ON THIS DRUG DEALER, SO I WENT UNDER-COVER.
ANYWAY, THE GUY GOT ALL WEIRD! LIKE, TOTALLY INTO SNIFFING MY HAIR AND STUFF.
SUPER SKEEVY, AMIRITE?! I MEAN, DUDE! STEP OFF.
AHA HA HA HA HA!
...
WHY IS IT I'M ONLY EVER POPULAR WITH GUYS?
No!
AHA HA!
I DON'T GET IT! IT'S TOTALLY UNFAIR!
...

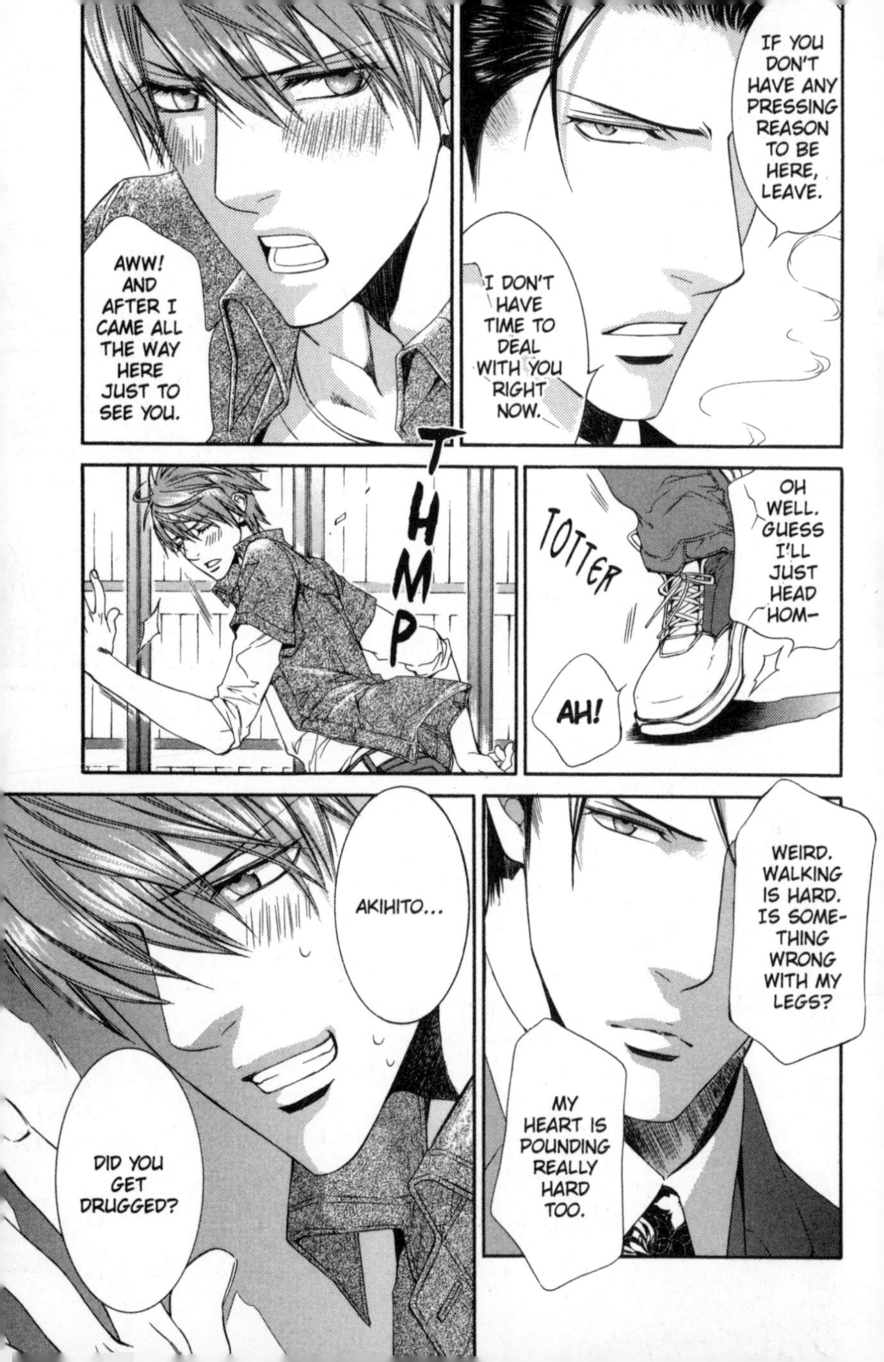
IF YOU DON'T HAVE ANY PRESSING REASON TO BE HERE, LEAVE.
I DON'T HAVE TIME TO DEAL WITH YOU RIGHT NOW.
AWW! AND AFTER I CAME ALL THE WAY HERE JUST TO SEE YOU.
TOTTER
OH WELL. GUESS I'LL JUST HEAD HOM-
AH!
THMP
WEIRD. WALKING IS HARD. IS SOME-THING WRONG WITH MY LEGS?
MY HEART IS POUNDING REALLY HARD TOO.
AKIHITO...
DID YOU GET DRUGGED?

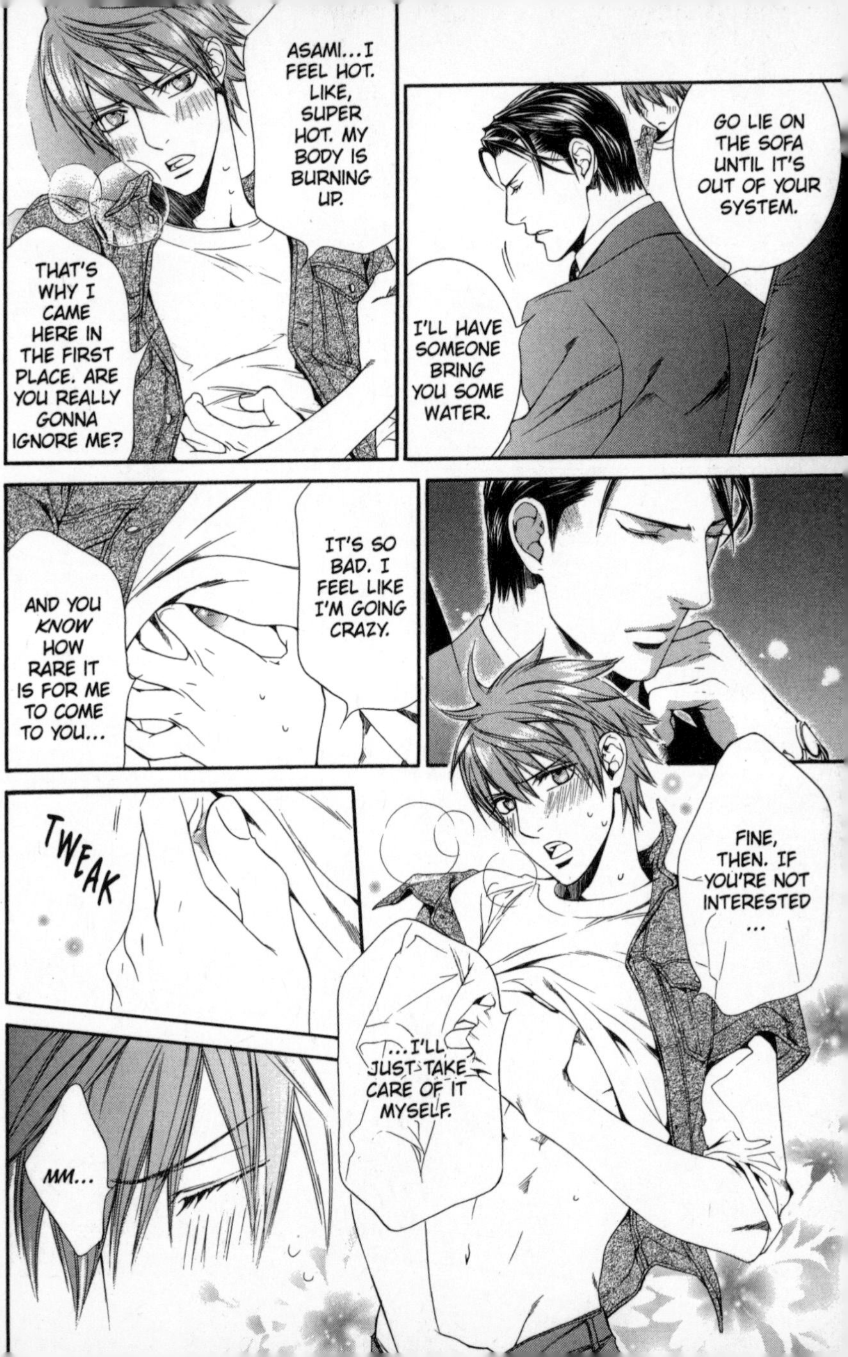
GO LIE ON THE SOFA UNTIL IT'S OUT OF YOUR SYSTEM.
I'LL HAVE SOMEONE BRING YOU SOME WATER.
ASAMI...I FEEL HOT. LIKE, SUPER HOT. MY BODY IS BURNING UP.
THAT'S WHY I CAME HERE IN THE FIRST PLACE. ARE YOU REALLY GONNA IGNORE ME?
IT'S SO BAD. I FEEL LIKE I'M GOING CRAZY.
AND YOU *KNOW* HOW RARE IT IS FOR ME TO COME TO YOU...
FINE, THEN. IF YOU'RE NOT INTERESTED ...
...I'LL JUST TAKE CARE OF IT MYSELF.
TWEAK
MM...

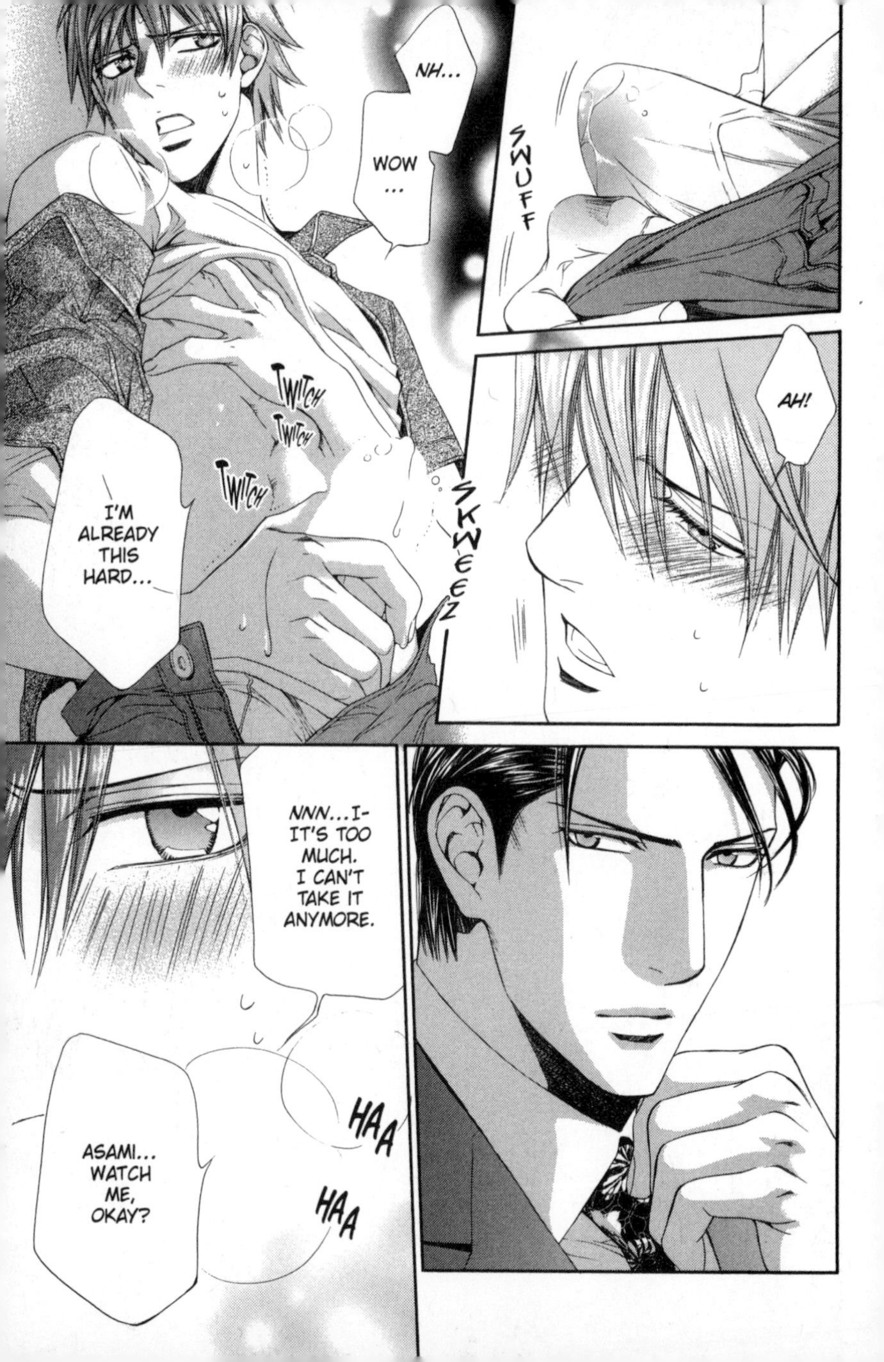
SWUFF
AH!
NH...
WOW...
TWITCH
TWITCH
TWITCH
SKWEEZ
I'M ALREADY THIS HARD...
NNN...I- IT'S TOO MUCH. I CAN'T TAKE IT ANYMORE.
HAA
HAA
ASAMI... WATCH ME, OKAY?

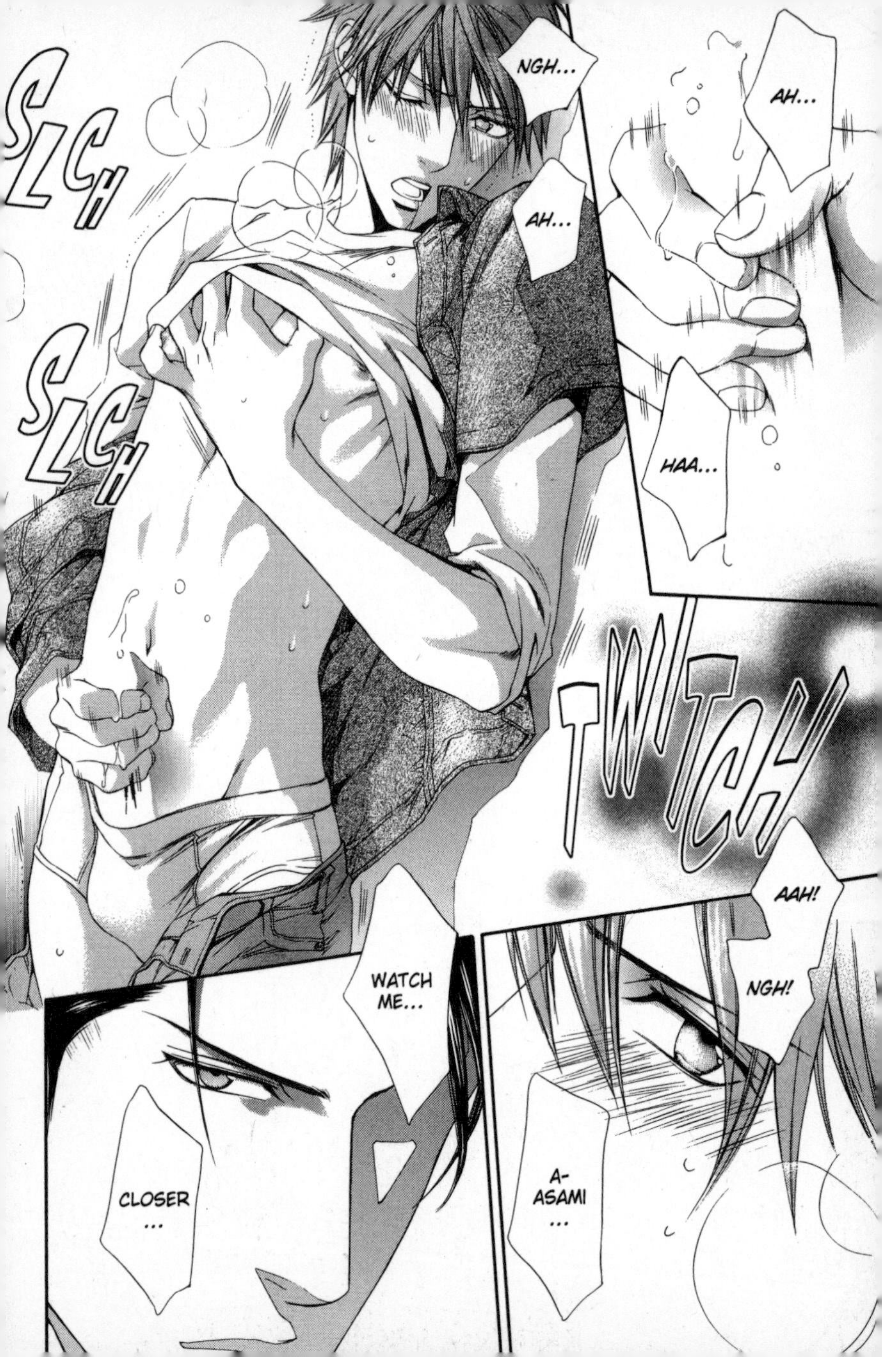
AH...
HAA...
NGH...
AH...
TWITCH
SLCH
SLCH
AAH!
NGH!
A-ASAMI...
WATCH ME...
CLOSER...

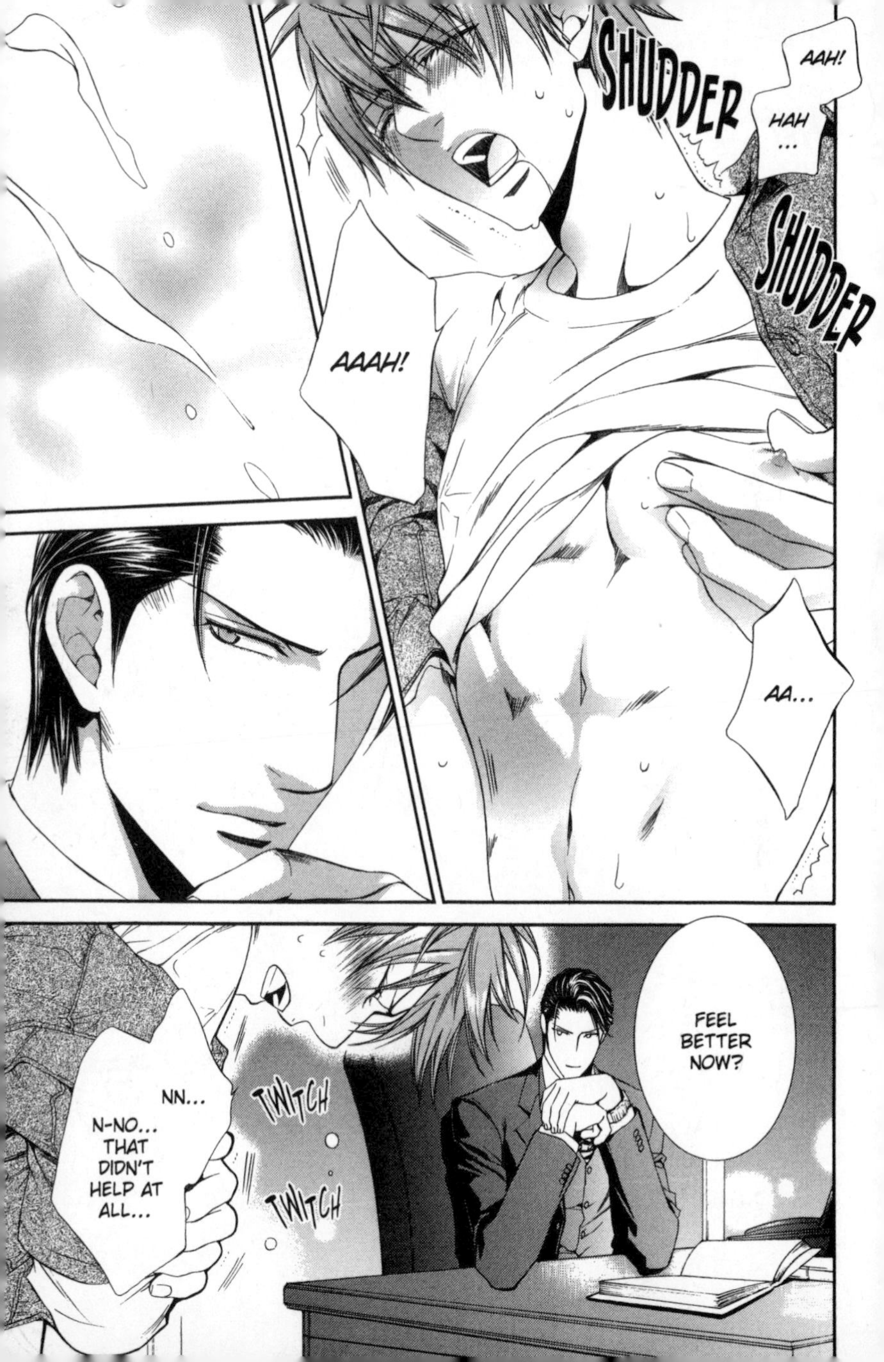
AAH!
SHUDDER
HAH ...
SHUDDER
AAAH!
AA...
FEEL BETTER NOW?
TWITCH
TWITCH
NN...
N-NO... THAT DIDN'T HELP AT ALL...

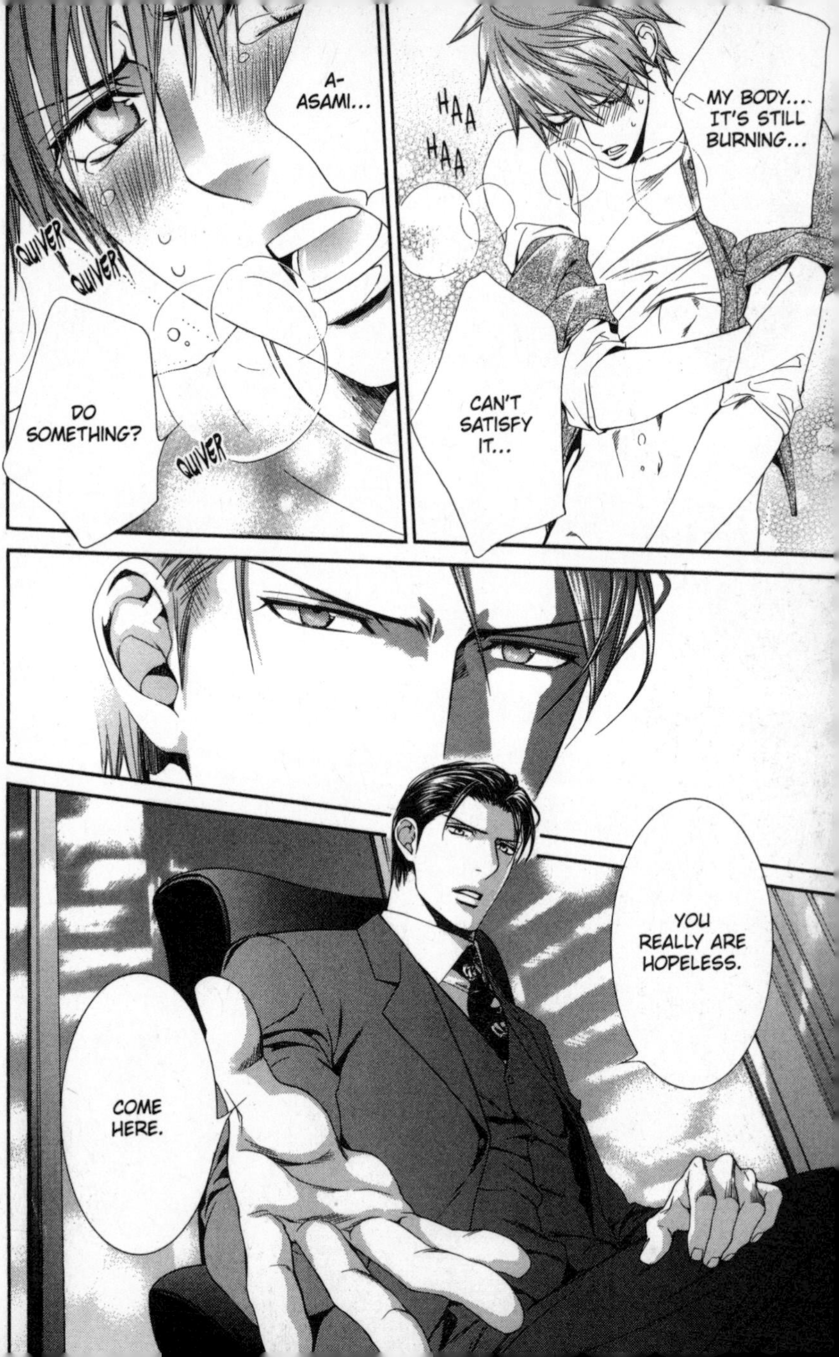
MY BODY... IT'S STILL BURNING...
HAA HAA
CAN'T SATISFY IT...
A-ASAMI...
QUIVER QUIVER
DO SOMETHING?
QUIVER
YOU REALLY ARE HOPELESS.
COME HERE.

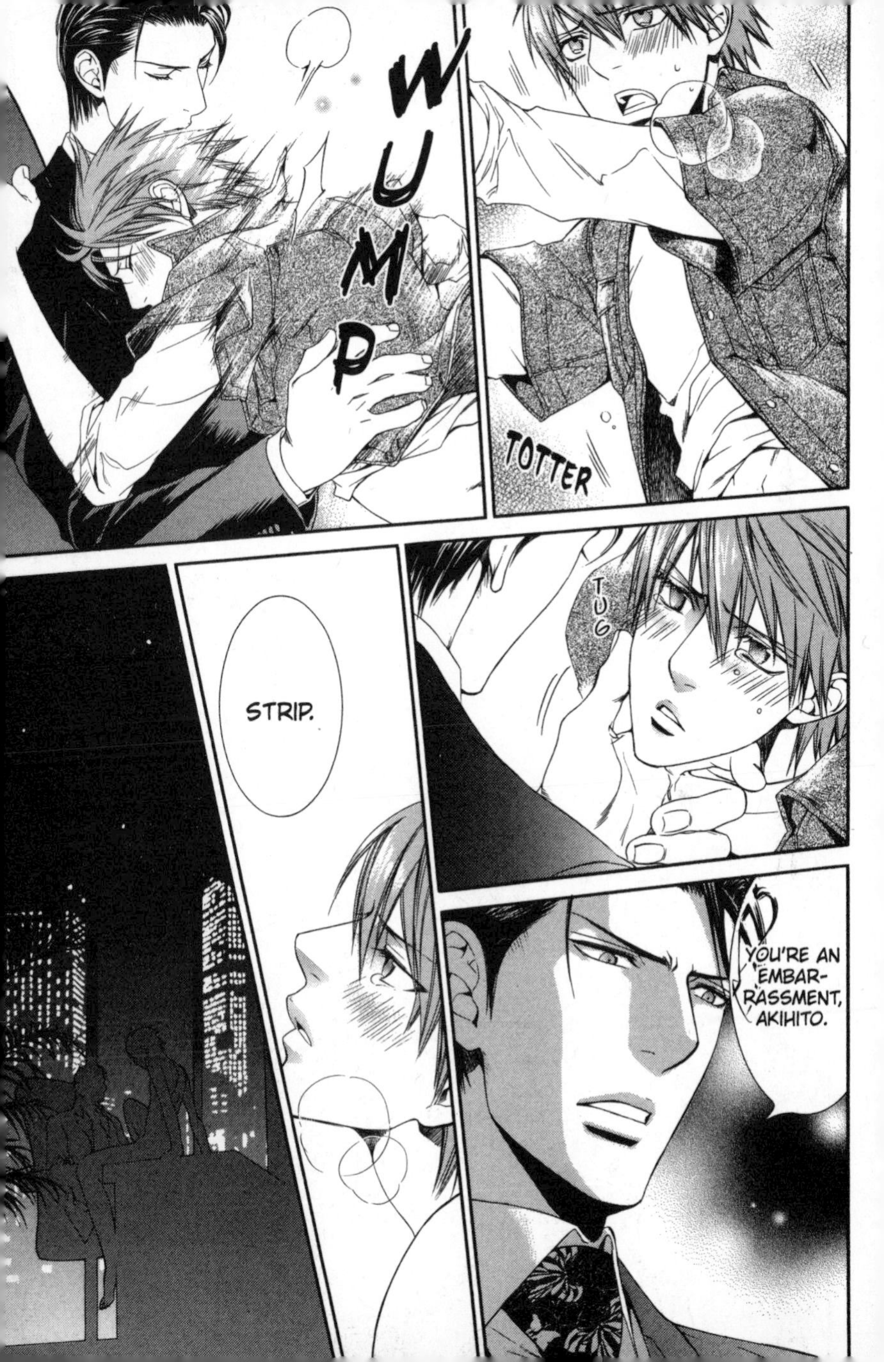
TOTTER
WUMP
TUG
YOU'RE AN EMBAR-RASSMENT, AKIHITO.
STRIP.

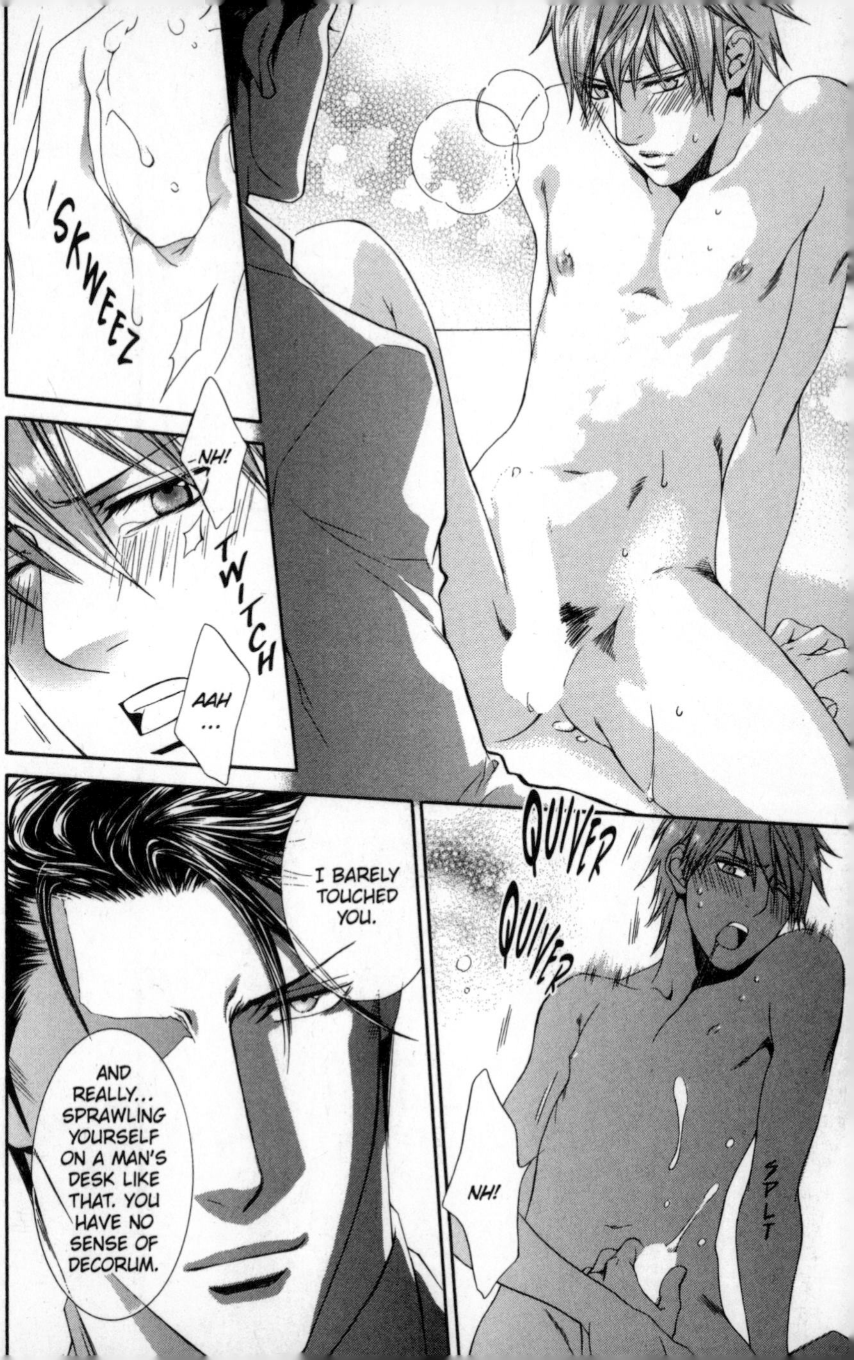
SKWEEZ
NH!
TWITCH
AAH ...
QUIVER
QUIVER
NH!
SPLT
I BARELY TOUCHED YOU.
AND REALLY... SPRAWLING YOURSELF ON A MAN'S DESK LIKE THAT. YOU HAVE NO SENSE OF DECORUM.

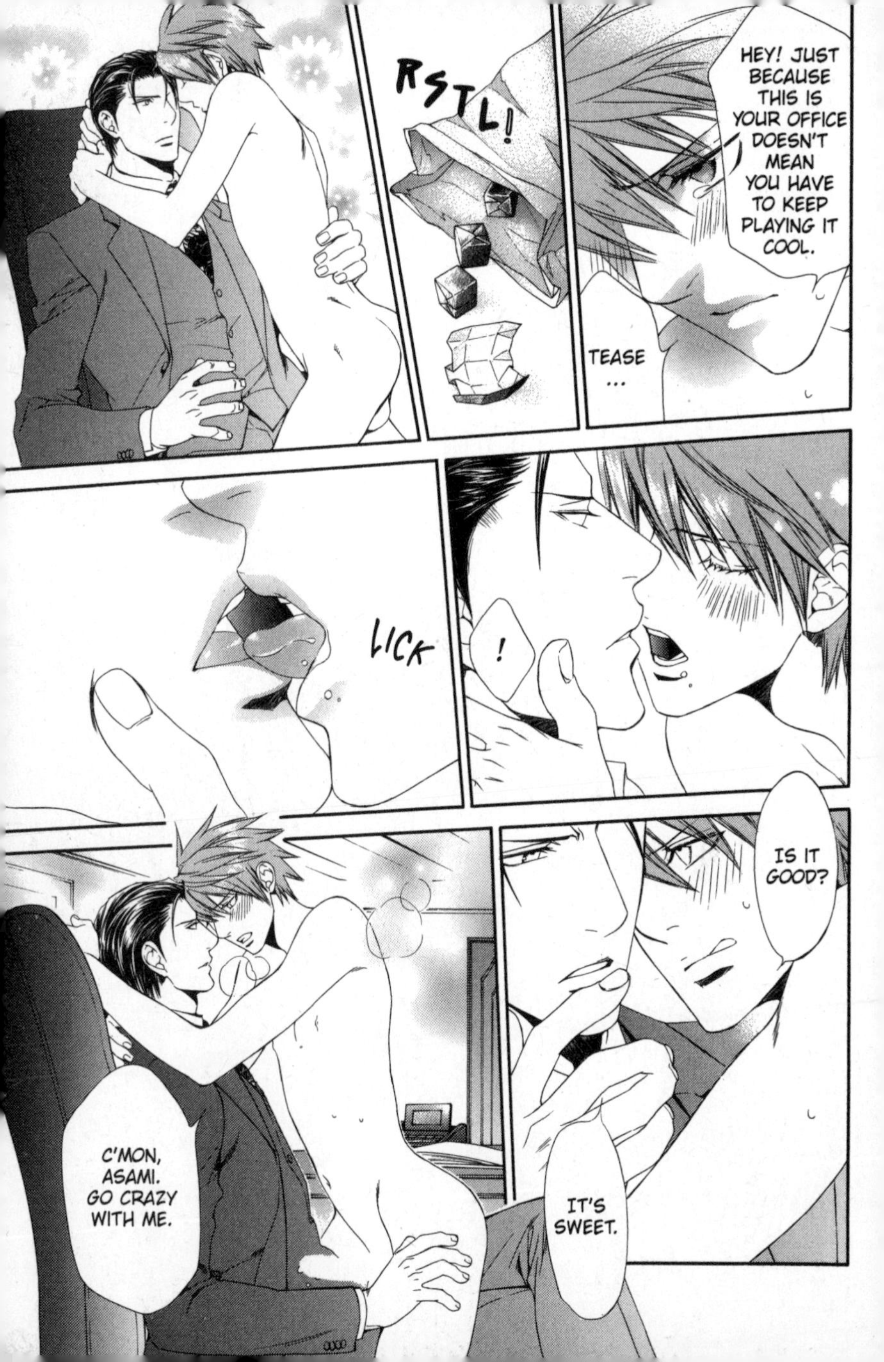
HEY! JUST BECAUSE THIS IS YOUR OFFICE DOESN'T MEAN YOU HAVE TO KEEP PLAYING IT COOL.
TEASE ...
RSTL!
!
LICK
IS IT GOOD?
IT'S SWEET.
C'MON, ASAMI. GO CRAZY WITH ME.

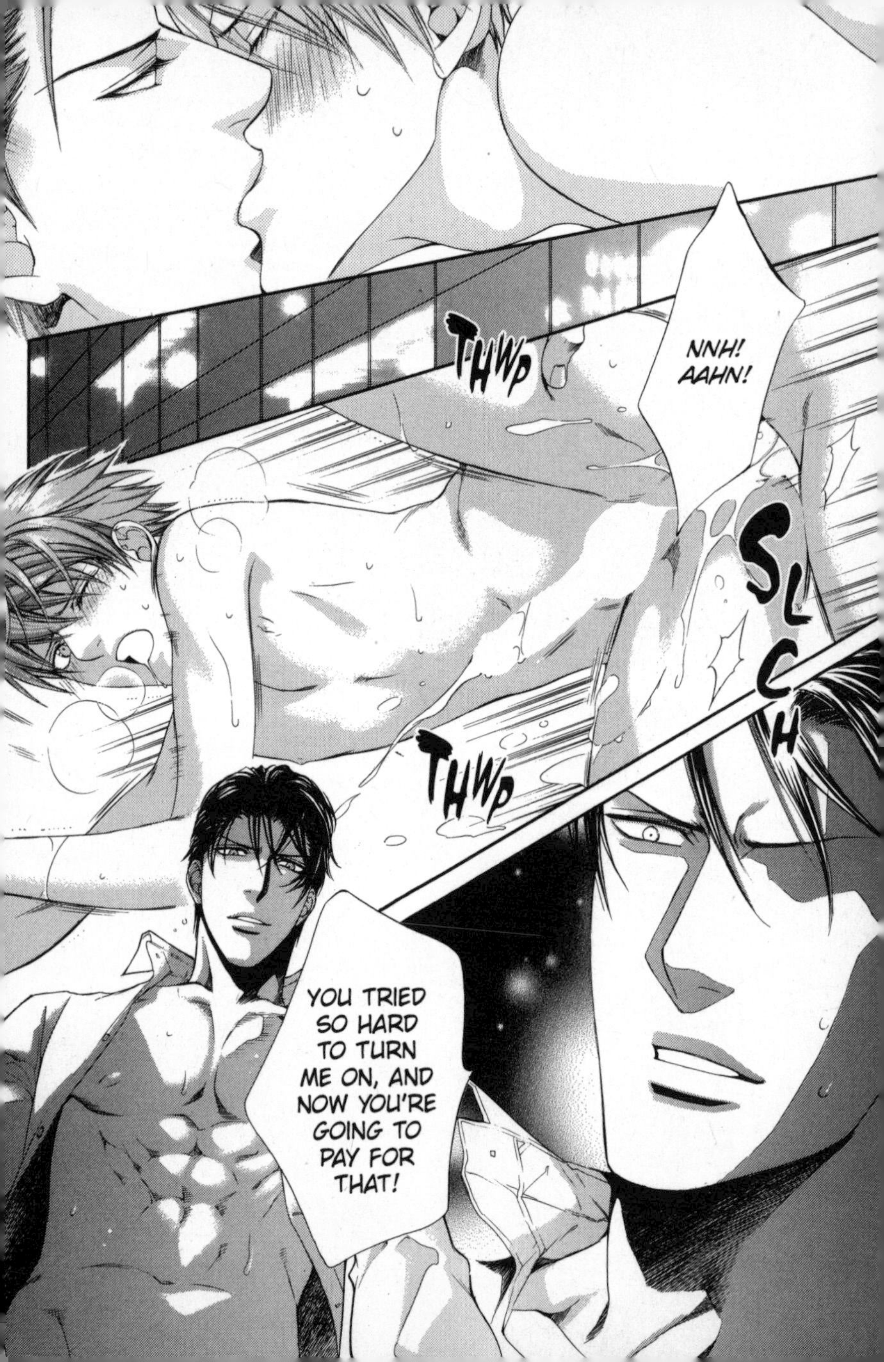
NNH! AAHN!
THWP
SLCH
THWP
YOU TRIED SO HARD TO TURN ME ON, AND NOW YOU'RE GOING TO PAY FOR THAT!

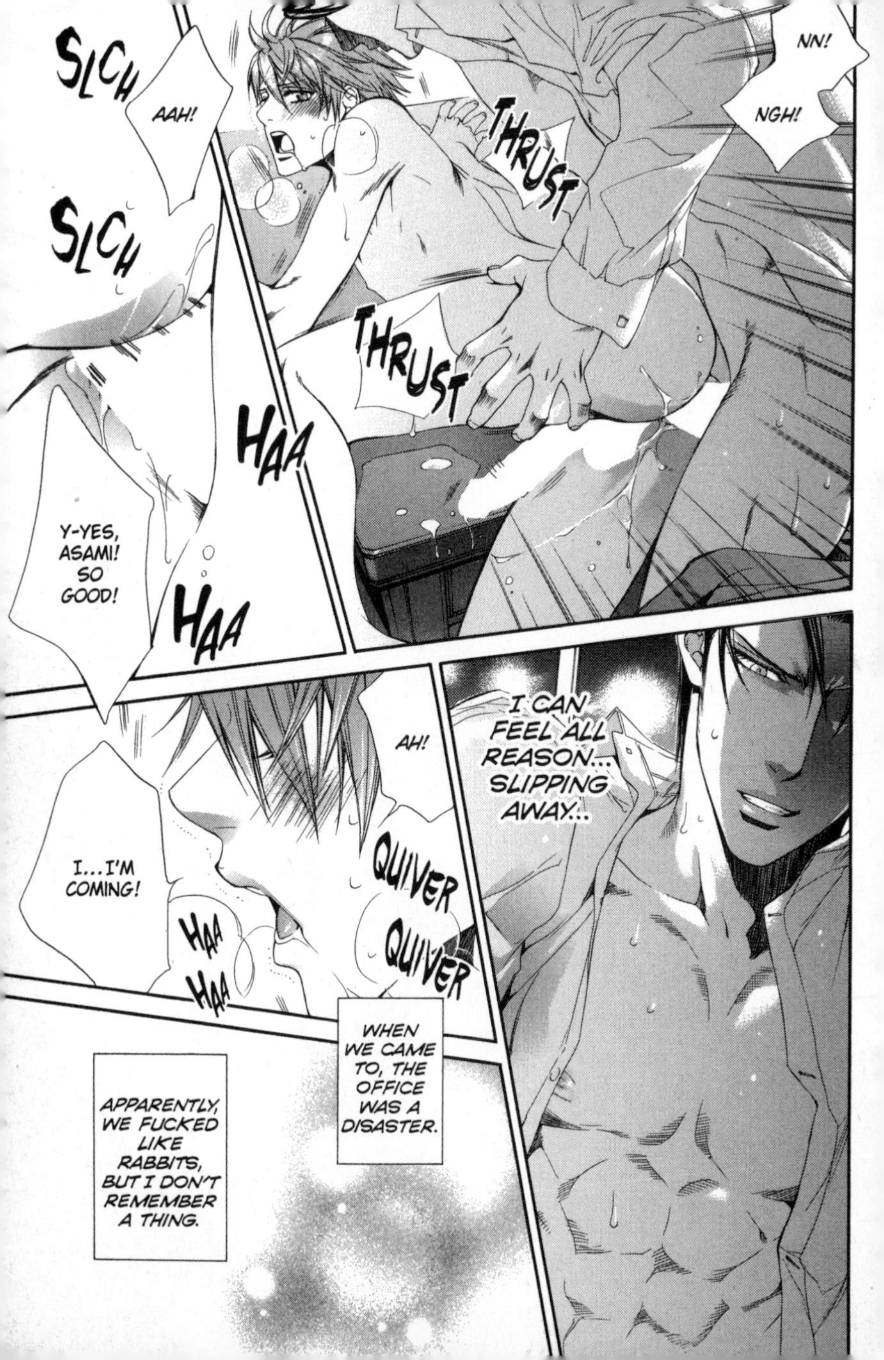
NN!
NGH!
THRUST
AAH!
THRUST
SLCH
SLCH
HAA
Y-YES, ASAMI! SO GOOD!
HAA
I CAN FEEL ALL REASON... SLIPPING AWAY...
AH!
QUIVER
QUIVER
I...I'M COMING!
HAA
HAA
WHEN WE CAME TO, THE OFFICE WAS A DISASTER.
APPARENTLY, WE FUCKED LIKE RABBITS, BUT I DON'T REMEMBER A THING.

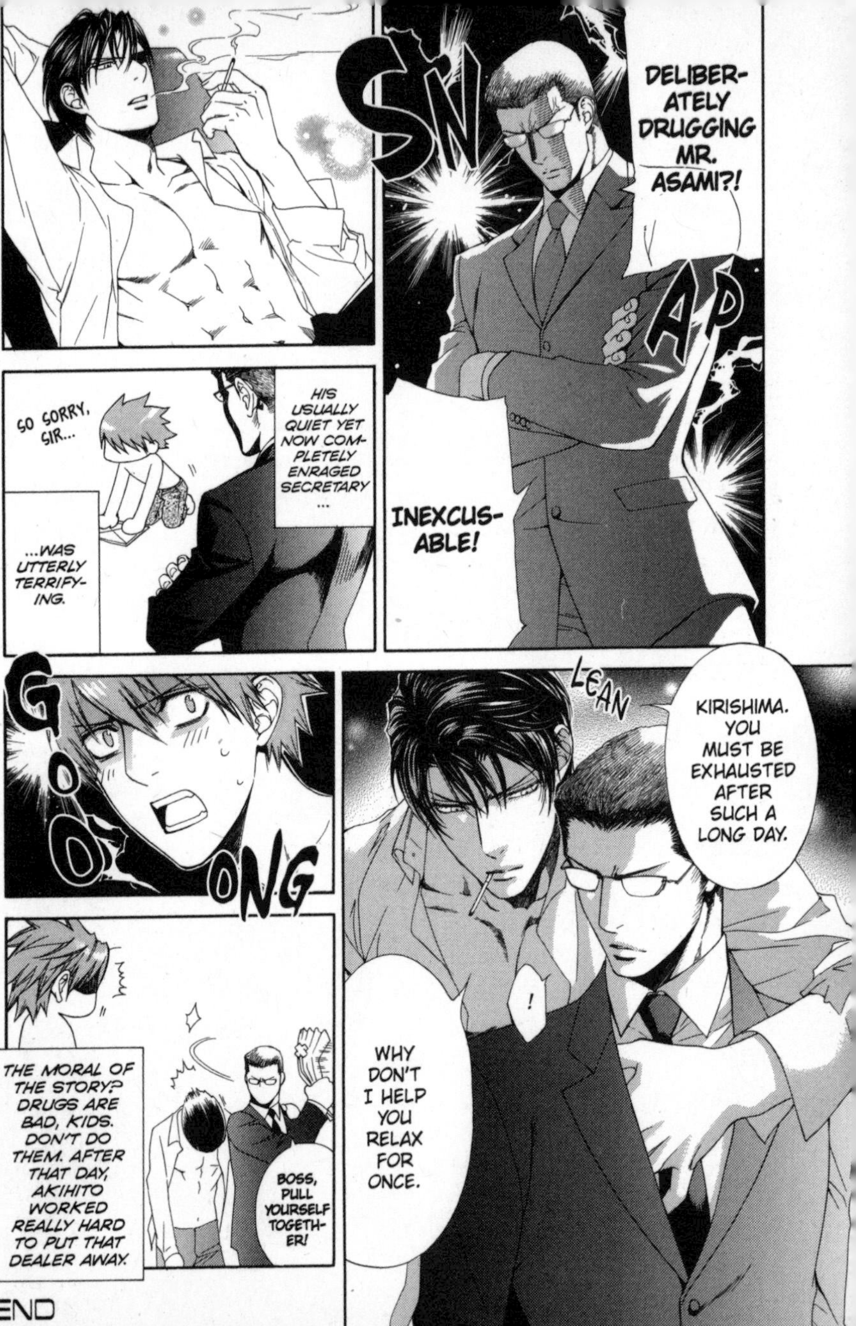
SN
DELIBER-ATELY DRUGGING MR. ASAMI?!
AP
INEXCUS-ABLE!
HIS USUALLY QUIET YET NOW COM-PLETELY ENRAGED SECRETARY...
SO SORRY, SIR...
...WAS UTTERLY TERRIFY-ING.
LEAN
KIRISHIMA. YOU MUST BE EXHAUSTED AFTER SUCH A LONG DAY.
!
WHY DON'T I HELP YOU RELAX FOR ONCE.
GOOONG
THE MORAL OF THE STORY? DRUGS ARE BAD, KIDS. DON'T DO THEM. AFTER THAT DAY, AKIHITO WORKED REALLY HARD TO PUT THAT DEALER AWAY.
BOSS, PULL YOURSELF TOGETH-ER!

END

• AFTERWORD •

★ Hello! Ayano Yamane here. Thank you very much for purchasing volume 8 of *Finder!* I hope you enjoyed this first volume in about two and a half years. This time, it took even longer than usual to pull together. I'm so sorry I kept all of you waiting this long. I'm all too aware of how disappointing I am on that front. Last time, I wrote how I'd put in even more effort this time...and then I promptly got sick. Not able to get enough pages done in time, I caused all kinds of trouble for my long-suffering editors and printers yet again. I'm so glad this volume is finally finished and out. While working on the art touch-ups, I was surprised at how bad some of it was. I know I do this every time, but I retouched a lot of the art in this volume! You can compare it to the magazine version—or, on second thought, please don't. T_T

On the story side of things, I apologize for the lack of lovey-dovey scenes in the midst of all the plot we're going through. Speaking as the one drawing this, spending so many chapters on all plot and no smut is actually kind of hard. I'd much rather be drawing cutesy things and lovely-dovey things and kissy-kissy things, but instead I have to hold back so I can finish drawing all the punching and shooting and blood spraying first. Continuing from last volume, Akihito finally finds the mentally frayed Sudo and gets ticked at how dumb he's being. I put extra effort into their catfight scene and Sudo getting off on Akihito's butt crack, as well as the sneak attack at the end of the volume. I was telling my editor about how I've always wanted to do some kind of scene where there's an escape through some hidden tunnel and the two share some fast and desperate love...and finally I was able to! Though the highlight is Kirishima coming to the rescue in his pj's. ^^ I feel like I didn't do enough with the scene where Akihito was strung up from the crane (violencewise), but well...this *is* technically a smut manga. Having the poor *uke* get beaten like a sandbag is much too *seinen* (just being prudent).

↖Continued...

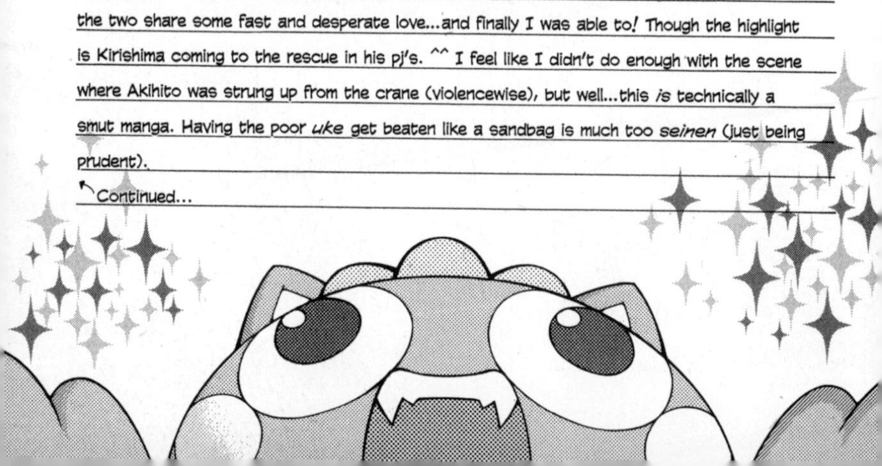

↘ Continuing...

Lately, censorship of erotic art is getting so bad that all the important bits wind up censored! I think that's unfortunate. I know there are many people perfectly satisfied with not seeing the naughty bits if the couple is in love and enjoying themselves, and that's okay. But personally I like my smut to be mind-blowingly hot and steamy! :D I want Akihito and Asami's relationship to have this continual will-they-or-won't-they sexual tension to it, so for the times when they *do* get together, I wish I could make it really intense and hardcore. ♡ Basically, please allow me the time needed to properly draw my smut... (← note to self: *make time!*)

The other day I was told *Finder* had hit its 15th anniversary, making me realize again just how long I've been drawing it. It's almost scary, actually. ^^; But by this point, there's just no fixing its pace, I'm afraid. I'm just going to keep chipping away at it little by little, as much as I can... Though I'm really sorry to everyone I'm making wait. I hope you all continue looking forward to Akihito's exploits as he tries not to get sucked into the black void that is the underworld and Asami as he wanders the line between love and hate, making even more enemies along the way! Perhaps a character or two fans have been clamoring for will make a reappearance!

In closing, to everyone who has loved this series from the beginning with saintlike patience and to everyone who is a recent fan, thank you so much for all of your letters and comments. Thank you for your presents, for your heartwarming comments on Twitter, and for never forgetting to submit the magazine's survey forms. Your warm and constant support is what gives me the energy to keep going! Without it, I would never have made it this far. Thank you so much!

I give all my gratitude to my supervisor and editors who know how to coax this slow artist along, and who provide interesting ideas and plans to help inspire the story; to the highly skilled assistants who get such godlike color pages out of this analog artist's work; to the printers and bookstores that wait so patiently for yet another late work; and to everybody else who helps these books get made. Going forward, I'm going to keep working hard and making things even more exciting, so I hope you all stick around for the ride!

やまねあやの拝.

2/29/16

Ayano Yamane

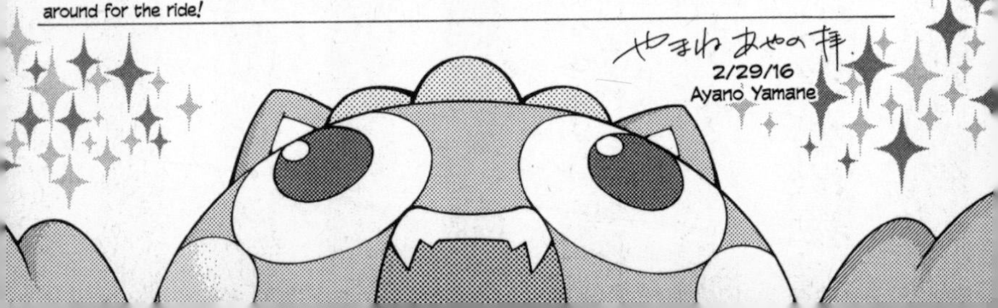

My Fair Prince

~A Night
of Celebration~

Deluxe Edition
Bonus

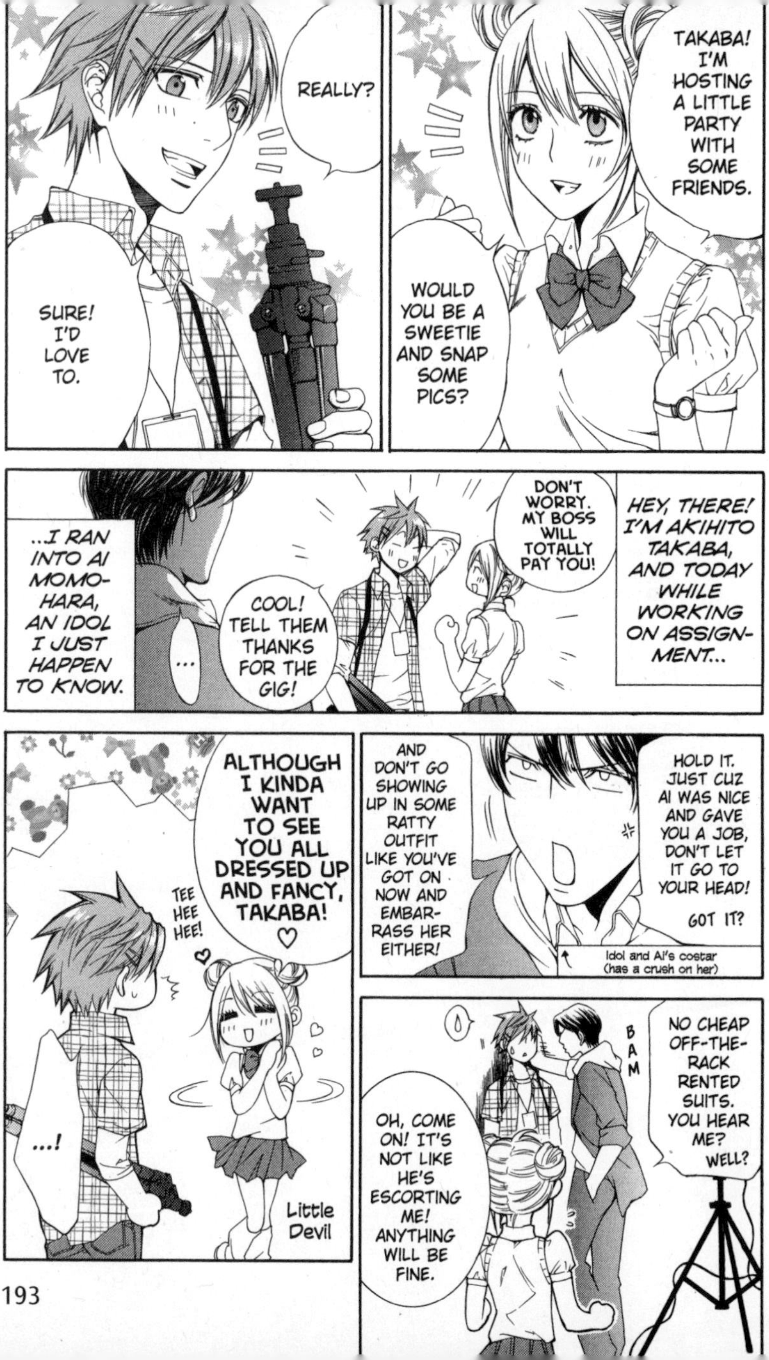
TAKABA! I'M HOSTING A LITTLE PARTY WITH SOME FRIENDS.
WOULD YOU BE A SWEETIE AND SNAP SOME PICS?
REALLY?
SURE! I'D LOVE TO.
HEY, THERE! I'M AKIHITO TAKABA, AND TODAY WHILE WORKING ON ASSIGNMENT...
DON'T WORRY. MY BOSS WILL TOTALLY PAY YOU!
COOL! TELL THEM THANKS FOR THE GIG!
...
...I RAN INTO AI MOMOHARA, AN IDOL I JUST HAPPEN TO KNOW.
HOLD IT. JUST CUZ AI WAS NICE AND GAVE YOU A JOB, DON'T LET IT GO TO YOUR HEAD!
GOT IT?
AND DON'T GO SHOWING UP IN SOME RATTY OUTFIT LIKE YOU'VE GOT ON NOW AND EMBARRASS HER EITHER!
Idol and Ai's costar (has a crush on her)
NO CHEAP OFF-THE-RACK RENTED SUITS. YOU HEAR ME?
WELL?
BAM
OH, COME ON! IT'S NOT LIKE HE'S ESCORTING ME! ANYTHING WILL BE FINE.
ALTHOUGH I KINDA WANT TO SEE YOU ALL DRESSED UP AND FANCY, TAKABA! ♡
TEE HEE HEE!
...!
Little Devil

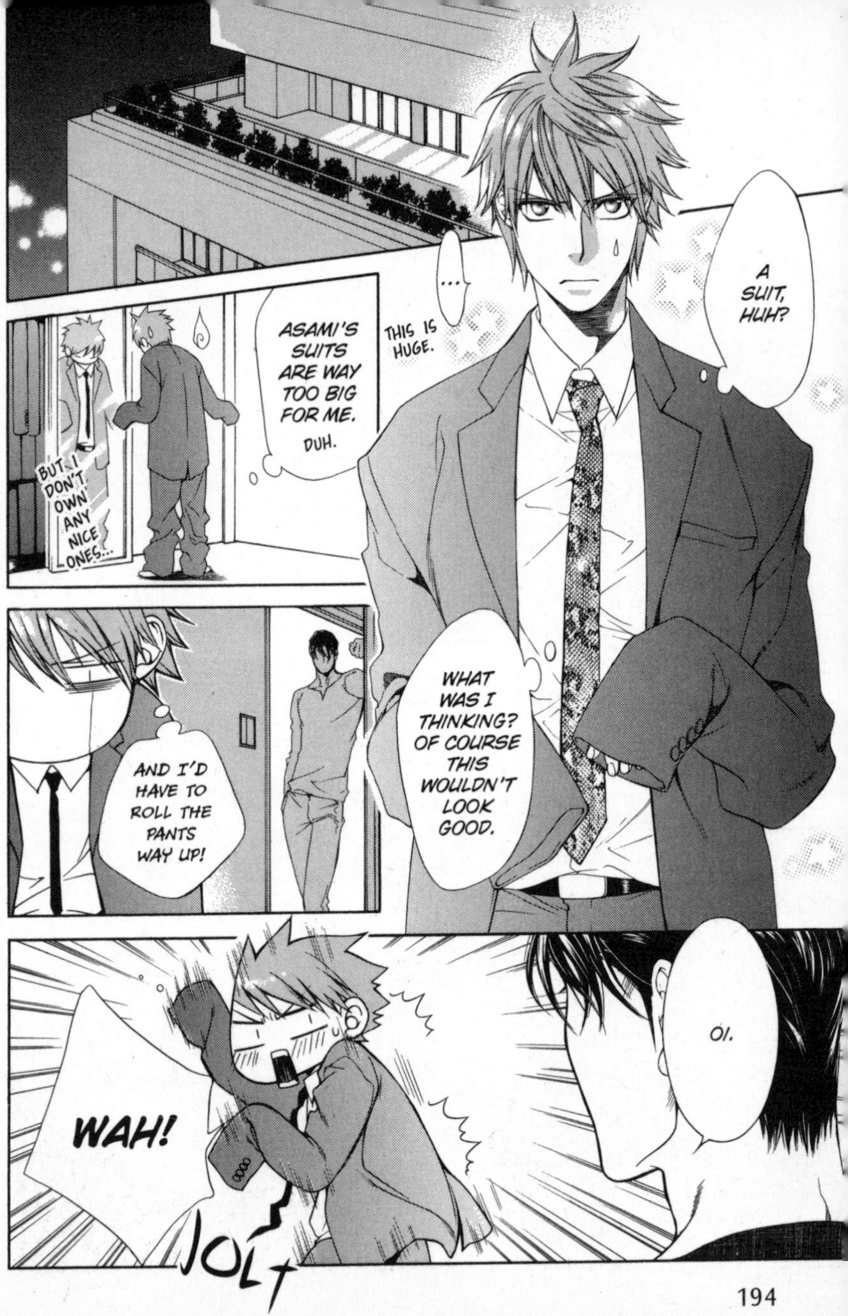
A SUIT, HUH?
...
WHAT WAS I THINKING? OF COURSE THIS WOULDN'T LOOK GOOD.
ASAMI'S SUITS ARE WAY TOO BIG FOR ME.
THIS IS HUGE.
DUH.
BUT I DON'T OWN ANY NICE ONES...
AND I'D HAVE TO ROLL THE PANTS WAY UP!
OI.
WAH!
JOLT

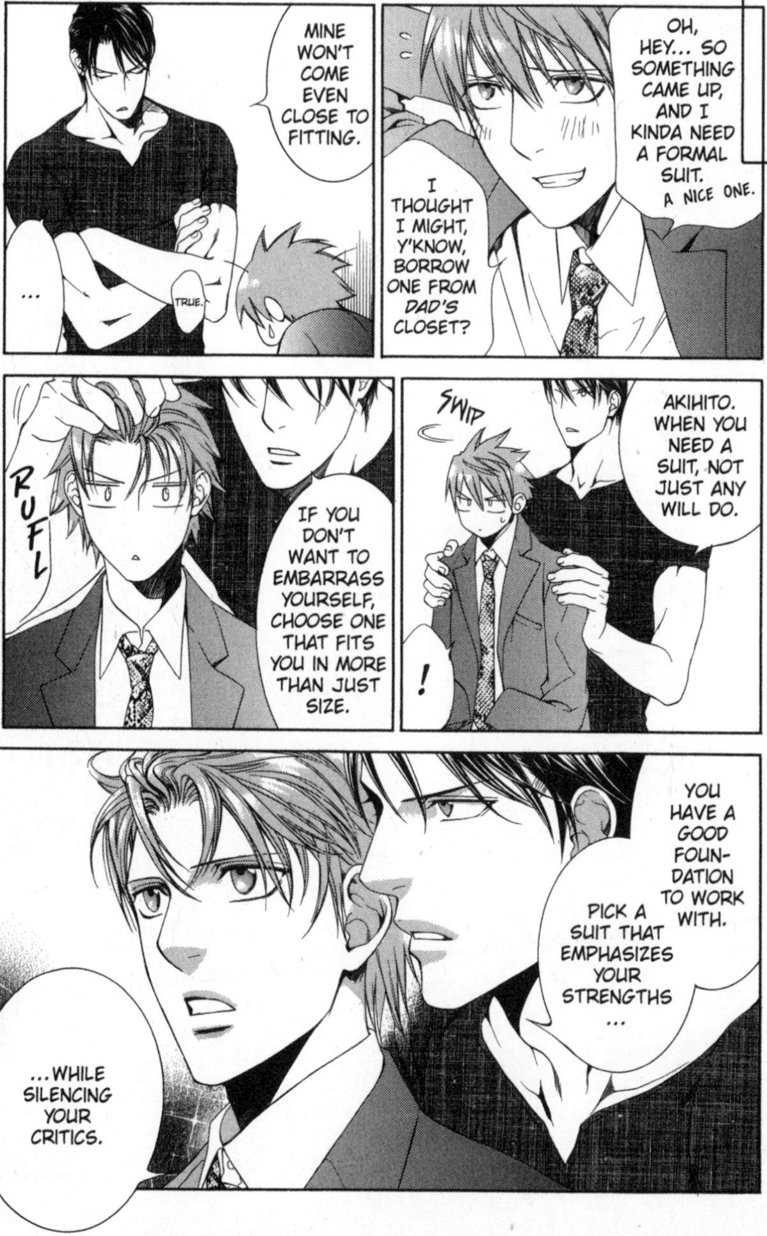
OH, HEY... SO SOMETHING CAME UP, AND I KINDA NEED A FORMAL SUIT.
A NICE ONE.
I THOUGHT I MIGHT, Y'KNOW, BORROW ONE FROM *DAD'S* CLOSET?
MINE WON'T COME EVEN CLOSE TO FITTING.
...
TRUE.
SWIP
AKIHITO. WHEN YOU NEED A SUIT, NOT JUST ANY WILL DO.
!
RUFL
IF YOU DON'T WANT TO EMBARRASS YOURSELF, CHOOSE ONE THAT FITS YOU IN MORE THAN JUST SIZE.
YOU HAVE A GOOD FOUN-DATION TO WORK WITH.
PICK A SUIT THAT EMPHASIZES YOUR STRENGTHS...
...WHILE SILENCING YOUR CRITICS.

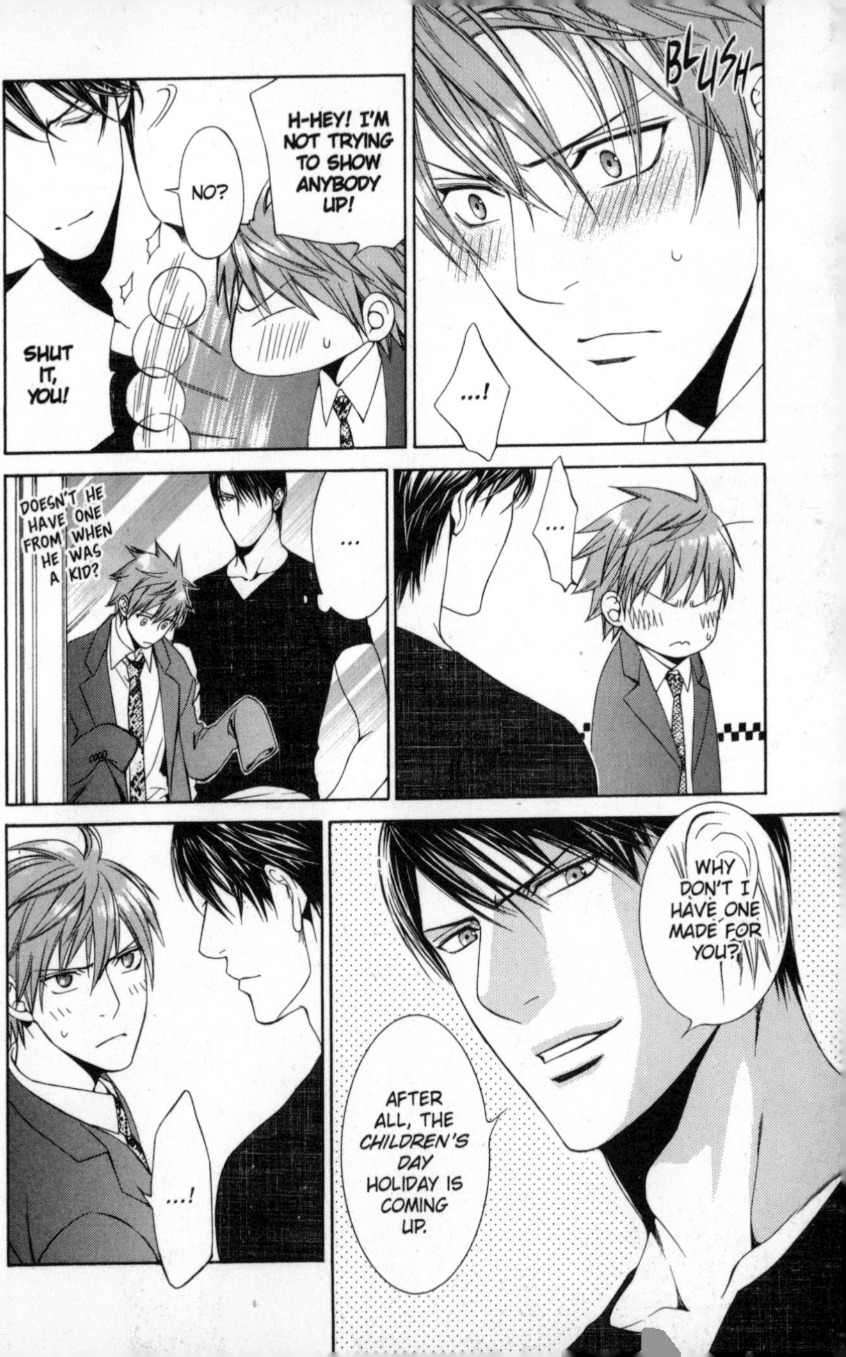
BLUSH
...!
H-HEY! I'M NOT TRYING TO SHOW ANYBODY UP!
NO?
SHUT IT, YOU!
...
...
DOESN'T HE HAVE ONE FROM WHEN HE WAS A KID?
WHY DON'T I HAVE ONE MADE FOR YOU?
AFTER ALL, THE *CHILDREN'S DAY* HOLIDAY IS COMING UP.
...!

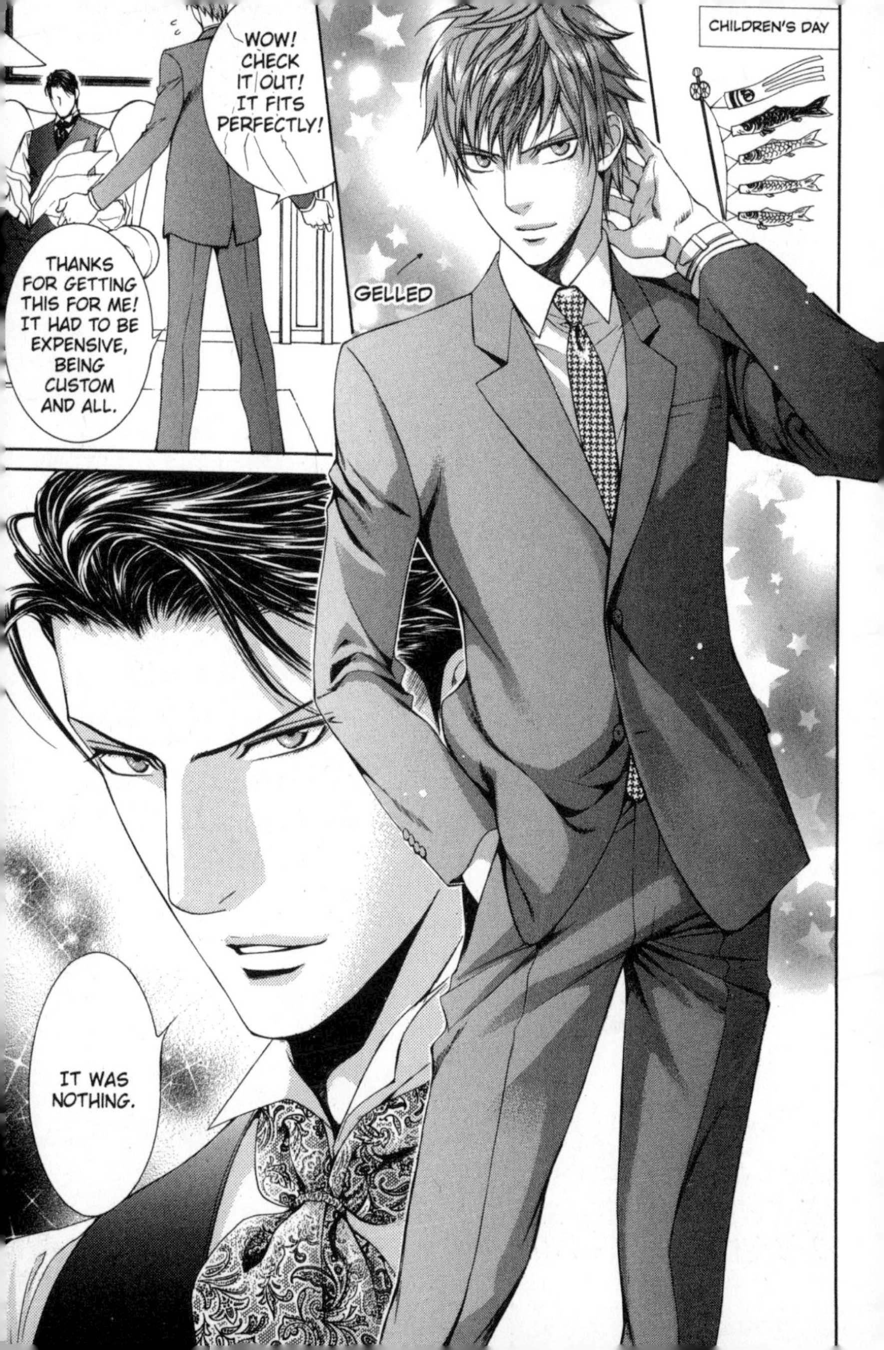
CHILDREN'S DAY
GELLED
WOW! CHECK IT OUT! IT FITS PERFECTLY!
THANKS FOR GETTING THIS FOR ME! IT HAD TO BE EXPENSIVE, BEING CUSTOM AND ALL.
IT WAS NOTHING.

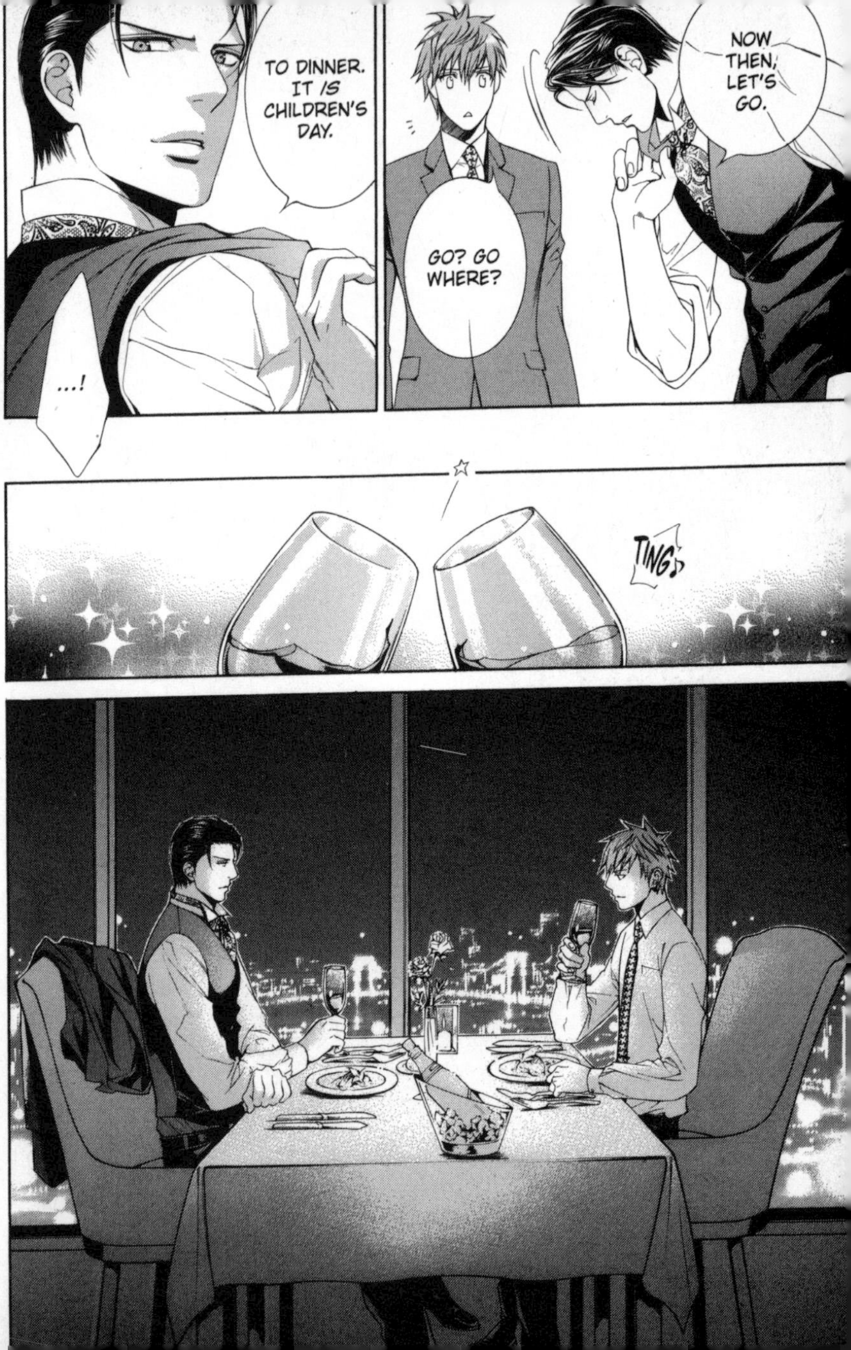
NOW THEN, LET'S GO.
GO? GO WHERE?
TO DINNER. IT IS CHILDREN'S DAY.
...!
TING♪

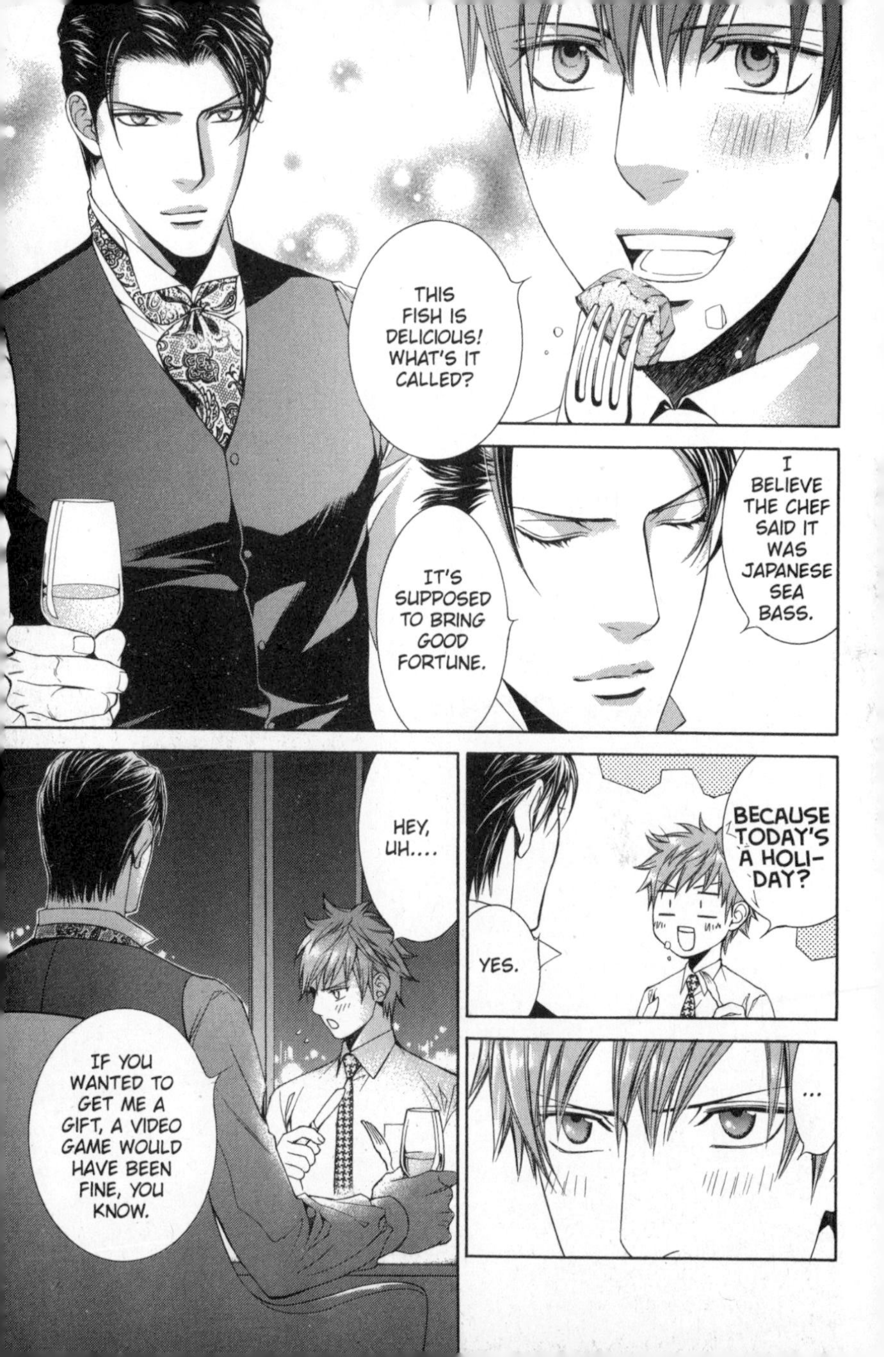
THIS FISH IS DELICIOUS! WHAT'S IT CALLED?
I BELIEVE THE CHEF SAID IT WAS JAPANESE SEA BASS.
IT'S SUPPOSED TO BRING GOOD FORTUNE.
BECAUSE TODAY'S A HOLI-DAY?
YES.
...
HEY, UH....
IF YOU WANTED TO GET ME A GIFT, A VIDEO GAME WOULD HAVE BEEN FINE, YOU KNOW.

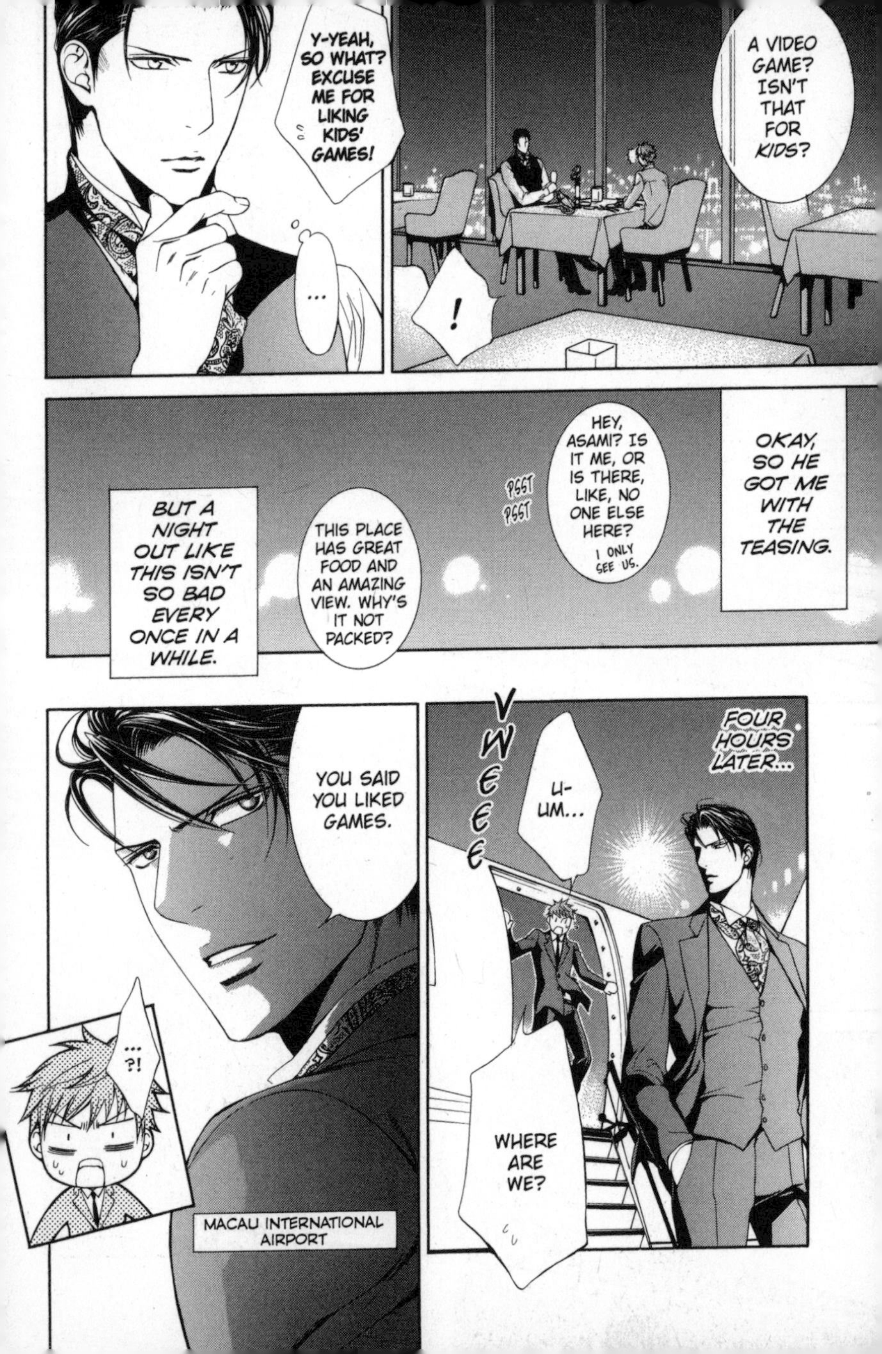
A VIDEO GAME? ISN'T THAT FOR KIDS?
!
Y-YEAH, SO WHAT? EXCUSE ME FOR LIKING KIDS' GAMES!
...
OKAY, SO HE GOT ME WITH THE TEASING.
HEY, ASAMI? IS IT ME, OR IS THERE, LIKE, NO ONE ELSE HERE?
I ONLY SEE US.
PSST PSST
THIS PLACE HAS GREAT FOOD AND AN AMAZING VIEW. WHY'S IT NOT PACKED?
BUT A NIGHT OUT LIKE THIS ISN'T SO BAD EVERY ONCE IN A WHILE.
FOUR HOURS LATER...
VWEEE
U-UM...
WHERE ARE WE?
YOU SAID YOU LIKED GAMES.
...?!
MACAU INTERNATIONAL AIRPORT

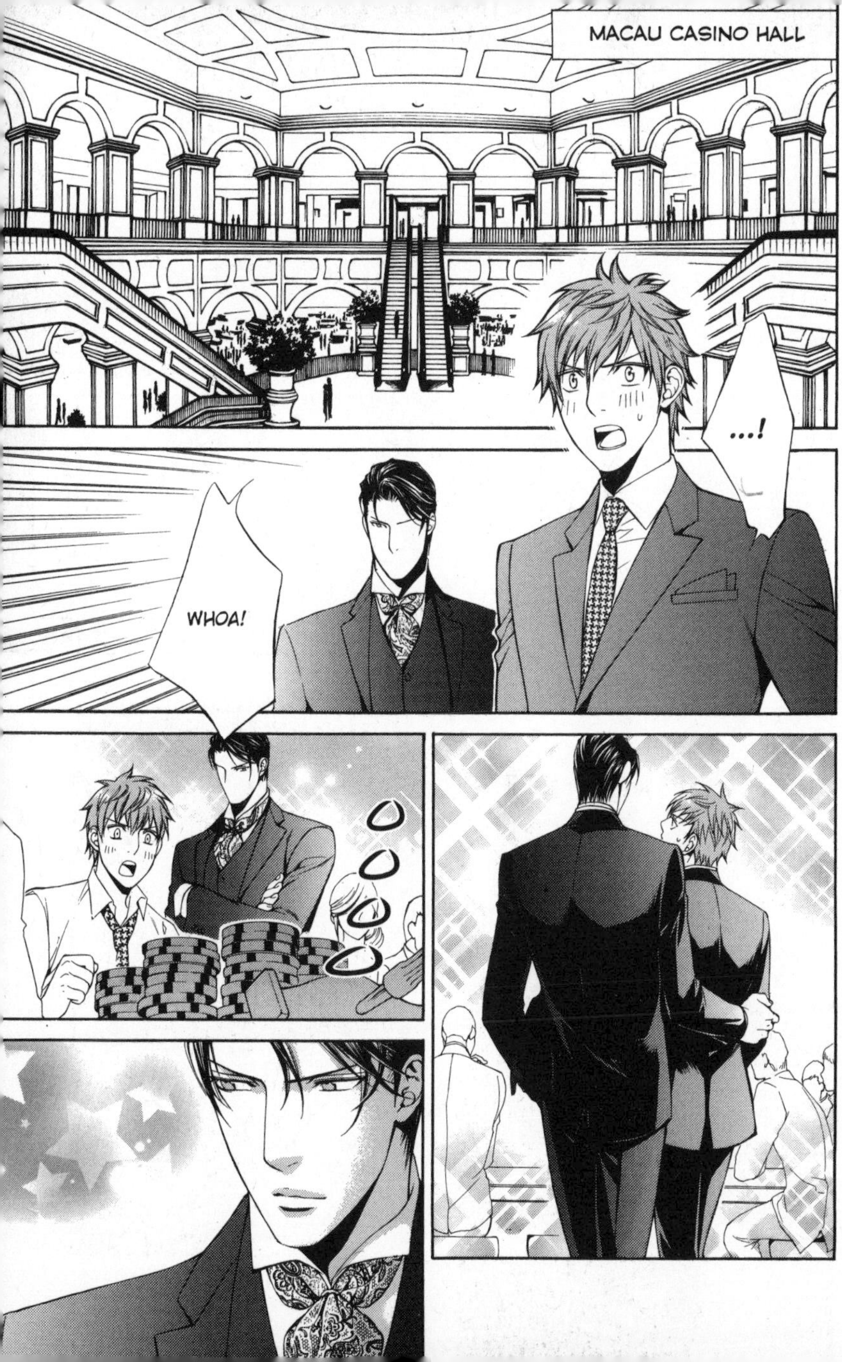
MACAU CASINO HALL
...!
WHOA!

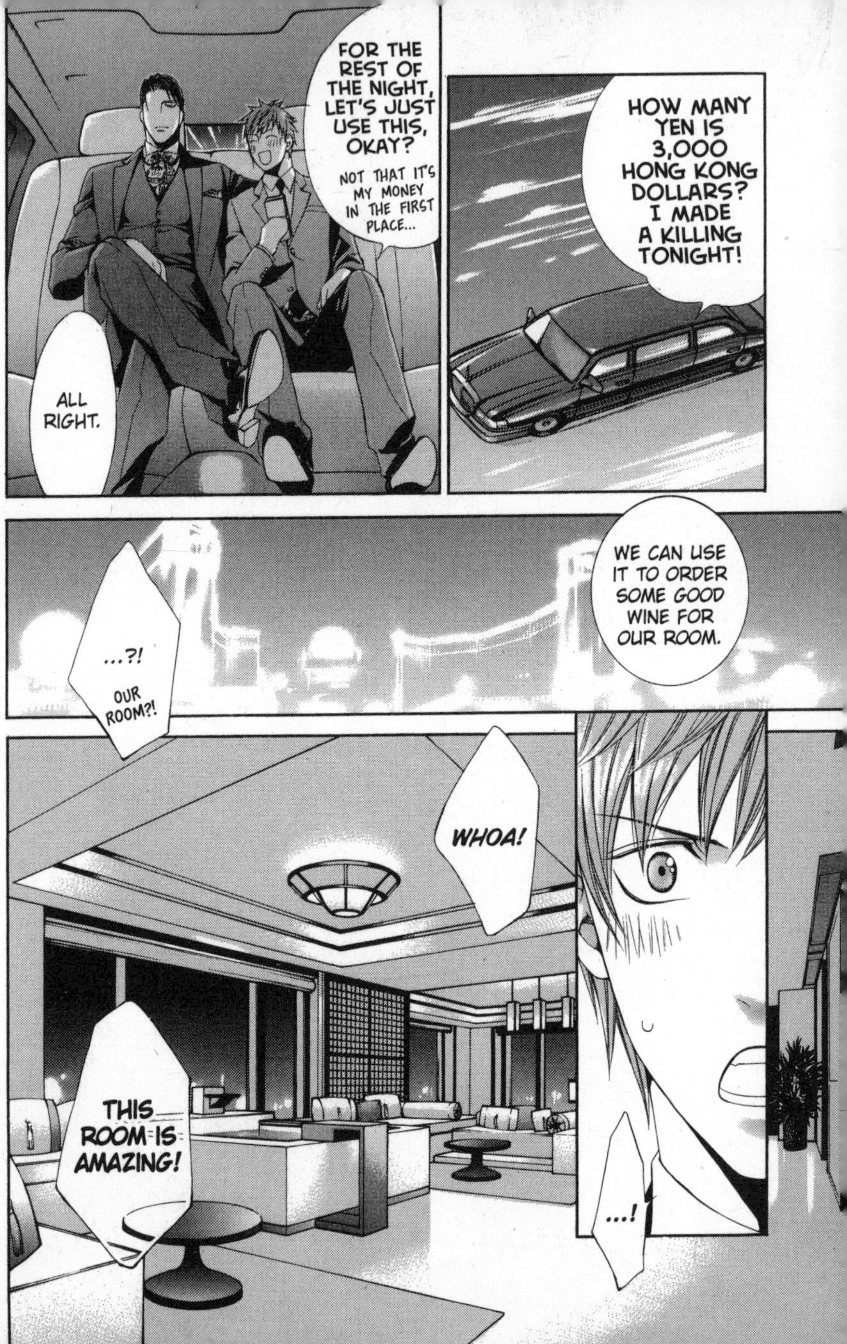
HOW MANY YEN IS 3,000 HONG KONG DOLLARS? I MADE A KILLING TONIGHT!
FOR THE REST OF THE NIGHT, LET'S JUST USE THIS, OKAY?
NOT THAT IT'S MY MONEY IN THE FIRST PLACE...
ALL RIGHT.
WE CAN USE IT TO ORDER SOME GOOD WINE FOR OUR ROOM.
...?!
OUR ROOM?!
...!
WHOA!
THIS ROOM IS AMAZING!

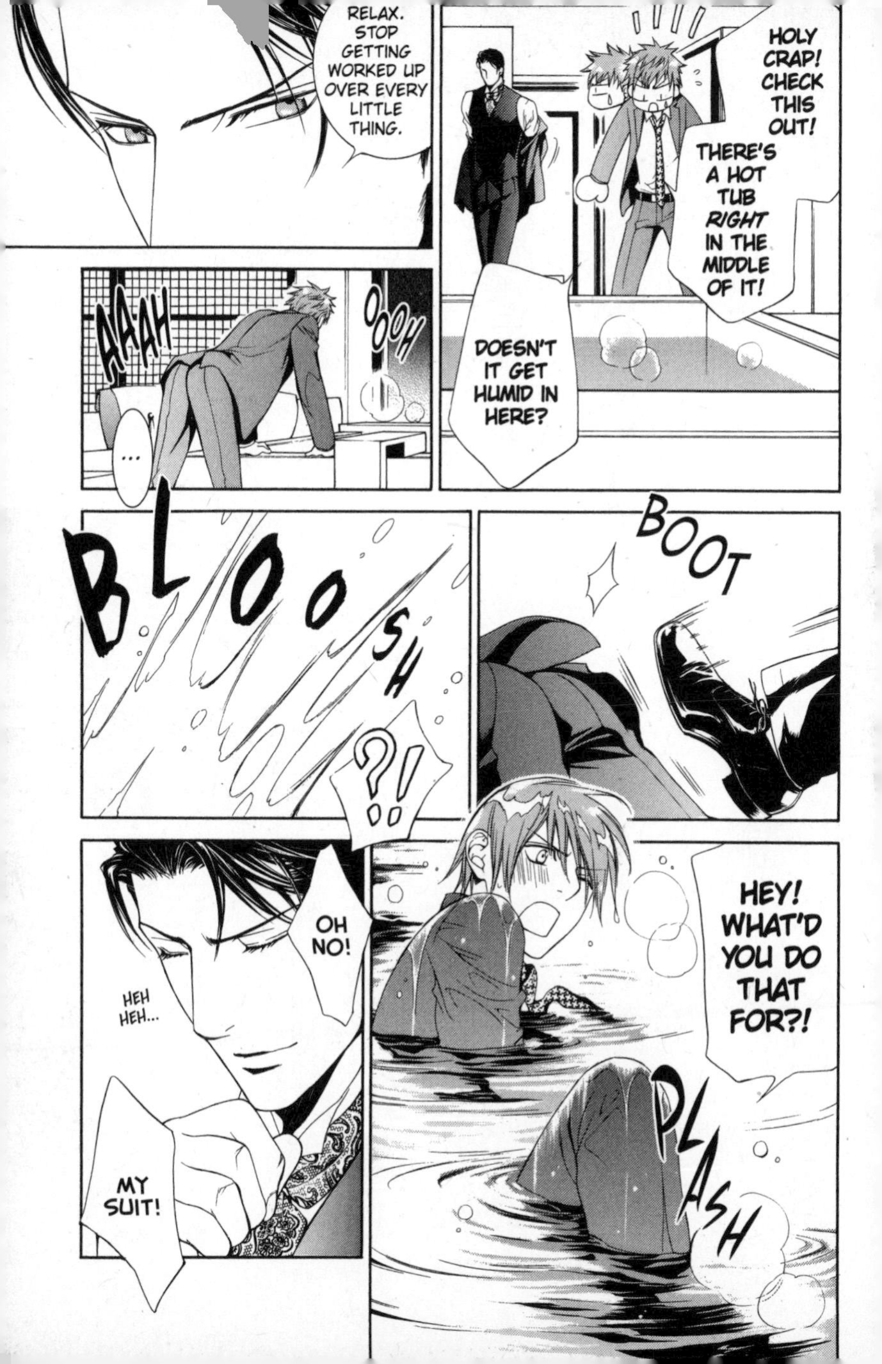
HOLY CRAP! CHECK THIS OUT!
THERE'S A HOT TUB *RIGHT* IN THE MIDDLE OF IT!
DOESN'T IT GET HUMID IN HERE?
RELAX. STOP GETTING WORKED UP OVER EVERY LITTLE THING.
AAAH
OOOH
...
BOOT
BLOOOSH
?!!
HEY! WHAT'D YOU DO THAT FOR?!
PLASH
OH NO!
HEH HEH...
MY SUIT!

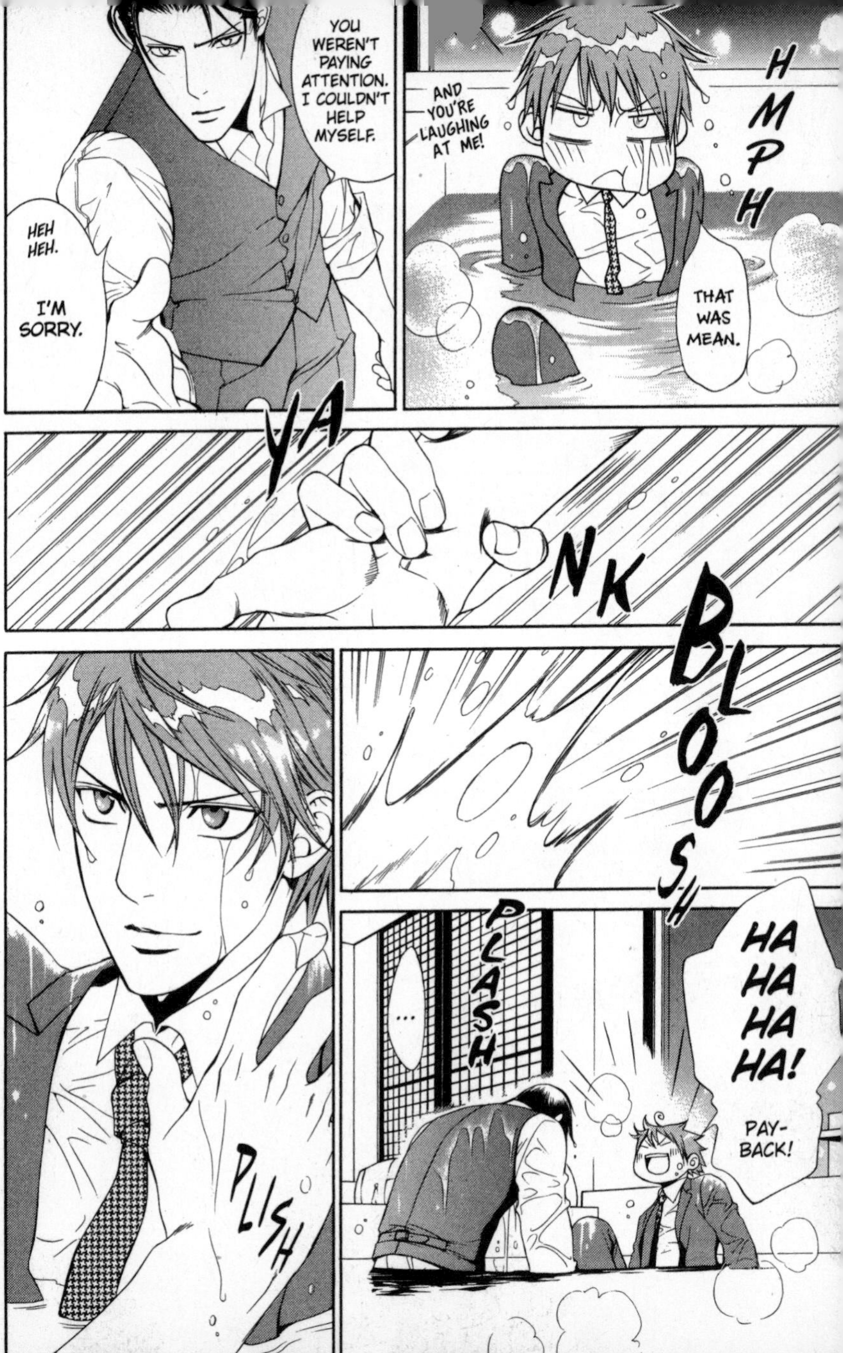
HMPH
AND YOU'RE LAUGHING AT ME!
THAT WAS MEAN.
YOU WEREN'T PAYING ATTENTION. I COULDN'T HELP MYSELF.
HEH HEH.
I'M SORRY.
YANK
BLOOSH
HA HA HA HA HA HA HA!
PAY-BACK!
PLASH
...
PLISH

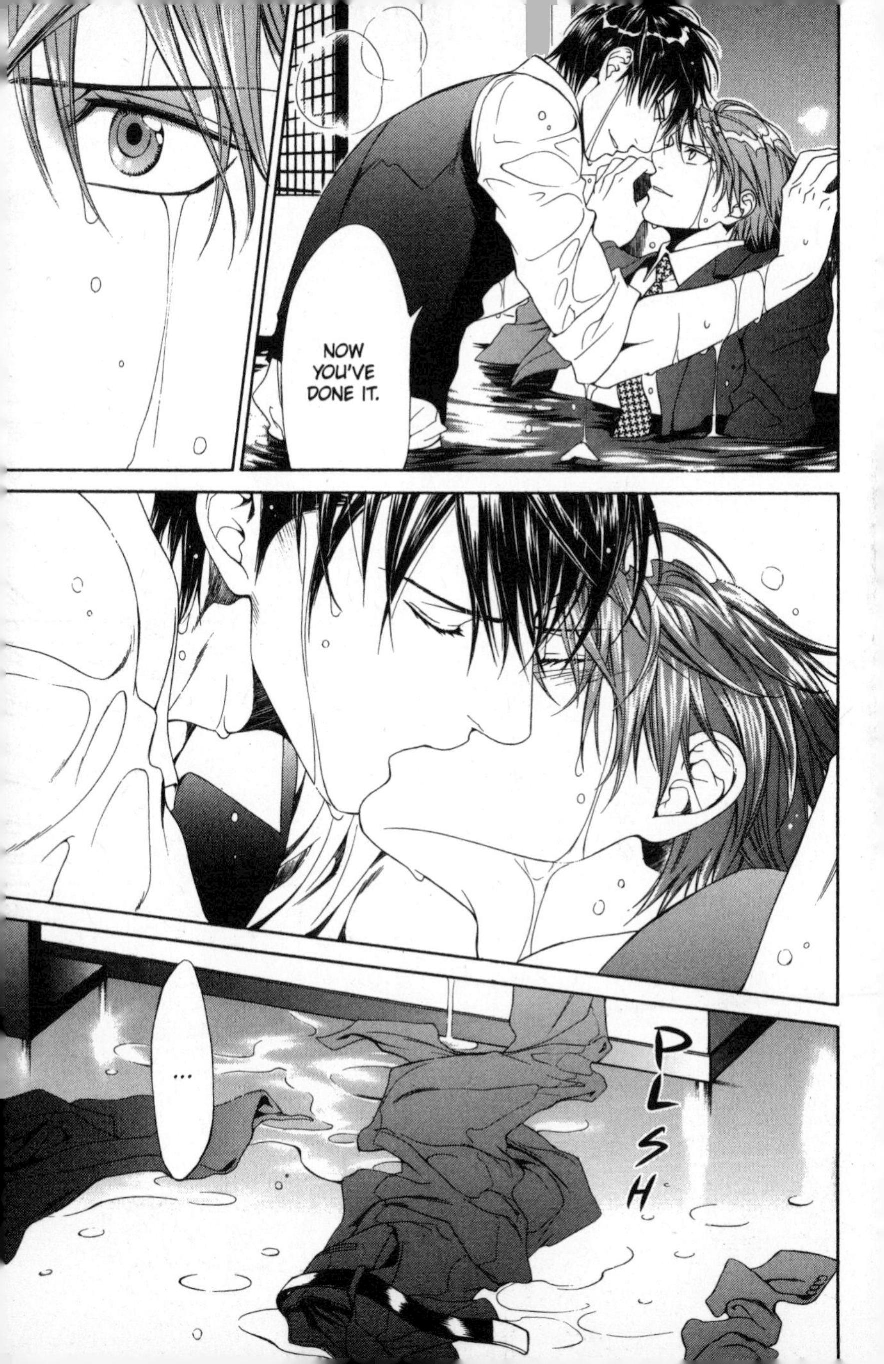
NOW YOU'VE DONE IT.
...
PLSH

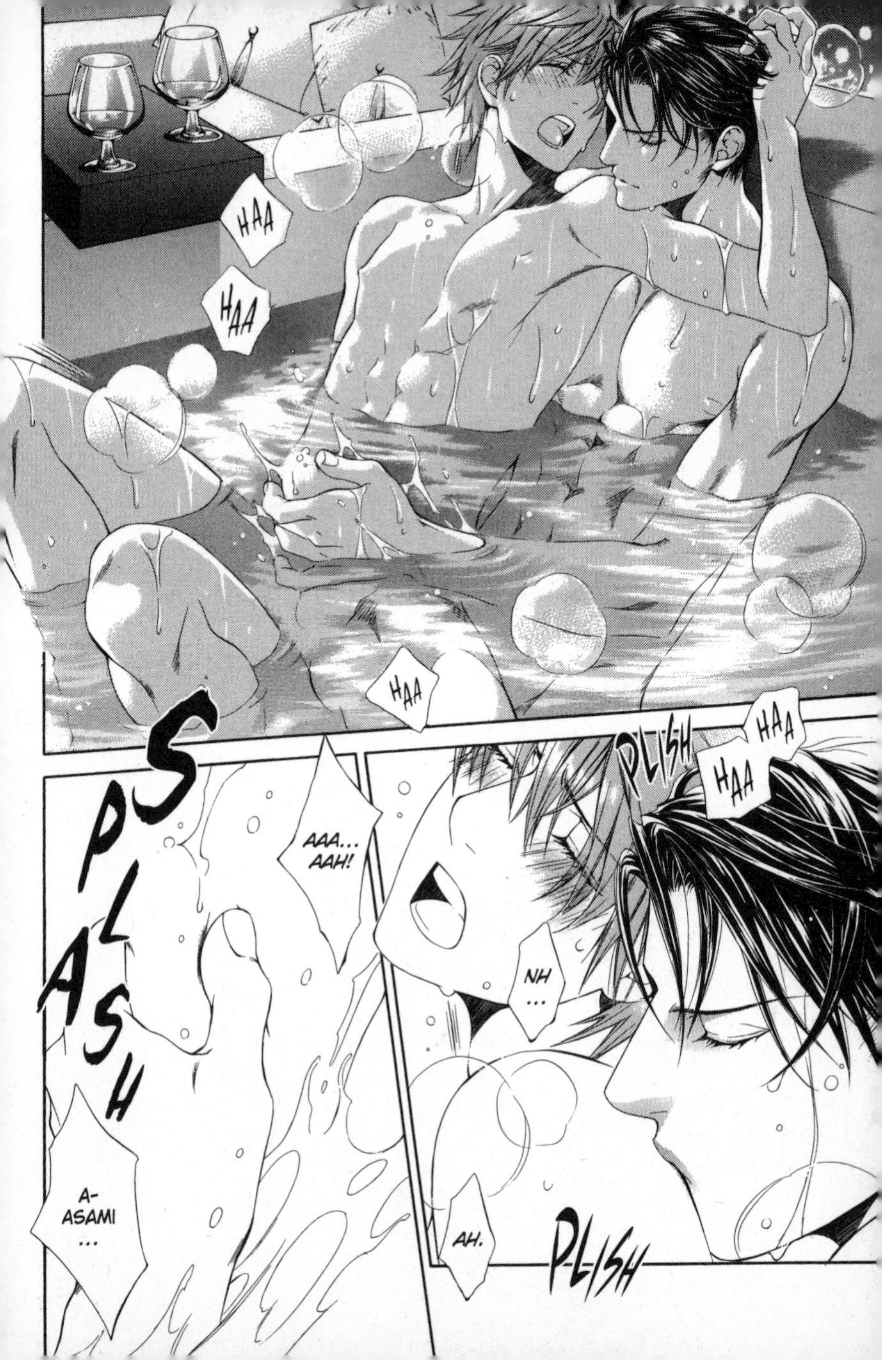
HAA
HAA
HAA
HAA
HAA
PLISH
NH ...
AH.
PLISH
SPLASH
AAA... AAH!
A-ASAMI ...

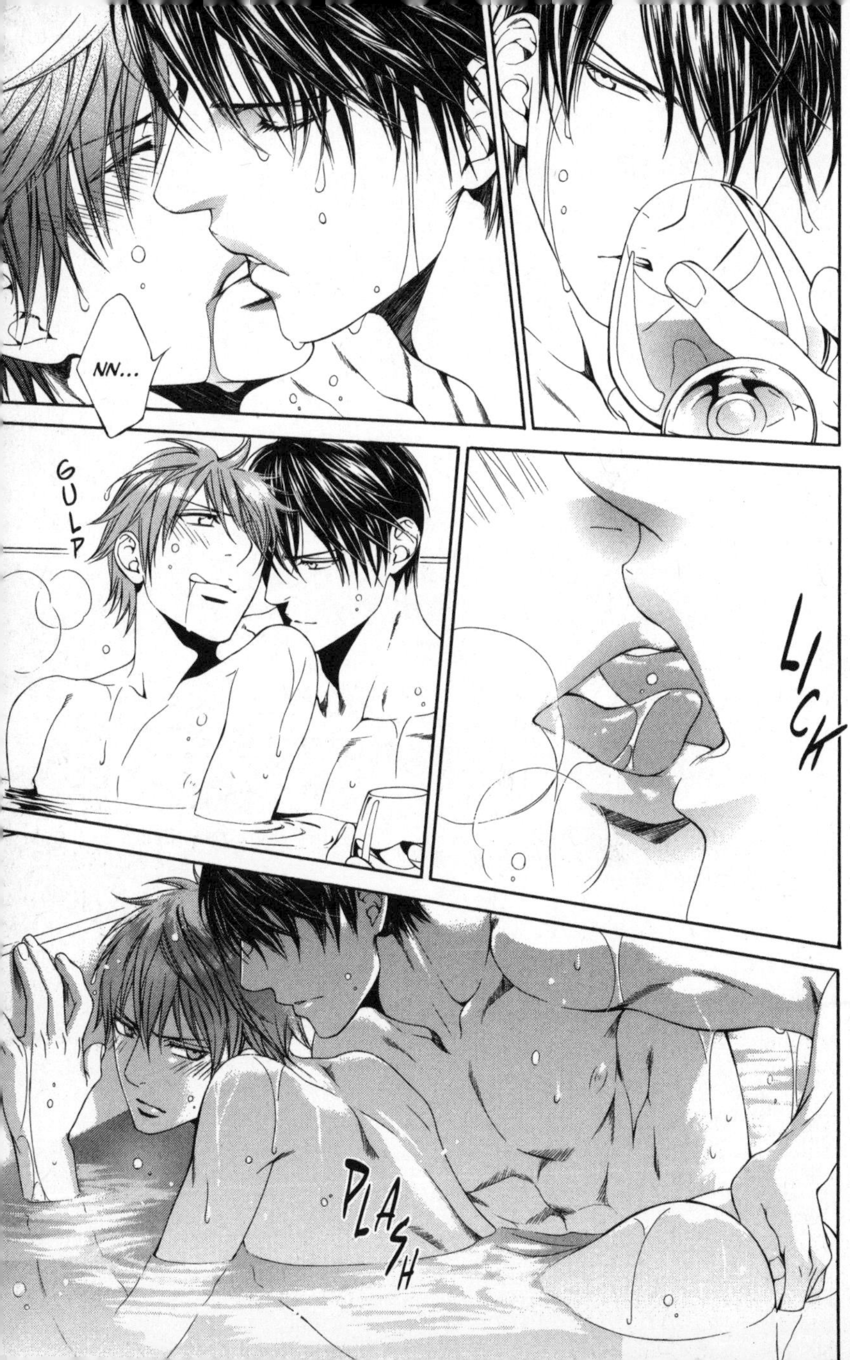
NN...
LICK
GULP
PLASH

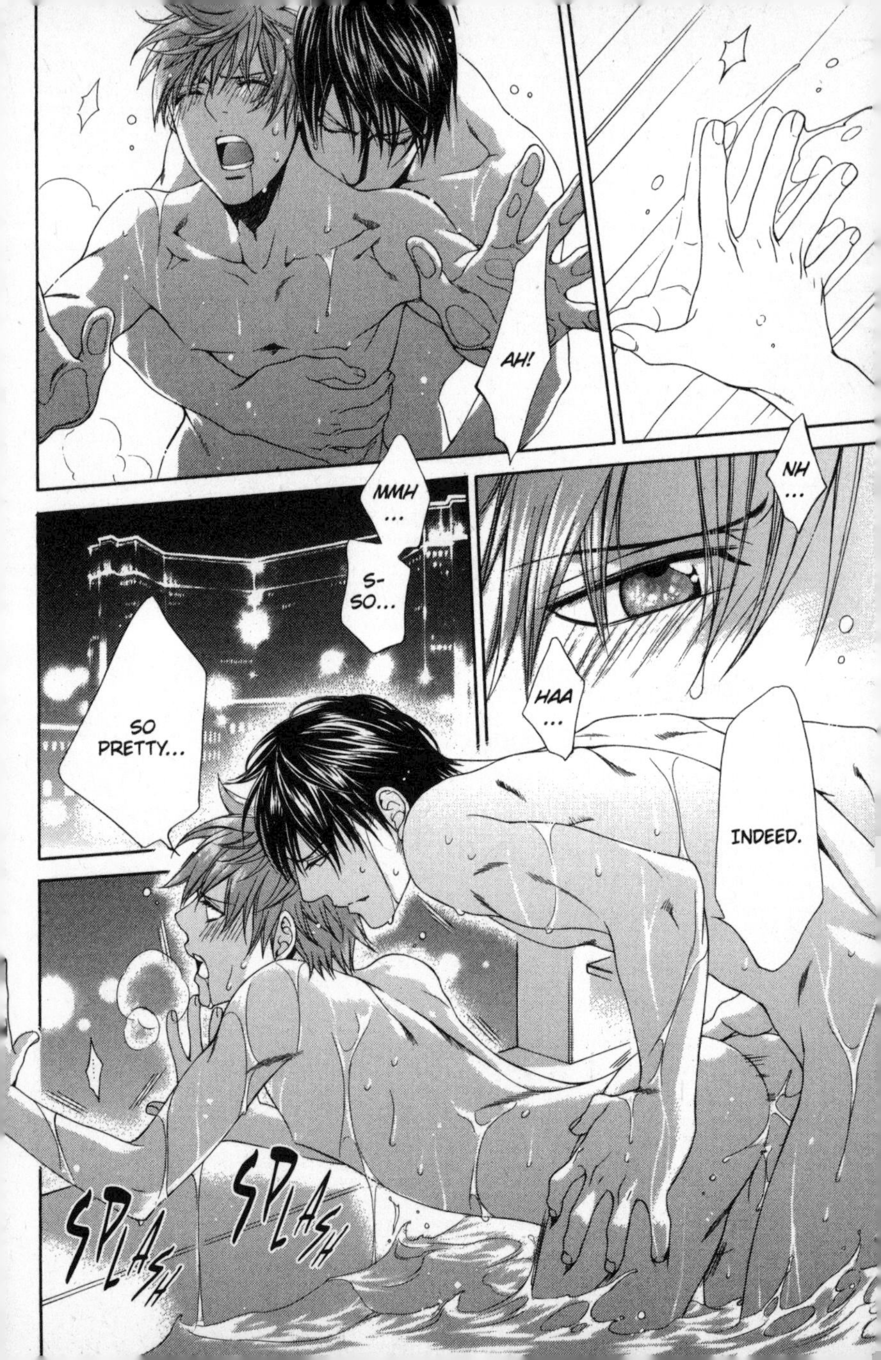
AH!
NH ...
HAA ...
MMH ...
S- SO...
SO PRETTY...
INDEED.
SPLASH
SPLASH

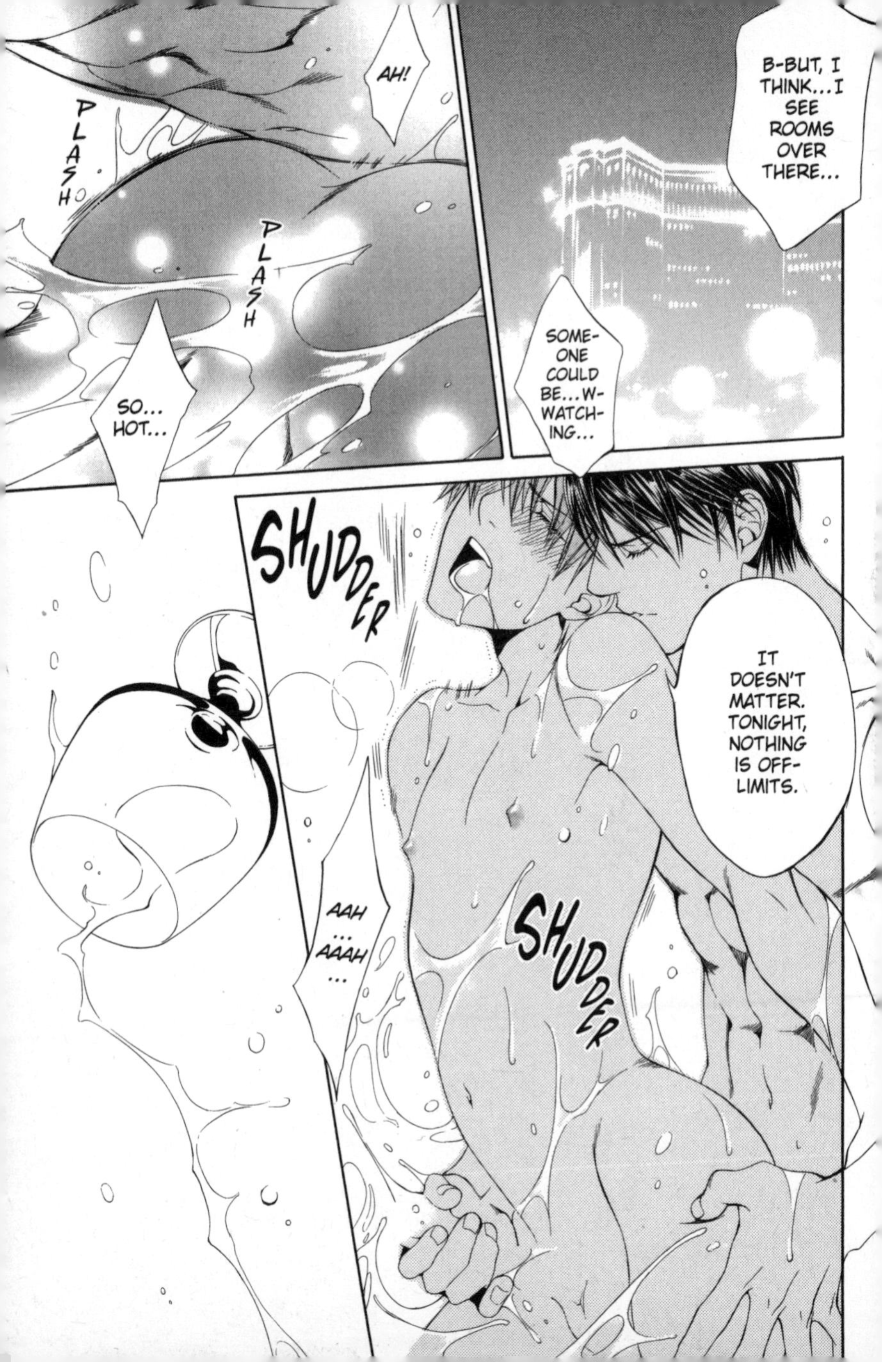
B-BUT, I THINK... I SEE ROOMS OVER THERE...
SOME-ONE COULD BE... W-WATCH-ING...
AH!
PLASH
PLASH
SO... HOT...
IT DOESN'T MATTER. TONIGHT, NOTHING IS OFF-LIMITS.
SHUDDER
SHUDDER
AAH... AAAH...

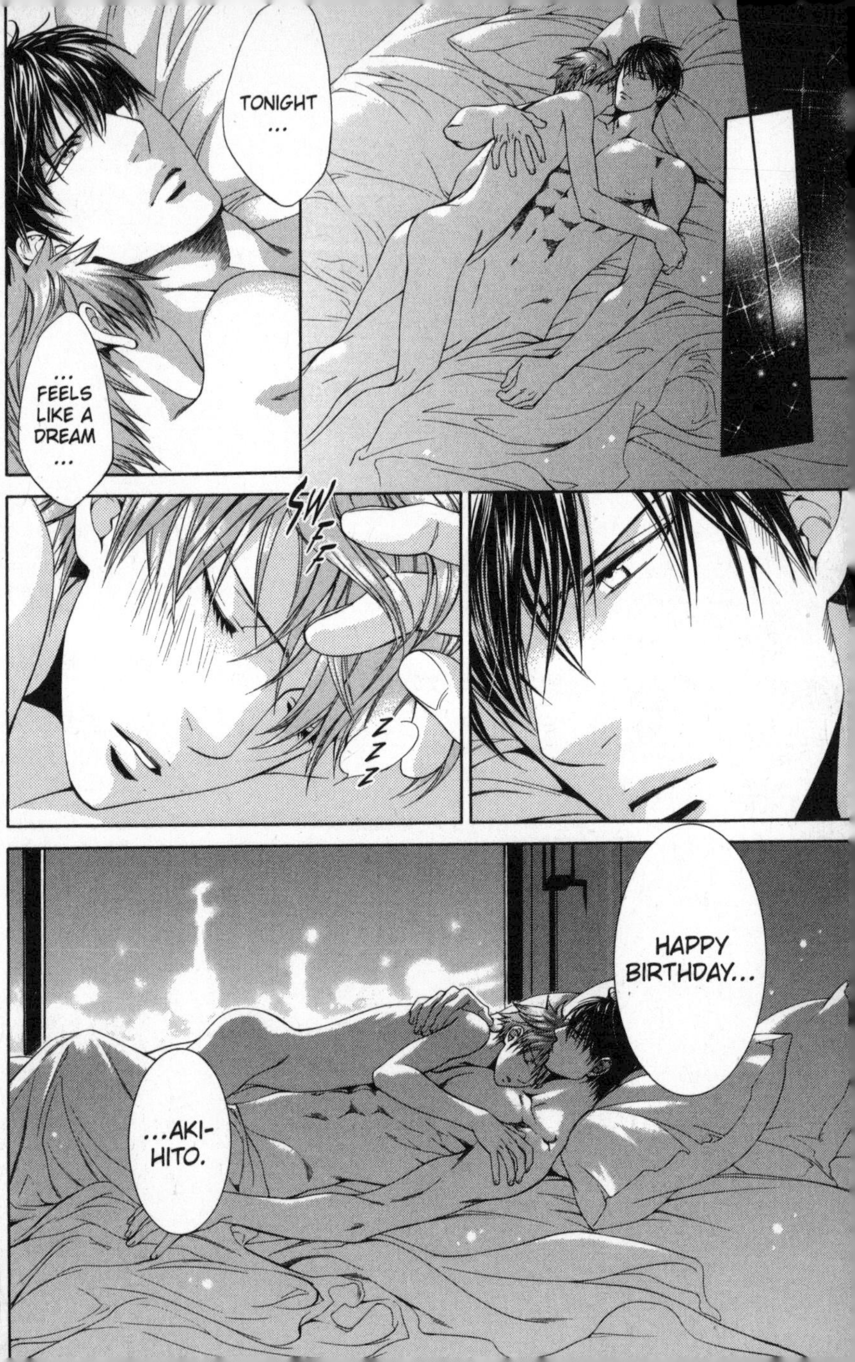
TONIGHT ...
... FEELS LIKE A DREAM ...
SWFF
ZZZ
HAPPY BIRTHDAY...
...AKI-HITO.

END

AFTERWORD

Hello! Ayano Yamane here. Another new volume, another new bonus story. They've become a tradition now. Did you enjoy this one? When the main storyline is short on smut or thick on violence, I like to think of these stories as my outlet for providing you all with a ray of sunshine and rejuvenating warmth.

This time, the new volume was scheduled to go on sale right around Akihito's birthday, so the story is a dreamy birthday surprise for the birthday boy himself! It's sweet, heartwarming, lovey-dovey, and made me go "*Aaaah!*" and "I can't! It's too embarrassing!" to my editor while drawing it. It's chock-full of lovely fanservice!

That sweet smile you get from watching a cutie getting all happy, blushy, and excited... That excitement over a full-course, red-carpet date with a fancy dinner, expensive presents, and a steamy surprise at the end... I wanted to present all of that with this one little story, and I hope you enjoyed it.

Thank you very much!

やまねあやの拝.

Ayano Yamane
April 2016

ANiMiX *Finder: Target in Sight* Jacket Art

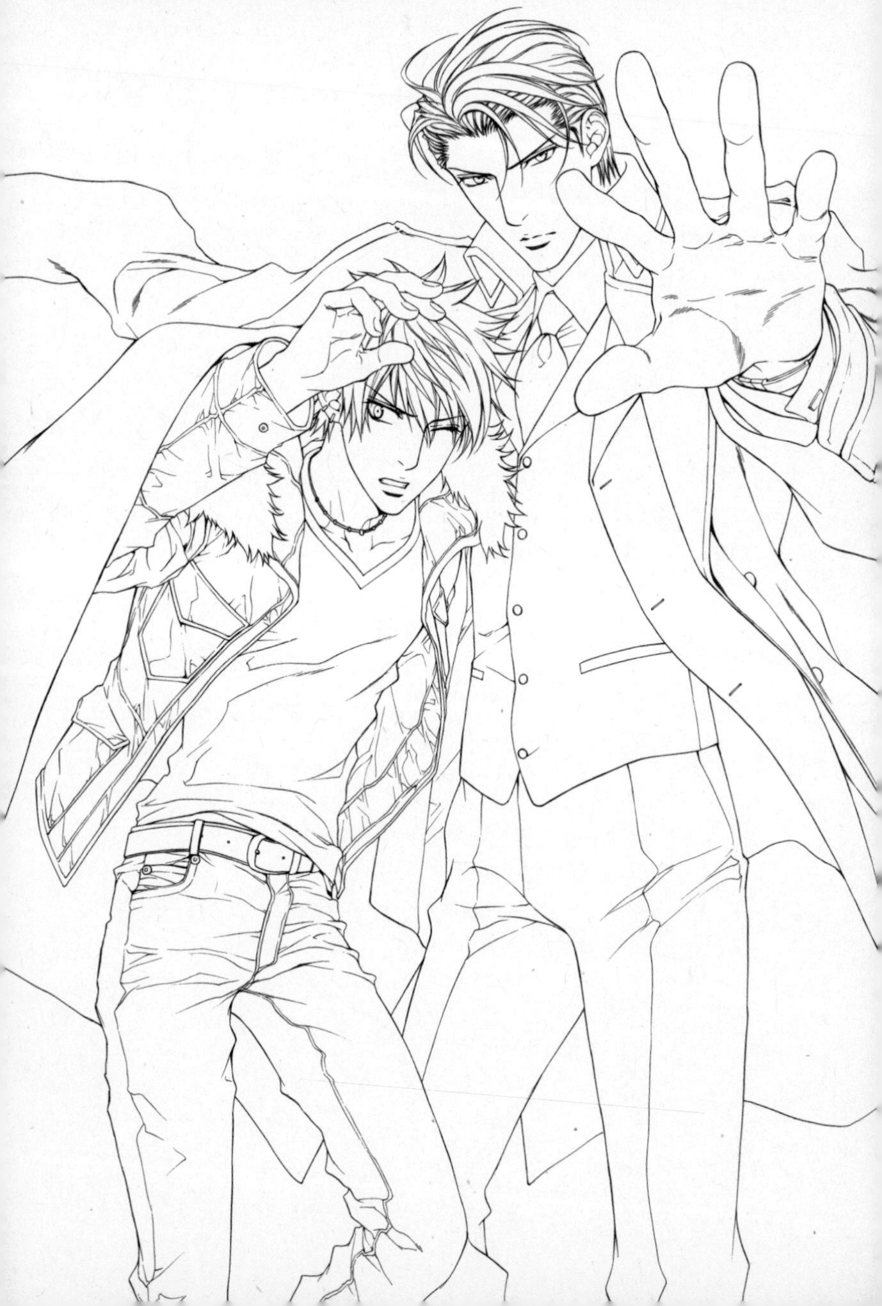

ANiMiX *Finder: On One Wing* Jacket Art

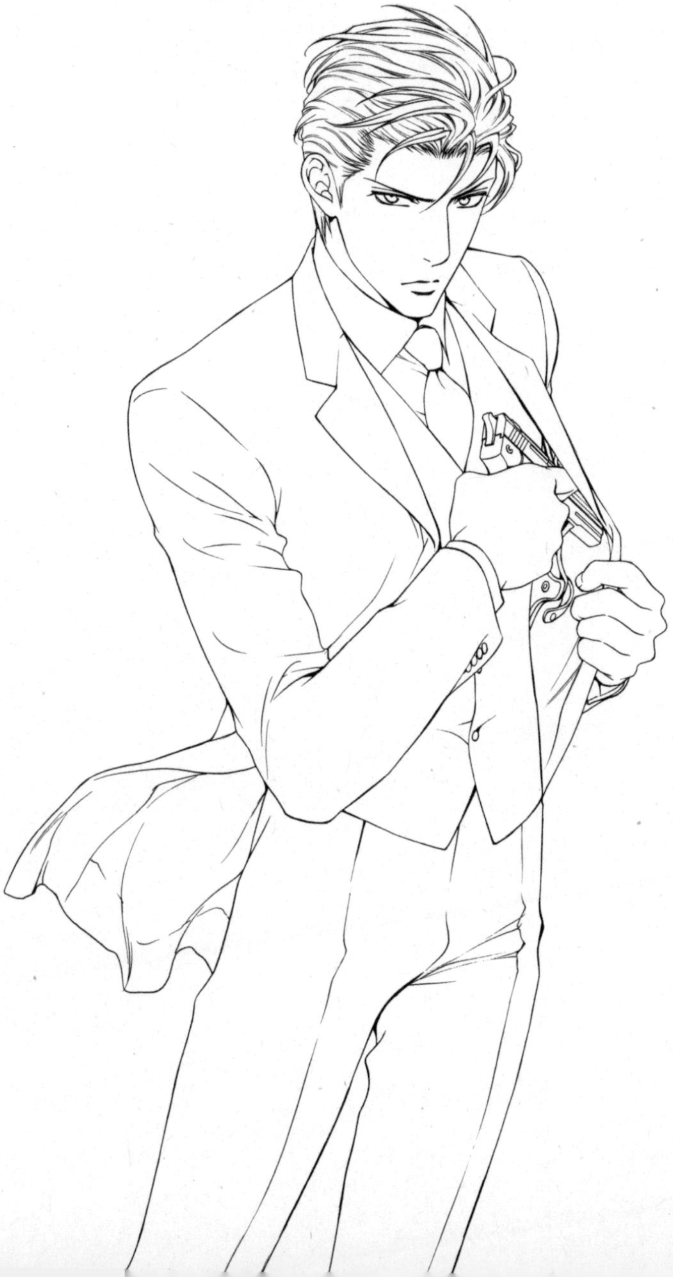

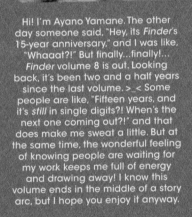

Hi! I'm Ayano Yamane. The other day someone said, "Hey, its *Finder*'s 15-year anniversary," and I was like, "Whaaat?!" But finally...finally!... *Finder* volume 8 is out. Looking back, it's been two and a half years since the last volume. >_< Some people are like, "Fifteen years, and it's *still* in single digits?! When's the next one coming out?!" and that does make me sweat a little. But at the same time, the wonderful feeling of knowing people are waiting for my work keeps me full of energy and drawing away! I know this volume ends in the middle of a story arc, but I hope you enjoy it anyway.

About the Author

One of the most popular boys' love mangaka to come out of Japan, Ayano Yamane is the creator of *A Foreign Love Affair* and the *Crimson Spell* series. She has also published *doujinshi* (independent comics) under the circle name GUN MANIA. A native of Awazi Island, she was born a Sagittarius on December 18th and has an A blood type. You can find out more about Ayano Yamane via her Twitter account, @yamaneayano.

Finder
Volume 8
SuBLime Manga Edition

Story and Art by **Ayano Yamane**

Translation—**Adrienne Beck**
Touch-Up Art and Lettering—**NRP Studios**
Cover and Graphic Design—**Shawn Carrico**
Editor—**Jennifer LeBlanc**

Finder no Mitsuyaku © 2016 Ayano Yamane
Originally published in Japan in 2016 by Libre Inc.
English translation rights arranged with Libre Inc.

libre

Printed in the U.S.A.

Published by SuBLime Manga
P.O. Box 77010
San Francisco, CA 94107

10 9 8 7 6 5 4 3 2 1
First printing, March 2017

SUBLIME
www.SuBLimeManga.com

For more information

on all our products, along with the most up-to-date news on releases, series announcements, and contests, please visit us at:

SuBLimeManga.com

twitter.com/SuBLimeManga

facebook.com/SuBLimeManga

SuBLimeManga.tumblr.com

SUBLIME
MANGA